Relevance Rediscovered
Volume I

An Anthology of 25 Significant Articles to Help Solve Today's and Tomorrow's Problems

NACA Bulletins and Yearbooks, 1919-1929

Selected by
Richard Vangermeersch

A project carried out on behalf of the
National Association of Accountants
Montvale, New Jersey

Published by

National Association of Accountants
10 Paragon Drive
Montvale, NJ 07645-1760
Claire Barth, Editor
Mandel & Wagreich, Inc., Cover

NAA Publication Number 89227
ISBN 0-86641-182-8

Foreword

This anthology, covering the period 1919-1929, is the initial volume beginning the commemoration of the 75th anniversary, in 1994, of the founding of NAA. Readers are being offered a once-in-a-lifetime opportunity — the opportunity to be able to explore the writings of leading member/practitioners of the National Association of Cost Accountants (NACA) from its inception. Contained in this volume are the great accounting ideas of the past, to help you solve today's and tomorrow's problems. There is no need to leave home. Just light the fire in the fireplace, settle down, and begin communicating with the great management accounting minds of the past.

But before you do, just a little perspective about NAA.

For more than 70 years, the National Association of Accountants has placed itself on the cutting edge of research in accounting practice. Since its founding in 1919 — for the express purpose of furthering education in the field of cost accounting (NACA Bylaws) — NAA, through research, discussion, and exchange of information with members, has dedicated itself to the continuing education of its members.

In furtherance of that goal, within a few months of its conception and organization the new society began to solicit from its members new concepts, developments, and practices in cost accounting. These, in turn, found their way into the Association's periodicals, such as the NACA Bulletins and Yearbooks.

When problems arose in the new accounting discipline, members who already had experienced similar situations were encouraged to describe their findings. The best summaries of practice were selected for separate publication as Accounting Practice Reports — more than 40 of which saw the light of print. In effect, the Association's early leaders strongly encouraged personal research and the sharing of findings.

Presented here are reprints of 25 articles from the period 1919-1929, selected by the researcher Richard Vangermeersch from the NACA Bulletins and Yearbooks. A synopsis of each article is given in the Introduction, along with some comments about the author and the applicability to today's and tomorrow's problems.

The reader should realize a number of benefits from a review of these articles. Some of them are:

1. Being placed in touch with good ideas that have been lost but that could be applied to problems of today and tomorrow.

2. Observing the proactive stance taken by management accountants in the successful adaptation of accounting to meet a new need.

3. Discovering that NAA has a rich and lustrous history—excellent contributions to accounting literature and practice—that should be revisited.

A final benefit—be sure to read the Introduction to this anthology by Professor Vangermeersch. He provides 10 reasons why management accountants should be involved with the study of these 25 articles.

Guidance in the preparation of this research report was kindly provided by the Project Committee:

Ann J. Rich, *Chairman*	L. Gayle Rayburn
Quinnipiac College	Memphis State University
Cheshire, Conn.	Memphis, Tenn.

This report reflects the views of the researcher and not necessarily those of the Association, the Committee on Research, or the Project Committee.

Patrick L. Romano
Director of Research
National Association of Accountants

Preface

Management accountants are not aware of the rich and long heritage of excellent articles published by the NAA in its early years. These articles are so good that they stand the test not only of today but of tomorrow. The articles selected for this anthology are really just a scratching of the surface for this time period.

I enjoyed immensely the opportunity to review this literature. As the NAA approaches its 75th anniversary in 1994, it is rewarding to note the excellence of its bulletins and yearbooks over the years.

Richard Vangermeersch, Ph.D., CMA, CPA
Professor of Accounting
University of Rhode Island
Kingston, Rhode Island

Acknowledgments

I would like to thank all those who helped with this work: Alfred M. King, managing director of professional and technical services of the NAA, for his support; Patrick L. Romano, director of research, for his guidance; and Anne Rich, professor of accounting at the University of Bridgeport and chair of the Project Committee on Anthologies to Help Solve Today's and Tomorrow's Problems, and her committee members – Gail W. DeLong, Mildred B. Stephens, and L. Gayle Rayburn – for their help. Claire Barth, associate editor for the NAA, is thanked for her fine job in the editing function.

About the Author

Richard Vangermeersch received a Ph.D. in accounting from the University of Florida in 1970 and a CMA in 1978. He was president of The Academy of Accounting Historians in 1987. Dr. Vangermeersch received an NAA Certificate of Recognition for 1975-76 and NAA Certificates of Merit in 1980-81 and 1982-83. He presented a paper, "Milestones in the History of Management Accounting," at the 1986 conference in Boston on Cost Accounting for the 90s.

Dr. Vangermeersch is also a CPA. He has been employed as a public accountant, an industrial accountant, a GAO auditor, an internal auditor, a training coordinator, and a federal systems accountant.

He joined the Bangor-Waterville Chapter of the NAA in 1969 and has been very involved with the Providence Chapter since 1971, serving as manuscripts director and as CMA director for that Chapter. The Providence Chapter awarded him its Distinguished Service Award in 1981.

Dr. Vangermeersch also has been involved with some NAA projects, as well as being a grader and writer for the CMA exam. He has taught at the University of Florida, the University of Maine, the American University in Cairo, and the University of Rhode Island.

Table of Contents

Relevance Rediscovered
Volume I

Introduction

Studying the past could help accountants to predict and control current and future events; however, they have tended to ignore the past in their professional reading, which most often is concerned with current regulations. Past accounting literature has been relegated to the "junk-heap." Academics have exhibited some interest in maintaining the past literature of financial accounting, but they have not shown nearly as great an interest in the past literature of management accounting. What a shame! What a waste! What a great deal of help not available to management accountants of today and tomorrow!

Relevance Lost: The Rise and Fall of Management Accounting, the recent book by H. Thomas Johnson and Robert Kaplan (Harvard Business School Press, 1987), traces the perceived loss of relevance of management accounting to a current society that is in tremendous need of a revitalized management accounting profession. The desire of manufacturers to become competitive again and the increasing factory automation have led us also to reexamine our roots. We were ahead of the competition during the 1920s. Cost and management accountants and the NACA (National Association of Cost Accountants — the NACA was renamed the NAA in 1957) had a lot to do with this competitiveness. This anthology lets the literature from the past light our way to the future. I would like to offer 10 reasons, not in any priority, why this past literature should be studied and also give some examples from it.

Reason No. 1

The study of management accounting literature leads to ideas that once were quite well developed but are now lost. Ideas sprout forth, are tried but, if not recorded systematically, are often forgotten after a time. Perhaps accountants have not been as quick to catalogue ideas as some other fields have. Hence, much of the brilliance and excellence of past literature may be only a dust cloth away. These ideas can jog your thought process — an "Aha!" experience may occur.

"Brief in Favor of Interest as a Cost" (Article 5), by Clinton H. Scovell, brings back the idea of the imputation of interest on invested capital as a legitimate, on-the-ledger expense. No one argued it better than Scovell. This controversial topic has never really died; in fact, it is of the timeless variety. With automated factories and few direct laborers, the idea needs revisiting.

"The Group Bonus and Labor Standards" (Article 20), by E. H. Tingley, then secretary of the National Association of Foremen, gives a refreshing look at how a group wage-incentive system can help quality control. With our current great emphasis on quality and how to improve it, this article is an especially important one. The use of a case study of a company also helps portray the idea.

One example of an idea that I have used is the machine hour rate method for a capital-intensive company. This method was well described in a 1926 article, "Cost Accounting Practice with Special Reference to Machine Hour Rate" (Article 21), that reprinted an earlier writing of Clinton H. Scovell, one of the NAA founders. The machine hour rate method is quite apropos for accounting for robots, for instance. "Incentives in Distribution" (Article 25), by Frederick D. Hess, gives many ideas to aid the management accountant in the distribution function. Examples from numerous companies are given. With the increased use of robots, it is critical to study descriptions of how earlier management accountants came to grips with automation.

One of the major goals of this anthology is to get the reader to try an idea a week from the readings. Thus, the articles were chosen with management accounting practitioners in mind. It is my job to get very busy management accountants to read these articles, so I have included an extensive introduction section and introductory comments to each article that give an overview of the article. The goal is to have this anthology become the basis for a CPE course in which management accountants would get credit for each idea tried, analyzed, and written up in a mini case study submitted to NAA.

Reason No. 2

The study of this literature gives you the opportunity to support your proposals with past writings. Your ideas might not be accepted on their own merit, but your listeners might be impressed with the fact that renowned accountants and other writers in the field held similar views. Management accountants need to learn the importance of using past literature to support a current position.

An example of this reason is R. R. Thompson's "Various Wage Systems in Relation to Factory Indirect Charges" (Article 16). This article is an excellent review of eight classic wage systems. A coverage of these systems was included in cost accounting texts until the early 1960s, so the accountant was once recognized as playing an important role in this area. A reading of the article might lead to a reinvolvement of management accountants in wage decisions. It would not hurt to reference this article in making your case for reinvolvement.

Another example is M. B. Folsom's "The Use of a Thirteen-Month Calendar" (Article 24). The system outlined by Folsom—who worked for Eastman Kodak, a pioneering company in the area of calendar reform—surely gives you a good source to quote in a possible argument for changing your company's time periods.

Reason No. 3

The study of this literature increases your ability to be verbal in management accounting. Accountants tend to be less at ease with words than others involved in the administration of organizations. Many students choose accounting as their major because they think they will be safe from ever having to read, write, and speak about their field. This lack of verbal ability is severely limiting for such people and, unfortunately, for the field of management accounting as well. Reading broadens horizons and exposes the reader to examples of good writing. Some of the articles that were especially well written are: "The Application of Selling and Administrative Expense to Product" (Article 8), by William Castenholz; "Standard Costs—Their Development and Use" (Article 15), by F. Brugger from General Electric; and "The Accountant's Relation to the Budgetary Program" (Article 23), by J. O. McKinsey. Two of these writers, Castenholz and McKinsey, were authors of many articles and books. Castenholz did a marvelous writing job in getting management accountants as interested in controlling marketing and administrative costs as they are in controlling production costs. Brugger gave a particularly forceful plea for standard costing, using the very successful General Electric Company as his example. McKinsey wrote the best précis of budgeting I have ever read. No wonder he attained the great status he did in consulting and the academic world. This literature is extremely well written and should inspire readers to give more attention to verbal ability.

Reason No. 4

The study of this literature enlarges your pantheon of accounting heroes. Accounting is probably the academic and professional field with the fewest, if any, heroes for its own members. Economists have John Maynard Keynes, Alfred Marshall, John Kenneth Galbraith, and Adam Smith; managers have Frederick Taylor, Douglas McGregor, and Herbert Simon. Who are the accounting heroes? If you name one or two, they will invariably be thought of as financial accountants in orientation. Heroes give you the courage to dare to be different, to rise above the current problems, and to propose a novel solution. Without heroes any profession is in deep trouble. Some of the heroes I observed in this literature are: Clinton H. Scovell in "Brief in Favor of Interest as a Cost" (Article 5) and in "Cost Accounting Practice with Special Reference to Machine Hour Rate" (Article 21); William Castenholz in "The Application of Selling and Administrative Expense to Product" (Article 8); T. H. Sanders in "Overhead in Economics and Accounting" (Article 17); and J. O. McKinsey in "The Accountant's Relation to the Budgetary Program" (Article 23).

Scovell was a strong and passionate fighter for his beliefs in accounting. He believed accounting made a difference, and he wanted that difference to be a positive one. Castenholz also fought strongly for his desire to have management accountants control marketing and administrative costs. Sanders, a professor of accounting at the Harvard Business School, is more remembered for his work in financial accounting, but his work in management accounting, when rediscovered, will make him a hero in that accounting field as well. Sanders was deeply involved in the NACA, as reported in Thomas Burns's and Edward Coffman's *The Accounting Hall of Fame* (Ohio State University, Columbus, Ohio, 1976). Tonya Flesher and Dale Flesher, in *Biographies of Notable Accountants* (Academy of Accounting Historians and Random House, New York, 1987), summarized McKinsey's work thusly:

> McKinsey should be revered by accounting educators for the fact that he authored the first budgeting book and the first managerial accounting textbook. Through his emphasis on principle instead of procedures, McKinsey was the first accounting author to base his writings on the uses of accounting data rather than on their preparation....(p.28)

These writers serve as fine role models for management accountants of today and tomorrow.

Reason No. 5

The study of this literature leads to an awareness of management accountants in action, through a number of case studies. Many of the case studies describe a successful change in accounting to meet a new challenge. These articles tell why the change occurred, how the change occurred, and what its effects were. Some of the case studies are covered in great depth. Each is useful in understanding the dynamics of the problems involved. The NACA members were writing to their colleagues in the field, telling them what had been accomplished in the writers' companies. This sharing of success must have provided much assistance to all members.

The number of case studies in this anthology is significant; they include: I. W. Kokins' "The Scrap Problem" (Article 7), William R. Donaldson's "Cost Accounting in the Production of Motion Pictures" (Article 10); Albert Bradley's "Financial Control Policies of General Motors Corporation and Their Relationship to Cost Accounting" (Article 19); and M. B. Folsom's "The Use of a Thirteen-Month Calendar" (Article 24). These writers were "hands-on" practitioners dealing with companies on the cutting-edge of managerial excellence.

Kokins wrote about GE's accounting goals – not only to record scrap properly but to reduce scrap and to increase its selling value. Donaldson stressed the importance of the job order concept to a fascinating industry, motion pictures. Bradley with GM and Folsom with Eastman Kodak described winning organizations in action. These case studies provide you with a feel for past reactions to situations that may be similar to your current one.

Reason No. 6

The study of this literature builds your general background in such areas as management, marketing, wage administration, and economics. Management accounting is an eclectic field; hence, it is interdisciplinary in nature. Management accountants should be willing to take ideas from other fields of knowledge and adapt them to the problems at hand. Without an appreciation of the literature of related fields the management accountant will be thinking in a vacuum.

Some examples of such interdisciplinary writings found in this anthology are: R. S. Kellogg's "The Use of Cost Data by Trade Associations" (Article 11); Hugo Diemer's "Methods of Supplying Cost Information to Foremen" (Article 13); J. W. Swaren's "Co-operation Between the Comptroller and the Engineer" (Article 14); E. H. Tingley's "The Group Bonus and Labor Standards" (Article 20); and James H. Rand, Jr.'s "The Profit Element" (Article 22).

These writers were certainly experts in their areas. Kellogg was secretary of the News Print Service Bureau. Diemer was then Director of Industrial Courses of the LaSalle Extension University. He also was chosen by Lyndall F. Urwick as one of the pioneers of management (*The Golden Book of Management*, 2nd edition, Urwick and Wolfe, Amacom, 1984, p. 14). Major Swaren was an engineer. Tingley was secretary of the National Association of Foremen. Rand was president of Remington Rand Company. These writers and articles enable you to come to grips quickly with another field in an action setting related to accounting.

Reason No. 7

The study of this literature shows the professionalism of the NAA and its members and its contributions to the literature. The NACA research studies, published in the bulletins of this period, are excellent examples of such professionalism. Pride in your professional organization and pride in your profession of management accounting are vital to your success and to the success of the profession.

Quite early in the history of the NACA it began publishing the NACA Research Studies. "Accounting for By-Products" (Article 2) was published in 1920, followed by "A Bibliography of Cost Books" (Article 4) in 1921. The organization published the text of four radio promotionals, "Radio Educational Campaign" (Article 9), in 1923. The 1920 research study discussed the three common methods of accounting for by-products, gave an illustration of each method, and gave pros and cons for each method. The research team then stated its preference. The 1921 research study shows how rich a heritage cost accounting had by 1920. I have found many of these books to be much more informative on many matters than subsequent literature. Here is a vast treasure chest of source material. The 1923 effort resulted in four radio scripts about cost accounting. These research studies and scripts are so good that they deserve to be known by every management accountant.

Reason No. 8

The study of this literature gives an awareness of the controversial topics in the field. These controversies may be timeless, as different situations will call for different solutions. The "Question Box" (Article 18) section of the 1926 Yearbook chronicled the debates on such questions as: "What is the basis for setting normal burden?"; "Should orders ever be taken below normal cost?"; and "When should a group bonus be used?". Other timeless topics are discussed in Gould Harris' "Calculation and Application of Departmental Burden Rates" (Article 1); in H. G. Crockett's "Some Problems in the Actual Installation of Cost Systems" (Article 3); in C. B. Williams' "The Distribution of Overhead Under Abnormal Conditions" (Article 6); and in Harry J. Ostlund's "Indirect Labor" (Article 12). Nothing has struck me more in preparing this anthology than the issue of timeless topics. Differences of opinion may always exist because there are no universal answers. Each company must fight out continually its current answers to these issues. Such debates bring management accounting to life and expand our horizons. Perhaps it is time your accounting department had a debate like those in the "Question Box" article.

Reason No. 9

The study of this literature should give you an incentive to build your accounting library by including other things than current tax regulations and current FAS statements. Take a look at your personal professional library now and see what is there. Are you satisfied with what you see? I doubt it. A rich literature base exists for the profession of management accounting, and not enough people know about it. "A Bibliography of Cost Books" (Article 4) gives a helpful start to such an appreciation of the literature.

Reason No. 10

The study of this literature makes one more flexible, more willing to attempt changes, and more valuable to one's employer — in short, a far stronger management accountant. You must challenge yourself to get involved now with reading some of these articles from the vast treasure chest of management accounting literature. Adopt a goal of one article a night and one idea to try from that article the next morning at work. You, your company, and the profession of management accounting will all be the better for it. The "Question Box" (Article 18) is the best example of an illustration of this reason.

The NACA bulletins were published sporadically from 1919 through 1921; starting in 1922, a bulletin was published twice a month on or about the first and fifteenth days. Most of these bulletins included one article, but some included more than one. The number of articles in the NACA yearbooks varied greatly from year to year; they were the papers presented at the yearly cost conference. For the first few years no introductory material was given on the article or the author by the NACA. This policy changed in 1924.

All the articles in the first 10 volumes of bulletins and yearbooks from 1921 through 1929 were reviewed. I also reviewed the NACA bulletins and yearbooks for the 1930s and 1940s so that I could choose an anthology from each decade with a minimum of redundancy. After much culling, these 25 articles remained for the anthology of the 1920s. The articles are presented in chronological order. The NACA introduction precedes the articles for which one was given; following the article, in certain instances, is a discussion section.

Review of Articles

(1) "Calculation and Application of Departmental Burden Rates," April 1920 Bulletin, Vol. 1., No. 3, Gould L. Harris, Lecturer in Cost Accounting, New York University

This article was the first substantive one appearing in an NACA Bulletin. It dealt with the issue of overhead (or "burden," in the parlance of earlier days). Gould L. Harris, a lecturer in cost accounting at New York University, considered burden amenable to control: "The impression is too widespread that burden is extremely elusive." He briefly traced the history of burden accounting and then presented a 12-step solution to the problem. He strove to differentiate between expense, burden, and overhead. Harris strongly favored departmental rates and utilized a detailed burden statement for each department. He stressed the importance of a close examination of each department so that proper departmentalization would occur. He then explained the journal, ledger, and statement procedure for the system.

We are probably, at best, operating overhead accounting systems at the level Harris described. It is possible that many current systems are at the fixed percentage method or at the blanket method. It is likely that present-day departmental burden statements are nowhere near as detailed as Harris'. You should study this article and measure your company's overhead system against it. Is overhead considered "elusive" in your company? Have you taken every opportunity to explain the system? Is your departmentalization reflective of good overhead control? This subject is a timeless one; it deserves a good debate from time to time.

(2) "Accounting for By-Products," August 1920 Bulletin, Vol. 1, No. 7, Research Department of the NACA

The NACA did not take long to publish a mini research study. Its seventh bulletin dealt with the accounting decisions inherent in recording of by-products. The article quoted A. Hamilton Church's classic definitions of spoilage, waste, scrap, and by-products. It also gave useful lists of different losses associated with defective work and of different classes of by-products. It was "...becoming more and more necessary to record by-product costs if the manufacturer is to decide intelligently whether he should scrap or sell the by-product at the time it arises, or rework it and enhance its sales value." The three common methods of accounting for by-products were discussed and illustrated. The research team then stated its preference for the third method—the total cost approach.

You can be of immeasurable help to management by inspiring greater control and profit maximization of the by-products. Accounting can greatly improve management's behavior toward by-products through a proper accounting for them. How long has it been since you have given some thought to this topic for your company? Does your company have a plan to convert spoilage into scrap and scrap into by-products? The article gives a much more detailed view of the problem than you find in a typical cost/managerial accounting text today. Hence, the article is more holistic in nature than the fractured treatment in textbooks. It is also more "hands on" as it involved NACA members. It is another example of "Accountants Serving Accountants."

(3) "Some Problems in the Actual Installation of Cost Systems," February 1921 Bulletin, Vol. 1, No. 8, H. G. Crockett, Resident Engineering Partner, Scovell, Wellington & Company

This article was written by H. G. Crockett, Resident Engineering Partner in the New York office of Scovell, Wellington & Company. That company was regarded by many as the premier management accounting consulting firm of its day. Its founder, Clinton H. Scovell, held a very significant place in the founding and early days of the NACA. Crockett stressed that the cost accountant should know why management felt a need to change its methods. "Local conditions necessarily have an important bearing on any situation, and there are so many governing factors of varying degrees of importance that each individual case can be decided only on its merits, after all of the factors have been brought out." He felt that whatever the answers chosen, the cost system should tie into the general books. The system was to be built *up* from the factory, not *down* from the accounts. Perpetual inventories were necessary. One could choose either a job order or process system, with an option of standard costs for each system.

Crockett then went on to detail both burden centers and burden distribution. Factors such as rental charges, machinery and equipment, power, steam and heat, light, repairs, general burden, shop transportation, and shop administration were discussed. Four methods of burden application were mentioned, as well as general administrative and selling expenses.

While not going into great detail in any one of the many topics discussed, Crockett does provide a great deal of food for thought on each one. I have found surprisingly little written about the "whys" of the costing system employed in companies. Perhaps the "whys" need some rigorous questioning. Again, consider these timeless and, hence, debatable questions. Can you describe the "whys" of your current system? Is your current system reflective of your current needs? Are you a slave to a computer package that does not fit? Crockett offers much help for these important questions.

(4) "A Bibliography of Cost Books," April 1921 Bulletin, Vol. 2, No. 10, Research Department, NACA

This article was prepared by the Research Department of the NACA and focused on the book literature; it divided the books into five classifications. Fifty-four were listed under the general subject of cost accounting; 69 were in general accounting and auditing, with some references to cost accounting; 59 were on industrial management but contained cost accounting sections; 135 were concerned with cost material for different industries; and 33 dealt with special phases of cost accounting.

I have used the books by A. Hamilton Church a great deal. They are well worth reading. Church's machine hour rate method has been the basis of a number of works in automated and robotics accounting that my colleague, Henry Schwarzbach, and I have written. We have taken Church's model and have extended the three-product cost system into a four-product cost system. (See "Why We Should Account for the Fourth Cost of Manufacturing," *Management Accounting*, July 1983.) Johnson and Kaplan stressed the works of Church favorably in their book, *Relevance Lost: The Rise and Fall of Management Accounting*. A sample of the other outstanding authors mentioned in the article are Holden A. Evans, Dexter S. Kimball, J. Lee Nicholson, Clinton H. Scovell, C. U. Carpenter, Hugo Diemer, Harrington Emerson, H. L. Gantt, Alex C. Humphreys, Frederick W. Taylor, C. E. Woods, C. E. Knoeppel, and Ewing Matheson.

Church, Kimball, Diemer, Emerson, Gantt, and Taylor are included among the pioneers of management chosen by Urwick in *The Golden Book of Management.* Do you recognize any of these names? Have you read any of the works listed? If you have, you are one of a select circle of management accountants.

It has not been easy to convince accountants that there already was a rich heritage of cost accounting literature by 1920. This article speaks mightily on this point. The NACA certainly thought so, or it would not have commissioned the study. You can improve your writing by referencing these works. You can improve your library by buying the reprints of some of these works. I have found many of these books more informative on many matters than books and articles on management accounting written since 1920. Try them; you'll like them.

(5) "Brief in Favor of Interest as a Cost," 1921 Yearbook, Clinton H. Scovell, Scovell, Wellington & Company

Clinton H. Scovell, founder of the accounting firm of Scovell, Wellington & Company, was a member of the NACA Special Committee on Interest as an Element of Cost. The committee decided not to reach a decision on the subject but to have one member present a "pro" paper and another member a "con" paper. Scovell agreed to prepare and present the "pro" paper. Note the debate style of the article.

Stephen Zeff reported in his article, "Some Junctures in the Evolution of the Process of Establishing Accounting Principles in the U.S.A.: 1917-1972" (*Accounting Review,* July 1984, pp. 447-468), that Scovell was one of the leaders of the "interest as a cost" movement. Scovell was very involved in the deliberation of the American Institute of Accountants (now the AICPA) on the topic in 1917. When the AIA rejected that argument, Scovell and others were among the leaders of the 37 men who met in Buffalo to found the NACA. Hence, it should be no surprise that this topic was discussed early on in the NACA. With the passage of FAS #34, "Capitalization of Interest Cost," the Financial Accounting Standards Board sent a clear signal that interest was not always to be considered a period expense. Scovell certainly would have used FAS #34 as a point in his favor. Scovell is a name that needs to be better known in the history of accounting.

Scovell relied heavily on economics and economists for his basic reasoning. It is interesting to note this economics base, as it is rarely given today. He expressed his theory thus:

> Interest on borrowed capital is a cost; so, too, is interest on owned capital. The mere fact that the one part of the investment carries contract interest, and the other only economic interest, is not ground for excluding the latter form from costs. *All* interest should be included.

He gave many examples of the importance of the inputation of interest—for instance, the purchase decision for a new machine and the decision to build up inventory. Scovell favored the use of the "ordinary interest rate on reasonably secured long-term investments in the locality." He described the accounting process for the imputation, which would yield many benefits to management, such as price justification. Scovell was willing to pull the imputation amount out of inventory to keep financial accountants and bankers happy. That was one of his responses to the opposition to the imputation of interest, of which there were 14 refuted points. What are your company's views on the imputation of interest? How much education would be necessary to have a meaningful debate? This article presents a point of view on a timeless topic that needs to be considered by all businesses, including yours. It is an idea whose time may have come again.

(6) "The Distribution of Overhead Under Abnormal Conditions," 1921 Yearbook, C. B. Williams, Nau, Rusk and Swearingen

C. B. Williams wrote this article during the brief but sharp recession of 1920-21. He placed much of his stress on the issue of pricing during an economic downturn, which had led to idleness. Should prices rise to reflect the increased overhead per unit or should prices be lowered to help alleviate some of the idle capacity? This is surely a timeless question. Williams stated the dilemma well:

> From the standpoint of the sales department, a price which is too high means that no business will be obtained. A short-sighted policy may dictate the quoting of low prices for no other reason than to secure business. On the other hand, if a price is quoted too low, it means future difficulties for the sales department and dissatisfied customers.

Williams favored a longer-term, normal capacity approach for setting overhead rates. He thereby differentiated between manufacturing costs and idle expenses. The idle cost should be deducted from gross profit so that management could see the effect of idleness. Does your company have a well thought out policy for pricing during downturns and booms? Is there a willingness to accept a negative capacity variance as a legitimate cost of the year? Do you feel your company gets carried away with price-slashing and consumer discounting during downspells? Does your company know the effects of indiscriminate price-slashing during downturns? If you have not thought much about the divisor of expected number of factor(s) used in your overhead computation, this article gives some food for thought.

(7) "The Scrap Problem," March 1, 1922, Bulletin, Vol. 3, No. 11, I. W. Kokins, Comptroller's Office, General Electric Company, Schenectady

This article is a mini case study of a very successful company. GE had adopted the accounting goals not only of properly recording scrap but of reducing scrap and of increasing the sales value of the scrap that occurred. There was a listing of three sources of scrap: vendor quality problems, avoidable scrap, and unavoidable scrap. "Ability to identify the vendor is of importance, particularly when similar material is purchased from a number of concerns, because such material can only be returned when the vendor is positively known." Workers were not to let carelessness about scrap become a bad work habit. Kokins then described a scrap control system.

A Scrap Ticket and a Scrap Transfer Slip were illustrated. The eight stages of scrap control were: (1) reporting defective material, (2) tagging, (3) reporting and tagging natural scrap, (4) collecting scrap, (5) accumulating space, (6) containers, (7) accumulating large lots of one-grade scrap, and (8) facilities and equipment. The functions of the salvage department were outlined, and the accounting aspects of scrap were well covered.

This article gives solutions to the ongoing problem of scrap. How long has it been since your company has taken a look at the scrap issue? Is scrap treated as a "red-light danger signal"? Have bad habits about scrap been ingrained in your company's employees?

(8) "The Application of Selling and Administrative Expense to Product," 1922 Yearbook, William B. Castenholz

William B. Castenholz, a writer of much note in management accounting and really someone in the "hero" category, focused attention on the accounting control of selling and administrative expenses. Castenholz had a mission to make accountants just as aware and as interested in marketing costs as they were in production costs. His writing was at a high level, as evidenced by this quote:

> I like to think of this one phase of activity, namely, marketing, in very much the same way that I do of production. We are in the habit of distributing overhead expenses in connection with production as nearly as possible in connection with some direct expense of production. There are direct expenses in connection with marketing;...

The failure to control direct marketing costs can lead to losses in that the price of the product must include some factors for marketing and administration. Castenholz then presented an example to illustrate his philosophy, a controversial method of accounting for product selling costs by a deferral procedure, although he stated that this might not be the final answer.

This article appears to be the first in NACA literature to detail an attempt at controlling nonproduction costs. Many articles followed until the late 1940s, when such literature appeared to decline noticeably. It is safe to assume that the reader could do well to adopt Castenholz's philosophy of devoting the same talents of cost analysis to marketing costs as to production costs. With the changes in the 1986 Tax Reform Act on putting some marketing costs to inventory, Castenholz's work becomes more significant than ever. Has this been done in your company? Do you think there is the same level of control applied to marketing costs as applied to production costs? Castenholz would have urged you to give this philosophy much thought and would have wished you well.

(9) "Radio Educational Campaign," July 2, 1923, Bulletin, Vol. 4, No. 20, NACA

The NACA, early in its history and also early in the history of radio, had a radio educational campaign with four programs: (1) "What Cost Accounting Means to Industry"; (2) "Advantages of Cost Accounting to Workers"; (3) "Advantages of Cost Accounting to Employers"; and (4) "Advantages of Cost Accounting to the Public." The goal was to illustrate how cost accounting plays an important role in broader economic problems. In the first broadcast, the NACA stated its educational objectives of narrowing the wide gap between management and labor by presenting facts without a selfish interest viewpoint. "On account of its being an association separate and distinct from employers and likewise from workers, and its object being educational, it is in a position to advance arguments which cannot be disputed on the score that it has in any way a selfish interest."

The second broadcast attacked the negative image workers may have about cost accounting. This broadcast stressed the workers' role in keeping down overhead and in relating suggestions for cost savings. The NACA called for the workers to add head work to their physical work. "We advocate no harder work, but rather the addition to the everyday work of the very powerful brain factor which is possessed to a remarkable degree by every worker in this country." The third broadcast focused on information given to management. There was a call to action. "The National Association of Cost Accountants, therefore, appeals to every employer to take immediate steps to see that his business is equipped with cost and production records whereby every employee in the company, foreman or worker, may have actual knowledge of what he is producing and how well he is progressing." The fourth broadcast defended industrial exchange of information of production effectiveness.

The early leaders of the NACA were very creative in these broadcasts. One could review the article with the thought that the NAA might redo the broadcasts from a management accounting viewpoint. Radio remains a very viable means of communicating such information. However, readers may find the scripts interesting from the viewpoint of increased communication among accountants, managers, and workers. It might not be a bad idea at least to think about how communications may be improved on these matters in your company.

Is your accounting department viewed as totally belonging to management versus having some feeling for the workers? Are you interested in bettering your relations with the "workers"? Is the climate right in your company for cooperation? Should the Institute of Certified Management Accountants and the NAA consider the same type of campaign for the CMA?

(10) "Cost Accounting in the Production of Motion Pictures," Dec. 1, 1923, Bulletin, Vol. 5, No. 6, William R. Donaldson, CPA, Member of Philip N. Miller and Company

William R. Donaldson wrote this article about cost accounting in the motion picture industry. While there were earlier examples of accounting for a specific industry—for example, foundries—in NACA literature, this article dealt with a more exciting product, at least to the general public. Donaldson did not describe a specific system in a studio but an ideal system that should cause discussion in the industry. Hence, this is one more example of a mini case study approach to informing other accountants of the happenings in a specific industry.

There was a description of the process of making a motion picture, from the story to the printing of the positive film for distribution. A typical organization chart was given, along with a chart of accounts. An interesting discussion of burden accounts and their distribution was presented. Donaldson made much mention of the need to develop a scrap value system for sets designed for a specific motion picture but still available for use for subsequent pictures.

> It was the custom generally to disregard this element on the theory that while the first picture will be heavy in cost, each subsequent one will "give and take" such used material and hence work out on the average....Where accurate information is required of the direct costs of sets for purposes of managerial control and of estimation of the costs of similar sets in future productions, it is essential that this element of scrap value be properly treated on the books.

Since the motion picture industry is still with us in an undiminished state of importance, this article is an excellent and eye-catching review of a job-order system. It shows how the job-order concept is of universal application and not limited just to the factory. It illustrates how burden accounts and allocation are also universal in nature. Do you have situations in your company like the "sets" in inventory? Is the job-order concept considered dead in your company? Should it be resurrected?

(11) "The Use of Cost Data by Trade Associations," 1923 Yearbook, R. S. Kellogg, Secretary, News Print Service Bureau

R. S. Kellogg wrote this interesting defense of the uses of collected cost data by his organization. This use of accounting data as input into a statistical study of industry is an example of the interdisciplinary use of accounting data. Kellogg felt that the trade association was the salvation of the smaller organization. He took great care to differentiate between using the cost data to fix prices and using the cost data to aid in finding inefficiencies. "As I said, it is to enable people to check their waste, to find out where their weak spots are and to give them information that will lead them to investigate their own condition, and if they are so disposed, to enable them to reduce their own operating costs."

This article gives you a chance to rethink your relationship with your trade association and with its important function of collecting cost data. The importance of avoiding the perception of price fixing is always a good point to remember. Do you agree with Kellogg that the trade association is essential to small business? Is your company a member of its trade association? If so, how does it use the statistics on cost data?

(12) "Indirect Labor," February 15, 1924, Bulletin, Vol. 5, No. 11, Harry J. Ostlund, University of Minnesota

Harry J. Ostlund defined indirect labor as all labor not directly charged against specific lots or units of the product. However, indirect labor did not mean unproductive labor. This was especially important since technology and machinery were resulting in a much higher percent of indirect labor to direct labor. Ostlund was worried about a rigid test of indirect labor to direct labor, which would lead to irrational management. It might be beneficial for the company to substitute indirect labor for direct labor.

> An increase in the proportion of indirect labor cost may be altogether favorable; especially is this true if in the case of direct labor working under a bonus system, the efficiency should be increased, when of course the added bonus would appear...in an addition to the indirect labor cost.

There has been an unfortunate tendency to aggregate indirect labor rather than control it by the types of service it performs. This trend has been accentuated by including not only the wages of indirect laborers but also by including some part of direct laborers' wages. Ostlund favored departmentalization to control indirect labor costs.

This article highlights how easy it is for companies to lose control of indirect labor costs by using that account as an indiscriminate dumping ground. Is indirect labor used as a dumping ground in your company? Does your company have a fairly rigid notion of the acceptable DL/IL ratio? Are seemingly rational decisions turned down because of this ratio? It may be that much work needs to be done with the accounting for direct labor.

(13) *"Methods of Supplying Cost Information to Foremen," June 1, 1924, Bulletin, Vol. 5, No. 18, Hugo Diemer, Director of Industrial Courses, LaSalle Extension University*

Hugo Diemer, a renowned figure in the history of management and one of the first 70 pioneers in management as chosen by Urwick, was concerned about the extent of accounting control information given to foremen. Six types of costs were discussed in the article. The first three – direct labor, direct material, and departmental overhead – could be controlled directly by foremen. The accountant should be sure that foremen participate in the daily network of control forms, so foremen cannot say they did not know a problem exists. Foremen should be made aware of the other three types of cost – general shop overhead, administrative and commercial overhead, and sales expense – for a broader picture of the business. Diemer also included 12 dominant characteristics of a group of foremen, as well as a chart to explain the foremen's role in controlling shop costs. Diemer concluded by stating "that it has been the writer's experience that in most cases, insufficient information as to costs is brought to the attention of the foremen."

This article is another example of the interdisciplinary nature of the NACA literature of the 1920s. It is also a reminder that the management decision as to how much information to give to foremen is a timeless issue. What are the relationships between accountants and foremen in your company? Can this relationship be improved by better communication? What is your opinion of Diemer's 12 characteristics of foremen and his chart on their role in controlling plant costs?

(14) *"Co-operation Between the Comptroller and the Engineer," November 15, 1924, Bulletin, Vol. 6, No. 6, Major J. W. Swaren*

Major Swaren wrote of the mutual interest the comptroller and the engineer have in capital assets. He felt engineers have three duties in a capital project. They first assemble all data pertinent to the task; they then design the project by the process of visualization of the model; and, lastly, they supervise actual construction. The comptroller should ask the engineer what information he wants collected on the job sheet and be sure that the job records are tied into the balance sheet. Another important matter of cooperation was the property records. Swaren stressed the importance of reproduction costs and realistic depreciation based on a careful measurement of useful life for tax, insurance, and planning purposes.

> The engineer has available deterioration meters, if the accountant desires accurate measure to determine his costs. And the consulting engineer demands accurate costs, including reproductive returns, in the interest of his clients, the security holders.

He also stressed the importance of engineering involvement in the property records.

This article is interdisciplinary in nature. The discipline in this case is engineering in its relationship to accounting. The article reminds one of the importance of cooperation between the engineer and accountant on capital projects accounting. This reminder is important to note, but of much more significance is the role the engineer was to play in the property records. It is very unlikely that engineers of today play anything like as significant a role in property record management and accounting as they did when Swaren wrote this article. Accountants have probably trivialized the property record function. It may be appropriate to reintroduce the engineer into property record management and accounting. What is the status of property record management in your company? Do engineers have any input into property management records? What is your opinion of the calculation of depreciation expense? Have you included engineers in this decision? Is it time to include engineers again in property management records?

(15) "Standard Costs—Their Development and Use," March 2, 1925, Bulletin, Vol. 6, No. 13, F. Brugger, General Electric, Pittsfield

F. Brugger wrote of the experiences of the Pittsfield plant of General Electric with its standard cost system. This system sprang from management's desire to see how the predetermined costs from the product decision process compared with actual costs. The system described was a very detailed one with a significant number of forms shown. Form E, Labor Operations Cards, and Form F, Material Operating Cards, are worthy of note. Brugger then discussed the uses and limitations of standard costs. He was in favor of changing standard costs at least once a year or sooner if significant changes occurred.

> Large differences between standard and actual cost cast doubt on the accuracy of the standards and consequently there should be no hesitancy in changing standards as soon as investigation shows that revision is necessary.

He felt the system worked best in a plant manufacturing a limited number of standard products in large quantities with very few main classes of material. Brugger found standard costing to be a strong control technique for executives, engineers, designers, and managers. Executives could get monthly reports of actual to standard with differences classified by cause. The author ended his article with a call for standard costing to be studied by all who wanted to increase the value of cost accounting.

The first major article on standard costs in the NACA literature is worth reviewing. It is extremely well written and, as such, gives an excellent example of the importance of verbal ability in accounting. It is also one more example of happenings at GE with a particular accounting issue. Are you happy with your company's use of standard costs to all products? When does your company change its standards?

(16) "Various Wage-Systems in Relation to Factory Indirect Charges," Dec. 15, 1925, Bulletin, Vol. 7, No. 8, R. R. Thompson, McGill University

R. R. Thompson posed a hypothetical situation of extraordinary demand with four alternatives and concentrated on the bonus or premium on workmen's wages as his solution. He stressed the fact that increased production per hour greatly reduces the indirect factory charges per unit of output.

> As the workman speeds up, and saves time, which is used for further production, so does the manufacturer get more production for his indirect factory charges, to repeat, a quantity of the indirect charges, hitherto used up entirely for a certain quantity of production, is saved and is used for further production. But all depends on the rate up to which the men will speed, and that depends, in the end, mainly on the hourly remuneration.

He then classified various bonus plans into three categories: (1) employer sharing in wages saved — the Halsey, Rowan, and Barth systems; (2) employer saves nothing in wages — the Ordinary Piece Rate System and the Bedeaux Point System; and (3) employer paying full rate plus bonus — Taylor Differential Piece Rate, Gantt, and Emerson systems. Thompson then gave one example for each of the eight different systems.

This article is an excellent review of eight classic wage systems. A coverage of these systems was included in cost accounting textbooks until the early 1960s, so the accountant was once recognized as playing an important role in this topic. Since a very important consideration is the lessening of indirect factory charges per unit of production, the accountant with his knowledge of these charges should be a prime contributor to the wage plan decision. Are you familiar with wage incentive systems? Do you play an important role in the wage system of your company? This article says you probably should.

(17) "Overhead in Economics and Accounting," April 15, 1926, Bulletin, Vol. 7, No. 6, T. H. Sanders, Professor of Accounting, Harvard University

Thomas H. Sanders is truly a hero in the history of management accounting, as well as financial accounting. He was president of the NACA in 1931-32, its director of publications from 1930-31, and its director of education from 1927-29. He authored two classic texts in management accounting, *Problems in Industrial Accounting* and *Cost Accounting for Control* (Burns and Coffman, *The Accounting Hall of Fame: Profiles of Thirty-Six Members,* 1976, p. 53). Sanders took a more philosophical, more economic, more policy-oriented view of the topic of overhead, in line with the comments in the Editorial Department Note. He described the march toward more capital-intensive production with subsequent problems of peak loads and idle capacity. He warned against cutting prices without having a reduction in costs due to better manufacturing and marketing methods. Instead he favored the establishment of a different class of customers for the product so that a lower price would not affect regular sales. Sanders' warnings on price slashing are worth noting:

> ...Moreover, it is not profitable to reduce prices if it is simply going to result in demoralizing the market by making buyers hold off in the expectation of still further reductions....
>
> ...In other words, lower prices will be a result of better manufacturing and marketing methods more often than they will be merely a course of increased output while business difficulties remain the same.

Sanders warned against the sales department's being out of close contact with the cost department on the issue of pricing the product to a different class of consumers. He was cautious about adding new products. Sanders favored the machine-rate approach for overhead allocation for situations in which the machine is the principal factor of production.

Sanders's philosophical and economics-oriented approach is a healthy change of viewpoint. His views on price cutting and new products are quite cautious. What is the role that the accounting department in your company plays in such matters as price cuts, new product pricing, and pricing the product for a new class of customers? Does the accounting department have the ability to question the marketing department? This article makes you think and also appreciate the importance of verbal ability in management accounting.

(18) "Question Box," 1926 Yearbook

Clinton H. Scovell, who was both NACA president in 1926 and chairman of the Question Box, drafted 16 topics for debate. Only five were debated. The first, and longest, debate centered on normal overhead policies, followed by a related topic of accepting bids below cost during idle times. About 25 pages were devoted to these topics. The next topic discussed was experimental work, then accomplishments for the year, and, last, the group bonus plan.

Most, if not all, of the 16 topics are timeless in nature. These issues need to be debated continually in all companies because there is no magic, all-time answer. Different times and different people call for some strategic changes in companies' policies on these items. Your company needs to debate some, or all, of these topics; surely your NAA chapter could well use a debate like this. When was the last time your company rigorously questioned its accounting policies on these and other matters? What other topics can you add to the 16 items in Scovell's list? Do you think that nonaccounting officials have enough accounting knowledge to participate meaningfully in the debate? Do you have a program to increase these people's knowledge of your accounting system? How many of your accountants are comfortable with this level of verbal ability?

(19) "Financial Control Policies of General Motors Corporation and Their Relationship to Cost Accounting," January 1, 1927, Bulletin, Vol. 8, No. 9, Albert Bradley, Assistant Treasurer, General Motors Corporation

Albert Bradley described General Motors, its decentralization policy, and its interdivisional committees. This article is one more example of a mini case study of a very successful company. The president of each division was given a free hand within a broad control framework. GM stressed a comprehensive scheme of forecasting. It favored departmental burden control, as established by A. Hamilton Church. Since forecasting was so crucial, fixed/variable analysis was employed. GM's policy of standard volume for burden distribution was described in great detail. Bradley then explained GM's rate-of-return process, which ended up with a standard price. He wrote:

> Whether a business is large or small, there is need of a policy in regard to the relation of capital investment to price of product, and the conditions under which additional capital is to be used to expand the business (either through retention of earnings instead of paying dividends, or from sale of capital securities).

Bradley ended the article with a defense of maintaining the standard price.

> Stability of prices is a condition under which industry prospers. The cost accountant is in a position to present information that is an essential part of an appraisal of the real economic situation of his own company, and thereby to act as a safeguard against action fundamentally unsound....

It is important to note Bradley's strong academic background, as well as the fact that he was prominently mentioned in Alfred Sloan's classic *My Year with General Motors* and later became Chairman of the Board of GM (Sloan, p. 98). GM has had the advantage of being a price-setter throughout most of its history. Whether your company is in such a position or not, you should know the steps in the GM standard price procedure. A need exists, perhaps in every business, to determine a procedure for total investment and a procedure for desired return on investment. GM's interdivisional committee procedure may be useful for your company. Does your company have the same rigorous interest in departmentalized overhead control that GM does? Are there profits and pricing goals for your company? Is interest on invested capital treated as an imputed cost to your company? What is your company's policy on price maintenance? What is your opinion of GM's interdivisional relations committees?

(20) "The Group Bonus and Labor Standards," April 15, 1927, Bulletin, Vol. 8, No. 16, E. H. Tingley, Secretary, National Association of Foremen

E. H. Tingley was an extremely well qualified person to write an upbeat article on a group bonus plan. His background in mechanical engineering and his new position as editor of the *Foremen's Magazine* represented an interesting combination. In the speech recorded here, he presented a sordid view of the early history of time study and presented the improved approaches to it. He then went into a description of the Delco System. The productivity gains were divided equally between management and labor.

> The fundamental principle is that the greatest gain comes to the employer only when the employee gains also, and when the responsibility for this gain is equally divided between management and the men. It must not be all on management or all on the men.

Delco, a GM subsidiary, printed a book on the plan to communicate it to workers. The bonus was based on a combined effort. Management benefited as overhead per unit was reduced by such steps as direct labor doing work formerly done by indirect labor. The group bonus plan led to a simpler and more accurate factory timekeeping system. Quality control was greatly benefited when workers realized that only good work counted. A very interesting and informative discussion followed Tingley's talk.

The group bonus idea fits well into the just-in-time environment of today. Has your company changed the roles employees play but not found an incentive system to reflect this change? Have you discussed the group bonus idea? What is the relationship between workers and foremen in your company? Do you have an informational booklet for your wage incentive system? This is one idea whose time might be back.

(21) "Cost Accounting Practice with Special Reference to Machine Hour Rate," June 1, 1927, Bulletin, Vol. 8, No. 19, Clinton H. Scovell, formerly Senior Partner, Scovell, Wellington & Company

This article was the best in the NACA literature on the scientific machine-hour rate system. As such, it is important to read. Clinton H. Scovell presented the situation of lessening direct labor and increasing indirect costs as the capital-intensive process continues. He regarded both the cost of building and of machinery to be primarily fixed in nature. He favored departmental burden rates and rejected plantwide rates or direct labor dollars and hours. He wrote, "The weakness of many cost systems is that important elements of indirect cost are thrown together in a 'general expense' account, concealing the leaks and wastes that reduce efficiency and curtail profits." Scovell's goal was to get the operating costs of machines at the same degree of accuracy as direct labor. He discussed the computation and disposition of idle time costs and then the effect on selling prices. A good example of the scientific machine hour rate system was given. An interesting discussion followed, focusing on the costs of idle time and pricing policies.

The scientific machine hour rate system fell out of vogue in cost accounting in the 1950s; it has come back as we have entered the era of robotics. The articles by Henry R. Schwarzbach and Richard G. Vangermeersch in the July 1983 issue of *Management Accounting* and by Allen H. Seed, III, in the October 1984 issue are examples of this revival of interest. Do you feel your overhead rate reflects reality? Do you believe that your overhead costs are driven by machines but your overhead rate is assigned by direct laborers? What happens when the last direct laborer dies? How do you assign overhead then? It is also interesting to note the holistic philosophy expressed by Scovell. He surely was a giant in the field of cost accounting.

(22) "The Profit Element," September 15, 1927, Bulletin, Vol. 9, No. 2, James H. Rand, Jr., President, Remington Rand Company

It is a rarity for a president of a major company, such as James Rand, Jr., of Remington Rand Company, to publish an article about cost accounting and cost accountants in an accounting journal. Accountants need to know how we stand vis-à-vis a manager like Rand. This interdisciplinary exchange is always refreshing and necessary. He started with a once traditional analogy of the Scottish influence on accounting and used Andrew Carnegie as his chief example of a cost-conscious manager—which Carnegie was, in terms of both unit cost and overall costs. Rand used the cost department of the National Cash Register Company as an example of what every cost department should aspire to.

> Today the National Cash Register Company has built up a cost department which is second to none, and which is used day in and day out, month in and month out, to check their selling prices; not only their manufacturing and operating costs, but their selling costs, the advertising costs; and every department of the business is checked against certain standards which have been set up. That department is actually a vital force in the business and is having a very commendable effect.

Rand discussed controlled expansion by merger, rather than "spread-eagle" growth. Cost departments aided in mergers by doing line of business analysis and were regarded as the department that had the most to do with profits. Rand felt the cost of selling was eating up the vitals of business. He warned against waiting until commitments were received for control to start. He was concerned about foreign competition. Rand wanted cost cutting to go from the top down.

Accountants have to aspire to the same role that Rand gave them in his company. Does your cost department actively apply cost principles to the conduct of the business? Are you too diffident and too silent about the things you know? Are you involved in merger studies to ascertain efficiencies? How do you control the costs of selling in your company? Is your role limited to paring costs on the lower levels of the organization chart? If your CEO does not have the same opinion of his cost accounting department that Rand did, you've got much work to do.

(23) "The Accountant's Relation to the Budgetary Program," 1927 Yearbook, James O. McKinsey

James O. McKinsey remains as probably the top expert on budgeting and accounting in the 20th century, with Glenn Welsch a very close second. He was a leading academic, as shown by his presidency of the American Accounting Association, as well as the founder of a world-famous consulting company. Flesher and Flesher summed up his accomplishments thusly:

> ...Through his emphasis on principles instead of procedures, McKinsey was the first accounting author to base his writings on the uses of accounting data rather than on their preparation. Indeed, McKinsey was one of those few individuals who operated at the frontiers of business research. His efforts in pushing back those frontiers have expanded the horizons for others. (*Biographies of Notable Accountants*, p. 28.)

Budgets, McKinsey wrote, are a statement of future accounts expressed in terms of units of responsibility. Budgeting was not to be an increase of a certain arbitrary percent; that process is a mathematical computation, not a budget. He presented the budget problem as a coordination between sales price, unit cost, and velocity of turnover. Sales programs were to be based on a well balanced production program and on market analysis. The accountant's role in all of this was quite broad—he served as the eyes and ears of the chief executive. The accountant not only reported to the executive but had to interpret the reports and assist him in formulating policies based on them. Personnel also had to be tied into the budgets. Monthly reports were to be presented in the spirit of helpfulness and cooperation. A budget procedure needed to be thought out carefully.

I have read no better précis of budgeting than McKinsey's. No wonder he attained the great status he did in consulting and academics. He is one more giant of management accounting. Are you the most competent person in your organization to collect, present, analyze, and interpret past information? Are you involved in the establishment of sales prices? Does your sales department push products that can be produced efficiently? Are you involved in the interpretation of accounting reports? Do you prepare the budget?

(24) "The Use of a Thirteen-Month Calendar," 1928 Yearbook, M. B. Folsom, Eastman Kodak Company

M. B. Folsom argued effectively for the adoption by business of a 13-period year. The number of workdays would be the same, as well as constant number of Mondays, Tuesdays, etc. in each period. Many false impressions are caused by looking at months with completely different days. He surveyed 60 companies that followed the 13-period year and gave flash reports from 25 of them. Folsom then discussed the international movement for the 13-period year, which was strongly supported by his boss, George Eastman. Eastman published a longer article in the NACA Bulletin of August 15, 1927, titled "Do We Need Calendar Reform?" In fact, the NACA endorsed the International Fixed Calendar in 1927.

This article should at least make you think about an issue that is probably a nonissue to you and your company. It might at least make you more cognizant of highlighting the number of workdays in the month when you compare months within the current year to the same month last year. Has dissatisfaction been expressed about your company's calendar? Are adjustments made for short and long months? If you were to propose a change, this article would be a good resource for you, especially the opinions given by those companies with the 13-month calendar.

(25) "Incentives in Distribution," 1929 Yearbook, Frederick D. Hess, Manager, Sales and Advertising Cooperative Foundry Company

This article was descriptive of many companies' solutions to the matter of incentives for sales personnel, distributors, and consumers. It is another article illustrating interdisciplinary interest in accounting. Eight company examples were given for sales executives, along with a brief history of profit-sharing plans, and three examples were given of nonfinancial incentives. Five company examples were given for distribution, along with examples for nonfinancial incentives. Nine company examples were given for consumers.

Accountants can add a great deal to these incentive plans because we bring a "hard-nosed," "did they work" attitude to them. The many actual examples used and the other ideas given should lead you to consider at least a few of them for your company. What role do you play in sales incentives? When was the last new idea tried for sales incentives?

(1) "Calculation and Application of Departmental Burden Rates," April 1920 Bulletin, Vol. 1, No. 3, Gould L. Harris, Lecturer in Cost Accounting, New York University

Calculation and Application of Departmental Burden Rates

Burden Subject to Scientific Calculation and Control

No feature of cost accounting is more difficult than burden distribution. Burden, however, can be calculated with a surprising degree of accuracy and can be scientifically controlled through the medium of departmental burden rates together with departmental burden and expense accounts. The impression is too widespread that burden is extremely elusive. Cost accountants can do a great deal to counteract this false impression by taking advantage of every opportunity to explain the modern methods of distributing burden.

A brief survey of the more important steps in the evolution of burden distribution will make it easier to understand the modern practice. It should be clearly borne in mind that in the following discussion a job-cost system is used as a basis of illustration.

Evolution of Burden Distribution

Fixed Percentage Method

What was probably the first method of distributing burden was very arbitrary and for that reason very inaccurate. This was known as the fixed percentage method. Under this plan manufacturing cost was found by adding, usually to the prime cost, a fixed percentage to cover manufacturing burden. To manufacturing cost was added another fixed percentage to cover selling and administrative burden. The addition to this cost figure of further percentages for profit furnished the figures for the arbitrary fixing of selling prices.

Blanket Rate Method

The next step in burden distribution which increased somewhat the accuracy of burden incidence was the use of blanket rates. At the beginning of each fiscal period blanket rates were calculated for the period. These rates were based on past or estimated figures for the *whole plant.* The following were some of the bases used for burden calculation and application under this plan:

1. Material Costs.
2. Direct-Labor Costs.
3. Prime Costs.
4. Direct-Labor Hours.
5. Machine Hours.

This rate was then applied during the current period as follows: Suppose a job whose prime cost was $30.00 consumed 20 direct-labor hours. Its burden cost would be: 20 × $0.50 = $10.00. The cost of the job summarized would be:

Prime Cost	$30.00
Burden Cost	10.00
Total Manufacturing Cost	$40.00

Both fixed percentages and blanket rates were open to serious objection. Neither method considered differences in equipment, machine hours, labor hours and labor costs which caused burden to vary among departments. Both methods ignored the fact that departments were the natural units for the calculation and application of burden.

Steps in the Calculation and Application of Departmental Burden Rates

The next step in the evolution of burden distribution was the use of departmental burden rates. This method is generally regarded today as the best method of applying burden to product. The steps involved in the calculation and application of departmental burden rates and in the preparation of Burden Statements (see Figure 1-1) may be summarized as follows:

1. Selecting equitable bases for the distribution of current burden incurred to direct (productive), indirect (nonproductive) and miscellaneous departments.[1]
2. Current charging of actual burden incurred to direct, indirect, and miscellaneous departments.
3. Current closing of actual burden incurred by indirect and miscellaneous departments into Department Burden Accounts for each direct department.
4. Predetermining standard departmental burden rates.
5. Applying standard departmental burden rates.
6. Preparing monthly Burden Statements.
7. Recording the differences between actual burden and applied burden under the caption "Balance Carried to Plant Burden Balances" in Department Burden Statements.
8. Transferring Plant Burden Balance of each department to a summary statement showing Plant Burden Balances of all departments.
9. Recording net result of this summary statement in the current Profit and Loss Statement before net manufacturing profit is ascertained.
10. Preparing journal entries to charge the total applied burden of each

[1]Some of these bases will be discussed in greater detail in a later article by the writer.

direct department to Work in Process Burden accounts; and to charge the individual jobs with their portion, the corresponding credit being made to the department burden accounts or to department credit accounts as explained below.

11. Preparing Burden Statements which show monthly comparisons of burden.[2]
12. Adjusting departmental burden rates when standard rates are no longer applicable to current conditions.

Departmental Burden Accounts

All manufacturing burden must ultimately be collected in departmental burden accounts for direct departments. Although some burden costs may be originally charged to indirect and miscellaneous departments, they are later cleared into direct departmental burden accounts and are added to the burden costs originally charged to such accounts.

Relation of Terms — Expense, Burden and Overhead

One of the difficulties in discussing all cost problems, including the one under consideration, is the lack of a standardized cost terminology. Many terms in common use have never been given established definitions which are generally accepted. The following distinctions between expense, burden and overhead have the merit of clearness although they are not always adhered to in present day practice.[3] The term expense might be applied to cost items (other than prime cost) when they are charged to expense accounts such as teaming expense and engineering expense. These accounts are split up and distributed ultimately to various departmental burden accounts. Expense accounts may first be closed into accounts which accumulate the expenses of indirect and miscellaneous departments. These accounts, in turn, along with "apportioned" expenses such as steam, electric power, compressed air and general expense, are ultimately closed into departmental burden accounts. As stated above, a departmental burden account is kept for each direct department. The term burden, therefore, would be used in connection with each account that accumulates all costs (other than prime costs) for each direct department. The term overhead would be reserved to indicate the fact that costs (other than prime costs) are "over" the product which passes through

[2]Some of these steps will be discussed in this article while others will be treated in greater detail in a subsequent publication.

[3]In connection with the work of the Committee on Standardization, we should like to have expressions of opinion from members on the definitions mentioned in this paragraph.

Figure 1-1

THE A. B. C. CORPORATION
Department No. 1
BURDEN STATEMENT
Month of January, 1920

	Other Dept. Labor	Own Labor	Material & Miscel.	Mo. Total	Last Mo. Total
Burden Labor:					
1—Foremen and Assistants					
2—Inspection Expense..........					
3—Timekeepers, Tool Cribs..					
4—Cleaning and Sweeping....					
5—Oiling Shafting					
6—Handling Product..............					
7—Work a/c Shop Errors....					
8—General Labor....................					
9—Idle Time............................					
10—Attendance Bonus............					
13—War Bonus					
Total	00000.00	0000.00	0000.00	0000.00	00000.00
Cost per Productive Hour......					
Maintenance and Supplies:					
15—Maint. of Machinery........					
16— " " Shafting, Pulleys, Hangers..					
17— " " Belts					
18— " " Electr. App.....					
19— " " Water, Air Power Lines....					
20— " " Furnace					
21—					
22—Other Maintenance					
23—Maintenance of Fixtures..					
24—					
25—Dies					
26—Hobs					
27—Mills and Drills................					
28—Files					
29—Steel Stamps.......................					
30—Other Non-Durable Tools					
31—Emery Wheels					
32—Lub. and Cutting Oils......					
33—Electric Lamps..................					
34—Gas					
35—Fuel Oil					
36—Other Fuel..........................					
37—Miscel. Shop Supplies......					
38—Welding Material..............					
39—Hardening Supplies..........					
40—Soda					
Total	00000.00	0000.00	0000.00	0000.00	00000.00
Cost per Productive Hour......					
Forward	00000.00	0000.00	0000.00	0000.00	00000.00

Figure 1-1 (con't)

Department No. 1
BURDEN STATEMENT
Month of January, 1920

	Other Dept. Labor	Own Labor	Material & Miscel.	Mo. Total	Last Mo. Total
Forward	00000.00	0000.00	0000.00	0000.00	00000.00
Proportioned Charges:					
Prop. of Div. Expense					
" " " Labor					
" " Elec. Power Exp.					
" " Steam Exp.					
" " Compressed Air Exp.					
" " Liability Insurance					
Total				0000.00	00000.00
Cost per Productive Hour					
Total Burden				0000.00	00000.00
Less Carried to Work in Process Burden 00,000 Productive Hours at .000 per hour				0000.00	0000.00
Balance Carried to Plant Burden Balances				0000.00	0000.00

COMPARATIVE COST PER PRODUCTIVE HOUR

	Prod. Hours		Burden		Cost per Hour	
	For Mo.	Total	For Mo.	Total	For Mo.	Average
January	0000.00	00000.00	00000.00	00000.00	000.00	000.00
February						
March						
April						
May						
June						
July						
August						
September						
October						
November						
December						

the shop and must be applied to the product before its final manufacturing cost can be calculated. If these distinctions between the terms expense, burden and overhead are held in mind, the technique of burden distribution will be more easily understood.

Predetermination of Standard Departmental Burden Rates

Before discussing the application of burden, let us consider the calculation of burden. The survey of a plant made by the cost accountant prior to the installation of a cost system may disclose that the plant is not departmentalized as well as it might be. If such a condition exists, proper departmentalization ought to precede the calculation and application of burden rates because burden is assembled by direct departments. The survey may bring to light also the fact that a proper division of expense accounts does not exist and that equitable bases for distributing expenses are not used. Those conditions like improper departmentalization should be corrected before burden can be scientifically applied and controlled. If the firm does not have correct departmental burden rates, then rates should be based either on past standard burden or on current burden during a period of sufficient duration to indicate what the standard burden is. Burden rates, therefore, are predetermined, i.e., averaged or estimated in advance of a fiscal period. Then they are applied during current periods. Burden rates should be standard or normal; that is, they should be based on burden costs which occur when production is standard or normal. It is not always an easy matter to determine standard production because it varies in different industries and in different plants in the same industry. A serviceable figure, however, is that production which is turned out when a plant runs 80 to 90 percent of its capacity. It is obviously unfair to use burden rates based on a single month's actual burden unless such burden is typical of the whole year. This is seldom the case. For example, the repairs made to an open-hearth furnace in a steel plant may be unusually high one month and very low the next. It would be both unfair and inaccurate to charge the product of the first month with a high burden rate and the product of the second month with a low burden rate, because neither rate would be standard. Furthermore, proper selling prices cannot be fixed without standard burden rates. After the standard burden (money amount) for a direct department has been ascertained, it is divided by some base such as normal direct-labor hours, or normal machine hours, or normal direct-labor cost — whichever basis best fits the conditions — in order to arrive at the predetermined burden rate for the department under consideration. Not that this rate is predetermined. Actual burden rates could not be calculated until the end of each cost period. If actual rates were used, however, product completed before the end of the period could not be costed until the close of the period. Thus, one desideratum of cost accounting, namely, prompt compilation and presentation, would be lost if actual rather than predetermined burden rates were used.

Theory of Burden Calculation

The general theory underlying the calculation of departmental burden rates is that a proportional relationship exists between the burden of each department and some basis. The major problem, therefore, is to select the basis best suited to existing conditions. The same basis is not necessarily used for all departments. The most satisfactory bases for the calculation of departmental burden rates are:

1. Direct-labor Hours.
2. Machine Hours.
3. Direct-labor Cost.

For the sake of illustration only one basis, namely, direct-labor hours, will be explained. Usually it is the best basis. It has been ascertained, let us say, that the standard manufacturing burden and the standard direct-labor hours in Department A have been $30,000 and 60,000 hours, respectively. The former divided by the latter would give $0.50 per direct-labor hour, which is the departmental burden rate.

Application of Departmental Burden Rates

After standard burden rates are predetermined for each direct department, they are applied to the product which passes through such department during the cost period. The number of direct-labor hours or machine hours, or the direct-labor cost—whichever burden basis is used—of each job in each direct department is multiplied by the burden rate of that department. This process is repeated for each department through which the job passes to give the applied burden costs. The detailed burden costs are entered on cost sheets for individual parts and assemblies, as the case may be. The total of applied burden is charged to Work in Process Burden accounts[4] and credited to Departmental Burden Credit accounts. Actual burden incurred during the period is distributed to Departmental Burden accounts in order to ascertain any difference between actual burden and applied burden. The treatment of these differences will be explained later.

---

[4]In modern cost systems it is sometimes advisable to open three work in process accounts, namely:

Work in Process Material
Work in Process Labor
Work in Process Burden

Frequently, however, only work in process account is used.

Contents of Burden Account

The following is a summary of what the illustrative departmental burden statement shows (see Figure 1-1):

1. Actual burden incurred.
   a. Burden labor (details).
   b. Burden labor (totals).
   c. Maintenance and supplies (details).
   d. Maintenance and supplies (totals).
   e. Proportioned charges (details).
   f. Proportioned charges (totals).
   g. Total burden.
2. Applied burden.
3. Difference between actual burden and burden applied through departmental burden rate.
4. Comparative table.

Actual burden charged during the period is entered in either the "Other Department Labor," "Own Labor," or "Material and Miscellaneous" columns, as the case may be. Indirect labor on work, plus burden on same, performed for department No. 1 by indirect workers of other departments is entered in the "Other Department Labor" column. The department's own indirect labor on work done in the department is entered in the "Own Labor" column. Indirect material and miscellaneous charges are recorded in the "Material and Miscellaneous" column. The individual items in these three columns are totaled at the bottom of the "Burden Labor" section. The individual items in the three above columns are cross-totaled and the sums are recorded in the "Monthly Total" column. The totals of the items for last month are entered for comparative purposes. The same general procedure is followed in filling out the "Maintenance and Supplies" and the "Proportioned Charges" sections. Then the total burden for the three big sections of the statement is calculated. The next step is to find the total of direct-labor hours (since this is the burden basis used in the sample statement) on all work in this department for the period. This figure is multiplied by the predetermined departmental burden rate based on direct-labor hours to give the applied burden which is charged to Work in Process Burden account and credited to the Burden Credit account kept for this department.

A question may arise as to the reason for using a burden credit account for each departmental burden account instead of crediting the latter itself with applied burden. The best reason in the writer's opinion is that the use of burden credit accounts insures the accumulation of totals throughout the year, thereby facilitating the prompt preparation of statements. If, when we charged Work in Process Burden account, we credited Departmental Burden account with the applied burden of the department, only a net balance for the month would remain in the latter account. After the repetition of this process monthly throughout the year, the preparation of a progressive statement for the year is troublesome. Another advantage of burden credit accounts is that they follow each other and accumulated totals can be shown when a trial balance is prepared. If applied burden were credited to departmental burden accounts, extensive analysis of these accounts would be required before the firm could ascertain how actual burden and applied burden were running month by month.

It should be noted, however, that no ledger accounts are opened to record plant burden balances shown in departmental burden statements to indicate the difference between actual burden and applied burden. Furthermore, these plant burden balances are too numerous to be entered in the Profit and Loss Statement. Hence they are arranged in a supplementary schedule which is keyed into the Profit and Loss Statement by a designating symbol. The net result of all plant burden balances is entered as a single amount in the manufacturing section of the Profit and Loss Statement before net manufacturing profit is ascertained.

Comparative Cost per Productive Hour

The "Comparative Cost per Productive Hour" shown on the departmental burden statement is a summarized table which shows (1) productive-labor hours, (2) total burden cost, and (3) burden cost per productive-labor hour. In the "For Month" column, under Productive Hours, is entered the productive-labor hours applicable to all work in the department for the month. The February figure added to the January figure, for example, would give the amount to be entered in the "Total" column opposite February. To this total figure would be added the productive-labor hours for March and the result would likewise be entered in the Total column opposite March, and so on. In other words, the total column is a running total column. The same general procedure is followed for the Burden columns.

The monthly costs, divided by the productive-labor hours for the month, gives the *actual burden cost rate per hour* for the month. The average burden cost (rate) per hour is figured every month for all months to date. The data in this table is necessary in making intelligent decisions as to whether or not burden rates should be revised.

Revision of Departmental Burden Rates

By the use of departmental burden accounts and burden credit accounts actual burden can be readily compared with applied burden. Any differences will be small if care is observed in setting standard departmental burden rates. The writer has in mind, for example, a plant with an actual burden of $2,000,000 and plant burden balances of only $12,000 for the year. In other words, the undistributed burden for the year was only 3/5 of 1 percent, which shows what can be done with scientific control of burden.

If plant burden balances are large and liable to continue so, the burden rates should be revised to fit the changed conditions. Otherwise, current costs will be inaccurate. Burden balances may be due, among other things, to changes in the volume of production and burden costs; and to idle machinery and equipment, and the like.

Note in Regard to Subsequent Articles

The chief purposes of the foregoing article are (1) to overcome the impression, which is too general, that burden is not subject to scientific calculation and control; and (2) to outline rather broadly all of the steps involved in the calculation and application of departmental burden rates, and in the preparation of burden statements. In subsequent issues of the "Official Publications" of the National Association of Cost Accountants, additional points, such as the following, will be taken up in detail:

1. Expense Debit Slip.
2. Selection of equitable bases for the distribution of current items of burden incurred to direct, indirect and miscellaneous departments, such as:
   a. Rent.
   b. Fire and Liability Insurance.
   c. Heat, Light and Power.
   d. Wages of Foremen and Superintendents.
   e. Telephone and Telegraph.
   f. Trucking Expense.
   g. General Expense.
3. Preparation of Burden Statements with illustrations.
4. Preparation of Plant Burden Balances Statement with illustrations.
5. Sample journal entries showing distribution of burden.
6. Sample statement showing monthly comparison of burden.

(2) "Accounting for By-Products," August 1920 Bulletin, Vol. 1, No. 7, Research Department, NACA

Accounting for By-Products

Scope of this Publication

The points covered in this publication may be broadly grouped as follows:

1. The meaning of the term "by-product."
2. Sources and classes of by-products.
3. The importance of accounting for by-products in modern industry.
4. General factors affecting by-product accounting.
5. The three chief methods of accounting for by-products.
6. Illustrations of accounting for by-products in certain industries.
7. The advantages and disadvantages of each method.

Meaning of the Term "By-Product"

A by-product has been defined as an article of value incidental to the manufacture of the main product of an establishment or made from the waste material arising from such manufacture.

A generally accepted opinion of the meaning of the term by-product, however, does not exist. One authority, for example, draws a distinction between spoilage, waste, scrap and by-products.[1] Spoilage, he says, is always accidental, although a certain percentage of spoilage may be inseparable from certain kinds of work; for example, the making of castings. Waste arises out of the manufacturing operation itself and is generally a variable quantity. This writer goes on to say that scrap is in the nature of by-product of low grade and is produced in the course of manufacture. He contends that waste has no market value; that scrap has a small value in comparison with the original cost of the material; and that spoilage has value only in as far as the spoiled material can be classed as scrap, all the rest being a loss. He defines by-products as that part of the material which has a value at the time it is rejected from the main processes. If it has no value, he would regard it as waste. So fine a distinction among terms is difficult to apply.

Classes of Defective Work Losses

According to another authority, the losses due to defective work may be classified as follows:

1. Labor and overhead required to salvage defective work.
2. Loss of material where salvaging does not realize full value from the original raw material used.

[1] A. Hamilton Church, *Manufacturing Costs and Accounts*, Chapter IX. McGraw-Hill Book Co.

3. Labor and burden entirely lost when material has to be scrapped.
4. Loss of the material value, being the difference between the original material used and the scrap value of what is spoiled.
5. Loss of profit on account of extra time taken on machines in salvaging material when other new material should have been produced for sale.
6. Loss of profit on material which has to be scrapped.

Items 5 and 6, of course, are not to be computed in the cost records. Nevertheless, a loss of profit due to these causes usually occurs because if it were not for the defective work, other material would be made and sold at a profit.

Classes of Products

One writer states that the products of many plants may be broadly classified into main and by-products. These products may even be called joint ones to indicate that the production factors of any enterprise are jointly required to manufacture them. Main products are sometimes known as primary products; and by-products as additional, minor or residual products.

Classes of By-Products

In the opinion of still another writer, by-products may be obtained from any one or more of the five following sources:

1. Sorting and inspecting raw material—the foreign or defective material not being allowed to enter the manufacturing processes.
2. Residues left after the main product is manufactured.
3. Substances removed in the purification of the main product.
4. Substances extracted which are not necessary to the manufacture of the main product.
5. Items not directly connected with or traceable to the material which enters the manufactured product, such as filings, shavings, sweepings, ashes, and exhaust steam.

It is evident that the above classification does not recognize distinctions among the terms spoilage, waste, scrap and by-products.

By-products can be classified also into two groups according to their marketable condition at the time they come into existence, namely: 1. Those that can be sold in their orignial form without any further expenditures for preparation; and, 2. Those which have to be reworked in order to get them ready for sale.

By-products are found chiefly in the continuous process rather than in assembling industries. Examples of continuous process industries are packing, chemicals, oil, coal and fine cotton. Consequently, by-products are usually accounted for by the process rather than the job cost system because the process system is used in continuous process industries.

Importance of Proper Accounting for By-Products

The problem of accounting for by-products is one of the developments in modern cost accounting brought about by better organization and management. Before the modern methods of reworking and disposing of residues in many of the manufacturing processes were discovered, the manufacturer relegated these residues to the scrap heap, thereby blindly throwing away profits. As the manufacturer found uses for them, some method for their accounting became necessary so that the manufacturer could know his costs in order to meet competition and to manage his business successfully. While as a first step, only the sales and not the costs of by-products may be recorded, it is becoming more and more necessary to record by-product costs if the manufacturer is to decide intelligently whether he should scrap or sell the by-product at the time it arises, or rework it and enhance its sale value.

During the war many manufacturers realized large profits from by-products but kept no record of their cost. In some cases these profits were large enough to pay the regular dividends and, because of this condition, manufacturers in many instances were tempted to increase the production of by-products. When better accounting methods led to recording the costs of the main product and by-product separately, it was often discovered that the extension of the manufacture of by-products turned out to be relatively unprofitable. Many by-products, however, rank nearly as high in importance as the main product. This is true, for example, in the packing, coal, oil and chemical industries.

Before accounting methods are selected for the recording of by-product costs, the management should decide what disposition is to be made of the by-products. Shall the waste be disposed of as such or reworked into some form of by-product with an enhanced value? An intelligent decision cannot be made without a knowledge of the cost of both by-products and main products. This is the case, for example, in the wood-working and the packing industries. If the by-products in the wood-working industries are charged with their legitimate costs, they often appear in a very unfavorable light. Often more labor and burden are expended in reclaiming material than is warranted by the loss that would result if the material were scrapped in the first place. This is particularly true in the metal industries since the development of electric and oxy-acetylene welding. In the steel industry, for illustration, it frequently is possible to infuse new material in defective places in material being processed, and it becomes a nice problem in many cases to decide whether this should be done. This possibility of using new material often leads to increased carelessness in workmanship because of the feeling on the part of the workers that defects can easily be remedied. It must be decided, therefore, in each case whether the defective work is to be reclaimed, converted into another product, or scrapped.

By-Product Asset Accounts

When a large part of the manufacturing activities of a plant is concerned with the production of by-products, segregated asset and cost accounts must be opened if costs are to be controlled and analysis of cost made possible.

The following list of assets used by one plant in the manufacture of by-products will give an idea of the importance of by-products in that plant:

1. By-product Foundations.
2. Primary Gas Cooler Building.
3. Primary Gas Cooler Apparatus.
4. By-product Building.
5. By-product Apparatus.
6. Booster Building.
7. Booster Apparatus.
8. Ammonia Building.
9. Ammonia Apparatus.
10. Sulphate Building.
11. Sulphate Apparatus.
12. By-product Pump Building.
13. By-product Pump Machinery and By-product Equipment.
14. Surplus Gas Meter Building.
15. Surplus Gas Meters.
16. By-product Platework.
17. Gas Pumper Building.
18. Surplus Gas Line.
19. By-product Piping.

General Factors Affecting By-Product Accounting

After a decision has been reached with reference to the disposition of by-products, the accounting methods for recording them are to be selected. To a great extent the method of accounting depends on (1) the character of the industry; (2) the volume and value of the by-product in comparison with those of the main product; and (3) the desire of the management to get accurate costs with a view to controlling them at their source. It is difficult to lay down any hard-and-fast rules for by-product accounting which can be generally followed, because each plant has individual peculiarities to be considered. The same method of accounting may not be suitable even for two plants in the same industry, because, for one reason, the product may not be processed in the same way.

The accounting for by-products, therefore, presents one of the most perplexing problems in cost accounting. Main products and by-products travel together through the shop up to a certain stage in the manufacturing processes, when a separation occurs. The difficulty in accounting for by-products lies in apportioning costs between the two classes of products up to the time the by-product breaks off or is divorced from the main product. Subsequent to that separation, no serious trouble need be experienced.

General Methods of Accounting for By-Products

Three general methods of accounting for by-products are discussed in this publication. They may be designated respectively as (1) No cost; (2) Preparation for Sale, Selling, and Administrative Cost; and, (3) Total Cost. They are referred to hereinafter as First, Second and Third methods, because the foregoing names are not generally used. The accounting technique in connection with each of them is briefly outlined first; then specific examples of each method are mentioned; and finally the advantages and disadvantages of each are discussed.

First Method of By-Product Accounting

The first method of by-product accounting, which probably is used more than any other, is to record only the sales and sales returns of by-products. One general account or a separate account for each by-product may be kept depending on the variety of by-products sold, and the extent to which the management wishes to go in obtaining data for analysis. The excess of sales over sales returns—that is, the net sales—is usually closed into the current profit and loss account, and entered in the "Other Income" or "Miscellaneous Income" section of the profit and loss statement instead of being treated as a reduction of "manufacturing" costs. This method may therefore be called the "No Cost" method, because the manufacturing costs, and the selling and administrative expenses of the by-products are not separated from the costs and expenses of the main products.

Second Method of By-Product Accounting

The second method of accounting for by-products differs from the first in that it records the cost of making by-products salable after they have split off from the main product, the expenses of selling them and the portion of administrative expense applicable to them. The advantage of the second method over the first, is that it gives more information, but neither the first nor the second method indicates the manufacturing costs of the by-products prior to the time they separate from the main products.

Third Method of By-Product Accounting

The chief feature of the third method of by-product accounting is that it separates the costs of by-products from the costs of main products, from the very first manufacturing step. Under the first two methods, the costs of main products and by-products are combined until the point of physical separation is reached. In many cases, however, it is difficult to calculate precisely the costs of by-products prior to physical separation and consequently, even under the third method, arbitrary initial cost values must often be assigned to by-products. In some cases these values are regarded as only the "material cost of by-products." They may, however, be the manufacturing costs if the by-products require no further treatment before sale. Under the third method, perpetual inventories of by-products are kept, which will show quantities and values. The method should not be adopted unless it will be practicable. This depends upon the degree of accuracy which can be attained without needless "hair-splitting" over details, and upon the relative value of the by-products in comparison with that of the main product.

Illustrations of First Method

The salient features of the accounting for by-products under the three methods have been described. Some specific illustrations of the different methods will now be discussed.

The first method is sometimes used for certain products in the chemical industry. In order, for example, to make a certain intermediate product, it may be necessary to make one which has little salable value without another manufacturing operation. When this operation has been performed, it may leave one part of the product that can be used in further processes, and another part with slight value in its present form. In this case the whole cost of the last operation is sometimes added to the cost of the first part. The second part of the product is sold as a by-product and its sale is recorded separately, but no manufacturing costs for it are recorded in the books.

If, taking another illustration, the manager of a machine shop wishes to show separately the cost of main products and the cost of by-products, then theoretically even turnings and borings should be credited to the costs of parts being machined. This, however, is rarely feasible because of the clerical work involved, and consequently only the sales, and not the costs of turnings and borings, are usually recorded.

Many by-products are of such relatively slight value and importance that the only practical method of accounting for them is to treat the proceeds of their sale as an item of miscellaneous profit. Although, in theory, they should be credited to the costs of the department which produces them, any benefits derived from this procedure would be offset by the cost of the clerical work involved.

First Method as Used in Shoe Industry

A modification of the first method is usually well adapted to the "Outsole, Innersole and Top Piece Cutting" department in a shoe factory, where stock such as outsoles, innersoles and heel top pieces are cut from leather. In this case, the by-product consists of damaged or undergrade main products, such as brands, heads, heeling, and half-heeling. At the beginning of a season, each one of the by-products is given an estimated value based (1) on the total value of shoes to be manufactured under contract, and (2) on the estimated market values during the season. As each lot of leather is cut up during the season, a cost sheet is opened on which is entered the total cost of material cut up and the quantity of good and defective pieces obtained. The fixed estimated value of the by-products is then deducted from the cost of the material cut up, the difference being the net material cost of the main product. In this case, the fixed estimated value of the by-product is not adjusted to record its actual cost. The labor and expense incurred in cutting and handling the material is assumed to be included in the fixed estimated value of the by-product material.

In the opinion of one writer, one of the reasons for this accounting treatment is that all the by-product is considered as waste which has a sorting value different from the main product. The profit or loss on the sales of by-product and main product, however, is recorded separately. Another reason for the above accounting treatment may be that the management wishes to keep the cost and volume of by-products to a minimum—the by-product being regarded as waste. In one shoe factory, the by-product was not more than 8% on all bottom stock cutting.

While this method of by-product accounting, whereby the proceeds received from the sale of the by-product are deducted from the manufacturing cost of the main product, is common, it nevertheless is unsatisfactory. It is even more erroneous to credit the proceeds to the overhead of the department which produced the by-product, because this method does not reveal either the correct costs or the "miscellaneous income" from the sales of products. Under this procedure, the sales figure is treated as a reduction of the cost of main product. Hence both the costs and profits of by-products are incorrectly recorded.

Illustration of Second Method

The second method of accounting for by-products is sometimes used in coke plants, where the principal by-products are gas and ammonia. The main product, coke, is charged with all costs up to the time the first by-product is extracted. Thereafter, the costs of the main product and the by-products are recorded separately. To be more exact, losses in weight of the coal consumed in the production of coke should be charged to by-products as a material cost. For example, if 100 tons of coal were consumed in producing 80 tons of coke, the cost of 20 tons should be charged to the by-products.

Summary of Third Method

Under the third method, by-products generally are charged with (1) material, at an arbitrary value if necessary; (2) labor expended on the by-product after it separates from the main product; (3) an equitable proportion of overhead; and (4) a proper share of selling and administrative expense, when these items are applied to the various products or classes of products on the basis of manufacturing costs.

Illustrations Showing Calculation of Material Costs of By-Products

The third method is used in the packing, steel and oil refining industries. Under it, the material costs of by-products may be ascertained, with varying precision, in several ways.

(1) The material cost can be accurately calculated if the business could, if desired, buy the material for the main products and by-products separately. In this case the approximate profit of the vendor is deducted from the purchase price of the material in order to ascertain the material cost to be recorded in the buyer's books.

(2) Arbitrary values can be assigned to residuals (by-products) extracted from the main products, if the residuals when extracted have a market value; such, for example, as a chemical of low degree of strength or concentration which is to be converted into another form. No part of any profit that might have been made if the residual were manufactured independently and not extracted, is included in the cost of residual. While the value of the by-product at the time it splits off from the main product is usually regarded simply as material cost, it consists in part of labor and overhead incurred prior to the time the by-product breaks off from the main product.

(3) The arbitrary values used, instead of being market values, may be those which are apportioned between the main products and the by-products,

when the two classes of products are capable of comparison by a *common standard*, such as the number of British thermal units. Such a comparison may be made, for instance, in plants which carbonize coal in order to get coke, the gas obtained being regarded as a by-product; or in factories where gas is the main product and coke is the by-product. Since the values of both products in these two cases are large, serious attempts should be made to approximate the values of each class in order to fix proper selling prices. Other units of comparison are board feet, used in the case of certain lumber industries; weights, used in the case of certain rubber products; and tons, used in petroleum refineries.

(4) If the value of material in by-products cannot be closely determined by any one of the three methods described above, it can be estimated by the procedure known as "working backward." This may be illustrated as shown in Figure 2-1.

Variation of Third Method

Many materials can be purchased with or without certain by-product contents. For example, there are ores which contain a major metal content and also one or more minor metals as by-products. A company desiring the major metal content may purchase the ores before or after the minor metal contents have been extracted. If raw materials which include by-products are purchased and the by-products are thereafter extracted, the material cost of the main product should get the full benefit of the charge to the by-product because the extraction of the by-product entails charges, such as labor and incidental supplies, which would not have been incurred if the raw materials had been purchased after the extraction of the by-products.

From the viewpoint of the total production cost, the point at which costs of the main products should be credited with the by-products is not of importance. If costs of by-products and main products are to be shown separately, however, labor and overhead as well as material costs should be recorded.

Methods of Calculating Labor and Overhead Costs of By-Products

In some cases attempts are made to calculate labor and overhead costs of by-products as well as the material costs. Accurate charging of labor and overhead may be more difficult than the charging of material. Sometimes labor and overhead are apportioned between the main products and by-products according to the weight or bulk of each class. In other cases, labor and overhead are distributed over main products and by-products according to respective selling prices. Obviously, a time basis for distribution cannot be used in cases where the main products and by-products have been in process for the same length of time.

Figure 2-1

COST OF MAIN PRODUCT UP TO SPLITTING OFF POINT

Material	$10,000	
Labor	8,000	
Burden	6,000	
Total		$24,000.00
Value of By-product per By-product Statement Shown Below		4,220.00
Net Cost of Main Product		$19,780.00

SUBSEQUENT COST OF MAIN PRODUCT

Value at Split Off Point		$19,780.00
Material	$1,000	
Labor	1,200	
Burden	800	
		3,000.00
Final Cost of Main Product		$22,780.00
Unit Cost of Main Product (300 units)		$75.93

COST OF BY-PRODUCT

Selling Price		$6,000.00
Deduct:		
Gross Profit, 10% of Selling Price	$600	
Administrative and Selling Expenses, 3% of Selling Price	180	
		780.00
Net		$5,220.00
Material, labor and burden cost from time of split off		1,000.00
Value at time of split off, to be credited to cost of main product		$4,220.00

SUBSEQUENT COST OF BY-PRODUCT

Value at split off point		$4,220.00
Material	$400	
Labor	500	
Burden	100	
		1,000.00
Final Cost of By-product		$5,220.00
Unit Cost of By-product (100 units)		$52.20

Time of Separation of By-Products from Main Product Affects Accounting

The separation of by-products from main products may be natural or artificial. If the separation can be controlled, the management must decide when to effect it. This managerial decision has a vital bearing on the cost accounting. For example, if for the sake of convenience in manufacturing the main product, the separation is not effected when first possible, then all the manufacturing costs subsequent to the earliest time when the separation could have been accomplished should be charged to the main product.

Objections to First Method

Executives sometimes are not anxious to recognize that by-products have a value, because of royalty complications. Their contention is that the manufacture of by-products and main products together requires more capital than the manufacture of main products alone. Consequently, they believe that anything obtained from the sale of the by-product is wholly profit, and should not be credited to the manufacturing cost of the main product.

One cost accountant contends that the manufacturing cost of the main product should not be credited with the proceeds received from the sale of by-products because the entries necessary in this case could not be made in the particular month when the operations on the by-products are performed. Therefore, he says, the above procedure would show a false cost. He claims, further, that where gross profits are shown yearly or periodically by products and departments, nothing worth while would be accomplished by crediting the sale of by-product to the main product, even though feasible.

Other objections to the first method are the following:

(1) The accounts do not reveal the separate costs of the main products and by-products. As a matter of fact, no attempt is made to calculate or even estimate the costs of by-products. These costs are buried in the accounts which show the manufacturing costs of the main products.

(2) The selling and administrative expenses necessary to dispose of the by-products and main products are not segregated.

(3) In the absence of manufacturing, selling and administrative costs, it is absolutely impossible to separate the losses or profits on by-products and main products.

Because of the deficiencies of the first method, selling prices cannot be fixed intelligently, and manufacturing policies cannot be based on facts.

Despite objections to this method of accounting for by-products, however, it may be the only practicable one for many plants, particularly small ones, where the separation of the costs of the main products from the costs of the by-products involves too much clerical work, or where no clearly defined basis of separation appears.

Criticism of First and Second Methods

Two very marked objections to both the first and second methods of by-products accounting in certain cases are that in the first place no physical inventories of by-products are taken; and in the second place no stock record sheets are kept for by-products. This failure to observe two fundamentals of cost accounting precludes the possibility of even approximating by-product costs. Still another objection is that entries for by-products are not recorded at the time of production, but only at the time of sale. As a result, a true cost history of the by-products does not exist. Because of these conditions, the first and second methods are conducive to loose and faulty accounting, and even to fraud. When adequate records for by-products are not maintained, workmen and, in some cases, executives have sold by-products and appropriated the proceeds for their own personal use. Furthermore, with inadequate accounting, no reductions in the manufacturing cost of main products are shown by the records, although the manufacture and sale of by-products does decrease the costs of the main products.

Advantages and Disadvantages of Second Method

The second method is applicable when the by-product has no salable value at the time it is divorced from the main product. But if it can be worked up into a marketable condition by incurring additional labor and overhead, these costs should be charged against it and deducted from the selling price in order to arrive at the profit. This method is applicable also to industries where the carrying of the by-product along with the main product prior to the separation of the two does not add appreciably to the cost of the main product. The second method of accounting for by-products is more accurate than the first, but it is not a great improvement, because the costs as recorded are not sufficiently complete to be of much practical use.

If the by-product is of so little value at the time it arises that it normally would be dumped, it often is manufactured and sold practically without profit in order to eliminate the cost of dumping. In that case, only the cost of getting the by-product into salable state should be charged to it.

If the manufacturer allows the by-product cost to remain as a part of the manufacturing cost of the main product, it means that the by-product at the time of separation would have no recorded cost value. If the by-product then is sold at market prices, the profit thereon will be overstated in the accounts because no cost value was placed on the by-product when it was divorced from the main product.

If this accounting method is followed, the selling price of the main product should, of course, be sufficient to cover the cost of the by-product and to provide a profit.

The following example illustrates the fact that the method of accounting for by-products may have a vital bearing on business policy: Suppose two competitors, A and B, are manufacturing the same line of furniture. Assume that A credits the manufacturing cost of his main product with an arbitrary value placed on his by-product, while B allows the value of the by-product to remain as part of the manufacturing cost of the main product. In this case the manufacturing cost of A's main product will be less than B's, and A might reasonably sell at a lower figure. Each would doubtless argue that the other's accounting methods are faulty. Unless A disposes of his by-product at a profit, he may incur a considerable loss.

Advantages and Disadvantages of Third Method

In many plants the tendency is to charge as little cost as possible to the by-product on the theory that it is entitled to the free use of the shop's equipment. Nothing could be more fallacious. No portion of a factory's output should be favored over any other. All output should be charged with its legitimate costs. This can be done correctly only under the third method of accounting. Another advantage of this method is that inventories can be priced more accurately.

One objection to this method, when the by-product cost is taken at market prices, is that the material cost of main products will be distorted by market fluctuations. An increase in the price of by-products due to a scarcity of or a large demand for them would reduce the cost of the main products because of market conditions which might be only temporary. For example, because of a temporary shortage, the price of sulphuric acid made by zinc manufacturers increased approximately 400% during the war. If the market price of the by-product varies in exact ratio with the market price of the main product, it is contended that no serious objection can be raised to using market prices in recording the material cost of by-product.

In some cases, a definite ratio is established between the cost of the raw material which enters the main product and the value placed on the by-product. For example, if the cost of raw material entering the main product is $20 per ton, the value set on the by-product may be $5 per ton. Now, if the price of the raw material increases to $30 per ton, the by-product can be charged and the main product credited at $7.50 per ton. This method should be followed if a large part of the profits are made on by-products, the price of which may increase disproportionately with the price of main products.

It should be remembered that the manufacturer of by-products usually expects to receive for them a price which will cover the cost of labor and overhead and allow a reasonable profit. Therefore, if the selling price covers these items, it is contended that no value should be placed on the material in the by-product for the purpose of reducing the cost of the main product. In cases of this kind, it might be well to consider the advisability of selling the waste material as scrap instead of working it into a marketable condition, unless the by-product is run to "get the machine time," that is, to absorb expenses which would otherwise have to be borne by the main product.

The argument that the utilization of waste material which otherwise might be thrown away does not decrease the cost of the main product may be met, however, by pointing out that just as the saving of labor or power by improvements in the process reduces the costs, so should an economy effected by putting into a by-product a material which cannot be used in the regular production reduce the cost of the main product.

If the by-product when it arises can itself be used in the further manufacture of the main product in place of material that could be bought in the open market, then the by-product is sometimes charged to the main product at the market price of the material for which it is used in substitution. Where, however, there is no equivalent material to be purchased on the open market, the best accounting method is to charge the main product with the manufacturing cost of the by-product. This eliminates the criticism that inventories of the main product are inflated if the main product is charged with the sale value of manufactured by-products that might include a profit, instead of with the manufacturing cost of the by-product.

The following objections have been made to this third method:

1. In some cases it involved too much clerical work.
2. It is difficult in many cases to determine the cost of the by-product even approximately.

In addition to these specific objections, a manufacturer may take the attitude that the cost of the main product is not really affected by the cost of the by-product. Further, there is the fear in some quarters that a reduction in the book cost of the main product, through credits for by-product costs, might lead customers who learned of it to demand a lower selling price for the main product.

On the whole, however, the third method is more logical and it gives information which is of vital importance in the administrative control of the business. A majority of the members of the Association who expressed their views on this matter stated their preference for the third method.

(3) "Some Problems in the Actual Installation of Cost Systems," February 1921 Bulletin, Vol. 1, No. 8, H. G. Crockett, Resident Engineering Partner, Scovell, Wellington & Company

Some Problems in the Actual Installation of Cost Systems

Many books have been written on the subject of cost accounting, but generally the chief object has been to establish fixed principles, describe various forms and methods in considerable detail, and to set forth the many reasons why every manufacturer should have a good cost accounting practice.

This article will forego all such discussion, and will be confined to an outline of the more important problems that must be solved during the installation of a cost system, and of the factors that should be considered in arriving at the solution of those problems.

Many cost systems have failed to accomplish the desired results because they were installed without an adequate conception of the problems involved or the factors that should have been considered. It is possible, therefore, that this brief discussion of this question may prove helpful to some of those concerned with the installation and operation of cost systems. The suggestions should be equally helpful to the professional and to the cost accountant directly employed in the factory concerned.

Specific Reason for New Methods

It may be taken for granted that in every factory some records already exist from which certain cost estimates or approximations have been made. Such methods as already exist may, and frequently do, require as much work to operate as the proposed methods; but the working out of the new plan, with the attending difficulties of changing from old to new methods, will necessarily entail some expense, perhaps a great deal. Therefore, there must be some very good reason to justify the management in authorizing this change, and it is the first duty of the cost accountant to find out what those reasons are and to give considerable study to them, if the new methods are to produce the desired results. The chief consideration is to know just what facts the management need to have set forth to assist them in determining policies.

It may be that better cost information is desired because competition has become more keen, and there must be more accurate knowledge of the cost of different articles and lines manufactured. The chief reason may be that waste and extravagance and perhaps even dishonesty have become the rule, and the management wishes to establish a close check on the performance of individuals in this respect. It may be that physical inventories have shown up large shrinkages from the values supposed to be on hand and a better control is desired; it may be that the present practice is generally sound but is not tied in with the general books, and for financial reasons it is desirable to have an accurate balance sheet and operating statement each month; or it may be a combination of any or all of the above reasons.

It is not within the premise of this article to attempt to lay down any definite rules to follow in any particular case, except possibly in a few instances where there can hardly be any question of the procedure to follow. Local conditions necessarily have an important bearing on any situation, and there are so many governing factors of varying degrees of importance that each individual case can be decided only on its merits, after all of the factors have been brought out. This article will attempt to point out what those governing factors are.

Engineering and Accounting Phases

There would seem to be no doubt that the cost records should be thoroughly "tied in" with the general books. You want either cost facts or cost estimates, and there can be no cost facts unless a definite and complete control is established between the general books and the cost records.

Starting from this point, it can readily be seen that there are two different phases to every cost practice. One is the cost construction or engineering phase, which establishes the foundation and develops the necessary cost information bringing the work up to the point of contact with the accounting records; the other is the accounting phase which takes the cost data and so interprets it through the accounts that the factory executives are given accurate information regarding all factory activities which they wish to have presented to them, and the financial and sales executives are presented with correct statements of financial condition and trading loss and gain as well as adequate statistics of sales, costs, and expenses by various classifications.

Importance of Proper Production Methods

It may be well to state at the outset that a satisfactory cost system must be built *up* from the factory, not *down* from the accounts; the problem must be approached primarily from a manufacturing and production and not from an accounting point of view. There must be an adequate conception of the relation of all manufacturing functions, both direct and auxiliary. Then, too, proper production and inventory control should be established either before the cost practice is established or at least concurrently.

Any cost system is only as good as the foundation on which it is built, and without proper control of inventories, manufacturing schedules and operations, and also some means of knowing that the basic records are dependable, the cost figures will be unreliable and may be misleading. Too little attention has been paid to this phase of the problem, and as a result many cost systems fall short of expectations in many respects. The costs of operation show surprising variations, for which there is no satisfactory explanation, and though inventory records may be in exact agreement with the control accounts, the materials in the stockroom have a disagreeable habit of falling short of the amounts called for on the records, and that means inventory adjustments which disturb any cost calculations.

There is much more to the problem than that of simple debits and credits. Of what use is it to know that costs are high, if at the same time the figures do not indicate where and why? Control of work in process is a comparatively easy matter, if there is proper production control, and work flows in an orderly way through the several operations; but it is a very different matter when there is no production control, when goods are diverted from one order to another without proper record, when deliveries from one operation to another or to finished goods are not properly identified, or when spoiled or defective work is not correctly accounted for because of lack of proper inspection.

Perpetual Inventories

Perpetual inventory records are valuable for cost accounting purposes, but that is perhaps the least important of their functions; nor is the utmost value obtained from these records if they show only quantities received, issued, and on hand. Unless they show requirements to meet sales schedules, quantities apportioned to orders and available for further orders, and maximum and minimum limits which will meet manufacturing schedules, and yet keep the investment in inventories at a low figure, when operations are on such a scale that the information is necessary, they are not giving full value for money expended. The additional information requires little extra effort beyond that necessary to keep records of receipts and disbursements and to keep them in agreement with the accounts, yet in many cases it can be made almost invaluable to the manufacturer. The investment in inventories can frequently be cut down to a considerable extent by the proper use of perpetual inventory records, and the accumulation of obsolete materials can be prevented.

It should be kept constantly in mind that a cost system is only a measure by which the operating results and the efficiency of the factory are gauged, and unless the manufacturing and production and planning problems are given due consideration and proper recognition, the costs will fail to indicate where it may be possible to effect economies, and will also fail to show the effectiveness of methods that were started in the expectation of reducing costs.

Kind of Costs Best Fitted to the Business

Assuming then that the production methods are sound, and that the work is properly planned and scheduled, or at least that steps have been taken to have proper methods started concurrently with, if not before, the actual starting of the cost practice, we may next take up the very important question of what kind of costs is best fitted to the business under consideration—order costs, process costs, or a combination of these two, with or without scheduled or standard costs used in connection with any of these plans.

During the course of many investigations the writer has frequently felt that proper consideration has not been given to this question. Sometimes the cost practice was established on the production methods which already existed, without giving thought as to whether or not those methods were designed to give the best results, and order cost systems were established where the cost of an individual order is of little or no value. Conversely, process costs have been established where order costs would serve the purpose better and where the inventory control of work in process would be more accurate.

The accountant will do well therefore to give a great deal of consideration to this question. If the manufacturer is engaged in a purely jobbing or contract business, there will be little choice but to establish order costs, but even where each order calls for something special, it frequently happens that the same materials are used and operations are the same up to a certain point, where a slight change has to be made to meet the particular requirements. For example, there may be many articles which will go through the same operations and be made on the same machines, with only slight differences in finish. Yet the materials must be kept entirely separate and cannot be confused with materials for another order, and therefore each order must be handled separately. Furthermore, it may be worth while to get order costs so as to obtain the relative cost of running a small order as against a large order, and to find out just where the size of the order ceases to have any appreciable effect on the unit cost.

A paper mill may have a variety of product, but operate only one paper machine, so that for that operation at least it might seem necessary to know only the total cost and total pounds produced, regardless of weight or color. Yet most paper mills find it worth while to get the cost of each order or run, if only for the purpose of determining the cost of handling short runs as against long runs.

In most cases it is undoubtedly easier to establish an accurate control of work in process through the use of order costs than through process costs, but it is not always possible to report material, labor or burden charges against definite orders or quantities, and even if possible it frequently costs more to get this record than the increased accuracy is worth.

If comparatively few articles are made and these are run practically continuously, then process costs will probably be the choice. As a matter of fact, it will probably be found that even where the order cost practice is established as the basis, there will be certain operations where it is necessary to obtain a process cost. That is, there will be certain operations where it is not possible to keep a record by orders of the material or labor, or burden, or perhaps any one of these three elements.

With either the order cost or process cost plan, it frequently is desirable to use scheduled costs. That means predetermining the standard cost of each article for material, labor, or burden and sometimes for all three of these items, and establishing the records so that there may be a comparison of actual performance with the standard, revising the standards when necessary.

This plan may frequently be used to advantage with order costs, and is nearly always used in connection with process costs. In fact it is exceptional when schedules or standards are not established for process costs, but cases do exist where it is not practicable, even if it is possible. The plan has the advantage of eliminating fluctuating unit costs from finished parts and finished goods inventories, and the very practical additional advantage of establishing a standard based on normal manufacturing conditions, which is the cost to be considered in fixing selling prices.

If the accountant will carefully consider all of the foregoing before deciding what kind of costs will be calculated, and in addition will consider how finished goods inventories are to be valued and sales costed, whether selling prices must be established long before manufacture or after, and whether they are established by lines rather than by individual articles, he can hardly go wrong in his decision.

Burden Centers

It is not necessary to point out that in any cost plan one of the most important things is to establish proper burden centers and rates, or to do what is technically known as developing the burden. There will be some advantage in having this done, or at least started, first, because this work necessarily requires considerable study of the various operations performed, and will bring to light many important factors which have a bearing on the method of compiling costs.

One of the first steps therefore is to divide the factory into production or burden centers, not necessarily according to physical conditions, though some attention will necessarily be paid to supervisional divisions, but according to operations or functions performed. This is a phase of work which requires careful study, as much depends upon the proper division of the factory. To consider the whole factory as one center, and to have only one burden rate, is no more to be condemned than to go to the other extreme and calculate a separate rate for every machine and work place in the factory. The latter method might seem to give absolutely accurate figures, but when we consider that under the best conditions many items of burden are estimated, at least as far as their distribution to centers or machines is concerned, that we are bound to have machines performing similar operations whose calculated burden rates will vary by only a few cents, and that frequently this difference of a few cents an hour in the rates can hardly be detected in the cost of the finished product, we must realize that this attempt at increased accuracy can easily cost more than it is worth.

It is unsafe to combine under one rate machines performing entirely different operations, unless they are machines that always work together as one unit, because something may easily happen to upset this arrangement. A revision of rates then becomes necessary, and it should be the object of any burden development to establish rates that will stand with as little and as infrequent revision as possible.

Burden Distribution

We now come to the question of how the various expenses of the business are to be distributed to the centers into which the factory has been divided, and also of how the burden of these centers is to be applied to the cost of the product as it passes through them. There is little difference of opinion regarding methods of calculating material and labor costs in any industry, and such differences as do exist relate to questions of the degree of refinement that is worth while rather than to questions of principle. When we get to the question of distribution and application of burden, however, we encounter marked differences of opinion as to methods to be followed, and even when there is an agreement as to methods there is always the question of whether it is worth while, because of the possible extra expense, to follow the procedure that is accepted as technically correct.

As between any two methods or bases for distribution of expenses to burden centers the accountant will of course have to form his own opinion, and the important thing is that he know what considerations should influence his decision and appreciate the extent to which the amounts involved may affect final costs. In the following paragraphs we will consider briefly some of the questions that should be raised before deciding on the basis of distribution.

Rental Charge

Assume that a manufacturer has a plant that consists of a group of buildings of varying types of construction, built at different periods to accommodate the expansion of the business. One or two of them may have been constructed to accommodate a particular operation or function, such as a power house, warehouse or foundry. The others are ordinary factory buildings, built to house the various manufacturing operations. It is probably correct in theory to calculate a rental charge separately for each building, because one building actually costs more per square foot than the other, but is any practical purpose served by showing the rental cost per square foot to be greater in one building than another, when the only reason for an operation's being in one building rather than another is because it happened to be started there, or because that is the proper location with reference to preceding and succeeding operations? The manufacturer would not think of moving an operation to another building simply because his rental charge was less in that building—there would certainly have to be a stronger reason than that.

On the other hand, is one floor of a building worth more than another? All floors of loft buildings which are rented to manufacturers are not rented at the same price, but light, elevator service, and accessibility to customers and employees have more to do with this than the usefulness of the space itself for the particular operations. We frequently find basements that are damp, dark, low-posted, almost useless for manufacturing but convenient, or at least useful, for storage space.

Machinery and Equipment Factor

There is hardly any question as to the basis of distribution of the fixed charges on machinery and equipment; since the charges are based on value, they would naturally be distributed in proportion to value. The difficulty will probably come in determining a proper classification of machinery and equipment items in the first place, and in determining the allocation of these items to centers. This will have little, if any, effect on the final costs, however, and is not worth a great deal of study.

Power

There is not much question about the distribution of power, except that some cost men make two charges, one for the fixed charges on the power transmission equipment and the other for the current itself. In this way there would be a charge to each burden center, each period, representing the cost of the power transmission equipment necessary to fulfill the needs of that department, but the charge for the current itself would vary with the actual power consumption. That refinement would probably pay in departments where the power was a very important factor of cost, but it presupposes that the actual consumption of power in a department is determined from meter readings, or else calculated on the basis of the rated horse-power of the machines and the actual hours operated. There is also the further question of whether the current should be charged to the department at a fixed rate, the power plant showing an underearned or overearned burden, or the total expense of the power plant distributed on a percentage basis, or on the basis of a calculation of the exact horse-power hour cost for each period.

Steam and Heat

The problem of steam distribution presents about the same problems as power distribution, except that when we come to the distribution of steam used for heating purposes, or rather to the distribution of heat, we encounter several additional problems. These have been treated rather slightingly by many cost accountants, on the theory that since buildings are frequently heated by exhaust steam from the engine, the heating really costs little or nothing. A more careful study of this question will reveal that this theory is not correct, and that heat may be a very important factor. The cost can be quite accurately ascertained if one wishes to take the trouble. One method is to assume that the excess of coal used in the winter months over the summer months represents the coal required for heating purposes only; another is to determine the cost by scientific tests of the cost of reheating the steam returned from the heating system. It must be recognized, however, that all areas are not heated uniformly. Storage departments may be little used and therefore require little heat, and other departments using furnaces and ovens for their processes furnish all the heat required. It is reasonable that a department should benefit by the fact that its operations require an oven or a furnace which gives out all of the heat required, but is that true of another department that happens to be located near these ovens or furnaces? For example, there are cases where whole floors, occupied by several departments, require no further heating than they get from furnaces, ovens, and muffles, located on the floor below.

The cost accountant may consider the area of the departments heated and use that as a basis for distribution, or he may think it worth while to ascertain the area of the radiation surface in each department.

Light

In considering the distribution of lighting expense, one method is to count the number of lamps in each department and to consider their wattage and the number of hours they are used, in order to arrive at the cost of lighting the various departments. No one will dispute that that is the correct method of calculating the actual cost of lighting any particular area, but is there any reason why one operation should be penalized because it happens to have been located on the first floor of a building where daylight is shut off by adjacent buildings, instead of on the top floor where there is plenty of daylight from all four sides? On the other hand, the operation may be one that requires close work and therefore a good deal of light, or it may be exactly the opposite. Furthermore, the total cost of light is a very small factor of burden in most instances, and the difference between a correct and estimated distribution will hardly be detected in the cost.

Repairs

The distribution of repairs offers no particular difficulty except that these repairs are apt to be somewhat intermittent. Some accountants estimate the total cost of repairs for the year and charge each department with a proportion of this charge each period, debiting the actual cost of repairs against the estimate or reserve. This plan certainly has an advantage when extraordinary repairs are required infrequently but cost considerable money.

Another question is whether the charge on a repair job should be the wages paid the man actually employed, to which will be added the proper burden rate, or whether all repair work should be charged for at a uniform rate per hour, including labor and burden, regardless of the wage rate of the man actually employed on the job. Unless the nature of the repairs is such that they require the services of a particular individual, skilled in that kind of work and earning a certain scale of wages, the method of using one rate of labor and burden has a good deal to recommend it. It is the basis of charging for repairs done by outsiders.

Direct Charges

Fortunately there are certain burden items that can be charged direct to the centers as the expense is incurred and therefore present no problem of distribution. Indirect labor, supplies, compensation insurance, and the like, are in this class. These factors require no discussion.

General Burden Items

There are a number of burden items, however, which are not so readily disposed of, because they can neither be charged direct from an analysis of the payroll or from requisitions, as can indirect labor and supplies, nor is there any accurate or scientific basis of distribution available as there is for steam, power, heat, or light. We refer to such factors as shop transportation, and shop administration. The latter item may be analyzed into superintendence, production and costs, industrial relations, and other subdivisions which are of sufficient importance to be shown separately.

Such factors constitute a general burden, which must be included in costs, but which in too many cases has not been given the study and consideration that it deserves. Its importance is apparent when we consider that the total amount of these general burden items usually forms a very large portion of the total burden of the plant.

Shop Transportation

Shop transportation presents difficulties of distribution only when there is a department or certain equipment used by all or several centers. In many small factories where the material is not particularly heavy, each department delivers its product to the next department with its own operating force, and therefore shop transportation becomes a direct charge to the center served. Where there is an industrial railway, overhead traveling cranes, or a special force organized to transport materials all over the shop, the problem is not so simple. The class of labor used in this work is frequently such that it is difficult to get accurate records on which to base a distribution, but tests can be made which should give the cost accountant sufficient data to make a distribution accurate enough for all practical purposes. In analyzing the results of these tests he should consider the following questions: Are all materials handled of a comparatively uniform weight and bulk, and can they all be handled with the same transportation equipment? Is all material handled the same number of times? The cost accountant will also have to decide whether the interests of true costs will be best served by adding the cost of shop transportation to the completed cost of the article on some common basis (probably weight or number of pieces) or whether the cost of operating the transportation department had better be redistributed to the various centers in proportion to the service rendered. With a fairly uniform product all going through the same operations the first method will be simpler and sufficiently accurate. With a diversified product where some items are handled more times and at a greater cost than others, the second plan will probably be followed, if the total cost of shop transportation is an item of sufficient importance.

Shop Administration

Shop administration, including as it may, superintendence, production, cost, timekeeping, industrial relations or personnel work, first aid, and such activities, presents one of the most difficult problems of distribution with which the cost accountant has to contend. These activities are organized for the benefit of the factory as a whole and frequently they form a very considerable portion of the total expense, yet because of their nature they offer no scientific basis of distribution to other centers, or for addition to the cost of the completed article.

Where this problem has been given study, the three most common methods or bases of distribution have been: (1) percentage of productive labor in the several departments; (2) productive hours; (3) number of employees; with perhaps the majority favoring the last method. It is doubtful whether any one of these methods will stand the test of scientific analysis applied to all the items making up the shop administration expense, and to all the kinds of service rendered by them. Obviously, the only way to obtain reasonably accurate results is to analyze the various items and consider each one individually, the final basis of distribution of the total expense reflecting the relation of each of the items to the several centers.

Shop superintendence, for example, which includes the wages of the superintendent himself and of the clerks who may be directly connected with his office and the accompanying expenses, is perhaps the most difficult item of all. Divisions like production, cost, and timekeeping are much simpler to analyze, but it is not wise to make snap judgments even for them if one wishes accurate results.

For example, it might seem offhand that the activities and the expense of the timekeeping department, which is almost entirely clerical hire, should be governed by the number of employees in the shop. It is generally true that with a factory and a timekeeping department fairly well established a general expansion of the business with an increase in the number of employees in all departments will call for a corresponding and proportionate increase in the timekeeping department, but when we consider distributing that charge to the various departments we have to take into account the kind of detail work which the timekeeping department has to do and the records they have to handle. For instance, in extending the wages of job tickets we may have a department of one hundred employees averaging not more than one order, and therefore not more than one job ticket, for an employee per day. On the other hand we may have a department of fifty employees averaging at least five changes of orders or operations per day calling for at least five job tickets per man, which means that the detailed records from this department which the timekeepers have to handle are two and one-half times as many as from the department of one hundred employees.

Furthermore in some departments labor is part of the burden rate and is charged direct to the center, and no records of actual labor on orders are necessary. There may be rather elaborate and complicated bonus systems in certain departments and some departments operate on piece work while others are on a day work basis. All of these circumstances affect the work of the timekeeping department and should be considered in prorating its expense to the other departments.

The production and cost divisions and the personnel and first aid departments offer similar problems of analysis. In all of these divisions, by far the largest item of expense is clerical hire and therefore it is important to analyze the work of the several clerks.

Relative Importance of Different Items

In all of these problems of distribution the cost accountant must first consider the relative importance in the final cost figures of these general burden items, and the error that might be caused by an inaccurate distribution of this expense.

It is a common criticism of cost accountants that they spend too much time in working out elaborate distributions of expenses which are unimportant in themselves and which do not permit of an accurate distribution. Undoubtedly some of that criticism is deserved, but it should also be remembered that once the basis for distribution has been worked out, it can generally continue in use for some time. The rates may remain unchanged for a year or longer because the relation of the services of these shop administration departments to the other departments does not change materially except when new activities are taken on or discontinued.

Burden Application

We now come to the very important question of how the burden which has been *distributed* to the centers engaged in the manufacture of the product shall be *applied* to that product. There are four rather widely used methods or bases, viz., the machine-hour rate, man-hour rate, the process or unit-of-product rate, and the percentage-of-direct-labor rate.

Machine and Man-Hour

The machine-hour and man-hour bases are operated in practically the same way, and in deciding upon which of these two methods to use the cost accountant should consider what is the dominant or controlling factor in production. If he accepts the theory that the hour basis is correct, then if the machine controls the production and the man simply operates the machine, the machine-hour basis will probably be used. In assembly departments, or where the operation is performed by hand, or where the machines used by different workmen are very similar, a man-hour rate will be used. Even where the machine-hour basis is accepted as the correct plan, if one man operates the machine, the record of his time will in most cases be the same as the machine time. In many cases, however, one workman will operate four or five machines and in other instances it takes two or three men to operate one machine. In such cases there will be no choice but to use the machine-hour basis, and unless labor is paid piece work, or there is some particular reason for keeping labor costs separate from burden, labor will probably be included as part of the burden and all covered in one rate per hour for the machine.

In some cases where one operator handles several machines, the wages of this operator are prorated to the orders on the basis of the production of the various machines. Before subscribing to such a plan the cost accountant should consider the work involved in prorating the labor, and decide whether the results are as accurate as those obtained by considering the labor as part of the total machine cost and including it in the one machine rate.

Process Rate

The process rate is used where it is not possible or practicable to get either man or machine time by jobs or kinds of work. The burden is then applied on the basis of a unit of product, such as pounds, or feet.

Percentage of Direct Labor

The fourth method of applying burden as a percentage of direct labor has been rather extensively used, particularly in factories where labor is paid largely on a piece work basis, probably because of its simplicity rather than its accuracy. The advocates of this method generally admit that it is not scientifically correct but claim that it is sufficiently accurate under the particular condition where it is employed, or where they have used it; in other words, that when reduced to an hourly basis the wage rates in the department are practically uniform for all employees, so that the burden is applied in substantially the same ratio as it would be if the hour rate were used. The cost accountant will of course want to be sure that no important error in costs will be introduced if this basis of burden application is used. He should also have in mind that while conditions at the time of making these tests or calculations may be such that the percentage-of-direct-labor basis will give approximately accurate results, these conditions are never stable. Even if piece work rates or basic wage rates do not change, the personnel in a department changes; new employees are usually paid a lower hourly rate than old employees, even though doing the same work and with just as much skill; and piece work and bonus rates have never yet been so accurately established that an individual employee makes the same hourly rate on each different operation. That being the case, it is evident that the product is not charged with burden in proportion to the time it is in the department, although most, if not all burden factors are proportionate to the time element.

General Administration Expenses

We have now covered, in a very broad and general way, the items of manufacturing cost, or the expenses that are incident to placing the goods in finished goods storage or on the shipping room floor. Many cost systems stop here, and the balance of the expenses of the business are guessed at, lumped together and added on some purely arbitrary basis.

A little study of this question will show that the only reason for such a procedure is that the items do not readily lend themselves to any scientific distribution or allocation to the product. On the other hand these general administrative and selling expenses frequently amount to a very considerable proportion of the total cost and should therefore be given the study necessary to insure that they are added to manufacturing costs on the proper basis.

Some manufacturers divide all of their expenses between manufacturing and selling, and everything that is considered manufacturing expense goes to make up manufacturing cost, leaving only selling expense to be added after the goods are delivered to the sales department. Others feel that there are certain functions or departments the expense of which cannot easily be divided as between manufacturing and selling, and had better be treated as general administrative or executive items.

In deciding which plan to follow, the cost accountant will have to consider whether the latter plan results in certain items being charged to manufacturing costs, and therefore to the finished goods inventory, which cannot properly be considered as a necessary expense of getting the product to that point. Generally speaking, also, none of the general administrative items permits of as accurate a distribution as even the shop administration items, and it is a fair question whether the ends of dependable costs are better served by treating them as a whole rather than individually.

Can the product be divided into lines, and do these administrative expenses follow this division? What relation do these expenses have to total costs? Does the material element in cost have any effect on these expenses? Does the labor element? Do these expenses or any of the individual items have any direct relation to the activities of certain manufacturing departments?

The cost accountant should first be sure that the issue is not clouded by including in this class items that very clearly belong either in manufacturing or selling (if he does not subscribe to the plan that all expenses are either manufacturing or selling). There is no established rule to guide him in his decision as to how he shall add this expense to cost. The bases usually adopted are percentage of total cost, percentage of direct labor only, and percentage of labor and burden. The writer is of the opinion that having made whatever division by lines seems possible, the basis of percentage of labor and burden offers the most satisfactory solution in the long run.

Selling Expenses

Selling expenses are not usually so difficult to analyze or allocate. They can frequently be divided quite accurately by lines, and having been divided in this way, each group of expenses will have a certain relation to the sales of that line. This relation may best be expressed as a percentage of sales or as so much per unit of product sold.

A division of expenses by salesmen or territories may furnish useful information, but it will be of no help in determining how these expenses shall be added as a part of cost. If freight is paid and treated as part of selling expense, it is possible to analyze this expense and apportion it to cost quite accurately; advertising can frequently be divided by lines; commissions offer no difficulties of distribution, if they are not in fact deducted from sales; and there are other items of selling expense that permit of as ready analysis by lines.

As stated at the beginning of this article, no attempt has been made to settle any questions of principle, or to establish any rules of procedure except in cases where a certain practice is practically universal among cost accountants. In the last analysis the success of the cost system depends upon the judgment exercised by the cost accountant in deciding these questions, but the chances that his judgment will be good are greatly increased if he has considered all of the factors involved.

(4) "A Bibliography of Cost Books," April 1921 Bulletin, Vol. 2, No. 10, Research Department, NACA

A Bibliography of Cost Books

Introductory Note

In presenting this bibliography of cost books to our members there are certain points which ought to be emphasized. In the first place the bibliography is restricted to books. We have purposely omitted pamphlets and other material. There is a considerable quantity of such material in circulation and we hope at a later date to issue a supplementary bibliography covering pamphlets and other literature of this type.

In the second place, no attempt has been made to indicate the relative value of the books listed. We hope to issue shortly a selected reading list which will indicate the sources of authoritative information on different phases of cost accounting, but at this time it was thought best to supply a list of books which would be as complete as possible.

The list is based on an extensive study of the published literature. It is probably too much to expect that no books have been overlooked, but we believe that most of the literature which has been published is included. Some of the sections are probably more complete than others. For example, there are not likely to be as many omissions in the section on general cost books as there are in some of the special sections such as the one dealing with particular trades and industries. We shall appreciate it if members will bring to our attention any omissions which they may notice.

For convenience the bibliography has been divided into five groups:

1. Books treating the whole field of cost accounting.

2. Books on general accounting and auditing which contain some references to cost accounting. In some cases these references are very short and are not likely to be of great value to the general student of cost accounting unless he is interested in obtaining the views of the particular author. In this section we have listed some volumes of accounting problems which contain cost problems.

3. Books on industrial management which contain passages devoted to cost accounting. Here again the same comment applies as in section 2.

4. Books dealing with cost accounting for particular trades or industries. In this section an attempt has been made to divide the books according to some of the leading types of industry.

5. Books dealing with some particular phase of cost accounting.

If this bibliography is used with due regard to its nature it should prove a useful guide to the general literature of cost accounting. It must be used with discrimination and the value of each book listed must be considered with relation to the date of its publication and the general nature of the subject matter. The books published abroad and those published some years ago may not be of as great practical value as some volumes recently published in this country, but they frequently present interesting material for historic or comparative purposes.

I. Books Dealing With the General Subject of Cost Accounting

ARNOLD, HORACE L. The Complete Cost Keeper.
The Engineering Magazine Press. New York. 1907 Edition. (Original Copyright 1899.) pp. 419.

BAUGH, FREDERICK H. Principles and Practice of Cost Accounting.
F. H. Baugh. Baltimore, Md., 1915. pp. 194.

BENNETT, G. E. Accounting — Principles and Practice. Vol. I.
Biddle Business Publications. New York.

BUNNELL, STERLING H. Cost Keeping for Manufacturing Plants.
D. Appleton & Co. New York, 1911. pp. 233.

CHURCH, A. HAMILTON. Manufacturing Costs and Accounts.
McGraw-Hill Book Company. New York, 1917. pp. 452.

COOK, CHARLES B. Factory Management.
Bookkeeper Publishing Co. Detroit, 1906. pp. 215.

DANA, R. T. and GILLETTE, H. P. Cost Analysis Engineering.
American Technical Society. Chicago, 1918. pp. 346. (Vol. 2 — Cyclopedia of Commerce, Accountancy and Business Administration.)

DICKSEE, L. R. Fundamentals of Manufacturing Costs.
Gee & Co. London, Eng.

EDDIS, WILTON C. and TINDALL, WILLIAM B. Manufacturers' Accounts.
Published by the authors, Manning Chambers, Toronto, Canada, 1902. (Third Edition.) pp. 199.

EGGLESTON, DEWITT CARL. Cost Accounting.
Ronald Press Company. New York, 1920. pp. 444. (Vol. III — Business Accounting.)

EGGLESTON, DEWITT CARL and ROBINSON, FREDERICK B. Business Costs.
D. Appleton and Company. New York, 1921. pp. 587.

ELBOURNE, EDWARD T. Factory Administration and Accounts.
Longmans, Green and Company. New York, 1921. (Third Edition.) pp. 811.

EVANS, H. A. Cost-Keeping and Scientific Management.
McGraw-Hill Book Co. New York, 1911. pp. 252.

FICKER, NICHOLAS THIEL. Industrial Cost Finding.
Industrial Extension Institute. New York, 1917. pp. 511. (Vol. 5 — Factory Management Course.)

GARCKE, EMILE and FELLS, J. M. Factory Accountants.
D. Van Nostrand Co. New York, 1914. (Sixth Edition.) pp. 248.

GLEDHILL, S.W. Practical Costing.
The Author, 26 Victoria Street. London, England, 1917. pp. 72.

HALL, H. L. C. Manufacturing Costs.
The Bookkeeper Publishing Company. Detroit, 1904. pp. 171.

HARRISON, G. CHARTER. Cost Accounting to Aid Production.
The Engineering Magazine Company. New York, 1921. pp. 300.

HATHAWAY, CHARLES E. and GRIFFITH, JAMES B. Factory Accounts.
American School of Correspondence. Chicago, 1913. pp. 71. (American Accountant's Library.)

HAWKINS, L. WHITTEM. Cost Accounts — An Explanation of Principles and a Guide to Practice.
Gee & Co. London, England, 1912. pp. 120.

JENKINSON, M. W. Cost Accounts for Small Manufacturers.
Gee and Company. London, England, 1907. pp. 56.

JOHNSON, G. Manufacturing, Bookkeeping and Costs.
Isaac Pitman and Sons. New York, 1918. pp. 120.

JORDAN, J. P. and HARRIS, GOULD L. Cost Accounting — Principles and Practice.
Ronald Press Company. New York, 1920. pp. 529.

KENT, WILLIAM. Bookkeeping and Cost Accounting for Factories.
John Wiley & Sons. New York, 1918. pp. 261.

KIMBALL, DEXTER S. Cost Finding.
Alexander Hamilton Institute. New York, 1919. pp. 338. (Vol. 10 — Modern Business Course.)

LEWIS, E. ST. ELMO. Efficient Cost Keeping.
Burroughs Adding Machine Company. New York, 1914. (Third Edition.) pp. 256.

LUNT, JULIUS. Manual of Cost Accounts.
Isaac Pitman and Sons. New York, 1920. pp. 124.

METCALFE, HENRY. The Cost of Manufacturers and the Administration of Workshops.
John Wiley and Sons. New York, 1907. (Third Edition.) pp. 366.

MILLENER, C. A. Cost Accounts.
Hunter Rose Company. Toronto, Canada.

MOXEY, EDWARD P., Jr. Principles of Factory Cost Keeping.
Ronald Press Company. New York, 1913. pp. 102.

NICHOLSON, J. LEE. Factory Organization and Costs.
Kohl Technical Publishing Company. New York, 1909. pp. 410.

NICHOLSON, J. LEE. Cost Accounting — Theory and Practice.
Ronald Press Company. New York, 1913. pp. 341.

NICHOLSON, J. LEE and ROHRBACH, JOHN F. D. Cost Accounting
Ronald Press Company. New York, 1919. pp. 576.

PREEN, H. Reorganization and Costings.
Simpkin Marshall. London, England, 1913. (Second Edition.) pp. 188.

PRICE, J. F. C. Factory Cost Accounts.
Educational Book Company. London, England. (Harmsworth Business Library, Vol. 2.)

RIDGWAY, A. CLIFFORD. Cost Accounts in Principle and Practice.
Isaac Pitman and Sons. New York, 1920. pp. 110.

SCOVELL, CLINTON H. Cost Accounting and Burden Application.
D. Appleton and Company. New York, 1916. pp. 328.

SEVERAL AUTHORS. Cost of Production.
The System Company. Chicago, 1907. pp. 196. (Vol. 3 – Business Man's Library.)

SEVERAL AUTHORS. Purchasing Manufacturing Costs.
American School of Correspondence. Chicago, Ill., 1910. pp. 342.

STRACHAN, W. Cost Accounts.
Stevens and Haynes. London, England, 1903. (Second Edition.) pp. 102.

STRACHAN, W. Cost Accounts: The Key to Economy in Manufacture.
Sweet and Maxwell. London, Eng., 1921. (Fourth Edition.)

THOMPSON, C. BERTRAND. How to Find Factory Costs.
A. W. Shaw Company. Chicago, 1916. pp. 191.

TIMKEN, FRANK H. General Factory Accounting.
Trade Periodical Company. Chicago, 1914. pp. 171.

UNCKLESS, L. How to Find Manufacturing Costs and Selling Costs.
Modern Methods Publishing Company. Detroit, 1909. pp. 90.

WEBNER, FRANK E. Factory Accounting.
La Salle Extension University. Chicago, 1917. pp. 345. (Higher Accountancy – Principles and Practice.)

WEBNER, FRANK E. Factory Costs.
Ronald Press Company. New York, 1911. pp. 611.

WILDMAN, JOHN R. Cost Accounting.
The Accountancy Publishing Company. New York, 1911. pp. 106.

WILDMAN, JOHN R. Principles of Cost Accounting.
New York University Press. New York, 1920. pp. 96.

WOODS, CLINTON E. Practical Cost Accounting for Accountant Students.
Universal Business Institute. (2 volumes.) New York, 1908.

____ ____ **Manufacturing Cost.**
The Business Man's Publishing Co. Detroit, 1904. pp. 191

____ ____ **Cost Keeping Short Cuts.**
Burroughs Adding Machine Co. Detroit, 1911. (Second Edition.) pp. 190.

____ ____ **Costs and Statistics.**
A. W. Shaw Company. Chicago, 1914. pp. 200. (Vol. 2 – Library of Office Management. Now published as a separate volume. Last printing 1917.)

II. Books On General Accounting and Auditing Which Contain Material On Costs

BAKER, JAMES W. 20th Century Bookkeeping and Accounting.
South-Western Publishing Company. Cincinnati, 1920. (Twelfth Edition.) pp. 233-238.

BASSET, WILLIAM R. Accounting as an Aid to Business Profits.
A. W. Shaw Company. Chicago, 1918. pp. 210-279, 307-309.

BEACH, E. H. and THORNE, W.W. The Science and Practice of Auditing.
Bookkeeper Publishing Company. Detroit, 1903. pp. 6-7, 18-61.

BENNETT, R. J. Corporation Accounting.
Ronald Press Company. New York, 1916. pp. 166-176, 352-364.

BENTLEY, HARRY C. Corporate Finance and Accounting.
Ronald Press Company. New York, 1908. pp. 150-165.

BENTLEY, HARRY C. The Science of Accounts.
Ronald Press Company. New York, 1911. pp. 191-250.

CARTER, R. N. Advanced Accounts.
Isaac Pitman and Sons. New York, 1920. pp. 566-640, 808-826.

CASTENHOLZ, WILLIAM B. Auditing Procedure.
La Salle Extension University. Chicago, 1918. Numerous references.

CHASE, W. A. Auditing and Cost Accounting.
La Salle Extension University. Chicago, 1911. (Higher Accountancy Principles and Practice.)

COLE, WILLIAM MORSE. Accounts — Their Construction and Interpretation.
Houghton Mifflin Company. New York, 1915. pp. 141-151, 270-327.

COLE, WILLIAM MORSE. Bookkeeping, Accounting and Auditing.
National Institute of Business. Chicago. pp. 347-375. (International Business Library.)

COLES, ARTHUR and COMINS, CHARLES. Company Accounts.
Isaac Pitman and Sons. New York, 1920. (Second Edition.) pp. 160-167, 168-182, 214-234, 242-247, 248-263.

CUTFORTH, A. E. Audits.
Gee and Co. London, England, 1914. (Third Edition.) pp. 87-133.

DAWSON, SIDNEY S. and DE ZOUCHE, R. C. Accounting.
Isaac Pitman and Sons. New York, 1920. pp. 38-47, 204-233, 248-256.

DAY, CLARENCE MUNRO. Accounting Practice.
D. Appleton and Company. New York, 1908. pp. 89-312.

DE PAULA, F. R. M. The Principles of Auditing.
Isaac Pitman and Sons. New York, 1919. pp. 82-97, 104-124.

DICKINSON, ARTHUR LOWES. Accounting Practice and Procedure.
Ronald Press Company. New York, 1918. pp. 190-211.

DICKSEE, LAWRENCE R. Auditing — A Practical Manual for Auditors.
Gee and Company. London, Eng., 1906. (Fifth Edition.) pp. 196-199, 232-237.
pp. 44, 53-57, 70-189, 208, 215-235, 255-262.

DICKSEE, LAWRENCE R. Bookkeeping for Accountant Students.
Gee and Company. London, Eng., 1906. Fifth Edition. pp. 196-199, 232-237.

DICKSEE, LAWRENCE R. (Author) and MONTGOMERY, ROBERT H. (Editor). Auditing — A Practical Manual for Auditors.
Ronald Press Company. New York, 1905. pp. 59-60, 71-73, 90-167, 179-180, 187-196, 212-217, 221-223, 396-509.

DICKSEE, LAWRENCE R. Advanced Accounting.
Gee and Company. London, England, 1916. pp. 253-272.

DOWLER, FRANK and HARRIS, E. MARDINOR. Auditing, Accounting and Banking.
Isaac Pitman and Sons. New York, 1919. pp. 206-210.

GILMAN, STEPHEN. Principles of Accounting.
La Salle Extension University. Chicago, 1916. pp. 346-371.

GREENDLINGER, LEO. Financial and Business Statements.
Alexander Hamilton Institute. New York, 1919. pp. 59, 60-61, 64-65, 69-70, 103, 107-108, 109, 197-198, 239, 276-277. (Vol. 22 —Modern Business Course.)

GREENDLINGER, LEO and SCHULZE, J. WILLIAM. Accounting Practice.
Alexander Hamilton Institute. New York, 1914. pp. 335-355. (Vol. 6—Modern Business Course.)

GRIFFITH, JAMES B. Corporation Accounts and Voucher System.
American Technical Society. Chicago, 1917. pp. 48-76. (American Accountant's Library.)

HATFIELD, HENRY RAND. Modern Accounting.
D. Appleton and Company. New York, 1909. pp. 293-315.

HEITMANN, HENRY. A Course in the Theory and Practice of Higher Accounting.
Eastman College. Poughkeepsie, N. Y., 1910. pp. 43-96.

HOOVER, S. R. Bookkeeping and Accounting Practice.
A. W. Shaw Company. Chicago, 1920. pp. 201-246.

KEISTER, D. A. Keister's Corporation Accounting and Auditing.
The Burrow Brothers Company. Cleveland. 1915. pp. 322-330, 374-380.

KESTER, ROY B. Accounting — Theory and Practice — Vol. 2.
Ronald Press Company. New York, 1918. pp. 49-60, 99-210.

KLEIN, JOSEPH J. Elements of Accounting.
D. Appleton and Company. New York, 1916. pp. 291-321.

LISLE, GEORGE Encyclopedia of Accounting.
William Green and Sons. London, Eng., 1903. Vol. 2. pp. 252-299. Vol. 5. pp. 1-5, 199-225, 336-344, 415-466.

LISLE, GEORGE. Accounting in Theory and Practice.
William Green and Sons. London, England, 1909. (Revised Edition.) pp. 52-63, 261-276.

McINTOSH, ROBERT J. Reference Book of Accounts for Manufacturing and Mercantile Companies.
Robert J. McIntosh and Company. Toledo, Ohio, 1914. (Second Edition.) pp. 25-145, 173-193, 215-244, 249-279.

MITCHELL, THOMAS W. Accounting Principles.
Alexander Hamilton Institute. New York, 1919. pp. 297-325. (Vol. 9—Modern Business Course.)

MONTGOMERY, ROBERT H. Auditing Theory and Practice.
Ronald Press Co. New York, 1905. (Trade Edition.) pp. 84-98, 116-122, 134-136, 209-212, 222-225, 235-292, 350-351, 358-361, 394-398, 401-429, 530-747.

MONTGOMERY, ROBERT H. Auditing Theory and Practice.
Ronald Press Company. New York, 1915. (Text Edition.) pp. 84-98, 134-136, 209, 235-292, 358-361, 394, 401-429.

PATON, WILLIAM ANDREW and STEVENSON, RUSSELL ALGER. Principles of Accounting.
The Macmillan Company. New York, 1918. pp. 482-524, 609-638.

PIXLEY, F. W. Auditors: Their Duties and Responsibilities.
Henry God and Son. London, England. (Original copyright 1906.) 1910 (Tenth Edition.) pp. 410-411, 412-413, 444-448, 489-511.

PIXLEY, F. W. Accountancy.
Isaac Pitman and Sons. New York, 1919. (Second Edition.) pp. 134-153, 202-220.

RACINE, SAMUEL F. Accounting Principles.
The Western Institute of Accountancy, Commerce and Finance. Seattle, Wash., 1917. pp. 131-164. (Accounting Student Series.)

RENN, G. B. Renn's Practical Auditing — A Working Manual for Auditors.
G. B. Renn. Chicago, 1905. (Second Edition.) pp. 55-100, 120-126.

RITTENHOUSE, CHARLES F. and CLAPP, PHILIP F. Accounting Theory and Practice.
McGraw-Hill Book Company. New York, 1918. (Second Edition.) Unit 2. pp. 110-115.

ROWE, HARRY M. Bookkeeping and Accountancy.
H. M. Rowe Company. Baltimore, Md., 1911. pp. 202-257.

RUSSELL, T. H. and JACKMAN, W. J. Bookkeeping, Accounting and Auditing.
International Law Business Institute. Minneapolis, 1916. pp. 131-162.

SALIERS, EARL A. Accounts in Theory and Practice Principles.
McGraw-Hill Book Company. New York, 1920. pp. 251-280.

SHERWOOD, J. F. Public Accounting and Auditing.
South-Western Publishing Company. Cincinnati, 1920. pp. 97-109, 131-132, 134-135, 145-156.

SOULÉ, GEORGE, Soulé's Accounts.
George Soulé. New Orleans, La., 1911. (Ninth Edition.) pp. 344-352, 394-429.

SPENCER, ENOS. Modern Bookkeeping and Accounting.
Enos Spencer. Louisville, Ky., 1909. (Fifth Edition.) pp. 113-120.

SPICER, ERNEST E. and PEGLER, ERNEST C. Bookkeeping and Accounts.
H. Foulks Lynch and Company. London, England, 1914. (Third Edition.) pp. 267-292.

STOCKWELL, HERBERT G. Net Worth and the Balance Sheet.
Ronald Press Company. New York, 1912. pp. 67-70, 73-76, 107-108.

WALTON, S. and GILMAN, STEPHEN W. Auditing and Cost Accounts.
Alexander Hamilton Institute. New York, 1913. pp. 219-454.

WILDMAN, JOHN R. Principles of Accounting.
The William G. Hewitt Press. Brooklyn, N. Y., 1913. pp. 203-208, 236-250.

WILDMAN, JOHN R. Principles of Auditing.
The William G. Hewitt Press. Brooklyn, N. Y., 1916. pp. 108-119.

____ ____ Office Methods and Accounting.

A. W. Shaw Company. Chicago, 1914. pp. 130-139. (The Library of Office Management — Separate book now — last printing 1917.)

Problems

BENNETT, R. J. Bookkeeping and Accounting Exercises.
American Book Company. New York, 1912. pp. 78-86. Part 2.

BROAKER, F. Vol. 1—American Accountants' Manual. Examination Questions.
Broaker and Chapman. New York, 1897. pp. 55-60.

COLE, WILLIAM MORSE. Problems in the Principles of Accounting.
Harvard University Press. Cambridge, Mass., 1915. pp. 47-48, 76-85.

EGGLESTON, DEWITT CARL. Problems in Cost Accounting.
D. Appleton and Company. New York, 1918. pp. 349.

ESQUERRÉ, PAUL-JOSEPH. Practical Accounting Problems.
Ronald Press Company. New York, 1921. pp. 98-120, 270-287.

FRIDAY, DAVID. Problems in Accounting.
The Ann Arbor Press. Ann Arbor, Mich., 1915. pp. 228, 289-290, 320, 330, 332-334.

GREENDLINGER, LEO. Accountancy Problems.
Key Publishing Company. New York, 1913. pp. 459.

GREENDLINGER, LEO and LOOMIS, JOHN R. Accountancy Problems.
Business Book Bureau. New York, 1911. pp. 393.

KLEIN, JOSEPH J. Student's Handbook of Accounting Based on (Klein's) Elements of Accounting.
D. Appleton and Company. New York, 1915. pp. 113-121.

MOREY, L. and CASTENHOLZ, W. B. C. P. A. Problems and Solutions.
La Salle Extension University. Chicago, 1918.

RITTENHOUSE, CHARLES F. and GREELEY, HAROLD DUDLEY, Illustrative Accounting Problems.
Ronald Press Company. New York, 1920. pp. 127, 130, 347, 351, 353, 355, 357, 367, 372, 380, 386. (Volume V—Business Accounting.)

SHARLES, F. F. Questions and Answers in Bookkeeping and Accounting.
Isaac Pitman and Sons. New York, 1921. pp. 224-240.

____ ____ C. P. A. Problems and Solutions.
Ronald Press Company. New York. 1914—Vol. 1—pp. 346. 1914—Vol. 2—pp. 375. 1915—Vol. 1—pp. 351. 1915—Vol. 2—pp. 361.

III. Books On Industrial Management Which Contain Material On Costs

ARNOLD, HORACE L. and FAUROTE, FAY L. Ford Shops.
Engineering Magazine Company. New York, 1919. pp. 31-63.

BABCOCK, GEORGE D. and TRANTSCHOLD, REGINALD. The Taylor System in Franklin Management.
Engineering Magazine Company. New York, 1917. pp. 47-63.

BRISCO, NORRIS A. Economics of Efficiency.
The Macmillan Company. New York, 1914. pp. 314-356.

BRISCO, NORRIS A. Economics of Business.
The Macmillan Company. New York, 1920. pp. 121-166.

CARPENTER, C. U. Increasing Production Decreasing Costs.
Engineering Magazine Company. New York, 1920. pp. 58-65, 343-358.

CARPENTER, C. U. Profit Making in Shop and Factory Management.
Engineering Magazine Company. New York, 1908. pp. 36-41, 116-124.

CHURCH, A. HAMILTON. The Science and Practice of Management.
Engineering Magazine Company. New York, 1914. pp. 427-481.

COPELAND, MELVIN T. Business Statistics.
Harvard University Press. Cambridge, Mass., 1917. pp. 402-684.

DE HAAS, J. ANTON. Business Organization and Administration.
The Gregg Publishing Company. New York, 1920. pp. 244-266.

DICKSEE, LAWRENCE R. and BLAIN, HERBERT E. Office Organization and Management.
Isaac Pitman & Sons. New York, 1920. (Fourth Edition.) pp. 136-177, 196-204.

DIEMER, HUGO. Factory Organization and Administration.
McGraw-Hill Book Company. New York, 1914. pp. 51-58, 142-149, 175-191, 212-224, 269-292, 292-304.

DRURY, HORACE B. Scientific Management—A History and Criticism.
Longmans, Green and Company. New York, 1915. pp. 30-52.

DUNCAN, JOHN C. The Principles of Industrial Management.
D. Appleton and Company. New York, 1911. pp. 262-280, 281-293, 294-316.

DURELL, FLETCHER. Fundamental Sources of Efficiency.
J. B. Lippincott Company. Philadelphia, 1914. pp. 152-191.

EMERSON, HARRINGTON. Efficiency as a Basis for Operation and Wages.
Engineering Magazine Company. New York, 1909. pp. 102-155.

EMERSON, HARRINGTON. The Twelve Principles of Efficiency.
The Engineering Magazine Company. New York, 1913. pp. 205-238, 371-397.

ENNIS, WILLIAM DUANE. Works Management.
McGraw-Hill Book Company. New York, 1911. pp. 8-99.

FISH, JOHN C. L. Engineering Economics.
McGraw-Hill Book Company. New York, 1915. pp. 33-108.

FRANKLIN, BENJAMIN A. Experiences in Efficiency.
Engineering Magazine Company. New York, 1915. pp. 53-66, 94-147.

GALLOWAY, LEE. Office Management—Its Principles and Practice.
Ronald Press Company. New York, 1919. pp. 265-289.

GALLOWAY, LEE. Organization and Management.
Alexander Hamilton Institute. New York, 1913. pp. 175-192. (Vol. 2—Modern Business Course.)

GANTT, H. L. Industrial Leadership.
Yale University Press. New Haven, Conn., 1916. pp. 109-128.

GANTT, H. L. Work, Wages and Profits.
Engineering Magazine Company. New York, 1913. pp. 253-292.

GANTT, H. L. Organizing for Work.
Harcourt, Brace and Howe. New York, 1919. pp. 23-40.

GERSTENBERG, C. W. Principles of Business.
Prentice-Hall. New York, 1918. pp. 754-794.

GOING, C. B. Principles of Industrial Engineering.
McGraw-Hill Book Company. New York, 1911. pp. 59-155.

HUMPHREYS, ALEX C. Lecture Notes on Some of the Business Features of Engineering Practice.
Stevens Institute of Technology. Hoboken, N. J., 1912. pp. 20-29, 53-61, 168-359.

HURLEY, EDWARD N. Awakening of American Business.
Doubleday, Page and Company. New York, 1916. pp. 18-24.

JACOBS, H. W. Betterment Briefs.
John Wiley and Sons. New York, 1909. pp. 171-196.

JENKINSON, M. W. The Workers' Interest in Costing.
Gee and Company. London, Eng.

JONES, EDWARD D. The Administration of Industrial Enterprises.
Longmans, Green and Company. New York, 1916. pp. 169-187.

JONES, FRANKLIN D. and HAMMOND, EDWARD K. Shop Management and Systems.
The Industrial Press. 1918. pp. 80-109, 238-271.

KENT, WILLIAM. Investigating an Industry.
John Wiley and Sons. New York, 1913. pp. 37-51.

KIMBALL, DEXTER S. Plant Management.
Alexander Hamilton Institute. New York, 1919. pp.52-91, 161-229. (Vol. 4—Modern Business Course.)

KIMBALL, DEXTER S. Principles of Industrial Organization.
McGraw-Hill Book Co. New York, 1913. pp. 110-168, 199-226.

KNOEPPEL, C. E. Graphic Production Control.
The Engineering Magazine Company. New York, 1920. pp. 151-255, 363-381, 413-419.

KNOEPPEL, C. E. Installing Efficiency Methods.
Engineering Magazine Company. New York, 1917. pp. 239-258.

KNOEPPEL, C. E. Organization and Administration.
Industrial Extension Institute. New York, 1919. pp. 129-130, 132, 229-245. (Vol. 1—Factory Management Course.)

LAWSON, F. M. Industrial Control.
Isaac Pitman and Sons. New York, 1920. pp. 30-114.

LEFFINGWELL, W. H. Scientific Office Management.
A. W. Shaw Company. Chicago, 1917. pp. 54-58, 116-123, 195-202.

LODGE, WILLIAM. Rules of Management.
McGraw-Hill Book Company. New York, 1913. pp. 34-38, 53-57.

MILLAR, THOMAS J. Management Bookkeeping.
Charles & Edwin Lagton. London, Eng. pp. 40-46.

NAYLOR, EMMETT HAY. Trade Associations—Their Organization and Management.
Ronald Press Company. New York, 1921. pp. 182-205. (Contains a cost system for a cover paper manufacturing association.)

PARKHURST, FREDERICK A. Applied Methods of Scientific Management.
John Wiley & Sons. New York, 1912. pp. 50, 89-114.

PARSONS, CARL C. Office Organization and Management.
La Salle Extension University. Chicago, 1917. pp. 261-267, 273-284.

SAMMONS, WHEELER. Keeping Up with Rising Costs.
A. W. Shaw Company. Chicago, Ill., 1915. pp. 192. Numerous references.

SCHULZE, J. WILLIAM. Office Administration.
McGraw-Hill Book Company. New York, 1919. pp. 133-137.

SCHULZE, J. WILLIAM. The American Office — Its Organization, Management and Records.
The Ronald Press Company. New York, 1914. pp. 272-298.

SEVERAL AUTHORS. Working Conditions Wages and Profits.
A. W. Shaw Company. Chicago, 1920. pp. 223-243.

SEVERAL AUTHORS. Production Records.
Business Training Corporation. New York, 1918. pp. 136. (Unit 5 of a Course in Modern Production Methods.)

SHEPARD, GEORGE H. The Application of Efficiency Principles.
The Engineering Magazine Company. New York, 1917. pp. 114-144, 324-356.

SMITH, J. RUSSELL. The Elements of Industrial Management.
J. B. Lippincott Company. Philadelphia, 1915. pp. 62-70, 243-255.

SPARLING, SAMUEL E. Business Organization.
The Macmillan Company. New York, 1906. pp. 134-160.

TAYLOR, FREDERICK WINSLOW. Shop Management.
Harper and Brothers. New York, 1911. pp. 115-121.

THOMPSON, CLARENCE B. Scientific Management.
Harvard University Press. Cambridge, Mass., 1914. pp. 420-430, 461-508, 544-568.

THOMPSON, C. B. The Taylor System of Scientific Management.
A. W. Shaw Co. Chicago, 1917. pp. 168. Numerous references.

WHITEFORD, JAMES F. Factory Management Wastes: And How to Prevent Them.
Nisbest and Company. London, Eng., 1919. pp. 123-144.

WILLIAMSON, J. GILMOUR. Counting-House and Factory Organization.
Isaac Pitman and Sons. New York, 1919. pp. 30-109, 132-151.

WOODS, C. E. Organizing a Factory.
A. W. Shaw and Company. Chicago, 1909. pp. 61-190. (The Business Man's Library — Vol. 6.)

IV. Books With Cost Material for Different Industries

Baking

MEGGISON, F. Bakers' Accounts.
Gee and Company. London, Eng., 1908. pp. 114. (Vol. 50 — Accountants' Library.)

Banking

DAVIS, J. F. Bank Organization, Management and Accounts.
Isaac Pitman and Sons. New York, 1919. pp. 70-149.

KNIFFIN, WILLIAM H., Jr. Practical Work of a Bank.
The Bankers' Publishing Company. New York, 1915. pp. 537-568.

LANGSTON, L. W. Practical Bank Operation.
Ronald Press Company. 1921. pp. 526-633. (Vol. 2.)

NIXON, ALFRED and STAGG, J. H. Accounting and Banking.
Longmans, Green and Company. New York, 1907. pp. 193-204 deal with manufacturing costs. pp. 244-260 deal with bank accounts. pp. 305-320 deal with hotel accounts and gas accounts. pp. 376-388 deal with collieries and building societies.

THOMAS, F. W. Cost Accounting in a Bank.
F. W. Thomas. Toledo, Ohio, 1910. pp. 52.

____ ____ **Cost Control as an Aid to Bank Management.**
A. W. Shaw Company. Chicago.

____ ____ **Accounting and Costs.**
A. W. Shaw Company. Chicago, 1918. pp. 225. (The Shaw Banking Service.)

Brewing

LANHAM, H. Brewers' and Bottlers' Accounts.
Gee and Company. London, England, 1916. (Vol. 44 — Accountants' Library.)

THORNTON, FRANK W. Brewery Accounts.
Ronald Press Company. New York, 1913. pp. 102.

Building and Construction

ARTHUR, WILLIAM. Estimating Building Costs.
David Williams Company. New York, 1917. pp. 211.

GILLETTE, HALBERT P. and DANA, RICHARD T. Cost Keeping and Management Engineering.
McGraw-Hill Book Co. New York, 1916. pp. 64-109, 127-339.

GILLETTE, H. P. Earthwork and Its Cost.
McGraw-Hill Book Co. New York, 1921. (Third Edition.) pp. 1346 — numerous references.

GRANT, H. D. Accounting for Contractors.
Biddle Business Publications. New York, 1921.

HAUER, D. J. Economics of Contracting.
Baumgartner. 1911. pp. 11-23, 261-264.

HAUER, D. J. Modern Management Applied to Construction.
McGraw-Hill Book Company. New York, 1918. pp. 117-130.

NISBET, A. G. Terminal Cost Accounts.
London, England, 1906. (Vol. 46 — Accountants' Library.) In English practice terminal costs are kept for engineers, contractors, bridge builders, and construction concerns.

RADFORD, W. A. Radford's Estimating and Contracting.
Radford Architectural Company. New York, 1913. pp. 887.

ROSS, G. ED. Cost Keeping and Construction Accounting.
The Ross System Company. Salem, Oregon, 1919. (Second Edition.) pp. 171.

SEABROOK, E. L. How to Make the Business Pay.
(A practical treatise on business management and cost accounting for contractors in sheet metal work, plumbing, heating, electrical work, and building construction, etc.) Sheet Metal Publication Company. New York, 1916. pp. 15-99.

TAYLOR, T. W. and THOMPSON, S. E. Concrete Costs.
John Wiley and Sons. New York, 1912. pp. 709.

WALBANK, JOHN A. Builders' Accounts.
Gee and Company. London, Eng., 1904. (Second Edition.) pp. 87. (Accountants' Library — Vol. 3.)

WALKER, F. R. Practical Cost Keeping for Contractors.
F. R. Walker. Chicago, 1916. pp. 723.

Engineering

BARKER, ARTHUR H. Management of Small Engineering Workshops.
Technical Publishing Company. Manchester, Eng., 1903. pp. 183-208.

BURTON, F. G. Engineering Estimates and Cost Accounts.
Technical Publishing Company. Manchester, England, 1900.

BURTON, F. G. Engineers' and Shipbuilders' Accounts.
Gee and Company. London, England, 1902. pp. 108. (Accountants' Library — Vol. 14.)

BURTON, F. G. The Commercial Management of Engineering Works.
The Scientific Publishing Company. Manchester, England, 1905. (Second Edition.) pp. 59-109, 271,364.

COLEMAN, T. E. The Civil Engineers Cost Book.
London, England, 1916. (Second Edition.) pp.381.

DAVIES, JOHN P. Engineering Office Systems and Methods.
McGraw-Hill Book Company. New York, 1915. pp. 228-284.

GILLETTE, HALBERT P. and DANA, RICHARD T. Mechanical and Electrical Cost Data.
McGraw-Hill Book Company. New York, 1918. pp. 82-145.

A GENERAL MANAGER. Engineering Estimates, Costs and Accounts.
Crosby, Lockwood and Son. London, England, 1896. (Second Edition.) pp. 255.

PEARN, S. and PEARN, F. Workshop Costs for Engineers and Manufacturers.
Technical Publishing Company. London, England, 1904.

SMITH, D. and PICKWORTH, P. C. N. Engineers' Costs and Economical Workshop Production.
Emmott Company. Manchester, England, 1916. (Second Edition.)

SPENCER, HENRY. Commercial Organization of Engineering Factories.
Spon and Chamberlain. New York, 1907. pp. 29-31, 32-62, 95-154.

SUGGATE, A. The Elements of Engineering Estimates.
The Technical Publishing Company. London, Eng. pp. 53-91.

Farming

CARD, FRED W. Farm Management.
George Sully and Company. New York, 1913.

CORNELL, C. D. Farm Accounts.
Isaac Pitman and Sons. New York, 1919, pp. 106.

LARSON, CARL W. Milk Production Cost Accounts.
Columbia University Press. New York, 1916. pp. 60.

ORWIN, C. S. The Determination of Farming Costs.
Clarendon Press. Oxford, England, 1917. pp. 144.

SCOVILL, H. T. Farm Accounting.
D. Appleton and Company. New York, 1918. pp. 429.

Foundries and Machine Shops

BELT, ROBERT E. Foundry Cost Accounting — Practice and Procedure.
Cost Engineering Company. Cleveland, 1919. pp. 271.

BEST, J. W. The Cost Accounts of an Engineer and Ironfounder.
Gee and Company. London, England, 1901. (Second Edition.) pp. 94.

DEAN, STUART. Shop and Foundry Management.
David Williams Company. New York, 1913. pp. 43-63, 69-87, 203-212.

FERGUSON, WILLIAM B. The Art of Estimating with Special Reference to Unstandardized Operations as in Jobbing Shops or Repair Work.
McGraw-Hill Book Company. New York, 1915. pp. 169.

KAUP, WILLIAM J. Machine Shop Practice.
John Wiley and Sons. New York, 1911. pp. 210-222.

KNOEPPEL, C. E. Maximum Production in Machine Shop and Foundry.
Engineering Magazine Company. New York, 1911. pp. 31-53, 95-127, 268-365.

PAYNE, DAVID W. Founder's Manual.
D. Van Nostrand Company. New York, 1917. pp. 587-632.

VAN DEVENTER, JOHN H. Handbook of Machine Shop Management.
McGraw-Hill Book Company. New York, 1915. pp. 227-333.

Furniture and Woodworking

TIMKEN, FRANK H. Accounting in the Furniture and Woodworking Industries.
Trade Periodical Company. Chicago, 1915. pp. 118.

BIGELOW, CARLE M. Installing Management in Woodworking Plants.
Engineering Magazine Company. New York, 1920. pp. 58-72, 201-226, 233-248, 259-314.

Garages

HOLLISTER, HORACE E. Practical Garage Accounting.
Garage Systems Company. Rockford, Ill., 1916. pp. 173.

____ ____ **The Accounts of a Motor Cab Company. Reprinted from Articles in the Accountant.**
Gee and Company. London, England, 1911. pp. 46.

____ ____ **How to Run a Retail Automobile Business at a Profit.**
A. W. Shaw Company. Chicago, 1918. pp. 69-122, 177-208.

Hotels and Institutions

BELL, S. A. A Report on Accounting Administration for Correctional Institutions.
Windermere Press. Chicago, 1914. pp. 91.

COLE, WILLIAM M. Cost Accounting for Institutions.
Ronald Press Company. New York, 1913. pp. 248.

DICKSEE, LAWRENCE R. Hotel Accounts.
Gee and Company. London, England, 1905. pp. 75. (Accountants' Library — Vol. 37.)

FLINT, C. A. Flint's Cost Finding System for Hotels, Restaurants and Cafeterias.
C. A. Flint. Seattle, Washington, 1917. pp. 168.

HUTCHINSON, J. HOWARD. School Costs and School Accounting.
Teachers College, Columbia University. New York City, 1914. pp. 151.

PIXLEY, FRANCIS W. Clubs and Their Management.
Isaac Pitman and Sons. New York, 1914. pp. 121-140.

THORNE, W. V. S. Hospital Accounting and Statistics.
E. P. Dutton and Company. New York, 1918. pp. 119.

——— ——— Hospital Accounting and Statistics.
Thompson-Brown Co. Boston, Mass., 1908. pp. 85.

Note: See also Nixon, Alfred and Stagg, J. H. under Banking in this section.

Jewellers

EDWARDS, ALLEN. Jewellers', Silversmiths', and Kindred Traders' Accounts.
For manufacturing jewellers, wholesale and retail jewellers and diamond merchants. Gee and Company. London, England, 1903. pp. 167. (Accountants' Library – Vol. 23.)

Lumber

JONES, ARTHUR F. Lumber Manufacturing Accounts.
Ronald Press Company. New York, 1914. pp. 112.

KELLOGG, R. S. Lumber Industry.
Ronald Press Company. New York, 1914. pp. 58-86.

——— ——— How to Run a Retail Lumber Business at a Profit.
A. W. Shaw Company. Chicago, 1917. pp. 75-145.

Mining

CHARLTON, W. H. American Mine Accounting.
McGraw-Hill Book Company. New York, 1913. pp. 367.

DICKSEE, LAWRENCE R. Mines Accounting and Management.
Gee and Company. London, England, 1914. pp. 100.

FINLAY, JAMES R. The Cost of Mining.
McGraw-Hill Book Company. New York, 1921. (Third Edition.) pp. 39-51.

GODDEN, D. and ROBERTSON, W. N. Australian Mining Companies Accounts.
Gee and Company. London, Eng., 1902. pp. 78.

IBOTSON, J. G. P. Quarry and Stone Merchants' Accounts.
Gee and Company. London, England, 1904. pp. 110. (Vol. 27 – Accountants' Library.)

JONES, E. HORTON. Smelter Construction Costs.
McGraw-Hill Book Co. New York, 1914. pp. 152.

LAWN, JAMES G. Mine Accounts and Mining Bookkeeping.
Charles Griffin and Company. London, England, 1909. (Sixth Edition.) pp. 147.

LOCK, FRED J. West African Gold Mining Accounts.
Gee and Company. London, England, 1910. pp. 134.

McGARRAUGH, ROBERT. Mine Bookkeeping.
McGraw-Hill Book Company. New York, 1920. pp. 118.

SKINNER, E. N. Mining Costs of the World.
McGraw-Hill Book Company. New York, 1915. pp. 406.

TAIT, G. W. Gold Mine Accounts and Costing.
Isaac Pitman and Sons. New York, 1912. pp. 93.

WALLACE, DAVID. Simple Mine Accounting.
McGraw-Hill Book Company. New York, 1909. pp. 78.

Note: See also Nixon, Alfred and Stagg, J. H., under Banking in this section.

Miscellaneous

CALVERT, ALFRED. Shipping Office Organization, Management and Accounts.
Isaac Pitman and Sons. New York, 1920. pp. 153-196.

CHANTREY, W. H. Theatre Accounts.
Gee and Company. London, Eng., 1902. pp. 83. (Accountants' Library – Vol. 5.)

CROSFIELD, A. W. E. Case and Freight Costs.
Isaac Pitman and Sons. New York, 1916. pp. 62.

DAY, JULIUS E. Stockbrokers' Office Organization, Management and Accounts.
Isaac Pitman and Sons. New York, 1921. pp. 104-231.

DOWD, ALBERT A. Tools and Patterns.
Industrial Extension Institute. New York, 1918. pp. 337-345, 421-428. (Vol. 4 – Factory Management Course.)

FOX, WILLIAM H. Accountants' Accounts.
Gee and Company. London, England, 1888. pp. 82.

GOULD, GERALD B. and HUBBARD, CARLETON W. The Cost of Power.
Fuel Engineering Company. New York, 1914. pp. 13-21, 105-120.

JOHNSON, GEORGE. Bookkeeping and Accounts for Grain, Flour, Hay, Seed and Allied Trades.
Gee and Company. London, Eng. (Accountants' Library – Vol. 10.)

LUND, J. and RICHARDSON, G. H.
Gee and Company. London, England, 1902. pp. 72. (Accountants' Library – Vol. 8.)

MACKEE, JOHN. Woollen and Other Warehousemen's Accounts.
Gee and Company. London, Eng., 1906. pp. 76.

MOXEY, EDWARD J., Jr., GREELEY, HAROLD DUDLEY, JEFFERSON, HOWARD M., GRUNDMAN, OTTO A. Practical Accounting Methods.
Key Publishing Company. New York, 1913. pp. 135-364 deal with various special fields of cost accounting, such as railway, city, gas, department stores, and brewery costs.

MYERS, DAVID M. Preventing Losses in Factory Power Plants.
Engineering Magazine Co. New York, 1915. pp. 508-560.

NORTON, S. V. The Motor Truck as an Aid to Business Profits.
A. W. Shaw Company. Chicago, 1918. pp. 33-78.

POLAKOV, WALTER N. Mastering Power Production.
Engineering Magazine Company. New York, 1921. pp. 300.

ROGERS, J. Newspaper Building.
Harper and Brothers. New York, 1918. pp. 265-308.

WOLFE, S. HERBERT. The Examination of Insurance Companies.
The Insurance Press. New York, 1910. Numerous references.

Motion Pictures

SCHAY, E. Manual of Goldwyn Branch Operations.
Published by Author. New York, 1920. pp. 50.

Municipal

ALLCOCK, JOHN. Municipal Accounts.
Gee and Company. London, Eng., 1903. pp. 190. (Accountants' Library – Vol. 21.)

EGGLESTON, DEWITT CARL. Municipal Accounting.
Ronald Press Company. New York, 1914. pp. 456.

HANDBOOK OF MUNICIPAL ACCOUNTING. Prepared under the direction of William H. Allen, Henry Bruere, Frederick A. Cleveland, by the Bureau of Municipal Research.
D. Appleton and Company. New York, 1914. pp. 318.

KELLY, A. A. Expert Estimator and Business Book. *Painting*
Prepared for the use of house and sign painters and interior decorators, etc. A. A. Kelly. Malvern, Pa., 1912. (Second Edition.) pp. 116.

VANDERWALKER, FRED N. Estimates, Costs and Profits, Exterior Painting, Interior Decorating.
F. J. Drake. Chicago, 1916. (Second Edition.) pp. 127.

—— —— Metal Worker, Plumber and Steam Fitter, Estimating, Cost Keeping and Profit Making. *Plumbing*
David Williams Company. New York, 1914. pp. 380.

DAVIS, A. E. How to Find Costs in Printing. *Printing*
Oswald Publishing Company. New York, 1914. pp. 120.

JOBSON, WALTER. Accounting for Printing Concerns.
Press of Jobson Printing Company. Louisville, Kentucky, 1914. pp. 106.

LAKIN-SMITH, H. Printers' Accounts.
Gee and Company. London, England, 1902. pp. 17. (Accountants' Library—Vol. 17.)

PORTE, R. T. How to Figure Costs in Printing Offices.
Minnesota Cost System Company. Minneapolis, 1914. pp. 134.

SWEETLAND, CHARLES A. Publishers' and Printers' Accounts.
American School of Correspondence. Chicago, 1909. pp. 91.

ADAMS, HENRY C. American Railway Accounting—A Commentary. *Public Utilities*
Henry Holt and Company. New York, 1918. pp. 465.

BROCKWAY, W. B. Electric Railway Accounting.
McGraw Publishing Company. New York, 1906. pp. 84.

EATON, J. SHIRLEY. Handbook of Railroad Expenses.
McGraw-Hill Book Company. New York, 1913. pp. 559.

EDWARDS, H. M. Electric Light Accounts and Their Significance.
McGraw-Hill Book Company. New York, 1914. pp. 172.

FISHER, J. ALFRED. Railway Accounts and Finance.
George Allen and Company. London, Eng., 1912. (Fourth Edition.) pp. 588.

FORSE, WILLIAM H., JR. Electric Railway Auditing and Accounting.
McGraw Publishing Company. New York, 1908. pp. 157.

HOOPER, WILLIAM E. Railroad Accounting.
D. Appleton and Company. New York, 1915. pp. 461.

JOHNSON, GEORGE. Electric Lighting Accounts.
Gee and Company. London, Eng., 1904. pp. 128. (Accountants' Library—Vol. 29.)

MAY, IRVILLE A. Street Railway Accounting.
Ronald Press Company. New York, 1917. pp. 454.

MULHALL, JOHN F. J. Quasi-Public Corporation Accounting and Management.
Corporation Publishing Company. Boston, Mass., 1905. pp. 28-175, 179-182.

McHENRY, E. H. Rules for Railway Location and Construction.
The Engineering News Publishing Company. New York, 1903. pp. 49-74.

SAKOLSKI, A. M. American Railroad Economics.
The Macmillan Company. New York, 1913. pp. 169-264.

SUFFERN, E. AND SON. Railroad Operating Costs.
Suffern and Son. New York, 1912. pp. 144. Vol. 2.

____ ____ **Gas Accounts.**
Gee and Company. London, Eng., 1905. pp. 112. (Accountants' Library – Vol. 7.)

Real Estate

HOPKINSON, JOSEPH. The Real Estate Accountant.
E. W. Rugg Company. Winnipeg, Manitoba, 1914. pp. 144.

MUCKLOW, WALTER. Real Estate Accounts.
Ronald Press Company. New York, 1917. pp. 357.

Retail Stores

BAYLEY, J. ERNEST. Drapery Business Organization, Management and Accounts.
Isaac Pitman and Sons. New York, 1920. pp. 30-38, 200-250, 251-288.

GOODWIN, FRANK E. Cost Accounting Pathfinder.
Midland Publishing Company. St. Louis, Mo., 1910. (Third Edition.) pp. 128.

SWEETLAND, CHARLES A. Department Store Accounts.
American School of Correspondence. Chicago, 1910.

WALKER, J. C. Retail Accounting and Store Management.
South-Western Publishing Company. Cincinnati, 1916. pp. 91.

CARTHAGE, PHILIP I. Retail Organization and Accounting Control.
D. Appleton and Company. New York, 1920. pp. 349.

Shoes

HEADEY, L. C. Boot and Shoe Costings.
Gee and Company. London, England.

SMALL, FREDERIC L. Treatise on Comprehensive Accounting Methods Adapted to Shoe Manufacturing and Other Industries.
L. & S. Printing Company. Boston, Mass., 1914. pp. 227.

Textiles

BARKER, A. F., and EBER, MIDGELY. Analysis of Woven Fabrics.
D. Van Nostrand Company. New York, 1914. pp. 229-253.

DAY, CLARENCE MUNRO. Silk Mill Costs.
Clarence M. Day. New York, 1912. pp. 70.

HARDMAN, A. H. Productive Costs in Cotton Spinning Mills.
Emmott and Co. London, Eng., 1912. pp. 132.

HEYLIN, H. BROUGHAN. Cotton Weaver's Handbook.
J. B. Lippincott Company. Philadelphia, 1908. pp. 137-161.

NICHOLS, H. W. Method of Determining Costs in a Cotton Mill.
H. W. Nichols. New Bedford, Mass., 1915. pp. 115.

NICHOLS, WILLIAM G. Methods of Cost Finding in Cotton Mills.
E. L. Barry. Waltham, Mass., 1900. pp. 70.

NORTON, G. P. Textile Manufacturers' Bookkeeping.
Simpkin. London, Eng., 1900. pp. 246-271.

V. Books Dealing With Special Phases of Cost Accounting

BAILLET, H. F. Overhead Expense and Percentage Methods.
D. Williams Company. New York, 1915. pp. 128.

CHURCH, A. HAMILTON. Production Factors.
Engineering Magazine Company. New York, 1916. pp. 187. (Overhead.)

CHURCH, A. HAMILTON. The Proper Distribution of Expense Burden.
Engineering Magazine Company. New York, 1912. pp. 144.

DICKSEE, LAWRENCE R. Office Machinery and Appliances.
Gee and Company. London, Eng., 1918. pp. 154.

FARNHAM, DWIGHT T. Executive Statistical Control.
Industrial Extension Institute. New York, 1917. pp. 37-55, 58-71.

FICKER, NICHOLAS THIEL. Shop Expense Analysis and Control.
Industrial Management Co. New York, 1917. pp. 236.

FLOY, HENRY. Value for Rate-Making.
McGraw-Hill Book Co. New York, 1916. pp. 235-311. (Depreciation.)

FOSTER, HORATIO A. Engineering Valuation of Public Utilities and Factories.
D. Van Nostrand Company. New York, 1913. (Second Edition.) pp. 147-218, 226-234. (Depreciation.)

FRANKLIN, BENJAMIN A. Cost Reports for Executives.
The Engineering Magazine Company. New York, 1913. pp. 149.

FREDERICK, J. GEORGE. Business Research and Statistics.
D. Appleton & Company. New York, 1920. pp. 251-268. (Presentation of cost reports.)

GARRY, H. S. Multiple Cost Accounts.
Gee and Company. London, England, 1906. pp. 97. (Accountants' Library — Vol. 42.)
Multiple costs used in plants making a number of articles whose cost and selling price vary considerably.

GARRY, H. S. Process Cost Accounts.
Gee and Company. London, England, 1908. pp. 152. (Accountants' Library — Vol. 49.)
Process costs used chiefly in chemical and allied industries.

GRUNSKY, CARL EWALD, and GRUNSKY, CARL EWALD, JR. Valuation, Depreciation and the Rate-Base.
John Wiley & Sons. New York, 1916. pp. 387. (Several references.)

HAYES, HAMMOND V. Public Utilities. Their Cost New and Depreciation.
D. Van Nostrand Co. New York, 1916. pp. 182-205 and other references.

HAZELIP, J. Multiple-Shop Accounts.
Gee and Company. London, Eng., 1903. pp. 114. (Accountants' Library – Vol. 24.)

HERZ, EUGENE. Controlling Profits – Simplified Efficiency Methods in Store Record Keeping.
Laird and Lee. Chicago, 1917. pp. 103.

LEAKE, P. D. Depreciation and Wasting Assets.
Isaac Pitman and Sons. New York, 1917. pp. 195.

LEE, JAMES M. Language for Men of Affairs.
Ronald Press Company. New York, 1920. pp. 267-364. (Presentation of Cost Reports.) Vol. 2 – Business Writing.

LUNT, JULIUS. Departmental Cost Keeping.
Gee and Company. London, Eng. In English practice departmental costs are synonymous with costs of intermediate processes as distinct from the cost of the complete manufacturing process.

MATHESON, EWING. The Depreciation of Factories, Mines and Industrial Undertakings and Their Valuation. (4th Edition.)
Spon and Chamberlain. New York, 1910. pp. 230.

McKAY, CHARLES W. Valuing Industrial Properties.
Industrial Extension Institute. New York, 1918. pp. 108-271. (Vol. 12, Factory Management Course.)

MITCHELL, G. A. Single Cost Account.
Gee and Company. London, Eng. 1907. (Accountants' Library – Vol. 47.) Single cost accounts applicable to a plant where a basis of measurement is readily provided, such as the ton, pound, barrel, etc.

PARKHURST, FREDERIC A. The Predetermination of True Costs and Relatively True Selling Prices.
John Wiley and Sons. New York, 1916. pp. 96.

PARKHURST, FREDERIC A. Symbols.
John Wiley and Sons. New York, 1917. pp. 165.

RINDFOOS, C. S. Purchasing.
McGraw-Hill Book Company. New York, 1915. pp. 107-162. (Stores.)

SALIERS, EARL A. Principles of Depreciation.
Ronald Press Company. New York, 1915. pp. 200.

TWYFORD, H. B. Purchasing.
D. Van Nostrand Company. New York, 1915. pp. 133-161. (Stores.)

TWYFORD, H. B. Storing.
D. Van Nostrand Company. New York, 1918. pp. 200.

WHITEHORN, W. J. Costing by Machinery.
F. Fleming, Dorking, England, 1916.

____ ____ Labor.
A. W. Shaw Company. Chicago, 1915. pp. 159-173. (Vol. 4. The Library of Factory Management. Separate book now. Last printing 1920.)

____ ____ Materials and Supplies.
A. W. Shaw Company. Chicago, 1915. pp. 216. (Vol. 3. The Library of Factory Management. Separate book now. Last printing 1920.)

—— —— **Operation and Costs.**
A. W. Shaw Company. Chicago, 1915. pp. 101-205. (Vol. 5. The Library of Factory Management. Separate book now. Last printing 1920.)

—— —— **Purchasing and Employment.**
A. W. Shaw Company. Chicago, 1917. pp. 86-92. (Formerly issued under title of the Library of Business Practice – Vol. 3.)

(5) "Brief in Favor of Interest as a Cost," 1921 Yearbook, Clinton H. Scovell, Scovell, Wellington & Company

Brief in Favor of Interest as a Cost

Interest on investment as a cost is sound in theory and practicable in operation.

I. Basic Agreement as to Interest in Selling Price

It is axiomatic that interest on investment must be included in the *selling price.* If the earnings do not produce more than the current rate of interest on safe securities, then as an investment the business is not worth while. The only question is as to what point is proper and convenient for interest inclusion.

II. Economic Interpretation of Interest

Distinction Between Interest and Profit

Some accountants contend that interest cannot properly be included in costs because it is a profit. Standard economic writings, however, are overwhelmingly in favor of making a clear-cut distinction between interest, the return to the capitalist, and profit, the return to the management.

The five typical citations following indicate how generally economists agree. The italics, which are ours, emphasize pertinent phraseology:

* * * *

J.A. Hobson: "The Industrial System," London, 1909, p. 9, paragraph 9: "*Profit* is the portion of the product left to the undertaker or controller of a business after the *expenses* of the factors of land, *capital,* and labor have been defrayed."

* * * *

Alfred Marshall: "Principle of Economics," 6th ed., London, 1910, Bk. V, Chap. IV, p. 359: "*Some technical terms relating to cost* may be considered here. When investing his capital in providing the means of carrying on an undertaking, the business man.....expects to be able under normal conditions to charge for each (product) a sufficient price; that is, one which will not only cover the special, direct, or prime cost, but also bear its proper share of the general expenses of the business, and these we may call its supplementary cost.... Supplementary cost is taken to include *standing charges on account of the durable plant in which much of the capital of business has been invested.*"

* * * *

Henry R. Seager: "Principles of Economics," New York, 1913, Chap. XI, p. 173: "The wages-of-management of the enterpriser is prospective. Normally it must remain after the other shares have been paid out of the money income, but *these other shares must be paid first.* In a shoe factory, or any other typical business, these other shares – all of them expenses of production in addition to the replacement fund which must be provided for as a matter of course—are: (1) rent for the use of land and natural powers; (2) wages to workers of different grades; (3) *interest for the use of capital;* (4) taxes....

"*If a business ties up on the average throughout the year capital goods worth* $100,000 *and the current rate of interest is five per cent,* $5,000 *should be charged as expense for interest.* This item should appear if capital belonging to the enterpriser himself rather than borrowed capital were used. When borrowed capital is used, the expense for interest is an actual outlay, when the enterpriser's own capital, it is a virtual outlay, since using the capital in the business prevents loaning it at the current rate to some other enterpriser."

* * * *

Edwin R. A. Seligmann: "Principles of Economics," 6th ed., New York, 1914, Chap. XXIII, p. 354: "The expenses of production...may ordinarily be classified into cost of raw material, wages, rent, *interest on the capital borrowed or invested,* taxes, and miscellaneous outlays like insurance, advertisements and transportation expenses....."

P. 357: "*The older writers confused interest with profit. Interest is the return from the fund of capital; profits are the return from the conduct of business enterprise,* irrespective of whether the enterprise deals with capital or labor or both. *Interest is a part of cost; profit is a surplus above cost.* Interest has a normal rate; profits may have an average rate but no normal rate.

"Just as a business man must deduct the rent or royalty of some patented machine used by him *before computing his profits,* so, if he buys the machine outright, he *must deduct the interest on the capital invested in the machine. Whether he uses his own capital or borrows it is immaterial; in the latter case it is loan or contract interest, in the former it is natural or economic interest.*"

* * * *

F.W. Taussig: "Principles of Economics," Revised Ed. of 1915, Chap. 50, p. 179: "We have tacitly assumed that so much only of a business man's income is to be regarded as profits as is in excess of interest on the capital which he manages. If he happens to borrow his capital, this is clearly true. He then pays interest to another, and only his net earnings over and above interest go to him as business profits. Usually his capital is partly borrowed and partly his own....On that part which is his own, he must indeed remember *that interest could be got at current rates without the risk and labor of actual management; and therefore he must reasonably reckon only the excess over such interest as his earnings of management or business profits.*"

Interest Is Charge for Use of Capital

A cost is incurred through the *use of capital.* Physical assets are constantly employed in production, and certainly their use cannot be provided free. It must mean a cost for interest, just as the use of land means a cost for rent and the use of labor a cost for wages.

Not Simply Interest on Borrowed Money

Interest on borrowed capital is a cost; so, too, is interest on owned capital. The mere fact that the one part of the investment carries contract interest, and the other only economic interest, is not ground for excluding the latter form from costs. *All* interest should be included.

Dividends Are Composite of Interest and Profit

Interest on investment is credited ultimately to the account (Loss and Gain) from which dividends are paid, but it should not be called a profit on the ground that only "profits" are properly divisible among stockholders. Dividends in the economic sense are a composite of interest for the use of capital and of profit for management. Stockholders expect to receive both recompense for providing capital and reward for sharing in management.

Depreciation Is Charge for Consumption of Capital

A depreciation charge is not a substitute for an interest charge. Depreciation is a cost for the exhaustion or consumption of assets, whereas interest is a cost for the use of the investment tied up during the period. The cost of production must include a charge for each item.

III. Practical Need for Interest Inclusion

According to economic interpretation, therefore, interest as a cost is theoretically proper. Moreover, cost accountants and business men deem interest inclusion practically necessary, for without it satisfactory solutions are lacking for these problems of management:

Measuring Relative Economy of Methods or Machines

In the simplest cases of buying new equipment, a manufacturer considers that he will tie up less capital, and thus keep interest cost lower, by purchasing the cheaper machine. In more complex cases, he may need to weigh an increase in interest against reductions in material and labor costs. For example, in the manufacture of candy, in construction work and in the manufacture of steel, high-priced machines can be used in place of many hand operations, but the relative economy cannot be accurately ascertained without the inclusion of interest in costs.

Checking Preliminary Estimates of Economy

A mere advance estimate of the relative economy of two processes does not require that interest be charged to cost in the accounting, but such a procedure is necessary in order to know that the estimate is realized. Furthermore, experiments do not always come up to expectations, and a falling off in the expected economy is detected more quickly if interest on the investment is a current charge.

The Time Element in Costs

Time has long been recognized by practical men as an important element of cost in numerous industrial operations; e. g., in the tanning and smelting industries. Other factors being equal, the longer of two alternative processes is the more costly. If the commodity is insurable and subject to taxation, charges for both of these elements must be included in costs. The greater cost for the longer time, however, is almost exclusively due to interest on the capital invested.

Distinguishing Between Kinds of Business or Lines of Sales

Business men need to know what returns they are making on their different operations or lines. To cite an example, many concerns, as one accountant has said, were wrecked by quarrels due to ignorance of comparative costs between the jobbing and the manufacturing parts, until it became apparent that each division should reckon into costs the interest on the investment involved. The manufacturer today may desire to favor an infant branch or line; but if he is wise, he does so with his eyes wide open to the actual cost, including interest on the capital required to swing the business.

Comparing Inventory Policies

If a manager is able through improved methods to conduct his business with a smaller inventory, he has less cost in carrying the goods. If, on the other hand, by reason of advancing prices he has to pay more to buy a given volume of inventory, he incurs a greater cost in carrying it.

When a manufacturer uses cheaper raw materials, he saves not only on their purchase price, but also on the capital cost of carrying the inventories (raw material, work-in-process and finished stock), which for the same volume will be smaller in value.

A manager may deliberately accumulate an unusually large inventory. The circumstances may seem to make this a wise policy; but he should calculate the interest cost, in order to secure a true conception of the value of one inventory policy over another.

Comparing Complete and and Incomplete Plants

In certain industries different plants show striking variations as to the number of steps in their manufacturing operations. Some machine builders buy their castings; others operate foundries. Some paper mills buy all their pulp, others manufacture it on the premises or at another property. Some automobile manufacturers make almost the entire car; others do hardly anything except assemble the component parts.

In view of the capital tied up, is it more profitable to manufacture certain parts than to buy them outside? The answer depends in part upon what a comparison of costs for manufactured parts and purchased parts shows. Such a comparison is inaccurate unless interest is included in manufacturing cost, just as in the price of the purchased parts.

Judging Owned and Rented Plants

Two plants with the same product, one owning and the other leasing property, need to include rent in costs to secure a true comparison. This is particularly important when both plants belong to the same company. Rent is the return on the factor of production called "land"; the reasons justifying its inclusion in costs also pertain to the interest return in the case of another factor, capital.

Weighing Varieties in Financing

Manufacturing enterprises present every variety of financing with bonds, notes payable, and capital stock. In any allied group some manufacturers are accustomed to include in costs the interest on *borrowed* money, and refuse to give up this practice unless they have something better. Moreover, many manufacturers insist upon the need of reckoning the cost of owned as well as borrowed capital. Experience shows that the only practical composition of views is to have all plants follow the theoretically proper method of including interest on the whole investment. Then differences in financing do not assume undue weights in comparative costs.

Making Uniform Cost Plans for Associations

The only way to secure uniform practice in association work is to provide for treating interest as a cost. The snag which an attempt at a uniform cost system without interest always strikes is that the manufacturers have decisions of policy to make, particularly as to buying new and expensive equipment and as to carrying large stocks of raw material or finished product, and to make such decisions they must consider capital cost. They know this cost is present, and they insist that it have its appropriate place in their accounting.

Handling Unearned Burden

Interest inclusion helps in the determination of manufacturing and selling policies during periods of curtailed production. Experienced cost accountants agree that for each operation the normal burden, based on normal activity, should be determined, and that with a partly shut-down plant the burden applicable to the idle time is a direct loss, and not an additional cost of the limited output. Current charges showing all the expense (including interest) of carrying the unused capacity are much more likely to arouse executives to action than a mere memorandum of approximate fixed charges.

IV. Rate of Interest is Readily Determinable

Another aspect of the practicability of interest inclusion has to do with the rate used. This is easily determinable when interest is clearly differentiated from profit.

Kind of Rate to Be Used

The manufacturer should charge not the rate of return (both interest and profit) which he expects to realize in his particular business, but rather the conventional interest rate which ought to be realized from any conservative investment in his territory. He is then entitled to something more in profit for his risk in running his particular business. What the rate of profit must be to attract the investment of owned capital depends on the industry. The amount is immaterial here.

Company's Security Rates Not Determinative

The conventional interest rate need not be equal to the actual rate of return on a company's securities. A corporation may be over-capitalized or under-capitalized, and either condition will permanently influence the dividend rate on the common stock. Moreover, this rate may vary widely from year to year according to the prosperity of the business. Nor should the "effective rate" on the preferred stock or bonds be a determining factor, for such a rate is a composite result of security of principal and income and market stability. These factors may in turn depend upon the age, the character, or even the reputation of the company or industry.

"Reasonable Expectancy" Rate Generally Understood

The conventional or "reasonable expectancy" rate varies in different sections and at different times. Nevertheless, business men at any place and at any time have a clear idea as to what the proper rate is. It is not the lowest interest rate known, on government securities with a minimum of risk, but the current rate which capital would be expected to earn if invested conservatively in high-grade securities.

Recommendation of Harvard Bureau

The Bureau of Research of Harvard University recommends the use of "the ordinary interest rate on reasonably secured long-term investment, in the locality in which the business is situated." The Bureau has determined from its inquiries that each locality seems to have a definite idea as to what constitutes a current rate.

Rate Variations Between Localities

The fact that the conventional rate may not be the same in different localities is not a valid reason for omitting interest from costs. The rates of wages vary, and rent varies. The cost of raw material, too, varies according to the different sources of supply and transportation facilities. Despite such variations these items are included in costs, and interest should be also.

V. Bookkeeping for Interest as a Cost

Accountants and business men who have successfully used interest as a cost follow two general methods.

Net-Investment Method

Under the "net-investment" method the credit is divided into (1) a credit to cash for the actual interest disbursement on borrowed money (bonds, notes payable and accounts payable), and (2) a credit to an income account, Interest is Charged to Cost, for interest at the agreed-upon rate on the capital owned. This second amount is reckoned on the "net investment" – that is, the difference between the sum of the assets (cash, notes and accounts receivable, raw materials, work-in-process and finished goods inventories, prepaid interest, insurance, etc.), and the sum of the liabilities (notes and accounts payable, and all accrued items). Plant and equipment assets are included unless the return on these is set up separately in a comparative rent account.

This method gives rise to objections. It introduces a variable element when differently financed plants are compared. It also makes an unwarranted contrast between borrowed and owned capital when one company is considered. The dollar owned in a given business does just as much work as the dollar borrowed, and the compensation should be the same. This is impossible under the "net-investment" method, with one or more rates on borrowed money, and the agreed-upon and probably different rate on the "net investment."

Another objection to the "net-investment" method is that it breaks down in a manufacturing establishment when the investment has to be subdivided so that the interest cost can be separately calculated for several subdivisions of equipment, and on two or more different inventories. Even in a merchandising business like the wholesaling of shoes or hardware, it would be indispensable to reckon fixed charges on inventories by classes, in order to measure results satisfactorily.

Flat-Rate Method

The method to be preferred in an industrial establishment requiring a careful subdivision of burden is that of using a flat selected rate upon all asset values. The interest is calculated as a debit through rent, equipment charges, inventory charges, etc., with a corresponding credit to Interest Charged to Cost. This is transferred each period to the Loss and Gain account, and is available for dividends if not offset by losses.

The accounting under either method is comparatively simple. No more work is involved in the financial books than is required for any accrual account, and on the cost accounting side one additional element in the burden rate does not cause any appreciable addition to the clerical work.

VI. Interest as a Cost Is Supported by Various Parties

The recognition which industrial accountants give to the theoretical propriety and the practical necessity of interest inclusion is supported by business men, labor and the government.

Attitude of Business Men

Business men generally regard a safe rate of interest as a cost of doing business, and they are thus helped to know what they can add for real profit without making the price unfair to the public or too high in the face of competition.

Professor William Morse Cole in the Journal of Accountancy for April, 1913, says: "On the announcement of the figure of profits under an agreement which makes no provision for interest, the first mental act of anyone interested in the business is to see what relation those profits bear to the capital—so as to see what are the excess profits over a reasonable return on the investment. Instinctively interest is a first deduction—partly because it has a definite basis that can be figured, and partly because it is one thing that everyone counts on."

Attitude of Labor

Interest as a cost is also deemed desirable by labor representatives. The more radical laborists, to be sure, hope to secure a large share of all earnings remaining after an established minimum return to capital. The more conservative element, however, believes that it is not sufficient to compensate the capitalist merely for the *use* of his money. This section of labor feels that able managers are entitled to a large profit, for only such a reward will attract the skill needed for increased production. What is accomplished by treating interest as a cost, therefore, is that the debate as to the proper share of labor in profits is *limited* to the real *profits* after interest, or to that residue of earnings which many business men may deem properly divisible according to management risk and labor reward.

Attitude of Federal Trade Commission

The principal government statement concerning interest inclusion was made by the Federal Trade Commission on July 1, 1916, in a pamphlet entitled, "Fundamentals of a Cost System for Manufacturers."

According to the commission, the cases where it is desirable to include interest in costs may be grouped under two heads: (1) where materials have to be stored for long periods under a seasoning process; or (2) where it is desired to show the effect of variations in the amount of capital employed and the term of employment.

As to a seasoning process the pamphlet continued: "The interest on the capital locked up during the seasoning process forms in a sense a direct part of the cost of the material. If the material were purchased in a seasoned condition, a higher price would have been paid, and this price would at least include interest and other carrying charges."

Regarding expensive equipment and the length of time to complete various processes, the pamphlet said: "It is impossible to get true relative costs unless consideration is given to interest on the capital employed."

In deference to financial accountants who feared an "overvaluation" of inventories because of interest inclusion in costs, the pamphlet compromised in these words: "It is recommended that where interest on investment is treated as an item of cost, the interest charged to the goods on hand be eliminated from inventory values, and that in preparing profit and loss statements, the amount of the interest charged to cost during the period be returned to income under the specific caption "Interest on Investment."

The Federal Trade Commission recognized clearly that interest must be reckoned, and made a part of accounting, if certain information was to be secured. The compromise as to a deduction of interest from inventories for financial statements, it is evident, was warranted solely by expediency and not because of any need for correcting an accounting error.

Most Convenient Settlement Is to Include Interest

The most convenient settlement of the interest question is to recognize the necessary practice of business men and industrial accountants. Accurate factory costs cannot be provided adequately or conveniently, and for all practical purposes cannot be provided at all, unless interest is reckoned into costs. No amount of theorizing will persuade manufacturers to give up their useful practice of including interest.

VII. Motives Actuating Proponents of Interest Inclusion

To emphasize the reasons prompting the advocates of interest as a cost, the following paragraphs are added.

Reconciling Economic and Business Costs

Economists, who favor interest inclusion, and financial accountants, who disfavor it, are both theorist about cost accounting. The choice between their views ought to lie with cost accountants, industrial engineers, and business men, for these are experienced in the matter. The decision would inevitably be given to the economists, for their theory is supported by the practice which meets industrial needs.

Interest advocates believe that business cost should be reconciled with economic cost. This is not foolish, for standard theory favors the idea. It is not impractical, for many accountants, engineers and business men have proved that it can be done.

Securing Accurate Cost Comparisons

Accuracy is the first requisite of cost work. Cost figures may not be worked out to six decimal places, but the non-requirement of "absolute" accuracy scarcely warrants the omission of an important factor. Men favor interest as a cost because they know from experience that without it comparisons often are misleading.

Standardizing the Basis for Costs

The proponents of interest inclusion also feel that this practice will help to secure accounting uniformity—that is, not the determination of one cost *result*, but the setting of a standard *method*. Uniformity along theoretically proper lines is one of the most important aims of modern accounting, and interest advocates are doing their share to see that it is realized. The experience of manufacturers' associations certainly justifies the belief that it can be realized.

Establishing Fair Selling Prices

Interest inclusion helps to establish a fair selling price, not because it leads to a standardized price but because, by securing the accurate cost, it eliminates ignorance and ruinous competition. Costs will vary between plants as will administrative expenses, selling expenses, and desired profits, so that no fixed rule can be laid down as to the exact part which cost plays in the selling price. Whenever the true cost is known, however, a more successful attempt can be made to fix a selling price that is fair to all concerned.

VIII. Objections to Interest Inclusion Answered

The objections commonly made by accountants who are reluctant to include interest in costs can all be refuted.

A. Economic cost cannot be reconciled with business cost.

Answer—The question is one of advisability, not possibility. There may be many considerations to influence a price below cost on inventory items, or a liberal reserve against inventory losses, but if cost is the basis of inventory valuation all of it should be recorded. Economic cost can be secured, for many manufacturers are actually figuring it by adding interest to the so-called business cost.

* * *

B. In mining, transportation, or manufacture by continuous processes, like the making of flour, cement, pig iron, or wood pulp, it makes but little practical difference whether the desired information is secured by reckoning interest on investment into cost, or by leaving it out and determining an average "profit" for the industry including a return on the capital.

Answer—This statement is substantially true as applied to the industries mentioned, but in most industries the manufacturers desire to include, and do include, interest in figuring costs for themselves. They are impelled to do this because rarely do they have a single product or a single process. More frequently they have a varied product (like (a) lead and silver, or copper and silver, from the same mine, or (b) a sale at a more or less advanced stage of manufacture, as with cloth unbleached or later bleached or still later cut up into retail lengths); or they have a varied process (like (a) automatic alongside of hand work, or (b) new types of machinery alongside of older types not yet discarded).

As Professor Cole says, "No comparison is possible between different establishments, between different periods in the same establishment, or between different methods in the same establishment, if capital investment in labor-saving or material-saving machinery is neglected; for the very purpose of such investment is to save cost in other directions, and to neglect the capital sacrifice, made in saving other costs, is to neglect in part the very aim of the cost accounting."

* * *

C. The provision of capital is a financial proposition, and has nothing to do with the production of goods.

Answer—Of course the provision of capital is a financial matter, but that capital therefore has nothing to do with production is a decided *non sequitur.* Here is a fundamental misunderstanding of the economic function of capital. Economists agree that capital is a prime factor with labor in production. Labor concerns human beings and is secured through employment agencies, but it is none the less a productive factor. Just so capital, although it is acquired in monetary units and is handled through financial channels, is not disassociated from production. The form, the manner of acquisition—these are immaterial; the vital point is that capital, just the same as labor, is *used* in production.

* * *

D. There is an actual outgo for labor, but not for capital owned.

Answer—The return to labor is wages, and the return for the use of owned capital is the interest element contained in the dividend rate. Under normal business conditions, therefore, the return to owned capital represents an actual outlay. It is made in different form and at a different time from that to labor, but it is none the less real. Under abnormal conditions the expected return to owned capital may fail to materialize on account of unproductive capacity, or losses due to sales or administrative policies. Interest deserves to be included in cost, however, for there is, whenever possible, an actual outlay representing the return for the use of capital owned.

* * *

E. A large amount of "futile clerical calculation" is necessary to include interest properly in costs.

Answer—Two points are involved here: the amount of the work, and its futility. As regards the first, interest can be included in costs just as easily as a rate for depreciation, taxes or insurance, with results completely justifying the slight effort. As to futility, the best judges of this are those who know by actual experience that cost accounting for interest gives extremely useful data.

* * *

F. The interest rate to be used must be chosen arbitrarily and is difficult to select.

Answer—The rate for interest is no more arbitrary and no more difficult to select than the rates for depreciation. As a matter of practical experience a group of business men are better informed and can come nearer to agreeing on a suitable rate of interest than they can on suitable rates of depreciation. For an interest rate to be used in cost accounting, nothing more is required than that it be reasonable and agreed upon by the persons concerned. This is particularly true when associated manufacturers are interested in establishing a plan of uniform accounting.

G. The interest inclusion theory means that capital shall be guaranteed a definite return.

Answer — The inclusion of interest in costs is not intended to create, and does not create, any legal guarantee of a definite return to capital, any more than the usual charges to cost and credits to reserves for depreciation guarantee an available fund to replace worn-out plant. The only insurance is merely the indirect, informal one that when all elements of cost are accounted for, the use of cost in fixing selling price is likely to be so much more intelligent that the reasonable expectancy of the desired return to capital is increased.

* * *

H. A credit to the account known as Interest Charged to Cost is fictitious, for it does not represent anything actually received.

Answer — Such a credit is no more fictitious than any nominal accrual (like depreciation). Modern accounting often estimates influences on business progress before they definitively materialize in dollars and cents. Just as a depreciation charge is a working estimate of impairment that must later be made up through an actual outlay of cash, so interest on investment is a working estimate of a cost which ultimately should be returned through income.

* * *

I. The inclusion of interest leads to an anticipation of profit.

Answer — This argument really begs the question, because it takes for granted that "interest" is profit. Such an assumption is contrary to standard economic theory. Moreover, even if objection is made to the inclusion of interest because it is an "anticipation," this objection can be entirely met by the simple device of taking out in total (if that course is thought to be conservative) what has been included in detail for the sake of making useful measurements.

* * *

J. The inclusion of interest leads to an inflation of inventories.

Answer — To use the word "inflate" again begs the question. There is no inflation resulting from including any element which is a cost. Since interest on investment is shown to be a cost, it logically and properly raises the value of manufactured goods as much as any other cost.

Any inventory of manufactured goods has used capital, frequently in huge quantities, in the process of conversion from raw material to finished product. It has also used capital in the possession of the producer before coming to the manufacturer, and the purchase price to the latter is higher accordingly. If it has used capital, it has, indisputably, a greater cost. If the manufacturing business has been sensibly managed, the product is worth what it has cost in capital in its last stage (manufacturing), just as much as in any previous (producing) stage. To be specific, the capital cost of converting seasoned lumber into furniture is just as inevitably an addition to its cost, and just as fair an addition to its inventory price, as the cost of seasoning it beforehand.

In short, it takes capital to manufacture, more or less capital according to the kind of product made, and according to the manufacturing policy pursued. Frequently a liberal use of capital diminishes other costs, and the too meager use of capital increases other costs. Interest on investment, as said before, is the conventional and logical way of expressing capital cost. Since one accepts an arbitrary charge for depreciation as a good asset in the cost of manufactured goods, the logic seems unavoidable that there should be no greater objection to an arbitrary charge for interest. One kind of cost is as good an addition as another.

Logically, therefore, no reason exists why an inventory should not be carried at all its cost, including as much as is due for interest on investment. This is the theoretically correct practice. If any adjustment of inventories on financial statements is made by eliminating the total interest (see last sentence of Section I), this step is altogether one of expediency in meeting bankers' demands, and not one of correcting an error in accounting.

* * *

K. Bankers insist upon scaling down inventories to exclude interest.

Answer—One must admit this practice on the part of some bankers, but must deny that their opinion should have preponderating weight on the general subject of including interest in costs. Bankers may insist upon underrating accounts receivable or estimating other assets too conservatively, but this fact should not influence the accounting. It should influence merely the adjustments that the owners may think it necessary or desirable to make in the statements prepared from the books of accounts. On the point of interest, as explained in Section I, an adjustment for the banker can be easily made by eliminating from the inventory the accumulated interest. It is better to do this than to leave an essential and calculable element out of costs.

* * *

L. If interest is included as a part of costs, the general disposition on the part of the public and labor will be to lay claim to part or the whole of the balance of income on the ground of overexaction or underpayment respectively.

Answer—The public or labor may make such a claim, and it may be valid, but the establishment of the claim is not made more certain by accounting for interest as a cost. In making such a claim under conditions of interest exclusion, the first step of the public or labor is to try to eliminate from consideration what it approximates as a fair return for the use of capital. In other words, neither the public nor labor is inclined to prejudice its case against excess profits by making an unfair demand for the interest return which properly belongs to capital. Any dispute as to residual profits, therefore, is decided upon its merits, whether interest is or is not included in costs.

* * *

M. Legal decisions are against interest inclusion, and government contracts during the war did not allow interest or rent.

Answer — That the courts and the government are slow to respond to economic thinking should not be an argument against trying to educate them. Great bodies move slowly, especially on new subjects. When an idea is theoretically correct and efficiently usable, one is justified in expecting that the courts and the government will eventually see the light. Indeed, some decisions favorable to the interest theory have already been made. (182 N. Y. Supp. — in re Ulrici's Estate; 160 U. S. 598; 257 U. S. 397.)

* * *

N. The objects sought in including interest in costs can be secured equally well by entering interest calculations in supplementary records.

Answer — This argument is not unlike the out-of-date argument, which would have kept accounts on an actual receipt and disbursement basis and reckoned accruals as statistical information "on the side." What is more important, however, the need for interest on investment in costs frequently arises under conditions which would make a detached calculation utterly impracticable, both because of the clerical difficulty and because of the impossibility of visualizing or comprehending the relationship between the detached calculation and the subject matter to which other fixed charges like taxes, insurance and depreciation would necessarily be related.

It may well be that the accomplished comptroller of some huge industrial corporation is in the habit of making precise calculations involving the exact use of economic theories, entirely apart from straightforward double-entry bookkeeping, and that these calculations can be practically applied and made to serve every need for information which arises in this connection. Anyone with a fairly broad experience with constructive accounting in a wide variety of industries, however, is justified in doubting whether an attempt of this kind could be expected to succeed with the ordinary manufacturer or his overworked chief accountant.

The manufacturer himself may not be actively interested in the mechanism, or the accounting practice or procedure, by which costs are determined, but the accountants who are responsible for the design, the installation and the successful operation of systems calculated to produce this information, have long since learned to avoid the snares and pitfalls of supplementary and detached records, and to tie the whole chain of information solidly into the general accounting.

The idea of co-ordinating general and factory accounting will no doubt be agreed to by nearly every practicing accountant in the United States. Since it can be applied so easily and so effectively to interest on the investment as well as to all the other elements of burden, and since there are so many reasons for including interest with the other calculations and none that will stand the test of analysis for not doing so, it is to be hoped that a greater number of accountants will in this respect progress in practical service to their employers or clients who want to know the facts.

(6) "The Distribution of Overhead Under Abnormal Conditions," 1921 Yearbook, C. B. Williams, Nau, Rusk and Swearingen

The Distribution of Overhead Under Abnormal Conditions

Ordinarily cost accounting has more important functions than to determine selling prices, therefore, in the distribution of overhead expense these other important things must be considered first. These are not ordinary times, however, and there are few manufacturers today who are not confronted with the problem of keeping their plants operating with sufficient volume to hold their organizations together and at the same time of not demoralizing their markets by quoting prices which cannot yield a profit at this or any other time.

The most important thing today and for next year is to stimulate business. In this price is an important factor. As I believe that we are most interested in the problems of today, I shall place more emphasis on selling prices than on some other effects of overhead distribution. There is more involved in setting a price than merely getting business. In the first place the price must provide for a profit to the manufacturer. This seems so evident as not to be worth mentioning, yet every manufacturer at times finds a competitor quoting prices which he is sure cannot yield a profit. We must keep in mind that the cost of production has to be met out of the price collected from the consumer or, if that is not sufficient, from the capital of the manufacturer, and when that in turn is exhausted, the difference is imposed upon his creditors.

One reason why the cost is sometimes taken from the capital of the manufacturer and from the creditor is that a price is set without a proper realization of the cost, thereby yielding no profit. In times like the present it may be equally true that the price set is too high, causing a loss of business and therefore an excessive amount of idleness, which may be the real cause for the depletion of the manufacturer's capital. It is a serious question whether the capital of many concerns is not being depleted to pay the cost of idleness, since prices are at levels which seek to collect this cost from the consumer.

If the manufacturer intentionally quotes a price which will not yield a profit, thereby hoping to obtain business which may temporarily keep his organization together, he must consider the effect of this policy upon future business. It is difficult to raise the price of a standard article unless the general tendency of all prices is upward. Assuming that this tendency will not prevail during the next few years, the manufacturer should be careful not to establish a price which will be used as a precedent and which it will be difficult to raise when business becomes normal.

I have in mind an instance where a price of 58¢ was quoted on a standard article at a time when business was hard to get and when the manufacturer was very anxious to keep a certain department operating. Later, when he sought to increase this price to 65¢ in order to make a profit, he met with serious objections from his customers to the price increase without any apparent increase in the cost of manufacture. His customers contended that they had assumed the quotation of 58¢ would stand unless and until there should be some change in the cost of manufacture. Knowing that the tendency was toward lower costs, they had made their quotations on the basis of a 58¢ price to them.

In the lowering of prices and the scramble to get as much as possible of the small amount of business offered, the manufacturer should be careful that the advantage which he may gain today is not lost to him when business becomes normal and he may expect to realize a normal profit. On the other hand, he should be careful not to lose customers by trying to make them pay for his idle expense.

From the standpoint of the sales department, a price which is too high means that no business will be obtained. A short-sighted policy may dictate the quoting of low prices for no other reason than to secure current business. On the other hand, if a price is quoted too low, it means future difficulties for the sales department and dissatisfied customers.

The question, then, is how to obtain a correct cost upon which to base sales prices. Labor and material cost can be determined at any time with a fair degree of accuracy and the method of obtaining them does not cause much argument. Overhead or burden costs, however, must be considered in relation to varying volumes of production. One way to apply this overhead properly is by means of normal overhead rates. To some it may seem unnecessary to discuss the difference between a program of distributing overhead to costs by means of normal overhead rates and one of absorbing all current overhead into cost regardless of the volume of production, yet I am sure that many manufacturers still use the latter unscientific and dangerous method.

Just recently I learned of a large producer of malleable castings who quoted on an order for castings and who when told that his price was too high, explained that he could make them at a lower price under normal conditions, but that at present his foundry was operating to only 30% of capacity and therefore he must obtain a higher price in order to avoid loss. He went so far as to refuse the order at a price which he admitted would be satisfactory if he were operating to normal capacity. Nor is this an isolated case. Was this man justified in refusing an order which would have returned his prime cost plus a reasonable amount for overhead and plus a profit? Had he accepted the order at a price which provided for a normal overhead charge, he would have received more than he paid out and therefore would have made a profit.

Whenever you exchange commodities or services and as a result have more assets than you would have had if the exchange had not been made, you have realized a profit. This is not a problem in accounting but in business. Again, if this foundryman had accepted the order he would have increased his volume of business and thus lowered his rate of overhead even on the basis of his own method of figuring. This would have enabled him to quote lower prices on additional business until finally his volume would have been at normal and he could have quoted a normal price.

Has a man a right to expect his customer to pay a higher price because business is poor? Certainly not! Should he accept business at a loss? Certainly not! Then how is he to quote a price which will stimulate business and at the same time not incur a loss on the business which he obtains? By recognizing the difference between manufacturing cost and idle expense. If the sales price is based on the cost of manufacture, idle expense excluded, instead of on the total expenditures, possibly it can be made low enough to attract buyers and at the same time not show a loss.

I contend that it costs no more to manufacture an article when only one out of ten machines is working than it does when all are working. The outlay may be more but instead of being cost of manufacture, it is cost of not manufacturing (other articles or more of the same article), and as such should properly be borne by the owners of the business, at least temporarily. In the long run the consumer must pay for the idleness of manufacturing units; but this should be reflected in the average price over a period of years rather than in an increased price when the idleness occurs.

For the purpose of this discussion I shall assume that we accept the principle of the normal rate. The natural question then is "What is a normal rate?" Most of us are familiar with the days when it was customary to add 100% for overhead. Without any knowledge of what his overhead expense was, to say nothing of a lack of knowledge as to how this expense should be applied, many a business man solved the problem to his own satisfaction by the expedient of adding 100%. In doing this he was unconsciously using a normal rate. Of course, the result was usually wrong because the rate was wrong. But this man was probably as nearly right as the man who, regardless of conditions, applied all of his overhead to costs and had a fluctuating cost as the basis of sales and manufacturing policies.

Another common method of applying overhead expense has been to divide the sum of a year's expenses by the direct labor for the year and use the resulting percentage as the overhead rate for the next year. This was an improvement over the 100% method and was also a method of using a normal rate. Of course, it was unsatisfactory because it did not take into account many important differences between departments and producing units. Although unsatisfactory, both of these methods showed a belief in the principle of normal rates.

Our purpose is to determine what a normal rate is and how it may be obtained. We shall discuss this from the standpoint of the average business which has not adopted the more scientific methods and has not built up scientific standards for all operations. I believe it is safe to say that 90% of all manufacturers do not use the so-called scientific methods of production control and cost accounting. Many, however, have a control and a knowledge of their business which meets their need, and which they would be unwilling to surrender. On the other hand, many are sadly lacking in a knowledge of their own affairs. I do not wish to be understood as being opposed to scientific management and control in industry. I believe every business concern should use the very best methods; but ours is a problem for the present, and the business which is not equipped with the latest and best methods must have some immediate answer to its problem.

Let us not overlook the fact that there has been much good in past methods. Occasionally some individual conceives the idea that everything in the universe is all wrong. If he happens to have some knowledge about a particular phase of business he proceeds to tell us how everything in connection with that phase is wrong. We do not take much stock in what he tells us because his criticism only seeks to tear down and does nothing to build up.

Two gentlemen by the names of Lenin and Trotsky once lived in the city of New York and conceived the idea that everything in the world was wrong and that it was their mission to correct it. Not being able to start among intelligent, clear thinking people, they took advantage of a situation in Russia, got enough of a following to seize the reins of power and then attempted to substitute a heavenly for an earthly condition. They succeeded in doing away with the earthly condition but, as you well know, what replaced it could hardly be called heavenly.

We have Lenins and Trotskys in every vocation and we have them in cost accounting. Through misguided judgment, they seek to destroy everything that has been done in the past. I am sure that the great body of business men and cost accountants will give little heed to their propaganda, because they realize that the way to make progress is to improve what you have, rather than to tear down without offering a workable substitute.

I believe there has been much good in past methods and that many of those present have developed plans which can easily be adapted to present conditions without great inconvenience or expense, and with this in mind I propose to suggest a method of applying overhead expense based on the present condition of the average business. We shall try sympathetically to allow for the shortcomings of the past as revealed by the present, with the hope that something may be accomplished which will meet the present needs.

What is a normal overhead rate? It is a rate which during a period of normal production and normal expense will absorb all the overhead expense of that period. In other words, it is a rate based on normal conditions of production and expense. Such a rate may be obtained by dividing a normal amount of expense by a normal volume of business for the same period. That is a simple statement; but to arrive at the result will not be so simple for the average concern. The most difficult thing to determine will be the normal volume of production.

Normal production does not mean possible production. In many cases it does not even mean possible production less proper allowances for repairs and other ordinary hindrances to continuous operation. A good illustration of some of the other elements which must be considered in establishing a normal rate will be found in a study of the coal mining industry. It is a condition of the coal business that more coal is demanded in winter than in summer and the operator has to provide facilities sufficient for his winter demand and suffer the resulting idleness in summer. During the winter months he is hampered by lack of cars and other hindrances so that frequently he finds it impossible to ship all that he can mine. Under such conditions the normal tonnage would not be the total tons that could be mined in a year but rather the tons that could be mined, loaded and delivered, considering the lack of demand in summer and the probability of car shortage and other hindrances to meeting the full demand in winter. Similar conditions may prevail in manufacturing industries where the normal output would be what the plant might produce, load and ship after considering in addition to lost time, repairs and similar hindrances, the irregularity of demand and the impossibility of making a shipment at the pleasure of the shipper.

Lacking scientific methods for determining the possible output from which to deduct allowances for all possible interruptions, the average business can at least establish its normal as the average of a certain number of years which the management considers representative of its business. If the several years preceding the war brought a volume of business to your plant that kept it as busy as you could ordinarily expect it to be, and there have been no material changes in the plant or methods, there appears to be no good reason why an average of these years should not be used to obtain a normal output.

This method may be criticized. It may be contended that it is unscientific; but after all are not established facts at least as reliable as untried theories? If you attempt to determine the output by other methods, you will doubtless refer to past experience in making various allowances and probably, in the end, you will make an allowance for contingencies that will bring your scientific figure close to the figures of the past anyway.

Will the average manufacturer of 1922-1930 be any different from what he was from 1906 to 1914? Will not human effort accompanied by human frailties operate much the same and obtain much the same results next year as it did last year? If this is so, will not past results be a fair basis for future calculations? Of course, where changes in methods take place, proper allowances must be made; but these allowances, based on the known differences between the old and the new methods, should not be hard to make.

Let us assume that our expense rate is to be a rate per hour of operation, although in some industries it would be based on tonnage or some other unit of production. Having selected a volume of output which we are willing to call normal, we must next determine the number of operating hours required to obtain this volume. This may be done either by analyzing the normal output according to operations and determining the time required for each operation on the basis of past records or engineering estimates or by using the same average hours of operation as were shown during the years selected as normal productive years. The simplest method of all would be to determine the number of hours a given unit operated during normal years without analyzing its output into operations, and then adjust this figure in accordance with any known changes.

The next step is to determine the normal operating expenses. Since we are not discussing labor and material cost, this term includes only those items which generally come under the head of overhead or burden. It will be helpful, if you have been in the habit of making a budget at the beginning of each year as a guide to the year's expenditures. If you have not done this, you have at least accumulated expenses in such classifications that they can now be analyzed for your present purpose. An analysis of these expenses for the years which were used to determine normal output will provide a basis for establishing normal expense charges.

In making up the expense budget each item of expense for each department should be considered separately. Past records should be an invaluable guide; but we must not overlook the importance of consultation with the factory superintendent and foremen. Certain fixed charges such as taxes, insurance, allowances for depreciation, and interest on investment (if you wish to include it), will be easy to calculate for the reason that they are fixed. If you have kept a record of repairs by machines or other producing units, you can with the help of the factory men set reliable allowances for repairs. You must consider the condition of the equipment at the present time in comparison with what it was when the figures were obtained, and also the present costs of labor and material. Such items as foremen, factory clerks and other indirect labor should be considered in the light of any changes in the plan of the organization, or in the rates of pay.

If records of past experience are not available, you will have to use your best judgment together with such helpful suggestions as you are sure to obtain from the factory men. Each plant will have its own peculiar conditions which must be given intelligent consideration in making up the expense budget. The expense arrived at by the budget divided by the number of normal operating hours will result in the normal rates to be used. These rates will be established in the divisions it is desired to use in applying overhead to cost.

It is important that a close check be maintained to determine the correctness of the rates established. A good way of doing this is to accumulate both the production and the expense figures in the same classifications as were used in setting the rates, and to compare these results with the standards. This comparison will disclose any considerable error in the budget figure. If the ratio of direct hours to production differs materially from the standard, it may disclose errors in the standard. On the other hand, it may be that the standards are correct and that differences indicate errors in the current practice.

When to the direct labor and material costs are added the overhead cost figured at the normal rates per hour, we have the total manufacturing cost. If the plant is only operating to 50% of capacity, only one-half of the overhead will be applied to cost. The remainder will be undistributed or unabsorbed overhead and will be understood to represent the extent to which the plant operated below normal production, in other words, idle expense or unused capacity.

In making a profit and loss statement under this plan, we should deduct the normal cost as explained above from the sales to show gross manufacturing profit. From this would then be deducted the unabsorbed overhead and other expenses, showing a result which might possibly be a loss. We should thus know what the profit was on the business which had been obtained and what the loss was because the plant was partially idle.

If the foundryman to whom I referred had used this method, he would have quoted a price based on normal operation. This would have obtained him the business, which would have yielded a profit, and which in addition would have absorbed part of the loss he was suffering because of partial idleness.

(7) "The Scrap Problem," March 1, 1922, Bulletin, Vol. 3, No. 11, I. W. Kokins, Comptroller's Office, General Electric Company, Schenectady

The Scrap Problem[1]

The chief purpose of this article is to discuss the methods to be used in reducing losses from scrap, with particular reference to plants in the electrical industry of some size.

Every manufacturing plant, whether small or large, has the problem of scrap to face. It may be either simple or complex, depending upon the size of the plant, the line of product and the variety of materials used in manufacturing. The contributing causes are defective and unsuitable material or product which falls short in performance of the service it is intended for; poor workmanship, accidental damage, etc. Briefly, the problem of scrap is always present, either as a result of operations through which the material passes, or defects in the material and product, or obsolescence.

Since all material that is scrapped represents an increase in cost, it is essential that efficient methods be used in handling it, so that scrap may be kept at a minimum, and correct accounting followed for the purpose of allocating the loss to individual lines of product. It is also true that correct accounting and comprehensive reports often point out inefficiency in manufacturing operations. In general it might be said that the higher the percentage of scrap, the larger is the loss of material, labor and overhead, and consequently more expense is necessary to handle the increased quantity of scrap for disposition.

To properly discuss the subject and to present a plan for taking care of the scrap problem, it is necessary to start with the source of scrap and follow it through the various stages until it is finally disposed of and properly accounted for.

I. Sources of Scrap

Scrap can be traced to three main sources—defective or unsuitable material purchased outside, avoidable scrap and unavoidable scrap.

1. Defective or Unsuitable Material Purchased Outside.

Defective material purchased outside can either be corrected and used or rejected and returned to the vendor. If it can be saved, the cost of correction should be charged back to the vendor, but this can be done only through

[1]The Association has issued three previous publications dealing with scrap, Volume I, Number 6, entitled "Distribution of Defective and Spoiled Material Costs," by C. H. Smith; Volume II, Number 13, entitled "A Method of Accounting for Scrap," by C. B. Williams, and Volume III, Number 9, entitled "Methods of Accounting for Waste in a Cotton Spinning Mill," by George D. Klimmer.

prearranged agreement. Otherwise it is the usual business practice to reject the material and bill it back to the vendor. However, any labor performed and expense entailed before defects are found represents a loss because such items, as a rule, cannot be charged back.

Ability to identify the vendor is of importance, particularly when similar material is purchased from a number of concerns, because such material can only be returned when the vendor is positively known. One method of identification is to assign different symbols to the vendors requiring that the material they supply should bear that symbol, or such symbol can be stamped on the material when it is received.

Defective material purchased outside, even though it can be rejected and billed back, is a source of loss because of the incidental expense. But by exercising care in placing orders with those vendors only who supply the best materials, using positive means of identification, and promptly rejecting defective material, it should not be difficult to keep the loss from this source at a low figure.

2. Avoidable Scrap. The scrap grouped under the general heading of avoidable scrap can be classified according to the following causes:

a.Obsolete (due to change in design), b. Surplus (due to over-ordering, ordering in error, or unbalanced production), c. Spoiled (due to errors in drawings), d. Spoiled (fault of operator), e. Spoiled (fault of operating conditions), f. Spoiled (from another department), g. Broken or lost, h. Defective (purchased outside), i. Failure in test, j. Due to cancellation of order or requisition, k. Extra labor (all labor, which would not be necessary under perfect manufacturing conditions), and l. Returned product (not marketable).

The classification of causes can be either reduced or extended to suit the requirement of the management. But it is desirable that it should be broad enough to permit easy analysis, and thereby assist in reducing or eliminating the loss by removing the cause.

Avoidable scrap is the most important class of scrap, in that its cost less the salvage value of material means a total loss.

3. Unavoidable Scrap. The term unavoidable scrap is to some extent self-explanatory. It includes worn out tools and equipment and all natural scrap, briefly all scrap other than that covered by the foregoing two broad classes. It might be well to arrange unavoidable scrap into three groups, and to consider each separately.

a. Obsolete and worn out tools and equipment when removed from service should be either put in shape and offered for sale to second-hand dealers, or disassembled and all good parts placed in storage as spare supply parts for similar equipment in active service. Only equipment and parts for which no use or ready sale can be found should be considered as unavoidable scrap.

b. Product that has been used for experimental purposes can occasionally be remodeled and sold as new product. When this is not practicable, it should be disassembled and all good parts placed in active stock and the remaining parts scrapped.

c .Borings, turnings, clippings, short ends, sweepings, etc., usually comprise the largest percentage of the total quantity of unavoidable scrap handled. There is generally no apparent loss connected with this group of scrap, yet it may be worth while to inspect it closely to determine whether it is really unavoidable. It may be found that the maximum use is not made of raw material. This may lead to transferring short ends from a department where they are useless, to another where they can be used to advantage. It may be found that by closer estimating of sizes of material used, correct proportioning of standard stock and eliminating wasteful practices, a reduction of scrap is possible, with a consequent reduction in material costs.

More could be said about the sources of scrap, and further classification of causes which lead to loss could be discussed in detail, but that is not the purpose of this article. As stated before, its intent is rather to dwell upon *methods* to be applied for the reduction of loss from scrap.

II. Handling Scrap

Scrap is usually looked upon as a nuisance. The word "scrap" itself implies something negligible and is conducive to indifference in handling, which leads to inefficiency and results in not obtaining the full value for the produced scrap. It is almost as important to handle scrap efficiently, as it is to prevent it. Scrap should usually stand out as a red light danger signal with respect to production, but, when once produced, it should receive sufficient attention because of a threefold effect:

a. Carefulness in handling scrap acts suggestively on the workers, leading to good habits such as tidiness, attentiveness and a better attitude towards work in general. This influence becomes an indirect factor in promoting higher efficiency.

b. Careful handling will mean no scrap lying around which takes up valuable working space and ties up capital.

c. Careful segregation at the source will reduce the cost of preparing scrap for disposition, and will also assist in obtaining better prices, thereby reducing the net loss from scrap.

Practically all scrap has a value in the scrap market when properly segregated into grades of unmixed and uniform quality. But mixed scrap brings comparatively only very low prices. For these reasons proper segregation at the source can not be too highly recommended. Of course, it would be poor economy to expend any money or effort in keeping scrap segregated, where the benefits derived would be offset by the expense of handling it.

The following outline of a system of handling scrap is probably not ample enough in scope to suit all industries, but it is adaptable to many, and more especially to the electrical industry, and is intended to meet the requirements of plants of some magnitude.

1. Reporting Defective Material Purchased Outside, and Spoiled or Obsolete Products and Parts (Avoidable Scrap).

In nearly every plant it is the practice to pass all raw material and product through an inspection routine. It would seem therefore that the inspector is the logical individual to report the case and to determine by cooperating with all concerned the advisability of saving the material or product through correction, or of passing on for other disposition.

To facilitate his work, the inspector can be provided with a form especially designed for reporting defects, obsolescence and all other causes. A carefully established list of causes can be printed on the form. The inspector should either put a check mark, or preferably use a punch to indicate the cause.

Form 1 (see Figure 7-1) is a scrap ticket which includes the ideas expressed above, and also shows the other information usually required to make the report complete. The scrap ticket is prepared in quadruplicate, each copy being of a distinctive color to make distribution easy. The form is serially

Figure 7-1

All Scrap tickets must be accounted for. Send void tickets to Dept

SCRAP TICKET — N° 000

Issued by. Dept Date. 19

✓	Check Cause involved	Shop Order N° Requisition N°	From.
	Obsolete Change in design	Name of Part	Drg N°
	Surplus material	Class or Type of Product	Pattern or Shop N°
	Spoiled Errors in drawings	Operations	Material
	Spoiled fault of operator		Quantity
	Spoiled, Fault of Operating conditions	Recommendation.	Weight
	Spoiled in Dept.		Cost of Mat. $
	Broken or lost in Dept.		Piece Work
	Defective Purchased outside	Reason detailed	Day Work
	Failed in test		Overhead
	Cancellation of Order or requisition		Total Cost $
	Extra Labor		Scrap Value
	Returned Product		LOSS $
Signed Inspector		Approved Foreman	
Responsibility assigned to		Labor ticket wanted	Price N°
		Completed part wanted	Signed Prod. Dept.
Signed		Stock wanted.	Signed Stock Dept.

numbered for the purpose of accounting for each set used. The following outline of the routine through which the ticket passes will readily show the important function it performs.

a. The inspector sends the four copies to the foreman, who in the majority of cases can immediately decide what action is to be taken.

b. All four copies should then be forwarded to the cost clerk for filling in of cost figures.

c. The copies are then sent to the production clerk for reordering material, figuring percentage of spoiled parts, estimating delays, etc.

d. The copies next go to the stock room for replacing spoiled material and for passing it into production.

e. The copies are then returned to the foreman for the issuing of labor tags to cover any additional labor. The intent is, that even though material should be passed out to the operator through some irregularity, no labor could be performed on it, until a labor ticket authorized by a waste ticket, is issued.

f. Finally the copies are distributed from the foreman's office. The first copy is sent to the cost department for calculating the percentage of loss to billing, and for preparing waste reports.[2] The second copy is sent to the salvage department for checking scrap received and for crediting the respective departments. The third copy is sent to the department or subforeman responsible for the loss. In the case of outside purchased material, this copy is sent to the purchasing department or individual handling rejections. The fourth copy remains in the foreman's file.

2. Tagging.

When material or product is found by the shop inspector to be defective, obsolete or unfit for use, his first step is to tie a tag to it, so that all further operations on it will be stopped until its final disposition is determined upon.

For easy distinction it is preferable to have three differently colored tags, a green tag for defective material purchased outside, a blue tag for all other defective material, which can possibly be saved through correction, and a red tag for material that is ordered scrapped.

Material purchased outside that has been "green tagged" as defective should not be removed from the shop floor, except on orders from the foreman or inspector. When correction is decided upon, the tag is removed by the inspector and the material is passed into production. When material is to be returned to the vendor the foreman issues an order for its delivery to the shipping department. When the vendor agrees to stand the loss, less scrap value, the green tag is removed by the inspector and a red tag is attached for delivery to scrap storage.

[2]This feature is discussed at length under the heading Absorbing of Scrap Losses in Costs.

Figure 7-2

SCRAP TRANSFER SLIP N° 000

From Dept To Dept, Date 19

Shop Order No	Quantity	Description	Weight	Price	Per	Amount

Signed

Form 2, Size (8 x 4)

"Blue tagged" material is held until the practicability of correction is decided. Then the tag is removed by the inspector and the material is passed into production or is replaced by a red tag and the material is delivered to scrap storage.

All "red tagged" material can be immediately removed from the floor to scrap storage.

3. Reporting and Tagging Natural Scrap (Unavoidable Scrap).

Natural manufacturing scrap does not need the attention of an inspector, but in a large shop there should be someone delegated to see that it is properly handled, i. e., well segregated, promptly collected, tagged, reported for delivery and removed from the floor. This individual should understand the classification of scrap grades in order to do this work intelligently.

One of the requisites for the efficient handling of natural scrap is the complete reporting of all transfers, chiefly for the purpose of allowing full credit at scrap value to the manufacturing departments.[3]

Reporting transfers can be simplified by the use of a special form. Form 2 (see Figure 7-2) will probably be adaptable in most plants without much modification.

The information called for in the headings of the columns on the form is considered necessary for correct accounting.

This scrap transfer slip can be issued either in triplicate or quadruplicate and in serially numbered sets.

[3]This point is explained under the heading Accounting for Scrap.

When filled out, the original is sent to the department or individual handling all scrap accumulations, the duplicate is retained in the originating department and the triplicate, made of heavy paper, is attached to the scrap and acts as a transportation tag. When it is desirable to consider the scrap as a direct credit to costs, a fourth copy can be supplied to the cost clerk for recording the scrap value in the cost ledger.

4. Collecting Scrap.

Systematic collection of scrap is important because it will prevent scrap from lying around, getting mixed and occupying valuable floor space. No specific method can be suggested as the best one to fit all cases because of the great variety of scrap. However, the principle that collection of scrap should be carried on systematically and economically, is applicable everywhere. One fact should be borne in mind, namely, that the quantity of high valued non-ferrous metals, such as copper, brass, aluminum, etc., is usually small. Therefore more care can and should be exercised in handling them to retain their high value. The ferrous scrap, such as iron and steel, is of low value and greater quantity, and requires more economical methods of handling.

5. Accumulation Space.

Proper spaces should be provided in shops where scrap can be accumulated for transfer to scrap storage, and nothing but scrap should be accumulated there. For easy checking and to prevent loss of good material, the red tagged scrap should be kept in separate containers and positively should not be mixed with natural scrap. This separation of the two classes will not entail any more expense and will simplify the handling and accounting for the natural scrap.

6. Containers.

The usual practice of collecting scrap in containers of a variety of shapes and sizes should be discouraged because of the following reasons:

a. They do not permit correct estimating of weights of scrap; b. they are inconvenient for handling in shops and transportation; c. they are unsafe and uneconomical, particularly wooden boxes, as they often break down with heavy loads, entailing the expense of reloading; and d. they cannot be economically stacked for storage, and thus occupy more space than is necessary.

Although the initial cost of uniform scrap containers may be looked upon as an unnecessary expense, it will be found that in the end, they will prove most economical, because they will be of assistance in handling scrap efficiently.

For collecting non-ferrous chips, clippings, etc., at the place where produced, each operator should be supplied with one or more small containers, and be held responsible for keeping the various grades of scrap separate and free from refuse. At regular intervals a laborer should empty the operators' containers into larger ones. The large containers should be labeled according to the grades they are intended to hold. Marks or level lines should be painted on them to indicate the weight of contents when filled to the respective mark or line. As a rule, scrap of uniform size and nature will run very near alike in weight. Thus the system of always using the same kind of container with level lines for the same grade, will eliminate the necessity of weighing scrap.

7. Accumulating Large Lots of One Grade Scrap.

The expense of handling and accumulating large quantities of steel and iron clips can be held at a minimum if large bins are constructed near a railroad track and adjacent to buildings where the chips are produced. The chips can be shoveled from floors into easily wheeled, large capacity tilting barrows and transferred to such bins for storage until enough is collected for carload lot shipments. Where the location does not allow such an arrangement, the chips should be collected in large containers for transfer to scrap storage, and should be emptied and returned to the shops. It may happen that the space on the shop floor is limited so that the use of large containers on the floor is prohibitive. This can be overcome by providing holes with strong trap doors in the main aisle which is usually kept open and by putting the containers in these holes under the floor. They should only be removed when they are full. A drop-bottom on such containers makes emptying easy. This is feasible only where crane service is available.

Scrap that is very bulky, irregular in shape, long and assembled will have to be handled as individual pieces or lots, and weighed either in shops where produced or on track scales when shipped. Even sweepings from shop floors have a certain value if they contain any metal. They can be put through a rotating mechanical sifter and graded into sweepings No. 1, 2, 3, etc., according to the percentage of metal contents.

8. Facilities and Equipment.

Many devices are used to reduce scrap to a convenient shape for consumption and shipping. The most noteworthy are the presses for baling skeleton punchings, wire, etc. The bales are often loaded directly into railroad cars by conveyor. Shears are used for cutting long scrap to charging sizes; magnetic separators for removing iron and steel from non-ferrous metals; lifting magnets for handling iron and steel; melting pots and dross reducing furnace for reclaiming tin, lead, zinc, etc., scrap and alloys derived therefrom.

There are other devices in common use, some of which are developed to meet particular requirements.

III. Disposition of Scrap

Scrap storage was mentioned in the preceding paragraphs. The term might be explained. It is an open space or building where scrap is accumulated until it is used or sold. In small factories it is usually a small open space. Larger factories should have a definite storage place where scrap is accumulated and prepared for profitable disposition. When the value of scrap disposed annually runs into large figures, then the establishment of a salvage department provided with building and adequate equipment is the most satisfactory solution.

1. The Salvage Department.

The duties of the salvage department are first, to prevent excessive scrapping at the source and second, to obtain the highest value with the least effort and expense for the scrap produced. It should be in charge of someone who will give his undivided attention to the scrap problem to forestall the undesirable attitude where no one knows much about scrap, and, therefore, nobody cares.

Should the volume of scrap be very large and the causes of loss numerous and complex, then such a department could be further divided into two distinct branches, one with particular duties of keeping scrap at a minimum and the other with the duty of handling scrap physically and preparing it for the market. Both branches, however, are so closely related that it is wise to place them under one head.

It is generally and instinctively known that scrapping usually means a loss, and in most cases some effort is made by those directly responsible for it, towards the prevention of recurrence. But possibilities of increasing the value of scrap sold are not as well known and frequently not even realized. Here is the opportunity for such a department to prove its worth. The underlying facts to keep in mind are, to know the scrap; its composition if it is an alloy; and to find a good market for it. Wherever practicable, the market value of scrap can then be further increased by preparing it to meet the consumers' requirements as scrap in shape for direct consumption will bring the highest price.

Based upon this point of view a salvage department can be constituted as a self-supporting organization, assessed with overhead and operated on an equal footing with producing departments. It should be invested with sufficient authority to induce better teamwork with other departments. Such an organization will relieve others from duties which are considered only side issues and hence often neglected. It will also be in better position to perform the following specialized functions:

a. While not relieving anyone from responsibility regarding conservation of material, it will analyze the causes of scrap and waste, based on information gathered from the scrap tickets, and will suggest means of reduction or possible elimination of loss.

b. Supervise handling of scrap in shops, paying particular attention to segregation and assist in developing inexpensive and efficient methods for collecting and transporting.

c. Prepare scrap for disposition, being on the alert to reclaim and place back into production all that is practicable, before selling any to dealers.

IV. Records and Reports

The last paragraph above suggests records and reports. The following are considered more or less essential.

1. One class of records are *summary sheets* on which the weights of scrap received shown on the scrap transfer forms and scrap tickets are to be compiled by departments and distributed according to grades. Totals for each department should then be recapitulated on one sheet and forwarded at the end of the month to the accounting department for crediting the respective departments with scrap value and charging the scrap account.

2. A scrap ledger should be maintained in the salvage department for debiting scrap classification accounts with scrap received (from summary sheets), and crediting the same with transfers and shipments of scrap (from material transfer slips and memos of shipment). A page is started in the ledger for each grade of scrap. On the left page all receipts of the grade are posted showing: a. the date of receipt, (b) summary sheet number, (c) department received from, (d) weight, (e) price, and (f) amount. On the right hand page all transfers or shipments are posted in the same order, showing the transfer slip or memo of shipment number and the purchaser's or consumer's name. The difference between the *weights* appearing on both sides at the end of a month should represent the weight of that particular scrap that is on hand. In this manner a book inventory of scrap on hand is maintained. This record will also serve for comparing prices on various shipments.

3. A record of purchasers can be maintained for statistical purposes, showing the kind of material they purchase, quantity, price and amount. The totals of this record should balance with the totals of grades transferred or shipped during the month, as posted in the ledger.

4. A car record book in which all shipments are entered in numerical order of the memo of shipment and showing all car numbers will be found valuable for tracing back to any data regarding outgoing scrap.

5. A monthly report of disposition of scrap should be compiled by the salvage department, showing under each purchaser's name the quantity, price and amount of each grade purchased, also the total weight of scrap disposed and total proceeds for the month. Opposite the price obtained for each grade, it might be well to show the percent it is of the basic market quotation price, (for example: if copper is quoted at 13c. lb. on date of sale and a grade of copper scrap was sold at 11c. lb., 84.61% of the market price was obtained). This ratio of price received for scrap to market price quoted for the respective raw material, will always show where the highest prices are obtained, regardless of the drop or rise in market quotations.

6. An annual summary of scrap can be compiled in two sections, one showing total weight and value of scrap sold to each purchaser, and the other total quantities and value of each grade of scrap disposed during the year. Both the monthly and the annual report are not essential but may prove valuable for comparison.

7. A scrap price list for crediting should be maintained. The prices should be based on market quotations minus the actual cost of handling.

V. Accounting for Scrap

In the preceding sections, different phases of the scrap problems were outlined with the reasons given for systematic handling, etc. The ultimate aim, however, of a system for handling scrap is to obtain correct costs and prevent loss.

The following system of accounting for scrap deals with the problem in general, and is built up to fit in with the methods of physically handling scrap already described.

1. Absorbing of Scrap Losses in Costs.

Careful and intelligent application of the scrap ticket outlined under "Reporting defective material, etc." will reveal all losses due to scrapping and permit calculation of a correct ratio of loss to product billed.

The copy of the scrap ticket sent to the cost clerk acts as a basis for summarizing all losses of material, labor and expense by lines of product. The provision of showing the order or requisition number on each scrap ticket simplifies matters in drawing a distinct line between losses incurred on special product manufactured for stock. Usually the loss on special product is chargeable direct to the cost of the order or requisition. The scrap tickets in such cases are to be stamped "absorbed in cost direct," and then filed.

All other scrap tickets are sorted and filed according to departments or lines of product. At the end of the month they are summarized on a "scrap report," provided with a column for each "cause" showing the loss of material, labor and expense. The extreme right hand column should show the total loss in each department or line of product. Directly under or next to this total there should be inserted the total cost of material consumed or the total cost of shipment of the line of product, and also the calculated ratio between the total cost of material consumed or total cost of shipments. This ratio should be added to the cost of the material consumed or the total cost of the product depending upon the basis used in calculating it. Where cost estimates are quoted on special orders or requisitions this ratio should also be considered in such estimates.

The scrap ticket form provides for separation of material, labor and expense, and deduction of scrap value, but the net loss only should be considered in costs. To calculate the scrap value correctly a list of up-to-date scrap prices should be maintained. Should the management desire to ascertain the loss for which each department is responsible, a report can be prepared, by sorting the scrap tickets and summarizing the data shown thereon according to respective departments. The scrap department should also include losses on special products.

2. Considering Scrap Value of Natural Scrap in Costs.

The "scrap report" covers only two classes of scrap, namely: defective material purchased outside and obsolete, spoiled, defective, surplus, etc., material and product but does not include the natural or common scrap. The natural scrap can be considered in costs under two methods:

a. Its cost may be calculated in the material costs of each *unit* or product, where a *large percentage* of the quantity of raw material used in one unit becomes scrap, or where the material used has a *high scrap value*. This method requires actual tests to be made by calculating the gross and net weight of a unit. The material charge minus the scrap value of the quantity scrapped becomes the net unit material cost.

b. Its cost may be calculated upon a percentage basis representing the ratio of natural manufacturing scrap to the total of each kind of material or line of product.

The scrap transfer form described under "Reporting and tagging scrap" will enable the salvage department to summarize the scrap received according to departments or lines of product and to submit such summaries to the cost clerk for the calculation of the ratio of scrap credit to be allowed in material costs.

3. – Scrap Account.

The ideal method of accounting for scrap is to establish a department with a complete set of operating accounts. In this manner the salvage department would not only bear its own expense but also a pro rata share of the general expense. The same set-up can be used as that for producing departments but the elements entered would differ in the case of material and direct labor.

a. The material account besides being debited with all scrap, would also be charged with tie wire used in baling, and other items of similar nature.

b. The direct labor account would receive charges for all labor performed in preparing scrap for disposition.

The direct expense charges would be similar to those of producing departments and the general expense would represent a fair share of fixed charges. The respective accounts would be credited in the usual way. The principal credits would come from summaries of transfers and shipments billed. Such operating accounts would permit of close analysis and proper control of expense. They would enable the manager to determine whether too much is being expended in recovering and sorting scrap in comparison with the value received. However, it is not always practicable or feasible to have a complete set of operating accounts. Then the best substitute is to open a scrap account, debited and credited as follows:

Debits

a. Scrap value of material and product reported by scrap tickets. From the summary of this class of scrap submitted by individual in charge of scrap. This scrap value is to be credited to respective departments, orders, or lines or product.

b. Scrap value of all natural scrap reported by scrap transfer forms, as submitted on summary sheet by the individual in charge of scrap. The credits to be distributed as above.

c. All labor used in preparing scrap for disposition.

d. Direct expense, such as salaries and wages, of others than laborers, and also expenditures for miscellaneous small tools and supplies.

e. Pro rata share of fixed charges.

Credits

a.Salvage value of scrap transferred to stock or other departments, obtained from a summary of stock transfers, debited to departments, orders or lines of product at fair value.

b. Value of scrap sold obtained from sales register covering all shipments of scrap to outside concerns.

c. Miscellaneous items.

At the end of the fiscal year, any balance in such account not representing physical scrap on hand, should be transferred to the profit and loss account.

The initial purpose of this article was to deal chiefly with fundamentals, as an attempt to lay out a specific system would fall short, in that such system would of necessity be too restrictive, debarring all features not specially included. The suggested methods, however, will permit modifications where required to meet local conditions. As a whole the use of the methods described may have some influence in perpetuating stricter conservation of materials and lead to a reduction of costs for the benefit of industry in general; and further, by inducing more efficient handling may increase the value of scrap and contribute to increased profits.

Perhaps, as a parting word it might be well to add, that scrap exists. Consequently handling it for ultimate disposition is inevitable. Makeshift handling and accounting for scrap is usually not only expensive but also precludes a rare opportunity for studying the efficiency of manufacturing operations, while the reverse is true when a well planned system is applied. It is plain, therefore, that the solution for meeting the scrap problem is an adequate system, which should have a place with other modern methods applied in well organized industries.

Summary

A Concise View of the Scrap Problem

1. Material purchased outside found defective after it has been placed in production means loss of material, if not rejected, labor and expense.

2. Material and product that is defective, spoiled, obsolete, lost, etc., means loss of material, labor and expense.

3. Material such as short ends, pieces, sheets, bolts, nuts, small parts dropped and scrapped, means loss of material, if more economical use were possible and practicable, and to a lesser extent labor and expense.

4. Natural (unavoidable) scrap, i.e., borings, turnings, clippings, sweepings, etc., means that cost is but slightly affected, and there is no apparent direct loss, but, if grades become mixed, salvage value is reduced, and a corresponding loss is incurred.

5. More scrap means larger loss, higher cost and more expense.

Solution

1. Prevent scrap at source by study and elimination of causes, and reclamation.

2. Handle scrap efficiently by proper segregation at point of origin, systematic collection and transportation, and preparation for profitable disposition.

3. Dispose of scrap for best returns by: maximum consumption of scrap within the factory, finding most profitable markets, and meeting the demands of consumers.

4. Account for scrap correctly by: considering losses and salvage value in costs, crediting scrap to material of individual lines of product and maintaining sufficient records for compilation of comprehensive reports.

The results will then be: less scrap by conservation of raw materials, lower costs through economies effected, less expense because the quantity of scrap handled is reduced, higher prices because of cleaner and well segregated scrap and correct accounts, whereby the material costs can be properly credited.

(8) "The Application of Selling and Administrative Expense to Product," 1922 Yearbook, William B. Castenholz

The Application of Selling and Administrative Expense to Product

One of the greatest absurdities that I know of in the distribution of selling expenses (that is, as it appears in the profit and loss statement that is prepared monthly) is the application of the actual monthly expenditures against those particular monthly sales.

There is absolutely no relationship, as a rule, between the things that are shipped and the actual expenses of the selling during that particular month so that it is necessary to always relate (if at all possible, and I believe it is possible in a majority of cases) against the shipments that are actually made each month, the expenses that are incurred in connection with the business which was shipped. Of course, in seasonable business, there is always an effort made to investigate that situation. That is, the selling expense is generally deferred and distributed against the shipments as they are made but as a rule that distribution, I have found, is not as scientific as it should be.

I like to think of this one phase of activity, namely, marketing, in very much the same way that I do of production. We are in the habit of distributing overhead expenses in connection with production as nearly as possible in connection with some direct expense of production. There are direct expenses in connection with marketing; there are direct road selling expenses and there are direct advertising expenses, in fact, we have almost a very similar situation at least in connection with marketing when compared with production. The marketing division takes the finished product, that is, material cost, the direct roadwork and the direct advertising (I mean the direct advertising which can be definitely allocated to a distinctive product), which corresponds with the direct labor in your factory.

Then again, we have the expenses of the management which is interested both in production and in marketing. We have all the indirect expenses arising out of those expenditures which are apportioned against the marketing division; we have the salaries of the sales manager, the advertising manager, the general publicity and all of those things which are the marketing division overhead corresponding to the factory overhead. Now if the overhead, which is the cause of certain activities, is distributed in the production department along the lines of those direct activities, why should not the marketing overhead be distributed on the basis of the direct marketing activity?

That, generally speaking, is the plan that I hope to develop when I discuss the details of the application of selling and administrative expenses to product.

Although cost accounting "per se" is confined to the computation of factory costs, that is, the manufacturing costs, price fixing demands the complete consideration of those additional expenses necessary to market the manufactured product and to administer the general affairs of the manufacturing business.

Very often, although a cost system may be nearly perfect and all possible factory economies may have been effected, a manufacturer may nevertheless show losses due to inadequate control over his selling and administrative expenses. The same keen analysis of selling and administrative operations should be had that obtains in factory cost matters. In fact, unless the same principles are applied in controlling selling and administrative costs, the entire advantage gained through efficient low cost production may be lost. In order not to overlook this danger some manufacturers have actually added selling and administrative costs to factory overhead, a course hardly to be recommended from an accounting standpoint.

A manufacturer is in business primarily to sell and one might just as logically consider all factory costs as selling expense. We must always distinguish carefully between the cost of manufacturing the goods sold, the cost of selling the goods and the cost of administering the general affairs of the business, which reflect its relations to the general public. Selling and administrative costs should therefore always be kept entirely distinct from factory cost and their tabulation and analysis should not form a part of the work of the cost accounting department.

All accounting, however, both cost and general, should be under one responsible head who should see to it that the same principles of analysis and economy are applied to the entire operating costs of the business; in other words, we wish to recommend a selling and administrative cost accounting department in addition to a production cost accounting department.

Selling and administrative costs are in a way predicated upon a correct knowledge of factory costs. When once the factory cost of a product is known, it becomes a fairly simple task to fix the amounts that may be spent for selling the product and for administrative purposes, so that a profit may still ensue from sales. Very often the accurate knowledge of factory costs is the salvation of an industry, in that such knowledge forces the introduction of economies and efficiency in selling and executive functions. A knowledge of what may be allowed for selling and administrative costs can generally be gained through an analysis of past performances. Let us assume a manufacturer making three distinct types of product, A, B and C, and that past conditions have indicated that these products must be sold at prices averaging $1,000.00, $980.00 and $900.00, respectively (a continuation of the same trade conditions being apparent); it was found that during the past year the sales reflected the following conditions:

Type	Quantity Sold	Average Unit Sales Price	Total Sales
A	200	$1,000.00	$200,000.00
B	250	980.00	245,000.00
C	300	900.00	270,000.00
	750		$715,000.00

The manufacturer concludes that since his plant was worked normally, he cannot materially increase his sales for the coming year and that therefore he estimates that the sales will be practically the same in quantities and values; he has determined, however, that he must make 10% on sales as a net profit after making due allowance for interest on borrowed money, which amounted to $3,000.00 for the previous year (6% on an average of $50,000.00). In order to assure himself of a 10% net profit on sales, he must know his factory costs; in fact, all of his calculations would be mere guesses if he did not know his factory costs. We are assuming, however, that he has an accurate cost system which revealed the following facts to him for the past year:

Type	Quantity Sold	Average Unit Cost of Sales	Total Cost of Sales
A	200	$600.00	$120,000.00
B	250	550.00	137,500.00
C	300	500.00	150,000.00
	750		$407,500.00

His gross profits on the three types of product sold were as follows:

Type	Sales Price	Cost of Sales	Gross Profit	Per Cent to Sales
A	$200,000.00	$120,000.00	$ 80,000.00	40 %
B	245,000.00	137,500.00	107,500.00	43.88%
C	270,000.00	150,000.00	120,000.00	44.44%
	$715,000.00	$407,500.00	$307,500.00	43.01%

If he is to make 10% on his sales he must make $20,000.00 on Type A, $24,500.00 on Type B and $27,000.00 on Type C product, or a total of $71,500.00; in other words, he must meet all of his costs, his interest charges and his selling and administrative expenses out of the difference between $715,000.00 and $71,500.00, which is $643,500.00. His factory costs are apparently known as amounting to $407,500.00 and his interest charges are estimated at $3,000.00; the balance available for selling and administrative expenses must therefore be computed as follows:

Budget available for all costs and expenses		$643,500.00
Deduct factory costs	$407,500.00	
Interest charges	3,000.00	410,500.00
Balance available for selling and administrative expenses		$233,000.00

To put the matter concretely, all selling and administrative expenses must not exceed $233,000.00 for the year if a net profit of 10% on sales is desired on a volume of $715,000.00. Having allowed $233,000.00 for selling and administrative costs it becomes a simple matter to determine how much of this is available for expenses of a variable nature, such as advertising, for example. Salaries of salesmen, commissions, officers' and office salaries are more or less fixed so that when a provision has been made for these expenses, the remainder of the budgeted amount may be considered as available for the variables in selling and administrative expenses.

We have seen that all of the above calculations are based upon one thing, namely, a knowledge of costs and that all estimates or calculations would be futile without that knowledge. In any calculation, however, no matter how certain one may feel of a continuation of past performances, certain amounts should be budgeted for contingencies; an entire allotment should not be fully hypothecated; in fact, only the minimum necessary to provide for efficient management and selling should be provided and every effort made to determine the maximum results are being obtained from the expenditures once they are in progress.

If, as indicated, a net profit of 10% on sales is desired, it is presumed that this percentage is expected on each type of product sold. It is possible, therefore, if factory costs on each type are known, to make proper provisions for at least the amount of selling expense necessary to adequately market each type, especially if separate selling forces are employed for each type or where each type may represent a different seasonal product. When, however, the sales force sells all products at all times it is not feasible to attempt a detailed application of selling expenses to the individual types of product, although the efforts of salesmen must be directed so as to secure the needed proportioning in sales.

If factory cost accounting does anything it must give the cost of sales for each type of product manufactured. In beginning the application of selling and administrative expenses therefore, we have a definite starting point, viz., the factory costs of each and all of the various products manufactured. The application of selling expenses is somewhat simpler than the application of administrative expense and it is therefore necessary to secure an analysis of administrative expense first.

Administrative expense is divisible into the following groups:

1. General Administrative supervision over all activities of a business, viz., (a) Purchasing, (b) Production, (c) Selling, (d) Financing, and (e) Accounting and Statistics.
2. Financing, Credits, Collections.
3. Legal and Corporate Expense.
4. General Office Expense — Telephone, Telegraph, Stationery, Postage, etc.
5. Accounting — Cost and General.

Taking the above grouping of administrative expense as fairly typical, our next problem is to distribute it on some fair basis as far as that is possible. In dealing with General Administrative supervision (our first group) the question of its proper proration is an important one. Do the executives give their time equally to the different elements of supervision or has each executive control over a single element or a logical combination of several elements? If, for example, the General Manager gave his full time to Purchasing and Production and the Treasurer devoted his time to Financing exclusively, leaving to the Secretary the Corporate Records and Accounting and to a First Vice-President the Supervision of Sales, the task of loading these supervisory expenses would be quite simple. In that case the General Manager's salary and expenses would become part of factory overhead, the Treasurer's salary and expenses would be charged to the second group of Administrative Expense, i. e., Financing, Credits and Collections, the Secretary's time and expenses would be divided between Group 3 (Legal and Corporate Expense) and Group 5 (Accounting), and the First Vice-President's activities would be translated into a charge to Selling Overhead. Departmentalization of this kind exists in many industries; in fact, a common plan of organization provides for Vice-Presidents, under the President and Board of Directors, who have charge of the various activities such as Production, Marketing, Financing and possibly Personnel arrangement.

For the purposes of this discussion we will assume such an organization with its various subdivisions as illustrated by the chart shown in Figure 8-1.

Using our chart, we must start with the expenses and salaries of the General Manager and his direct assistants. If possible these outlays should be allocated to the functions with which general management is concerned; if we assume all of the functions to be of equal importance then one-fourth of the general management cost should be charged against each of the four general operating groups, i. e., Production, Marketing, Financing and Personnel; if, however, these groups are of varying importance, the relative importance of the groups must be fixed upon some arbitrary but common sense basis and the distribution made in accordance therewith. The portion charged to Production will become part of factory overhead; we need not worry therefore about this element because it will appear in the various product costs of sales. We must deal, however, with the portions charged to Marketing, Finance and Personnel, and for the time being may consider them as Marketing, Finance and Personnel overhead expenses, respectively. In view of the fact that Accounting (both Cost and General) and Statistical work may be viewed as existing primarily and intentionally for general management purposes, the salaries and expenses of the entire accounting department should be included as part of the General Management outlay, although it may properly be distributed to the various functions on an independent basis; it would surely be found a simple task to determine all direct charges for cost accounting so that that portion could be readily charged to the Production unit as factory overhead. The remainder of accounting expense should be charged to General Administrative Overhead.

In view of the fact that Selling expense, both direct and indirect, should be allocated to product as closely as possible and that therefore all general overhead

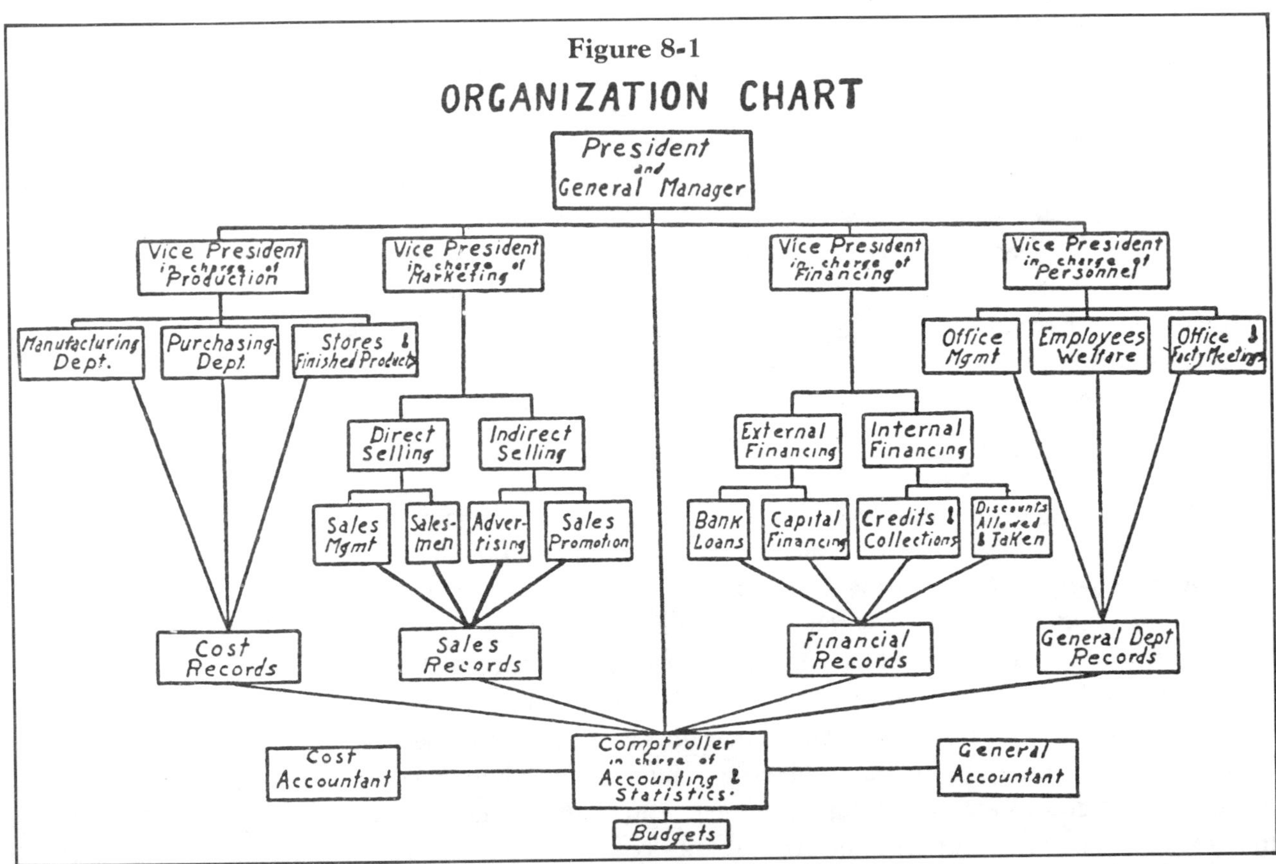

Figure 8-1

should as far as possible be analyzed into portions chargeable to the various functions, our second step is to make such an analysis and distribution. Our components for this task are the following:

1. The expenses of the Personnel Department, which also now include some General Management expense.
2. The expenses of Financing (to which has been added a portion of General Management and Personnel expense).

Personnel expense may not exist in all industries but many progressive manufacturers feel that personnel relations are of sufficient importance to warrant the creation of a department whose tasks are to promote proper relations between the employees and the employer, to foster such welfare work as will produce agreeable working conditions and to generally cement together the individuals of the various groups into a harmonious whole; in other words, the Personnel Department exists primarily for the purpose of developing an "esprit de corps." The Personnel Department expense confined largely as it is to the affairs of individuals in their relation to the industry as a whole should be distributed to the various groups or departments (Production, Marketing and Financing) on the basis of the average number of employees in each department.

Financial expense exists in order to properly finance the various functions and activities of a business and its distribution should therefore be on the basis of the financial requirements of these functions. Whatever earnings may accrue to the finance department may well be deducted from its expenses so that a net amount may receive consideration. After applying to the Marketing division the expenses of maintaining a credit and collection department the remainder of Financing expense should be distributed to the Marketing and Production departments, respectively, on the basis of the direct expenditures of these departments, the direct costs consisting for this purpose of the total payrolls, purchases, insurance, taxes and all cash expenditures in the Production Department and the total selling payrolls and advertising disbursements in the Marketing Department. The amounts of financing expense thus all absorbed will become Production Overhead and Marketing Overhead.

Our analyses and distributions thus far have left us only two functions to deal with, namely, Production and Marketing. After all, are not these two functions the real cardinal functions of a manufacturing business and are not all other activities contributory to these two? We do not have executive functions merely to go through the motions of administration; we do not make loans or raise money in other ways merely because we are able to exercise such propensities. A manufacturing business is administered, controlled and financed in order to produce goods and to sell them. It is for this reason that we have finally loaded all administrative and financing expenses on to Production and Marketing. In other words, after applying whatever is proper to the Production Department, the remainder of all so-called commercial expenses must be regarded as necessary to properly market the commodities produced. In fact, there is nothing else to do — after goods have been produced the only problem remaining is the distribution of the product and all efforts are given either directly or indirectly to accomplish that distribution.

To summarize our plan of distribution up to this point, we now have the following picture:

(1) Production Department has been charged with all direct costs, a portion of General Management expense, a portion of Personnel expense and a portion of Financing expense. All of these costs will appear in the Cost of Finished Product and in the Cost of Sales of the individual types of products manufactured.

(2) Marketing Department, which includes the direct and indirect expenses of its own operation, has been charged in addition with portions of General Management, Personnel and Financing expenses.

The two above departments now include all expenses of a direct nature as well as the entire expense group which is usually characterized in accounting as Administrative expense. The cost department furnishes us with the entire cost of sales, including that portion of Administrative expense absorbed by the Production department, so that nothing further remains, for discussion, than the distribution of Marketing expense to products sold.

The Application of Marketing Expense to Product Sales

The application of Marketing expense to the various types of products sold will depend almost entirely upon the character of the selling organization and its advertising. To illustrate this point we will assume two types of organization, one in which each salesman sells one type of product and another in which each salesman sells all products.

1. Where Each Salesman Sells One Type of Product

Under these conditions the direct road-selling expenses may be lodged against each product sold and an average cost per unit established. Such an average will be created by taking the total units of each product sold during a normal year in a given territory by the various salesmen selling each particular product and dividing the number of these units into the total annual road expenses (salesmen's salaries and expenses). If the sales manager devotes his time exclusively to supervision over salesmen then his salary and expenses should be distributed first to the various territories in proportion to the road expenses indicated for the various territories, and secondly to the products sold within each territory on the basis of the product road expenses distributed to such product sales. If the sales manager also devotes his time to advertising, then only a portion of his salary and expenses will be prorated as suggested; the proportioning between selling and advertising should probably be on the basis of the relative annual costs of these two functions.

Advertising expenses should be distributed in accordance with space utilized by the various products in trade journals, newspapers or catalogues, although the accounting procedure in making the distribution may differ with the various forms of advertising. It may as in the case of road expenses be first applied territorially and then to product; this would be advisable in the case of catalogue circulation. Catalogues should, of course, be handled as an inventory account and selling expense charged only as the catalogues are mailed; in mailing the territorial divisions should be noted. The products illustrated and described in the catalogue would be charged on a space basis at the time the credit to catalogue inventory would be made. The annual expense thus created could be translated into a unit product catalogue advertising expense. Newspaper and trade journal advertising, unless deferred, for special reasons, should also be charged to product in much the same way. General advertising or promotional advertising must be prorated either on the basis of the costs of direct product advertising or upon a combination of direct product advertising and direct road selling costs.

The Marketing Department overhead expense composed of portions of general management and personnel department expense plus any indirect expense created in the Marketing Department itself should, as far as possible, be distributed to product on the basis of the direct selling costs, which may be either the direct road selling costs for each product or a combination of the latter with the direct product advertising costs.

2. Where Each Salesman Sells All Products

To secure an approximately accurate loading of direct road selling expense to individual products it would be necessary to require each salesman to record at least weekly the time he has devoted in securing orders for each product. Although such a plan would have its limitations it would be far better than a proration on the basis of relative sales either by values or units. Again a plan based upon relative costs of sales would be unfair because the costs of producing articles bear no relation to the efforts of selling. The proposed plan calling for a weekly distribution of time need not be made burdensome to the salesman if the requirements are reasonable; certainly, the salesman is the best judge of his own activities and if his honesty of purpose may be assumed there is little reason to doubt that his time reports would furnish the best basis for his expense distribution to product.

Even where salesmen sell all products, the advertising could probably be split up in the same manner as heretofore discussed. Advertising would probably be individual. Again, as in our first case, all overhead selling expense would be prorated on the basis of the direct selling costs per product.

The Product Selling Cost

After having applied all marketing costs to product, a unit selling cost per product can be readily determined both for each product generally as well as for each product territorially. Our next problem is therefore to provide the proper accounting procedure.

In the speaker's opinion, the following procedure would be desirable:

1. Charge all expenditures for marketing to a General Ledger controlling account entitled "Deferred Marketing Costs," the latter controlling account to be properly analyzed and detailed in an Analysis Ledger as follows:

   (a) D. M. C. General Management Expense Portion.
   (b) D. M. C. Personnel Expense Portion.
   (c) D. M. C. Financial Expense Portion.
   (d) D. M. C. Sales Management Expense.
   (e) D. M. C. Advertising.
   (f) D. M. C. Salesmen's Expenses.

   (D. M. C. stands for "Deferred Marketing Costs.")

2. Charge to a Controlling Account entitled "Product Marketing Costs" the pre-determined selling cost per unit for all units of the various products actually shipped and billed each month and detail these charges in an Analysis Ledger as follows:

   (a) P. M. C. Product A.
   (b) P. M. C. Product B.
   (c) P. M. C. Product C.

   (P. M. C. stands for "Product Marketing Costs.")

The offsetting credit to the above charge might well be called "Provision for Product Marketing Costs" and represents in reality that portion of the Deferred Marketing Costs applicable to actual shipments made and thus absorbed. The credit is not made to the detailed deferred charges in order that the actual expenditures reflected in the deferred charge accounts may remain intact, thus obviating the need of later expense analysis when the regular Profit and Loss statement is prepared in standard form.

At the end of any year, if the pre-determined unit cost of marketing has been approximately correct, the "Deferred Marketing Costs" account will be in close agreement with the "Provision for Product Marketing Costs" account and at any rate they must be closed one against the other; differences after closing will represent either under or over absorbed Marketing Costs.

To make the proposed plan of marketing costs distribution of real value, it is almost essential that a detailed budget system be provided. The budget would naturally be based upon very much the same data used in establishing the annual product unit marketing cost. The budget should provide for monthly and in some cases seasonal control. A budget, coupled with a plan or plans for measuring the efficiency of salesmen and of advertising would certainly in time create not only standards of direct selling but of general marketing management.

In connection with any plan for the tabulation of marketing costs it is essential that definite forms for measuring selling efforts be installed. At the beginning of this paper we have indicated how the broad general allotments for selling and administrative expenses may be fixed. These general appropriations should be budgeted in detail so that specific amounts (based upon careful investigations) may be allotted to cover the marketing costs for each product in each territory. To judge how effectively the funds are used implies a careful check up of all marketing efforts. Real standards of direct selling must be created and care must be exercised in varying these standards in accordance with changing and variable conditions. For example, a manufacturer having one plant only and having a wide territorial distribution of his product cannot measure the efforts of all his salesmen by one standard; he must divide his sales field into zones representing a home zone, a zone of normal competition and a zone of difficult competition. Salesmen must be grouped according to these zones. However, in all events, the criteria of a salesman's efficiency are the gross profits he can make for his employer on a standard or better volume and the selling costs per unit of product. A salesman's efficiency sheet must therefore show at least the gross profit and the unit selling cost by zones; a comparison of salesmen within the same zones will then furnish a clue as to the relative value of services. Variations from established zone standards should also appear on this salesman's efficiency sheet and in addition it would be desirable to indicate the delivery date of orders, the rating of the customers and cancellations. The latter information will indicate the salesman's ability to take orders for prompt delivery, to sell to customers of financial standing and his power to permanently impress the customer.

Conclusion

It is not our intention to give the impression that the recommended procedure is the "sine qua non" of marketing costs distribution. Our idea has been rather to suggest possible methods of proration under certain assumed conditions, feeling that thereby the necessary modifications may suggest themselves where conditions are difficult. At any rate it is the hope of the speaker that this virgin field of "Marketing Cost Accounting" will receive the earnest attention of cost accountants who have thus far felt that their prerogatives were confined entirely to the Production Costs.

(9) "Radio Educational Campaign," July 2, 1923, Bulletin, Vol. 4, No. 20, NACA

Radio Educational Campaign

Broadcastings by National Association of Cost Accountants

During the past two months the air has literally been full of cost gospel. Through arrangements with thirteen broadcasting stations throughout the United States a series of four popular talks on cost accounting were broadcasted under the auspices of the NACA.

These talks were not intended to deal with the technical phases of the subject but were designed to emphasize the economic value of cost accounting to industry, to employees, employers, and to consumers. The titles of the talks were: "What Cost Accounting Means to Industry," "Advantages of Cost Accounting to Workers," "Advantages of Cost Accounting to Employers," and "Advantages of Cost Accounting to the Public."

The purpose of this campaign was to correct a popular misconception that cost accounting is a technical procedure which is related entirely to the internal records of business and has no direct bearing on the broader economic problems. Such a conception is entirely untrue. If the consumer had a real understanding of what sound costs in industry mean to him in dollars and cents, he would bring the full weight of his opinion to bear on American manufacturers and distributors in order to compel them to operate their affairs upon the basis of accurate cost data.

Furthermore, many of our industrial problems and the differences between employers and employed arise solely from a lack of facts. If workers understood what costs mean to them they would take greater interest in their work and much wasted effort might be eliminated. Wider publicity among workers of accurate facts relating to the costs of production and distribution would not only solve but would also prevent many industrial deadlocks which cost the consuming public millions of dollars a year.

This campaign was prepared and organized by J. P. Jordan, our National President, and its success was due to his untiring efforts in preparing the material and arranging for its distribution.

In order that there may be a permanent record of these talks and in order that our members may have an opportunity to read them, the four talks are reproduced exactly as they were broadcasted from the following stations: WEAF, New York City; WGI, Medford Hills, Mass.; WHAZ, Troy, New York; WLW, Cincinnati, Ohio; WCX, Detroit, Michigan; WJAX, Cleveland, Ohio; WIAO, Milwaukee, Wisconsin; KPO, San Francisco, Calif.; KWH, Los Angeles, Calif.; WLAG, Minneapolis, Minn.; KJR, Seattle, Washington; WGR, Buffalo, New York; and WEAN, Providence, R. I.

What Cost Accounting Means to Industry

Broadcast No. 1

The National Association of Cost Accountants is an organization only three years old, but already having a membership of over 3,000. It is not in any sense a business organization but is wholly educational. The main objects of the Association are to develop and improve the science of cost accounting, and to serve all who are in industry, both employers and workers, by spreading the gospel that facts and facts only should be the guide of all business transactions. When actual facts have been known to both employers and employees it has rarely been the case that serious disputes have arisen, causing loss of time and money to both parties.

The determination of the cost of any product has long since passed from simply trying to find out what an article costs for the purpose of fixing the selling price into a much broader and infinitely more valuable phase of assembling facts which are valuable equally to both the employer and the employee. Cost Accounting recognizes the fact that 98% of all human beings are honest; that they take an honest pride in their work; and that they are anxious and glad to have what they accomplish made a matter of actual record, particularly where the employer insists upon his workers being compensated and advanced on the basis of actual facts rather than through the personal likes and dislikes of his foreman and superintendent.

We all must admit that conditions in industry are today generally far from ideal, and that there still is a wide gap between the great mass of workers and the majority of employers. We hear and read many explanations of this condition, but in practically every dispute which arises a careful analysis will reveal the fact that neither side in the dispute will agree as to the actual conditions which exist, and regarding which the dispute has arisen. This condition exists entirely on account of the absence of adequate records which honestly, fairly and accurately reflect the true conditions in the industry or plant where trouble has arisen.

In almost any other branch of activity we find records brought to the finest point of development wherein no point of doubt is left, which records are anxiously awaited, scanned and implicitly believed by the millions of people who see them. An instance of this is found in baseball. Every move of a baseball player is recorded; every play is noted; every game is analyzed; and the results accomplished by every team is a matter of the very finest piece of record procedure. After a season is closed our newspapers are full of enormous tabulated statements by percentage whereby every league, team and player is shown in terms of figures, from which tables the public and the team owners decide who is the greatest player of the year and what player leads in the various star activities in which they excel.

We find the same in football, tennis, basket ball, golf and other sports.

People to the extent of thousands will choke streets in front of bulletin boards watching the records of a world series game or a football game. Yet in our every day life, industry in general has not yet awakened to the fact that records of accomplishment in connection with production and the cost of production may be made just exactly as interesting as the sports just mentioned. The coal strike, resulting in the appointment of the commission to find the real facts in connection with the coal industry is a wonderful example of lack of knowledge which is more or less prevalent in each individual industry in the country. It is pretty safe to prophesy that when this coal commission completes its work it will bring out facts which will clearly indicate the basic difficulties in the industry, the knowledge of which should make comparatively easy a permanent solution which will greatly benefit all three interested parties, the public, the operators, and the workers.

The National Association of Cost Accountants is in a most advantageous position for bringing to the attention of the public, the employers and the workers the enormous benefits to be derived from knowing the actual cost of production, the word "cost" being used in its very broadest sense. On account of its being an Association separate and distinct from employers and likewise from workers, and its object being educational, it is in a position to advance arguments which cannot be disputed on the score that it has in any way a selfish interest. It is in a position to show to workers where it is to their greatest profit to cooperate in every possible way in the assembling of accurate figures, as it can be proved that these figures rightfully used will mean lower cost of production at the same or greater wages, with the result that the same or greater wages will buy more goods and thereby give to all a far greater value to be secured for every dollar earned.

It is in a position to show the employers that they cannot possibly expect to properly manage their business affairs with any degree of fairness and success unless they are guided by actual figures, accurately giving them the results accomplished by their various departments and the personnel in each department. That each employer must insist that his foremen and superintendents be guided in their work by these actual records of results, thereby eliminating the great majority of causes for disputes which have arisen in the past on account of unfair dealing which was largely the result of ignorance of conditions, rather than from premeditated desire to invite trouble.

It is in a position to show to the public that added cost of disputes can be eliminated to a very great degree if it would get solidly behind a movement to insist that industry, plant by plant and as a whole, should take most decided steps to continuously and adequately record results.

In three succeeding broadcastings we will show the great value of adequate cost accounting to every person in this country. On.................... we will broadcast

the Advantages of Cost Accounting to the workers. On......................we will broadcast the Advantages of Cost Accounting to the employers, and on.........
.....we will broadcast the Advantages of Cost Accounting to the public.

The matter of accounting for cost of production is one that requires the cooperation of management and worker alike, and it is believed that if the advantages to be received by all are really understood, this cooperation would become very general and would accomplish most wonderful results. Everyone hearing this and succeeding messages has a real responsibility in connection with the cost of production and should take this responsibility very seriously.

The headquarters of the National Association of Cost Accountants is at 130 West 42nd St., New York City. Anyone desiring to know more of their work may get full details by addressing the National Association of Cost Accountants, 130 West 42nd St., New York City.

Advantages of Cost Accounting to Workers

Broadcast No. 2

Last.................. evening we broadcasted from this station the objects for which the National Association of Cost Accountants are working in connection with industry. Our message tonight is the Advantages of Cost Accounting to Workers.

The Accounting for Costs in its broadest sense means a great deal more than is realized by the majority of people, and in fact means a great deal more than is realized by a very great number of employers. There have been many cases in the past where Cost Accounting has been regarded by the workers and unfortunately by many manufacturers as being a process of assembling figures from the standpoint of getting something on somebody. Any information obtained for the sole purpose of criticism frequently does much more damage than good and we hope to convince you that accurate cost accounting is of equal value to both workers and employers.

The National Association of Cost Accountants advocates the principle that 98% of all human beings are honest. Therefore every effort should be made to establish records which will give to this great number of honest people the opportunity to have the results of their work shown in definite and usable figures, in order that the management of each company may know who deserves commendation and who is producing the best results for his company. The day of regulation of industry on the basis of personal likes and dislikes of foremen and superintendents is past.

In every manufacturing institution there is a constant opportunity for promotion. Two factors contribute to this matter of promotion, the first being that the normal growth of almost every company requires more supervision, thereby creating new and higher jobs; and second, the normal changes brought about through resignation or shifting to other positions automatically make these positions available to others.

As advancement to a different nature of position does not always come to every worker, the natural question will arise as to what benefit Cost Accounting is to workers who stay at the same position. Before answering this question, one point must be cleared up in the minds of every worker irrespective of who he is or what he does. This point is that there is an unlimited amount of business for every company who can sell at prices which meet competition and better still, at prices which will stimulate consumption. For instance, if suits of clothes sell for $50 when they ought to sell for $30 it is but natural for the public — and that means every one of us — to wear a suit longer than we would if we could buy it for $30. Therefore less suits are made at the higher cost. Reduce the cost, and more suits will be used and everyone has the same or more work. The same reasoning applies to shoes, shirts, dresses and to all kinds of goods.

Now — If each one of us as a worker does everything in our power to reduce costs by saving or helping to save wasted time and material, our wages may remain the same or increase, and we may buy much more with the money we earn. This is not theory, but is a cold fact.

When the rates of wages are taken under consideration in any industrial plant, the consideration of these wages is very largely influenced by that portion of the cost of the product other than the direct wage cost involved. To the great majority of workers these expenses are absolutely unknown, and naturally do not receive very much consideration.

To the management, however, all these expenses, which are known as overhead, have an enormous bearing on the wage rates that can be paid to the workers and still keep the cost of the product where it can be sold. And in the past, many managers have failed to enlist the interest of the workers in assisting to keep down these costs in order that sufficient savings can be made to justify the management in paying the most satisfactory wage rate to the workers.

The workers in any industrial plant know more about where money can be saved than the management itself can ever know. The mistaken idea in the past has been for workers to countenance wastes of this sort on account of the sole thought that men have got to live, and to live must have a job. If this waste is saved, costs decrease, more business comes and everyone works just the same.

Workers ask the question as to what they can do to cut costs. This, of course, depends on the kind of work each one is doing, but a number of instances will be cited. A machine operator can so interest himself in what he is doing that he will first of all do his work as nearly perfect as possible. As many operations are bound to produce some defective work the operator can, in a great many cases, separate defective work from the good work, being absolutely fearless of the results if he has a shop management which is fair and square. Doing this will save a large part of the inspection expense. It will safeguard the product to such an extent that there will be fewer returns from the field after it has been shipped to the customer; the product as shipped out will attain a higher plane of quality; the sales department can sell with less expense because they have a better product to sell; and the better product will bring sales by its own reputation. How many have thought of all these consequences which mean less cost and more sales by little acts that can be done right at the machine every minute during the day? Machine operators can be more careful with their machines in the matter of keeping them in shape; properly oiled; reporting to the foreman defects which should be remedied at once before greater damage takes place. This kind of interest will reflect directly in the reduction of maintenance costs, thereby cutting down a goodly share of this part of the overhead.

The cooperation of workers in cutting down costs can have but one result on a management that is honest and fair, and this result will be satisfactory wages for the ones who take this interest in the business. This does not mean that anyone is to work any harder at all, in fact, harder work is absolutely unnecessary. It does mean, however, that those who are working should see that head work is mixed with physical work and that the moves made count for actual accomplishment, rather than for waste.

If the cost of product is reduced, this means that selling prices are reduced and that everyone can buy more for a dollar than he could if the cost in general remained where it was. So it should be apparent to anyone that the cooperation of workers with the management in the reducing of these costs, will have a most direct return in the pockets and bank accounts of the workers themselves.

The National Association of Cost Accountants as an educational organization of workers bespeaks the interest and cooperation of workers of all kinds in the matter of the cost of production. We advocate no harder work, but rather the addition to the everyday work of the very powerful brain factor which is possessed to a remarkable degree by every worker in this country. Industry needs the heads as well as the hands of every worker; and if they all would fearlessly throw in the head work, costs would come down, and individuals would profit both in wages received and in what can be bought with these wages.

Next................. we will broadcast the Advantages of Cost Accounting to Employers, and the following week....................the Advantages of Cost Accounting to the public in general. It will pay everyone to hear these broadcastings.

The headquarters of the National Association of Cost Accountants is at 130 West 42nd St., New York City. Anyone desiring to know more of their work may get full details by addressing the National Association of Cost Accountants, 130 West 42nd St., New York City.

Advantages of Cost Accounting to Employers

Broadcast No. 3

Last................. evening we broadcasted from this station a few facts as to the Advantages of Cost Accounting to Workers. This evening we will speak of the Advantages of Cost Accounting to Employers, and this will be found equally interesting to everyone.

Fifty years ago the manufacturing of this country was mostly done in small plants scattered throughout the country, the majority of which were operated by the owner himself who was in direct charge of all branches of the work. In fact, the owner was on the job from early morning until late at night, knew everyone personally, and conducted his affairs by a personal contact which gave him first hand knowledge not only of all that was going on, but also of each man who worked for him. This was a most ideal condition, and everybody did his best because he knew that he was getting a square deal; for the "old man" knew everybody, and just what each was doing.

Business grew and these plants became larger and larger. In this growth the great value of the personal contact of the business was overlooked, as the foremen and superintendents handled the workers from an entirely different angle than the owner formerly did and not being backed up by records, they handled matters as best they could, and many times in a manner to best suit their own interests, irrespective of the actual performances of the workers. In other words, the owner of the business having lost the personal contact with his men failed to substitute methods of recording actual performances whereby he could insist that his operating men would handle the workers purely on a basis of merit rather than as a result of personal likes and dislikes.

During this period countless cases of injustice occurred, and it was but natural that thousands of disputes arose which had a most serious effect on the relations between employers and workers.

As time went on, progressive managers recognized the fact that something had to be done to replace the old personal knowledge which the employer formerly had in the earlier days, and as a result much more attention was given to the matter of plant records, particularly those in connection with the cost of production.

The National Association of Cost Accountants is actively behind the idea that no industrial management can hope to reach the greatest measure of success until they make the fullest use of records of production and cost throughout the entire organization. The old thought that any publicity at all of cost and production figures is running the risk of allowing information to leak out of the plant, with detrimental effects to the business, is an absolute fallacy. No two shops are alike; and even if they were, the operating or conversion costs have now become a matter of frequent interchange between plants manufacturing like products with great benefit to all.

The most unfortunate part of the whole problem is that so few employers realize in the first place what is meant by costs and cost records. Altogether too many think that cost records simply mean the cost of the product manufactured in its entirety, including material, labor and overhead. Cost figures as advocated by the National Association of Cost Accountants go very much further than simply to tell the cost of the product. The great volume of cost in the overhead should be systematically analyzed by departments and operations whereby each indirect department of the business may be treated practically the same as a producing department.

The burden of each operating department such as, for instance, the machine shop, the forge shop, the weaving room, the knitting room and other like direct producing departments, should each have its monthly statement whereby the foreman in charge may know exactly how he operated for the month.

Comparatively few employers or managers have realized the enormous possibility in supplying their operating foremen with these cost statements. The great majority of plants of any size are organized in a way where maintenance and repair work, for instance, is concentrated in a department by itself. This department will send men around the plant working on various repairs, and a great deal of repair work will be done in the headquarters of the maintenance crew. This department is altogether too often divided up on a percentage basis to the various operating departments and nobody has any detailed check on the amount of money spent on important repairs.

By having a set of standing monthly orders for each direct and indirect department, this repair work will be charged up to the proper standing orders of the *department for which the work was done.* Each month the foreman of each department will receive a statement of these costs, and it will be most surprising to the manager who has never operated in this way to see the effects that such figures have on each foreman.

The monthly statement of cost in connection with handling product, time keeping, tool and store keeping, inspection and all such items bring to each foreman a means of working out all kinds of reforms whereby these costs may be reduced. Guesswork and doubts are eliminated, and the foreman knows just exactly how his department is running in overhead expense, and furthermore he knows that the superintendent and the general manager know exactly the same thing. And with this knowledge, it is only human for him to exert every endeavor to make this record just as clean as it can possibly be made. How many employers listening in are giving their foremen these facilities?

The National Association of Cost Accountants is most strenuously advocating the use of standards in connection with production whereby constant comparison may lead the way to betterment of processes and constructive work in connection with the various operations in the plant. Employers have failed to realize that 80% of slack production and high costs is the fault of the employers themselves in not knowing the facts. By far the great majority of workers, probably 98%, are ready and willing to make their work count to the fullest extent if they are given the opportunity and the backing to do so.

The National Association of Cost Accountants, therefore, appeals to every employer to take immediate steps to see that his business is equipped with cost and production records whereby every employee in the company, foreman or worker, may have actual knowledge of what he is producing and how well he is progressing. It is inconceivable that a business can be properly run without it; and the employer who sees to it that these records become the guide of his business, is magnifying his managerial ability almost in proportion to the number of employees in the company.

Next .... evening we will broadcast the Advantages of Cost Accounting to the Public, and we hope that everyone who has heard this and past broadcastings will be sure to listen in.

The headquarters of the National Association of Cost Accountants is at 130 West 42nd St., New York City. Anyone desiring to know more about its work may get full details by addressing the National Association of Cost Accountants, 130 West 42nd St., New York City.

Advantages of Cost Accounting to the Public

Broadcast No. 4

We have already broadcasted during the last three weeks a great deal of what the National Association of Cost Accountants is doing in connection with industry, including the Advantages of Cost Accounting to Workers and to Employers. This evening we will broadcast the Advantages of Cost Accounting to the Public, and the public includes us all.

We have heard a great deal during the last few years of the high cost of living, but we have not heard as much as we should have in connection with how these costs were made up and why they are so high. We read of strike after strike resulting from disputes where somebody must be right and somebody wrong. It is impossible for both to be right. In how many of these cases has there been a true detailed statement made public as to the exact position taken by each side, giving proofs to substantiate the positions taken? We will have to admit that such a thing has rarely been known.

The National Association of Cost Accountants is in reality an organization of the public, all of its members in their private capacities, whether in industrial or professional work, being a part of the great organization of American industry working under the direction of management as do all workers. The Association itself, however, is primarily educational and is under the dictation of no one excepting its own elected officers and members, and as such is actively spreading the gospel that we have reached the time where costs of production must be known and further, must be used for the guidance of management in all of its decisions.

The public little realizes the enormous percentage of the cost of the product which is concentrated in the indirect costs. These indirect expenses, called overhead, include all expenses other than the direct wages paid for producing the product and the direct material which enters into the product. This expense is made up of hundreds of items which are the most difficult to control in any business whatever. A little here, a little there added together make an astounding total which, in perhaps the majority of industries, amounts to more than the direct wages paid.

Cost Accounting as advocated by the National Association of Cost Accountants is of a far different nature than has been the case in the past. The public, being the customer, is entitled to know more about what it is paying for, and what enters into the cost of the goods which it buys. It has been said and probably is true that the fault of 80% of lack of production and high costs, where existing, rests with management on account of its failure to actually know what are the true facts. This may be a rather serious arraignment of the management of such plants, but it is a well known fact that there still exists a lack of appreciation on the part of management in general that all employees should be taken into more or less confidence as to the cost of the items which make up the total cost of the product manufactured.

Too many men are in managerial positions who are there because their family controls the stock of the company or because of some other personal connection, and are not in their positions because they have earned them or because of any capabilities whatever which fit them for the job. Naturally in such cases as this it is pretty difficult to expect results which have a beneficial effect in the reduction of cost of product and the bringing of prices to the level where they belong.

Other managers are just the opposite and are doing everything within their power to so regulate the production in their plants that the lowest cost is reached. These managers believe in paying good wages, improving the status of workers, and assisting workers in doing the best for themselves. This class of managers embraces those who want to cooperate with other plants of the same industry, standardize methods of cost and production accounting and do everything in their power to reduce costs, in order that the goods may be sold with profit to the stockholders but also at the lowest possible price to the public. These managers have formed themselves into associations whereby a systematic betterment of knowledge may be accomplished. We are referring here to those associations which are absolutely honest, who confine their activities to the improvement of current practices and are far above the class of those who use such advantageous intercourse in an improper manner.

The public can do nothing better than to encourage the interchange of ideas within an industry, as it is bound to have a direct and beneficial effect on the cost of production with a resultant decrease of selling prices at good profits to the plants.

As stated before, the public is paying the bill in everything it buys for inefficiency and for thousands of disputes which result from inefficient and unguided operations. It is inconceivable that the great majority of these disputes would ever come to an open break if both sides were fully posted in respect to all of the facts in connection with the case. And far less would be the liability of open breaks if management in general provided proper cost accounting methods, taking into their confidence the foremen to a considerable extent and the workers to a sufficient extent whereby everyone in each plant has a clearer conception of all the transactions which take place. Certainly a cooperative arrangement of this sort cannot help but obviate 99 out of every 100 disagreements which otherwise would take place.

Organizations of workers could do no greater service to industry than to take an actual and constructive interest in the records of production and cost with which they are concerned, cooperating in saving unnecessary costs, and thereby maintaining good wages and working conditions by actual cooperation and assistance, with the guidance of figures furnished by the management. Workers of all degrees have responsibilities beyond working with their hands. If they would recognize this responsibility, and place their mental ability at the disposition of their employers and take steps to create conditions whereby they could give to their employers greater results through knowing where these results could be produced, most remarkable consequences would follow.

The National Association of Cost Accountants is an educational organization and is doing everything within its power to spread the gospel of adequate cost accounting and the full use by both employers and workers of the figures obtained from cost accounts, in a cooperative campaign to reduce costs; not by working any harder, but by eliminating waste and inefficiency and getting far more for the dollars that are paid out.

The headquarters of the National Association of Cost Accountants is at 130 West 42nd St., New York City. Anyone desiring to know more about their work may get full details by addressing the National Association of Cost Accountants, 130 West 42nd St., New York City.

(10) "Cost Accounting in the Production of Motion Pictures," Dec. 1, 1923, Bulletin, Vol. 5, No. 6, William R. Donaldson, CPA, Member of Philip N. Miller and Company

Cost Accounting in the Production of Motion Pictures[1]

Little published data are available on the principles and the practices of cost accounting in the production of motion pictures. Such a condition is easily understood, for the industry is a comparatively new one and its methods have but recently approached any basis of stabilization. This "infant industry" — born within the lifetime of most of the readers of this article — has had a prodigious growth. Today, it is one of the foremost in the country, motion picture theatres in the United States alone numbering about 15,000, the attendance at which is estimated at over 50,000,000 per week. As a mass agency of popular appeal the "movie" takes its place with the daily newspaper and the public library, the contribution it has made to civilization and the influence it wields in the life of the people being most aptly described in the following excerpt from an article in the *New York Times*, July 1, 1923:

> " ' Of all inventions, the alphabet and the printing press alone excepted, those that have shortened distance have done the most for humanity', wrote Macaulay. When he wrote he referred particularly to the application of steam to land and sea travel. He did not refer to — by the nature of the case he could not foresee — that system of the shortening of distances which operates not by transferring the individual to far places and peoples, but by bringing those places and peoples to the individual. This the motion picture theatre has done, and the system of distribution is such that hundreds of thousands of people are literally witnessing the same scenes, participating in the same dramatic action at the same time.
>
> "In estimating the mental influence of the moving picture theatre, it is well to remember that when one goes to the movies today he does not sit down only with his neighbors. He mingles with peoples from all parts of the earth."

Realizing that so little has been told of the story of that matter-of-fact but nevertheless most important phase of this great and fascinating industry — accounting for the cost of the photoplay — this article attempts to outline the principles and the practices applicable thereto, going into some detail in the hope that thus may be established the basis for developing, under the auspices of the National Association of Cost Accountants, further contributions to this branch of cost accounting. Most of the members of the Association will find that the manner of making a motion picture is so different

[1]This article is based upon a paper read before a meeting of the New York Chapter.

from the processes in the fundamental industries with which they are occupied that there is little they can borrow to solve their own problems. This is the excuse, therefore, for presenting this story in somewhat different fashion than prior official publications.

Division of Activities

The motion picture industry is divided into three major activities: Production, distribution and exhibition. Several of the larger organizations (three of which have their stock listed on the New York Stock Exchange) engage through numerous subsidiary corporations in all three activities, maintaining studios on the Pacific Coast and in the East, distributing exchanges in twenty-five to thirty key distribution and railroad centers in the United States; and owning large theatres in the principal cities and towns. Furthermore, these organizations through their foreign subsidiaries carry on operations in all countries of the world. Some organizations maintain studios and exchanges only, their product being exhibited entirely in independently owned theatres. Other smaller organizations merely produce, distributing through independent companies or the distributing branches of the larger organizations, usually on the basis of a percentage sharing in the gross rentals with a guaranteed advance from the distributor equivalent to the cost of production.

How a Picture Is Made

Like all things theatrical the making of a movie has a curtain of glamour thrown about it, which is naturally the part of good business, as in the popular phase it is designed to amuse — to create illusions and to stir the imagination. In brief, then, stripped of its glamour, this is how a photoplay is made: A suitable story must first be secured — one with lots of action and good situations. It may be an original one or it may be based upon a book or magazine story. Stories are ofttimes picked with leading actors or actresses in mind to play the principal roles and these parts must conform, or be made to conform, to their types and characteristics. In many instances, of course, where the book rather than the star is to be the appealing feature, the play must be cast to conform to the characters of the book. A skilled writer with a knack of visualizing a story is set to work to prepare what is called "the continuity." This describes in detail each scene in sequence, so that the document when completed presents the writer's idea of the whole picture as it should be projected on the screen. A director is selected to make the picture, and he and the continuity writer get together and discuss the continuity and exchange ideas. They call in the cameraman who is to do the photography, the technical man or art director, as he is called, who is to design and arrange the settings, furnishings, costumes, mechanical effects, etc., and the assistant director who among other things is to assist in finding suitable players for the minor parts, and sometimes also the star when he or she possesses ability along lines of preparation. The continuity is then studied and discussed with each one's particular field in mind. When the continuity is in final working form, it is indexed to show each scene which must be enacted on each set or background, frequently fifty and more scenes occurring on the same set. A production schedule is compiled to show the dates when the respective sets and exterior locations are to be available, and when the photography on those sets should commence. Well-organized companies have a business manager for each production. His duties are to estimate the cost to produce the picture, to watch expenditures and to be the financial guide, so that the picture may be produced as economically as possible and within the budget set for it. Up to the date when the first photography is to be done, each of the persons mentioned is busy in preparing his part of the work. The star is fitted to new clothes and costumes; the technical man and his assistants design the sets, select the "properties"—i.e., the furnishings, draperies, costumes, etc.—either out of the studio's stock or in the local stores from which properties may be rented. He also consults with the location man to discover suitable outdoor places conforming to the requirements of the continuity. If such are not available, then he must arrange to have them constructed on the "lot,"i.e., in the fenced-in open land adjoining the studio, where replicas of French villages, New York streets, etc., may be erected. The cameraman plans lighting and photographic effects. The director works with and supervises these assistants, selects his cast and generally studies the continuity and its proper unfolding. When all this has been arranged and construction of the interior and exterior scenes is underway in accordance with the plans, the photographing or "shooting" as it is called begins. There is ordinarily no sequence to the shooting; the last scene in the play may be the first shot. As a rule the set or location which is first available determines where the photography shall commence.

The director rehearses and takes and retakes the same scene in many ways and shadings, at first following the continuity and then using his own imagination when he feels that the scene can be improved. It is also customary to take "still" photos of the important scenes to use in advertising, and for lithographs, etc. All the action taking place on one set or location, whether at the beginning or end of the story itself, is usually done in sequence. At the end of each day's work in the studio or immediately upon return from location, the negative film is delivered to the laboratory (the stills to the so-called "Still Room"), where it is developed and positive prints made which are projected on the screen the following evening to enable the director and his assistants to discuss each "take," and decide upon which is the best. If none is suitable, the director orders a retake and the cast is re-assembled and goes through the same scene until it is satisfactory. The set may then be "struck,"i.e., torn down to make room on the studio floor for another set of the same or another picture. Exterior sets are as a rule left standing as the ground space is not generally necessary for immediate use. They are struck or altered when the space is needed.

When photography has been completed, it becomes necessary to cut the scenes and arrange them in the order called for by the continuity. Ofttimes, scenes are longer than it was expected and it is essential then to eliminate many of them so that when finally cut and titled, the footage will be within the amount planned. For example, average feature pictures run about six reels or 6,000 feet; extraordinary productions which constitute a whole evening's entertainment, run about 12,000 feet. "Titles" are made and photographed—i.e., insertion of the words necessary to explain the situation or show the dialogue ensuing. Many times, so-called "Art Titles" are prepared, i.e., titles with decorative borders or backgrounds. The negative is then complete and turned over to the Head Office—the cost being transferred from the studio to the Head Office books. (Frequently, two negatives are taken of large and important productions to facilitate foreign distribution; and, when stored and shipped separately, to afford insurance against loss by fire, etc.) From the negative as many separate positive films are printed as are required for distribution throughout the country, from 80 to 100 sets or more. This latter service is ordinarily performed in independently conducted laboratories which specialize in this work.

The cycle from the time the director takes active charge to the delivery of the completed negative to Head Office is about two months for the average feature picture. Extraordinary productions of course take much longer time.

Major Considerations in Design of System

It should be kept uppermost in mind that photoplays are in no sense standard, and that as a result a comparison of costs between them is of only relative value. Furthermore, price setting (ordinarily one of the predominating reasons for securing accurate information) is not determined by the cost of the picture. Any system of accounts installed in a studio, however, should be sufficiently complete and accurate to serve as a proper control of assets and liabilities, including a perpetual inventory of stores and fixed assets, and to permit compilation of reasonably accurate costs of productions made. Since a unit is not standard, no attempt was made in the early years of the industry to strive for accuracy in costing out productions, and producers were content to run their accounts on a cash disbursement basis.

The very unique situation exists of "consuming" many thousands of feet of lumber, hardware, valuable furnishings, costumes, etc., to manufacture sets and yet having them all still on hand and almost as good as new when the picture is completed and delivered. The product of the motion picture "factory" is nothing more than a narrow strip of negative film several thousand feet in length from which positive copies may be made for use in the projection machines of the exhibitor. Condensed into this footage is $100,000 and more, expended for salaries and wages, for lumber, hardware, properties, etc., and for the fixed charges of the studio. Much of the left-over materials may be used on subsequent pictures or sold, and represent real asset values. It was the desirability of reflecting some fair value for these assets that induced producers to correct this deficiency in the statements they furnished their bankers. Even then, until recently it did not become important to differentiate carefully the costs entering into the respective pictures being processed at any one time. Following the crisis of 1920 and the period of shutdown of most studios, the industry was deflated with the result that prominent directors, stars and authors are in a sense in partnership with their producers, receiving part of their compensation in a percentage of the income after the picture has cleared its cost. With this sort of arrangement on the increase, it is becoming more and more important to ascertain just what is the correct cost of the individual photoplay.

Outlining any system to be installed in a business that is truly an art, where the products and their component parts are in a great measure entirely dissimilar and where the real value to be measured is rather the "idea" and the brain effort expended to crystallize it into photographed action, makes the problem a peculiar one. To set up in a production the cost of "ideas" is impossible, though a considerable portion of the huge amounts expended as salary is paid to persons for the purchase of such ideas and their translation into photographs. While such a person is present in the studio presumably employed upon a certain production, he may be actually formulating ideas for use in succeeding ones. This is further complicated by the fact that during what may be termed "lost time" (when the employee is absent or unassigned or when he is resting between the completion of one picture and commencement of a new one, a frequently occurring situation representing large items of cost) such ideas will continue to be formulated and will be embodied in future productions, together with ideas developed entirely outside of "office hours."

Chart of Accounts

This outline of the "manufacturing process" forms the basis for the system of accounts and records built around a studio's operations to effect the general purposes outlined.

The chart of organization reproduced (see Figure 10-1) requires no extensive comment. It represents a typical departmental and divisional arrangement of a large studio, working on say eight to twelve pictures at a time, which is equivalent to turning out a product costing about $5,000,000 or $6,000,000 per annum.

Two typical statements appear in Figures 10-2 and 10-3.

Sources of Charges to Productions in Process

Salaries — Star, Artists, Directors, and Staff: These charges are obtained from weekly distribution of time as reported by department heads. A form

Figure 10-1

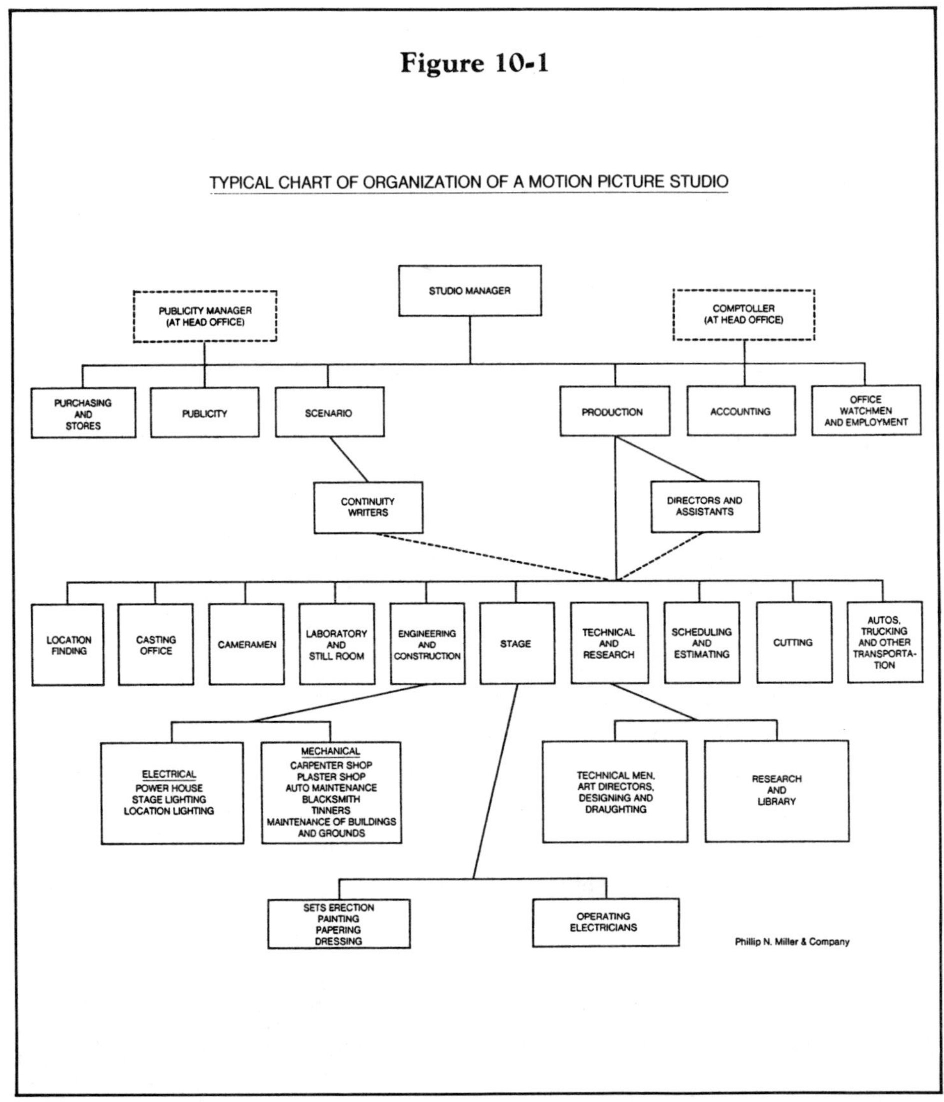

Figure 10-2

**Typical Statement of Cost Items
Comprising a Motion Picture Production
(Subsidiary Ledger to Control Account in Studio General Ledger
Inventory of Production in Process)**

Account Number	Item	
01	Salaries - Star	
02	" - Artists	
03	" - Director and Staff	
04	" - Extra Talent	
05	Sets - Interior:	
	(a) Material	)
	(b) Labor	)
	(c) Properties - Stock	)
	(d) " - Rented	)
	(m) Miscellaneous	)
06	Sets - Exterior:	)
	(a) Material	)
	(b) Labor	)
		)Separate accounts for each set
	(c) Properties - Stock	)
	(d) " - Rented	)
	(e) Autos and Cartage	)
	(f) Railroad Fare	)
	(g) Hotel	)
	(h) Lunches	)
	(j) Location Rental	)
	(m) Miscellaneous	)
07	Properties not Chargeable to Single Set	
08	Costumes - Stock	
09	" - Rented	
10	Animals	
11	Electric Current and Expense	
12	Negative Film	
13	Positive Film	
14	Laboratory Expense	
15	Still Expense	
16	Titles	
17	Cutting	
18	Book	
19	Scenario and Continuity	
20	Miscellaneous	
21	Apportioned Stores and Wardrobe Departments Salaries and Expenses	
22	Apportioned Stage Overhead Salaries and Expenses	
23	Apportioned Other Indirect Salaries and Expenses	

may be designed which will become the Accounting Department record and serve in itself as the payroll and distribution.

Salaries—Extra Talent: This item is obtained from Daily Report of Extra Talent Employed. The Assistant Director or Business Manager lists the names

Figure 10-3

Typical Chart of Asset and Liability Accounts of a Motion Picture Studio

ASSETS

CURRENT:
- Cash in Bank
- Petty Cash Fund
- Extra Talent Cash Fund
- Advances to Assistant Directors and Business Managers
- Accounts Receivable
- Loans and Advances Receivable-Employees
- Inventories:
  - Productions in Process
  - Scenarios and Continuities in Process
  - Scenarios and Continuities Completed
- Raw Stores and Supplies
- Negative with Cameramen
- Positive in Laboratory
- Unexposed Negatives in Still Room
- Rights to Books, Plays and Stories

FIXED ASSETS:
- Land
- Buildings
- Camera Equipment
- Electrical Equipment
- Machinery and Tools
- Office Furniture and Fixtures
- Autos and Trucks
- Properties and Costumes
- Less - Corresponding Reserves for Depreciation
- Construction in Process

DEFERRED CHARGES:
- Fire etc., Insurance Prepaid
- Life Insurance on Stars and Directors Prepaid
- Taxes Prepaid
- Unassigned Salaries
- Extraordinary Repairs
- Miscellaneous

LIABILITIES

CURRENT:
- Accounts Payable
- Extra Talent Payable
- Unclaimed Salaries and Wages
- Accrued Items

LONG TERM:
Loans Payable - Secured by Mortgages

HEAD OFFICE CONTROLLING ACCOUNT

DEFERRED CHARGES OR CREDITS:
- (Burden - Under or Over Absorbed)
- Electrical Current and Expense
- Use of Autos and Trucks
- Sale of Laboratory By-Products
- Stage Overhead } When absorbed on
- General Overhead } predetermined rate.

of the extras reporting. They are paid a full day's compensation even if engaged but part of the day or though not called upon to act. On dismissing talent for the day, they are furnished with vouchers entitling them to call at the Cashier's Office for their pay. The vouchers issued should agree with the list turned in to the Accounting Department. Entry is made *charging* Productions in Process with total of the list and *crediting* Extra Talent Payable. The cashier draws from the general cash the total of the daily list.

As vouchers are exchanged for cash they are stamped "paid" and checked off the list. After about ten days the list is returned to the Accounting Department with the paid vouchers and the cash for the unpaid items. Entry is then made clearing these accounts by *crediting* Extra Talent Cash Fund and *charging* Extra Talent Payable for the amount of the day's list. The cash returned is *charged* to the general funds and Unclaimed Salaries and Wages *credited*, the unchecked items on the daily lists constituting the detail of the account. Subsequently presented vouchers are paid out of general cash and charged to the Unclaimed Salaries and Wages account.

Extras hired on location are paid out of funds advanced to Assistant Directors or Business Managers, and the *charge* to pictures is made from reports or disbursements made on location turned in from time to time.

Sets — Interior — (a) Material: The material cost of interior sets is obtained from Requisitions for Material showing the items drawn and the picture and set chargeable. Requisitions are forwarded to the perpetual inventory clerk, who prices, extends and deducts them from stores cards. A weekly summary furnishes the basis for posting to pictures and individual sets, and to proper debit and credit controlling accounts.

(b) Labor: The labor cost of interior sets is obtained from Job Time Tickets. Carpenters, painters, plasterers and other studio workmen ring clock cards at the Studio entrance. At the close of the week these cards show attendance, and when rated and extended form the basis for the pay-roll in the customary manner. All time should be accounted for by separate job tickets showing hours spent on individual sets. Job tickets are issued to employees by foremen or their assistants, indicating the work to be done and the picture and set chargeable, and are rung in on job clocks at the commencement and conclusion of work. Job tickets are extended and balanced with the clock cards at the close of a payroll period, it being necessary also to account for idle time. Payroll and distribution form the basis for entry *charging* Productions in Process and *crediting* Accounts Payable — Payroll.

(c) Properties — Stock: The cost of properties issued from stock for interior sets is obtained from Requisitions for Stock Properties, Costumes, etc. Requisitions are forwarded to the perpetual inventory clerk who prices, extends and makes entries on his cards, moving such cards into an "Out" file as record

of their withdrawal from stock. A weekly summary is the basis for *charging* pictures and individual sets, and *crediting* proper Reserves for Depreciation. On return of "props" the "Return Memo" is forwarded to the inventory clerk who removes the card from the "Out" file and replaces it in the "In" file.

Most studios carry many thousand dollars worth of valuable articles in stock, consisting of furniture, rugs, draperies, house furnishings and utensils, doors, windows, "flats" (for walls), gowns and sundry costumes. It was (and to a great extent still is) the practice to charge the production for which these articles were originally purchased or constructed with the entire cost thereof. Many of these articles may be used over and over again, frequently without change and sometimes with slight alterations, repainting, etc. The practice of charging the entire cost to the first production manifestly overcosts that production and undercosts subsequent ones making use of these stock articles.

This condition, coupled with the fact that these articles will actually produce income through rental to other producers (in accordance with the custom of studios to rent "stock props," as they are called, to each other), seems to require the formulation of some method by which fairer and more accurate absorption can be made. Stock props, costumes and scenery are a part of the fixed assets and as such should be depreciated. But depreciation as used here has not the usual significance, for the very age and shabbiness of some property may make it even more valuable than if new. Properties and costumes will be reused less often in proportion to their striking and bizarre character. A maid's costume of black dress, apron and cap can be used a dozen times, whereas a gorgeous dancing gown of exotic design can be filmed in but one picture. Similarly, a common kitchen chair can be used many times, while a medieval throne can be used but once. This is not due entirely to adaptability to the general nature of the pictures produced, but more particularly to the fact that the "movie-fan" dislikes to see a repetition of gowns or furnishings, commenting that "Susi Somebody wore the same dress in her last picture," or that "Harry Hairbredth has that same big chair in his room that he had in the picture he was in last winter." In theory each picture should be charged with a proportion of the cost of the props it uses, plus some small allowance for the regular depreciation of the stock as a whole. Such a calculation is most intangible, but the rule provides the basis for arriving at a method that seems to be the best under the circumstances. When a property is purchased or constructed, determine about how often it may be used, and with this as a base, fix a rate for each use which will absorb slightly in excess of its cost over the estimated times of use, charging this rate to the respective productions either as a "weekly rental" charge or in one lump amount. The credit side of this entry acts as a "Reserve for Depreciation" offsetting the gross asset account on the balance sheet.

Many studios absorb depreciation on stock props, costumes, etc., as a charge to the burden account on a percentage basis of 20% to 33 1/3% per annum. While this is the easiest way, it does work inequity between pictures. For example: A picture in which most of the action occurs in the "great outdoors," drawing but little on the studio stock, is charged equally with a picture in which most of the action takes place in "interiors" in the studio, drawing heavily on the studio's stock. Where it is the practice to charge depreciation into "stage overhead" on a percentage basis, and thereby absorb into productions making use of stages, this inequity is not quite so patent, but nevertheless it may well be that one type of picture requires rented props almost exclusively, while another is able to make use of the studio's stock. In such a case it is evident that the former picture would bear a double burden.

When properties are rented to other studios, the net profit should be *credited* to Head Office to be picked up as an item of profit and loss. Against the gross rental received should be *charged* the depreciation (same type of charge as made to the cost of a picture using the article), the proper reserve for depreciation being credited.

(d) Properties — Rented: The cost of rented properties is obtained from the copy of the Rental Order, showing notation of receiving clerk that articles have been received. A weekly rent is paid to the lessor for this service which is a *charge* to Productions in Process, and a *credit* to Accounts Payable, liability and charge being booked at once and usually in advance of receipt of lessor's invoice. The invoice when received is matched against and attached to a copy of the Rental Order.

Since retention during subsequent weeks involves additional liability, a diary system should be maintained to enable a check up of unreturned props with a view to returning them promptly, or if necessary to hold them over, to form the basis for an entry *charging* Productions in Process and *crediting* Accounts Payable. In its simplest form this record consists of an extra copy of the Rental Order filed behind guide cards of the date returnable. As props are returned, the return receipt should be forwarded to the same clerk who originally handled the requisition and who refers to his file and stamps opposite each item the date of return. The day preceding the expiration of the week he examines the file for the succeeding day, and in conference with the proper operating man, determines if any or all of these props (against which no return date appears) can or will be returned. Additional rental for props held over is then charged to Productions in Process and *credited* to Accounts Payable through a "Hold Over" memo invoice.

Sets — Exterior — (a) Material: The cost procedure for the material cost of exterior sets erected on the lot is the same as for Interior Sets.

Sets erected on location are charged through a report of the Assistant

Director or the Business Manager of all the expenditures made for material.

(b) Labor: For the labor cost of exterior sets erected on the lot, the same cost procedure as for Sets Interior is followed, except that use of a job clock may not be feasible, in which case handwritten time for commencing and finishing job must be accepted. Labor on location is usually paid out of the fund advanced to the Assistant Director or Business Manager. Forms should be provided, similar to a payroll record, to support these expenditures.

(c) Properties — Stock: See Sets — Interior for treatment of Stock properties.

(d) Properties — Rented: For rented properties of sets on the lot, the same cost procedure as for Sets — Interior is followed.

Sets on location are *charged* through a report of the Assistant Director or Business Manager of expenditures made for rented props.

(e) Autos and Cartage: The cost of the item Autos and Cartage is derived from the Report of Autos and Trucks used. Weekly reports are made to the Accounting Department of the time spent by each auto and truck, and the picture chargeable. Predetermined rates per hour of use are set for the different machines, which take into consideration the entire operating expenses — gas, oil, chauffeur's salary, depreciation, etc. Rates are multiplied by the hours used and Productions in Process is *charged, credit* being made to Auto and Trucks Burden Account into which all actual expenses are charged as incurred. (See Burden Accounts, Figure 10-4).

Expenditures made on location for hired transportation are charged through the report of the Assistant Director or Business Manager.

(f) Railroad Fare, (g) Hotel, (h) Lunches, (j) Location Rental: These four items are usually chargeable through a report of the Assistant Director or Business Manager of expenditures made on location. Location Rental is paid sometimes by check direct from Studio, in which case entry is passed on proper authority to *charge* Productions in Process, and to *credit* Accounts Payable.

Properties Not Chargeable to Single Sets: See under Properties for treatment of cost of properties not chargeable to single sets. The reason for this account lies in the fact that sometimes certain props are not confined to any one set, but may be used on several.

Costumes — Stock: The cost of costumes taken from stock is obtained from Requisition for Stock, Properties, Costumes, etc. See comments under Sets — Interior — (c) Properties — Stock.

Costumes — Rented: See comments under Sets — Interior, and Sets — Exterior — (d) Properties — Rented.

Animals: The charge for animals ordinarily comes through the payroll, the name of the trainer who cares for the animal being shown, viz.: "John Jones and Dog." It may also come through as a daily charge similar to extra talent;

or where hired apart from trainers or owners (for example, a canary) it may be covered by a Rental Order.

Electric Current and Expense: The cost of electric current and expense is taken from the Report of Operating Electrician. This report made out by the

Figure 10-4

BURDEN ACCOUNTS

The following is a list of burden accounts and the method of apportioning each item.

Nature	Method of Apportionment
Electrical Current and Expense	By predetermined hourly rate
Autos and Trucks	By predetermined hourly rate
Laboratory Salaries and Expenses (Less-Sale of laboratory by-products)	Footage processed during period
Still Room Salaries and Expenses	Number of Prints made during period
Wardrobe Salaries and Expenses	Costume cost during period
General Stores Salaries and Expenses	Cost of Material requisitioned during period
Property Stores Salaries and Expenses	Cost of Properties (Stock and Rented) during period

Nature	
Stage Overhead: Watchmen Wages County, City and State Taxes on Plant Repairs to Buildings and Equipment (Other than electrical) Depreciation on Buildings and Equipment (other than electrical) Insurance	Some studios used predetermined rate per day for each stage (or part thereof) occupied. Others combine with "General Overhead."
General Overhead (Items not chargeable direct to Pictures): Salaries and Expenses - Executive do. - Office and Employment do. - Purchasing Dept. do. - Production Dept. Salaries of Artists, Directors etc. while Unassigned, in excess of ordinary rest period Cartage Electric Current and Expense for Office Telephone and Telegraph Postage Legal Employees' Liability Insurance (may be directly charged) Miscellaneous and General	Costs for period, less star salary and cost of book. or (Where use of normal burden is feasible) - Predetermined Rate per camera day based on normal camera day capacity and estimated normal burden - unabsorbed amount to be charged to Profit and Loss.

operating electrician assigned to the picture is in handy card form and is turned in daily. It lists the various types of lamps and lighting devices and opposite each item is shown the hours of service. Predetermined rates are set in consultation with the lighting engineer. These rates combine all elements of electrical expense: Kilowatt consumption, hours of life of tubes and arcs; depreciation of wiring, power house machinery and similar equipment; repairs; salaries of electrical workers (other than the operating electricians who are assigned to specific pictures); etc. Daily reports are rated and extended, weekly summary forming the basis for entry *charging* Productions in Process and *crediting* Electrical Current and Expense Burden Account. Into this latter account are *charged* all the actual electrical expenses as incurred.

Negative Film: The cost of negative film is obtained from the Laboratory Receipt for Exposed Negative. Copy of this form, the original of which goes to the Cameraman on delivery of his exposed negative to the Laboratory, forms the basis of entry (by weekly summary) to *charge* the picture with the cost of the raw negative exposed and to *credit* the Cameraman, who has previously been charged with the footage and value of the raw negative stock drawn from stores. Copy of Cameraman's Daily Report is turned into the Laboratory with the negative. This report shows each "take" and instructions for disposition, i.e., "N. G.," "Print," "Hold," etc.

Positive Film: From Laboratory Weekly Report which shows the positive footage consumed for each picture, entry for the cost of a positive film is made *charging* Productions in Process and *crediting* Positive in Laboratory, it having previously been charged with footage and value of the raw positive stock drawn from stores.

Laboratory Expenses: From Laboratory Weekly Report *charge* is made of the laboratory expense for the week. Total expense of laboratory, per the books, is *credited* by distribution over the negative and positive processed on a footage basis, after giving effect to the estimated reclaim value of waste hypo, etc. On sale of waste, actual return is credited to the same account as was charged when the estimate was set up. Excess debit or credit balance is deferred and adjusted from time to time.

Still Expense: From Still Room Weekly Report the cost of still expense for the week is *charged* to the various pictures on the basis of prints made, Still Room Expense Account being *credited*. The cost of negative plates used is also *charged* through this report and Still Room Stock *credited*, as it was previously charged with the quantity and value of the negative plates drawn by it for sub-stores.

Titles, Cutting and Book: From pay-roll distribution of Title Department and from Requisitions for Raw Materials and Supplies the cost of titles is obtained; from pay-roll distribution of Cutting Department the cost of cutting is determined; and from voucher authorizing purchase the cost of "book" is ascertained.

Scenario and Continuity: By transfer from account Scenarios and Continuities Completed and from pay-roll distribution of Scenario Department when scenarist or continuity writer works with director in production, the cost of scenario and continuity is determined.

Scenarios and Continuities are written prior to production, as described near the beginning of this article. The time spent thereon is *charged* through the asset account, Scenarios and Continuities in Process, to the particular story worked on. When finished, this account is *credited* and Completed Account *charged,* from whence it is transferred on commencing production into picture cost. Should the story be sold or scrapped the account is closed out to Profit and Loss through transfer to Head Office account.

Apportioned Stores and Wardrobe Departments, Salaries and Expenses: The cost of this item is obtained from distribution of actual expenses on basis respectively of amount of requisitions filled (Stores Summary Distribution) and of costume cost during period.

Stage Overhead: (For detail accounts of Stage Overhead see Burden Accounts, Figure 10-4).

From Weekly Report of Stage Use showing pictures and sets occupying stages and portions thereof, extended at predetermined rate per day for each stage, the stage overhead is obtained. Actual expenses of the nature shown in the schedule are *charged* against the credits arising through use of predetermined rates.

When Stage Overhead is combined with General Overhead, the accounting is as shown in Figure 10-4.

General Overhead: (For detail accounts of general overhead see Burden Accounts, Figure 10-4).

The method of absorbing the general overhead of a studio offers a wide field for discussion. One thing seems true, however, that the common practice in other industries of using the basis of direct-labor hours or direct-labor value or machine-hours is not applicable here.

Two separate practices are followed. Each has its advantages and disadvantages. Both are presented to the reader and he may make his choice. One method is to absorb overhead on the basis of the total of all costs of each picture for the accounting period, less the salary of star and the cost of "book." This cost of course, is the cost before adding the apportioned general overhead. Salary of star and price of "book" are omitted as these costs are in ratio to the already advertised and selling value rather than to real worth from the viewpoint of pure production. This method has been investigated in detail by the writer and in the particular studio seemed to very fairly measure the indirect effort and expense. It has the effect of carrying into inventory each period the entire general overhead. Our friends who are staunch supporters of standard costs and normal burdens may not like this method. For them there is the other method of determining camera day capacity, estimating normal burden, and arriving at a rate per camera day, using say a factor of 80% of capacity. The unabsorbed burden by such method would find its way direct to Profit and Loss.

It is possible to conceive of several other treatments of general overhead. A prominent producer has a weighted scale manner of absorption, taking in the burden on one percentage for say the first $10,000 of direct cost for the period, another percentage for the second $10,000 and so on. At any rate, we have followed the cost of a picture down to this final step. Experience shows that each company's production problem is sufficiently different to warrant dissimilar methods of apportioning general overhead. This one thought should be kept in mind; namely, the increasing tendency toward using the "cost of a picture" as a basis for measuring advances by distributors and for stating the amount which a production must return to the producer before commencing to share rentals with stars, directors, authors, etc., makes it advisable to carry into the cost of each particular picture every element which can possibly be classed as an expense of production.

Lost Time

Two interesting questions, namely, lost time and scrap value of sets, have not been brought out in the discussion of the detailed accounts. They have been deferred purposely to this point so as not to confuse the reader in developing logically the items of picture cost.

Treatment of "lost time" on the books of account allows some latitude. Several methods have been suggested by motion picture executives and public accountants. A rather arbitrary method must be used, and it is felt that the most practical way under all the circumstances is to absorb the amount of salary while a picture is in process into the cost of production to which the employee has been assigned. Salaries paid to employees while unassigned or awaiting commencement of a new production, should be deferred and charged into the cost of the new production, with this exception, that should the rest between pictures be of longer duration than the ordinary period of time, then the excess over normal should be charged into the general studio burden account and absorbed into costs through that medium. It may be argued that the rest following a production is more properly chargeable to that production. It will be found in practice that it is important to close costs immediately on completion of the negative, and since on the average the cost of the rest will be quite equitably distributed against various pictures, if charged in the manner proposed, no great harm results from this practice.

Scrap Value of Sets

As pointed out, after an interior set is struck, a large part of the lumber, etc., may be restocked and used on succeeding pictures. It was the custom generally to disregard this element on the theory that while the first picture will be heavy in cost, each subsequent one will "give and take" such used material and hence work out on the average. Where accurate costs are not sought and particularly where costs of individual sets are not secured, this question is not of vital importance except that the balance sheet reflects only such value for this material as may be buried in the cost of the pictures produced. Where accurate information is required of the direct costs of sets for purposes of managerial control and of estimation of the costs of similar sets in future production, it is essential that this element of scrap value be properly treated on the books. Several methods are suggested: (1) On striking a set, value the material and put through a "Return to Stores" slip, charging stores and crediting cost of the particular set. (Lumber in standard sizes may be restocked and revalued as second-hand lumber in three or four value classifications, depending on the physical condition and equivalent roughly to what it would cost to acquire such lumber elsewhere.) (2) Another method has been suggested by which a stores account, "Second-hand material in sets," should be opened to which will be charged (when material is requisitioned) that proportion estimated to be the scrap value of the set when struck. For example, charge 60% to the cost of production and 40% to the "Second-hand" account. In this way the periodic costs of pictures reported to the Head Office will not be inflated by the value of the material to be returned to stores when sets are struck. On striking, the material returned to stores is cleared out of "Second-hand material in sets." If this account is carefully watched, but little adjustment will be required on taking the physical inventory at close of the fiscal year. The method to be followed depends very much on the size and scope of the particular studio's operations. Several other methods may be suggested but it is sufficient to outline the problem to this extent, leaving the particular treatment to the judgment of the accounting executive as to the simplest and best system in his own case.

The above discussion covers interior sets. Exteriors usually remain standing until the ground space is required for another set. On striking or altering, if any salvage value be present, the Head Office should be credited with the amount thereof as an item of Profit and Loss. From time to time it is possible to make use in another picture of exteriors left standing. Cost of altering should be charged to the new picture. Whether the new picture should also be charged with a "rental" for the use of the set, is questionable. Occasionally, producers permit other producers to make use of their standing exteriors on payment of a rental charge. This is an item of sundry Profit and Loss. It is possible that in some studios where an independent producer is permitted to make his picture along with the company's own product (because of his contract to distribute that picture through the company), a rental charge for use of exteriors might be proper.

Job Orders

Orders for the making of stock props, for sundry construction, for equipment installation, etc., are accounted for by job orders. Like all factories, for proper control of repair, construction work, etc., a "plant order" or "job order" system should be installed. Time and material expended should be charged to the proper order through time cards and requisitions. When completed, these orders should be closed out to proper accounts. Balances in expense orders, including standing orders, may be closed out periodically into the proper burden accounts.

Purchases and Rentals

Purchases and rentals should be controlled through a Purchasing Department, and all oral and rush orders should be confirmed by proper purchase orders and rental order forms. Copies should be forwarded to the Receiving Clerk and to the Accounting Department for use in checking receipt of goods and in passing invoices for payment.

A copy of each Receiving Slip should be forwarded to the Accounting Department for matching with orders and invoices. Due to irregularity in receipt of invoices and to the practice of closing costs and reporting to the Head Office weekly, some studios set up the liability from the Receiving Slip itself as soon as received, pricing it from the Purchase or Rental Order data, making whatever adjustment may be necessary, if any, on receipt of the invoice.

Conclusion

The system as described in this article is not in effect in any one particular studio. It is a compendium of the salient features of several systems and outlines what seems to be the best practice. True, it is somewhat complicated as compared with the simple cash disbursement plan of many small producers, but as cost accountants of varied experience must admit, it is a "babe in arms," when compared with the systems required to compile costs in many industries. Any system cannot be much less complex than the processes which it attempts to record, and a glimpse into the inner workings of a large studio with five or six pictures in course of "shooting," and as many more in preparation or in cutting, will soon convince the skeptic that things are not done in simple operations as might appear from the speed and apparent ease in which scenes are reeled off on the silver screen. It is just as satisfactory to shoot on the stages at night as it is during the day, and enthusiastic directors know no stopping point when things are going right. With mob scenes on schedule, stages are jammed with extras; lights are sizzling on and off; the bell is clanging for silence; gorgeous ball-rooms rise before one's very eyes—the product of high speed carpentry; wondrously gowned women flit across the scenes; the crisp instruction of the director echoes across the stage; and the camera clicks in rhythmic accord gathering into itself a stirring tale of love and adventure.

Complicated as the system may be as applied to a large studio, the smaller producer can refine it and reduce it to the barest essentials for his own particular purposes.

Just as in most factories and shops, when volume and repetition of operations become prevalent, we are able to introduce machinery to smooth the task and to increase the "per man" output, so in the accounting department in dealing with volume of repetitive transactions we can try to apply machinery to its work. Fortunately, a rather unique application of bookkeeping machines is possible which lessens the "cost of cost accounting" and speeds up the periodic closing. This system (originally designed for Metro Pictures Corporation and now installed in other large studios) enables direct posting from accounts payable and journal vouchers to voucher register and to ledger accounts to be charged and credited, beside reflecting continuously the balances in such accounts. The studio general ledger itself and all subsidiary ledgers are kept by machine. Daily proof of postings is obtained through the accumulator wheels and, when ready to close, balances of accounts to be apportioned are available without further effort. In addition, Cash Disbursement records are kept by machine; the filling out of checks, check register and posting to proper charge accounts are all made by one operation. Similarly, Cash Receipts record is compiled and posted by the same operation.

It would take too much space to describe in detail how this mechanical bookkeeping is done, but those acquainted with the principles of this kind of machine can picture fairly well how it operates. Suffice it to say, that the company mentioned, with an accounting staff of nine persons, closes its costs weekly as of Saturday and on the following Tuesday or Wednesday has its financial statement and report of operations in the mail on its way to its New York Head Office.

Before concluding the writer desires to appeal to those more particularly concerned in this field of endeavor. There is no reason why available data should be as scarce as they are. If the cost accountant in the motion picture field is to occupy the important place that others of his profession hold in other businesses, and if the science is to be advanced in its application to this phase of industry, he should freely and fully offer his ideas and his experiences. It is desired that this article evoke discussion. It affords a good opportunity to those who disagree with parts of it to state their views, and to those who have more to add to build upon its foundation.

(11) "The Use of Cost Data by Trade Associations," 1923 Yearbook, R. S. Kellogg, Secretary, News Print Service Bureau

The Use of Cost Data by Trade Associations

The subject really assigned to me three or four months ago was entitled, "The Proper Use of Cost Data by Trade Associations."

As it is put on the program the subject of this session reads: "How Far Is It Proper for a Trade Association to Distribute Cost Information Among Its Members?" Some question might perhaps be raised as to whether I am the best person to speak on a subject of this kind. Persons occasionally get their labels mixed up and the right person gets into the wrong box, and vice versa; and that reminds me of a fable I ran across the other day. I call it a fable because it is old, to the effect that Mike says, "I was crossing the bridge the other night and met Pat O'Brien, and I said, 'Pat, how are you?' He says 'Pretty well, thank you, Brady; how are you?' 'Faith and my name is not Brady.' 'And my name is not Pat O'Brien;' and then we looked at each other, and, begorrah, it was neither of us."

Some question might perhaps be raised as to why I should speak about the legitimate use of cost data by a Trade Association. I am not a lawyer, which I am thankful for. I am not a cost accountant, which I am also thankful for; and in view of these two circumstances, I rather think I am qualified to speak on the subject. At any rate, I am going to do it. But when we come to talking about what a Trade Association can do, I think in the first place we have got to follow the example of Mr. Stevenson this morning in setting up certain standards and definitions, and so, to start with, I want to quote the most authoritative definition we have as yet as to what a Trade Association really is.

What a Trade Association Is

There is an organization of Trade Association Secretaries covering the United States which is called American Trade Association Executives. Less than a year ago they adopted a definition as to what a Trade Association is. It is quoted in the book just published by the Department of Commerce upon Trade Association activities. This definition is: "An organization of producers or distributors of a commodity or service upon a mutual basis for the purpose of promoting the business of their branch of industry and improving their service to the public through the compilation and distribution of information, the establishment of trade standards and the cooperative handling of problems common to the production or distribution of the commodity or service with which they are concerned."

That is what constitutes a Trade Association according to present standards and practices, and what I shall say this afternoon, after I get through saying a little more about the theory underlying legitimate Trade Association work, ties up with that standard definition.

There are various types of industrial services existing in this country which are not Trade Associations. Some of those are of a most excellent character; they are doing very helpful and entirely legitimate work. There are others of a different character, and the Supreme Court has had its say as to some of them. The Department of Justice and the Federal Trade Commission has had its say as to others.

The outstanding accomplishments of American Trade Associations have been in two very important fields; one, the development of standards of commodities and services; and second, the compilation of facts, and that takes in statistics of every kind, including cost statistics. We get the benefit of trade standardization daily from the bed we sleep in, unless we happen to be beyond standard length, the paper we read and the breakfast we eat in the morning, and our means of travel to our daily task, afoot or awheel. We get the benefit of standardization clear down to the coffin we are buried in and the insurance policy we leave behind us. Those things are all standardized, for human beings cannot live together without standardization.

The Necessity for Statistics

Then there are statistics and statisticians of a good many kinds and varieties which we do not need to amplify very much except to say that statistics are as necessary to a navigator on the sea of business as compass, sextant and barometer to the navigator on the high seas. There are submerged reefs and rocky shores, doldrums and whirlpools which must be charted, channel buoys to be set and lights to be maintained if the good ship industry is to be steered in a safe course with its cargo of satisfaction for a multitude of human needs. When the course is not charted or the compass not used or the lighthouses left in darkness, catastrophe follows. A poor navigator may, with good luck, make a successful trip, but only an expert with a level head can carry a cargo through a hurricane. Just as the atmosphere is subject to periodic cyclonic disturbances, so there are cycles in the industrial world. We have not been able to pick up a trade journal or newspaper in the last few years without reading about cycles, but after all is said and done, overproduction leads to prices below cost, to lessened production, to higher prices and again to overproduction. I think that situation is going to remain with us as long as human beings are what they are now. Wave is bound to follow wave and action is followed by reaction. The best we can do is to put ourselves in shape to withstand these periodic shocks and carry through them safely. In a state of free competition, as little as 5% under or oversupply may bull or bear a commodity market. Monopolies and artificial restrictions upon commerce are illegal, and, more than that, they are abhorrent to our sense of justice and contrary to our conception of freedom, but blind competition may be as disastrous as no competition in its ultimate effects. It is for this reason that we must know all the surrounding facts if we are to have intelligent competition and competition which gives us service and permanent benefits, rather than unintelligent competition which may do tremendous harm.

It is only upon a basis of facts that it is possible for the public to be served in the manner the present day public demands of us. Facts are sometimes disconcerting, but they are never so damaging as the gossip which circulates in the absence of facts. Business done by daylight is permanently more successful than that done in darkness, and while the public may reap a temporary advantage from blind competition of either buyers or sellers, the public in the long run pays the bills for all economic losses. Big business, as it is popularly called, represented by the great business organizations, companies and corporations, usually has adequate and ample means of its own for securing necessary data and statistics, but it is only through Trade Associations that the smaller operators are able to be informed from day to day of the actual conditions and able to put themselves in shape to meet situations which arise.

It is only through the Trade Association, I say, that the smaller operator has his chance of survival in intelligent competition today; the Trade Association is the salvation of the smaller organization. But it is clearly established and everywhere recognized by intelligent men, that there are certain things that competitors under our system of legislative enactment, may not do. They may not fix prices by agreement, or limit output or divide territory, and any organization that is proceeding on the assumption that any of these things may be done in any direct or indirect manner, is going upon an absolutely false assumption and will get into trouble if it keeps at it.

But commerce and industry assert that they have the inherent right to collect and distribute through their trade organizations, statistics as to the volume of production, shipments, stocks, orders, costs, wage rates and market conditions as to their own and competing commodities—all reports to be impartially compiled by a trained Association executive and supplied without coloring by him to all who have a legitimate interest in the matters dealt with. Carrying this out, Trade Associations have an opportunity for great service to their members and to the public through the study of all items of cost and the setting up of honest cost standards. Here is an example, for instance, that has arisen in one particular field. We have heard a tremendous outcry in the last two or three years about the condition of the farmer and the small amount that the farmer was getting in return for his labor and his expenditure of capital. We had a congressional committee on agricultural inquiry that made as thorough an investigation as a committee has ever been known to make of that character in the country, and that committee found that out of the dollar the consumer pays for a product that starts on the farm, the farmer gets 20 cents; the manufacturer gets 17 cents; that the profits of the retailer, wholesaler and manufacturer take 14 cents, and that selling and distribution costs take 49 cents of it. Here is a great field for effecting economies, possibly not very much in production but certainly a great deal in distribution; and yet solutions of these problems can never be worked out and put into operation without the most accurate kind of cost studies and market analyses. The problem cannot be solved in any way without the application of correct principles of that character. That is only one example, which can be multiplied many times.

Uniform Cost Systems

We have heard a great deal about uniform cost systems, and I want to say right here that I do not like the term very much; we have seen too many cases in which, instead of a *uniform cost system*, groups of more or less irresponsible people have got hold of it and transformed it into a *system of uniform costs*. Get that, and leave it alone. There is a tremendous difference. A uniform cost system is all right if it means the setting up of honest cost standards upon a uniform basis, but if it is used for the purpose of setting up a system of uniform costs, you have got something that is entirely wrong and illegitimate. There have been too many cases where so-called uniform cost systems have been introduced by so-called accountants, and they have not been used for the honest determination of costs, for the purpose of reducing costs and effecting economies in operation, but they have been used for the purpose of fixing or raising selling prices, and I submit that their use for that purpose is something which no member of this organization wants to have anything to do with, and I know perfectly well it is something that no member of this organization has any intention of having anything to do with, but there have been a lot of cases of that sort where, under the guise of cost accounting, we have had very flagrant examples of price fixing carried on through so-called Trade Associations. If you want any more information on that score, you can go into the Supreme Court decisions, you can go into pending cases brought by the Department of Justice, you can go into cases now under consideration and orders recently issued by the Federal Trade Commission; they are all in existence and can be easily found, and you will find behind a number of them, working under the guise of a uniform cost system, just the same old purpose of fixing prices. They tried to sugar coat it over a little, but the coating has been dissolved in some cases.

Association Responsibility

It needs to be realized that many men, business men, used to individual freedom, have utterly failed to realize the difference between what each may do for himself and what he may not do in agreement with his fellow competitors. That is where the trouble lies; what is legitimate in the case of the individual may turn out to be criminal conspiracy if done by two or more individuals acting together. Trade Association executives in every capacity, managers, secretaries, cost accountants, legal advisors, or what not, are in duty bound to protect their organizations from foolish ventures of this sort, and that, I think, needs to be a little more realized than it has been in some cases. I heard of a case this week where a business organization, according to its sworn statement of not many months ago, showed liabilities of $116,000, and on the basis of that statement was supposed to be solvent. They recently got into such difficulties that, if their prominent competitors agree, they may perhaps be able to save the organization from going on the rocks. If they do not, it will be the end of them. When this firm was audited by really honest auditors from outside the organization, they found that instead of liabilities of $116,000 they had liabilities of $394,000, and when asked for the explanation as to why they showed only $116,000 liabilities in their sworn published statement, they said that the other liabilities had been kept off their books by advice of counsel. So, after all, sometimes even if a man carries a label of some particular kind of profession, he may still be a scoundrel. So, as I say, trade association executives have a particular responsibility to be borne clearly in mind in every matter of this kind. Going back to what I said previously, there is a great deal of freedom that the individual may exercise, entirely legitimate, which has to be to a considerable extent curtailed when he works in agreement with his competitors; the line has to be clearly drawn.

Standards of Service

The handling of cost data by a trade association should be on the same basis as all its other statistical work; it should be on the same general basis as its statistics on production and orders and stocks on hand and everything of that character. In cost statistics handled by a trade association, there should be no guess work; there should be no advice as to selling prices or profit margins; there should be no agreements as to fixed charges of any kind, because competent legal counsel will tell you it is just as illegal to agree upon certain fixed charges in relation to the product as to agree upon the selling price of the entire product. They are the same character, only different in degree. There must be no averaging of estimates to establish mythical costs which in reality conceal any profit. In other words, it devolves upon Trade Association executives quite frequently to tell the truth even if they find it rather unpleasant.

I ran across this the other day; when asked as to the responsibility of a fellow lawyer in Springfield, it is said Lincoln once wrote: "He has in his office a table worth $1.50 and a chair worth 50 cents. He has a bouncing baby boy worth $150,000. There is also a rat hole that will bear watching." And I submit that an Association executive has to watch for rat holes, particularly in the handling of cost data. Trade Association service in cost determination should be of as high grade as that given by well-known firms of public accountants and equally impartial, and that is not always an easy thing to do, particularly when you remember the human relationships and the human nature involved in Association membership. It is a pretty high standard, and yet it is a necessary standard for the handling of cost data or any other statistical data by a Trade Association if it is to be kept above suspicion.

Helping to Reduce Costs

The handling of cost data by a Trade Association in this manner is of value to industry in a great many ways, but in particular in doing these four things: First, exposing incorrect methods; second, revealing uneconomic processes; third, checking wastes; and fourth, directly growing out of these other three, the indicating of new opportunities for reducing costs. Inherently they all come out if the work is carried on correctly. Direct service of this sort to an industry is indirect but nevertheless tangible service to the public which buys the product of the industry, and will react to public benefit. That is the test of trade association work in this country which, in the future, will be supplied constantly by the public authorities. Is the work of your organization of benefit to the public? If it is, it is going to be sustained, but that test has got to be met.

Methods of Comparison

In the opinion of the members of the News Print Service Bureau, the manufacturers of news print paper in North America, cost service of this character is helpful to them. I am not saying that it would be in any other operation; I am saying that in their opinion it is helpful to them when operating costs are compared monthly upon a standard basis. Samples of the forms upon which information upon operating costs is exchanged through the Bureau office every month are in a folder on your seats this afternoon. The original forms, of course, are much larger; they had to be reduced to fit the printing necessities of the proceedings of this meeting. The first form (see Figure 11-1) is for the comparison of operating costs in the manufacture of news print paper. It covers both the current month specified and the cumulative operating costs for the year to date. You will find running across the top, company 1, company 2, and so on, as far as is necessary; underneath monthly and cumulative parallel columns and at the left the items of cost which are put into these parallel columns, all of which are based upon a standard accounting system prepared by the best talent we could get to prepare it. I said this is a conversion cost statement or operating cost statement. It represents the operating cost involved in tranforming wood pulp into news print paper; in other words, there is no cost for pulp in that statement and there is no sales and shipping expense at the end of it. We take the cost that the operating man has some control over; we show it up in this form in order to put his costs for these particular items parallel with these other companies and thus find out what the weak spot may be. That is the purpose of it. As I said, it is to enable people to check their waste, to find out where their weak spots are and to give them information that will lead them to investigate their own condition, and if they are so disposed, to enable them to reduce their own operating costs. We do not know in a single case what the total cost of any of these firms is, and we do not care. That is none of our business, but we take this section right out of their costs, that will be of direct and immediate benefit to the operating man.

There are sub-totals given on the right-hand side of the form for the more important items. There is a final weighted total based upon the number of tons involved, and below that there is a great deal of statistical information which is proving very interesting.

You will note the form for a similar report upon the cost of making groundwood pulp (see Figure 11-2), one of the constituents of new print paper, but in that cost of making groundwood pulp there is no cost of the wood that goes into it; it is purely an operating cost. Figure 11-3 is a similar form for exchanging reports upon the operating cost of making sulphite pulp, all based upon the same standard system. Figure 11-4 has to do with steam; Figures 11-5, 11-6 and 11-7 have to do with a system of reports upon operating efficiencies in which there are no dollars and cents involved at all; in which the whole test is made as to the losses in production in percentage of ideal or ultimate possible production due to a large number of causes. In the center of each of these seven sheets you will find a summary sheet which groups particular items so that the executive who wishes to look only for the main things can get them in the summary sheet, and the operating man can get the details from the larger sheet. The reports go out with the

Figure 11-1
News Print Rolls
Comparative Statement of Conversion Costs
Per Ton

Average cost based on total tons produced UNFINISHED ROLLS
FINISHED ROLLS
MONTH CUM

		CO. 1		CO. 2		CO. 3		CO. 4	
		MONTH	CUM.	MONTH	CUM.	MONTH	CUM.	MONTH	CUM.
	UNFINISHED ROLLS								
1	LABOR - SUPERINTENDENTS								
2	BEATERS AND MIXERS								
3	MACHINE ROOM								
4	INSIDE								
5	MISCELLANEOUS								
6	TOTAL LABOR								
7	POWER ELECTRIC								
8	WATER								
9	STEAM								
10	WIRES								
11	MACHINE CLOTHING								
12	BELTING								
13	LUBRICANTS								
14	SUPPLIES								
15	REPAIRS-LABOR								
16	MATERIAL								
17	REPLACEMENTS - LOSSES ETC.								
18	SUB-TOTAL								
19	DEPRECIATION								
20	TAXES								
21	INSURANCE								
22	MANUFACTURING BURDEN								
23									
24	TOTAL								
	FINISHING								
25	LABOR								
26	WRAPPERS								
27	CORES								
28	SUPPLIES								
29	REPAIRS LABOR								
30	MATERIAL								
31	MISCELLANEOUS								
32	TOTAL								
	STATISTICAL								
33	COAL - LBS. PER TON OF PAPER								
34	COST " " " "								
35	STEAM - LBS. PER TON OF PAPER								
36	COST " " " "								
37	FILLERS - LBS. PER TON OF PAPER								
38	COST " " " "								
39	ALUM - LBS. PER TON OF PAPER								
40	COST " " " "								
41	COLORS - LBS. PER TON OF PAPER								
42	COST " " " "								
43	SIZE - LBS. PER TON OF PAPER								
44	COST " " " "								
45	FURNISH % - GROUNDWOOD								
46	SULPHITE								
47	OTHER FIBERS								
48	FILLERS								
49	TOTAL FURNISH %								
50	% MOISTURE IN PAPER								
51	% OPERATING HOURS TO TOTAL HOURS								

Figure 11-2
Groundwood
Comparative Statement of Conversion Costs
Per Ton

Average cost based on total tons produced UNFINISHED ROLLS
FINISHED ROLLS
MONTH CUM

		CO. 1		CO. 2		CO. 3		CO. 4	
		MONTH	CUM.	MONTH	CUM.	MONTH	CUM.	MONTH	CUM.
	SLUSHING								
1	LABOR - SUPERINTENDENTS								
2	WOOD HDLG IN GRINDER ROOM								
3	GRINDERS								
4	SCREENS								
5	INSIDE								
6	MISCELLANEOUS								
7	TOTAL LABOR								
8	POWER - WATER								
9	ELECTRIC								
10	STEAM								
11	PULP STONES								
12	BELTING								
13	LUBRICANTS								
14	SUPPLIES								
15	REPAIRS LABOR								
16	MATERIAL								
17	REPLACEMENTS - LOSSES ETC.								
18	SUB-TOTAL								
19	DEPRECIATION								
20	TAXES								
21	INSURANCE								
22	MANUFACTURING BURDEN								
23									
24									
25	TOTAL								
	DECKERING								
26	LABOR								
27	POWER - WATER								
28	ELECTRIC								
29	WIRES								
30	SUPPLIES								
31	REPAIRS LABOR								
32	MATERIAL								
33	REPLACEMENTS - LOSSES ETC.								
34	TOTAL								
	LAPPING								
35	LABOR - WET MACHINES								
36	HYDRAULIC PRESSES								
37	PILING								
38	MISCELLANEOUS								
39	TOTAL LABOR								
40	POWER - WATER								
41	ELECTRIC								
42	WIRES								
43	MACHINE CLOTHING								
44	SUPPLIES								
45	REPAIRS LABOR								
46	MATERIAL								
47	REPLACEMENTS - LOSSES ETC.								
48									
49	TOTAL								
	STATISTICAL								
50	% OPERATING HOURS TO TOTAL HOURS								
51	% TOTAL SCREENINGS RECOVERED								
52									

Figure 11-3
Sulphite
Comparative Statement of Conversion Costs
Per Ton

Average cost based on total tons produced RAW SLUSH
DECKERED SLUSH
LAPPED STOCK
MONTH CUM

		CO. 1		CO. 2		CO. 3		CO. 4	
		MONTH	CUM.	MONTH	CUM.	MONTH	CUM.	MONTH	CUM.
	SLUSHING								
1	LABOR - SUPERINTENDENTS								
2	CHIPPING								
3	ACID MAKING								
4	DIGESTERS								
5	BLOW-FITS								
6	SCREENS								
7	INSIDE								
8	MISCELLANEOUS								
9	TOTAL LABOR								
10	POWER - ELECTRIC								
11	WATER								
12	STEAM								
13	BELTING								
14	LUBRICANTS								
15	SUPPLIES								
16	REPAIRS LABOR								
17	MATERIAL								
18	REPLACEMENTS - LOSSES ETC.								
19	SUB-TOTAL								
20	DEPRECIATION								
21	TAXES								
22	INSURANCE								
23	MANUFACTURING BURDEN								
24									
25	TOTAL								
	DECKERING								
26	LABOR								
27	POWER - ELECTRIC								
28	WATER								
29	WIRES								
30	SUPPLIES								
31	REPAIRS LABOR								
32	MATERIAL								
33	REPLACEMENTS - LOSSES ETC								
34	TOTAL								
	LAPPING								
35	LABOR - WET MACHINES								
36	HYDRAULIC PRESSES								
37	PILING								
38	MISCELLANEOUS								
39	TOTAL LABOR								
40	POWER - ELECTRIC								
41	WATER								
42	WIRES								
43	MACHINE CLOTHING								
44	SUPPLIES								
45	REPAIRS LABOR								
46	MATERIAL								
47	REPLACEMENTS - LOSSES ETC.								
48									
49	TOTAL								
	STATISTICAL								
50	COAL - LBS PER TON OF SULPHITE								
51	" " " "								
52	STEAM - LBS PER TON OF SULPHITE								
53	" " " "								
54	SULPHUR - PER TON OF SULPHITE								
55	" " " "								
56	LIME - LBS PER TON OF SULPHITE								
57	" " " "								
58	LIMESTONE - LBS PER TON OF SULPHITE								
59	" " " "								
60	% ACTUAL PRODUCTION TO CAPACITY								
61	% OPERATING HOURS TO TOTAL HOURS								
62	% TOTAL SCREENINGS ARE COVERED								
63	NUMBER OF DIGESTED COOKS								
64	AVERAGE TIME PER COOK								

Figure 11-4

Steam
Comparative Statement of Conversion Costs
Per 1000 lbs delivered

Average cost based on 1000 lbs. Steam Delivered
MONTH CUM

		CO. 1		CO. 2		CO. 3		CO. 4	
		MONTH	CUM.	MONTH	CUM.	MONTH	CUM.	MONTH	CUM.
1	LABOR - SUPERINTENDENTS								
2	FIREMEN								
3	FIRE CLEANERS								
4	COAL HANDLING								
5	ASH HANDLING								
6	MISCELLANEOUS								
7	TOTAL LABOR								
8	COAL								
9	FUEL OIL								
10	REFUSE WOOD								
11	ELECTRIC STEAM								
12	LUBRICANTS								
13	SUPPLIES								
14	REPAIRS-LABOR								
15	MATERIAL								
16	REPLACEMENTS-LOSSES ETC								
17	POWER-ELECTRIC								
18	SUB-TOTAL								
19	DEPRECIATION								
20	TAXES								
21	INSURANCE								
22									
23									
24	MISCELLANEOUS								
25	COST PER 1000 LBS GENERATED								
26	BOILER HOUSE STEAM								
27	COST PER 1000 LBS DELIVERED								
	STEAM DISTRIBUTION								
28	1000 LBS. TO PAPER MILL								
29	1000 LBS. TO SULPHITE MILL								
30	OTHER USAGES								
31									
32	TOTAL DELIVERED								
33	USED IN BOILER HOUSE								
34	TOTAL 1000 LBS GENERATED FROM AND AT 212° F								
	STATISTICAL								
35	TONS COAL CONSUMED								
36	TONS REFUSE WOOD CONSUMED								
37	GALLONS FUEL OIL CONSUMED								
38	TOTAL EQUIVALENT TONS COAL CONSUMED								
39	LBS WATER EVAP PER LB OF COAL AS FIRED								
40	LBS STEAM GENERATED PER DOLLAR								

Figure 11-5
Statistical and Efficiency Reports
Paper Mill

MILL	Mach.	OPERATING HOURS: Schedule of	OPERATING HOURS: Actual	OPERATING HOURS: % Operating Hours	MILL LOSSES: Breakdowns %	MILL LOSSES: Power %	MILL LOSSES: Labor Stock %	MILL LOSSES: Total %	SPEED: Standard	SPEED: Actual Avg.	SPEED: Speed Efficiency %	TRIM: Capacity	TRIM: Actual Avg.	TRIM: % Trim Loss
2	1													
	2													
	3													
	4													
	Month													
3	1													
	2													
	Month													
4	1													
	2													
	Month													
5	2													
	3													
	4													
	5													
	6													
	7													
	8													
	9													
	Month													
6	1													
	2													
	3													
	4													
	5													
	Month													
7	1													
	2													
	Month													
8	Month													
9	1													
	2													
	3													
	4													
	Month													
10	1													
	2													
	Month													
11	1													
	2													
	3													
	4													
	Month													

Figure 11-6
News Print Service Bureau
Statistical and Efficiency Reports
Machine Equipment

MILL	MACH.	POUNDS OF PAPER									
		PER SQ. FT. OF WIRES		PER LB. OF JACKETS		PER LB. OF 1st. FELTS		PER LB. OF 2nd. FELTS		PER LB. OF 3rd. FELTS	
		MONTH	CUM	MONTH	CUM	MONTH	CUM	MONTH	CUM	MONTH	CUM
1	1										
	2										
	3										
	4										
	5										
	6										
	7										
	AVERAGE										
2	1										
	2										
	3										
	4										
	5										
	AVERAGE										
3	1										
	2										
	AVERAGE										
4	1										
	2										
	AVERAGE										
5	2										
	3										
	4										
	5										
	6										
	7										
	8										
	9										
	AVERAGE										
6	1										
	2										
	3										
	4										
	5										
	AVERAGE										
7	1										
	2										
	AVERAGE										
8	1										
9	1										
	2										
	3										
	4										
	AVERAGE										
10	1										
	2										
	AVERAGE										
11	1										
	2										
	3										
	AVERAGE										
12	1										
	2										
	3										
	4										
	5										
	6										
	7										
	8										
	AVERAGE										

Figure 11-7

Statistical and Efficiency Reports
Steam Plant

MONTH CUM

	CO. 1		CO. 2		CO. 3		CO. 4	
	MONTH	CUM.	MONTH	CUM.	MONTH	CUM.	MONTH	CUM.
1. Steam Pressure (Lbs. per Sq. In.)								
2. Temperature of Steam								
Degrees Superheat								
(a) Quality of Steam								
% Moisture								
3. Feedwater (a) Temperature Entering Boilers								
(b) Temperature Entering Economisers								
(c) Increased Temperature Due to Economisers								
4. Flue Gas (a) Temperature Leaving Boilers								
(b) Temperature Leaving Economisers								
(c) Decrease of Temperature due to Economisers								
5. % Moisture in Fuel (a) Coal								
(b) Wood								
6. Fuel Used (as fired) (a) Coal								
(b) Wood								
7. Fuel Used, (dry) (a) Coal								
(b) Wood (Equivalent Coal)								
(c) Fuel Oil (Equivalent Coal)								
8. Equivalent Dry Fuel Used (Total)								
9. Equivalent Dry Fuel Used per Sq. Ft. of Grate Surface per Hour								
10. Total Weight of Water Fed to Boilers								
11. Total Weight of Steam Generated								
12. Percent Loss in Steam Generation								
13. Apparent Evaporation per Lb. of Equivalent Dry Fuel Used								
14. Factor of Evaporation for Water Entering Economisers								
15. Total Equivalent Evaporation from and at 212°								
16. Equivalent Evap from and at 212° per Lb. Equiv. Dry Fuel Used								
17. Equivalent Evaporation from and at 212° per 10,000 B. T. U.								
18. Equivalent Evap. from and at 212° per Lb. of Combustible								
19. Equivalent Evaporation per hour per Sq. Ft. of heating Surface								
20. Boiler H. P. Hours (a) Rated								
(b) Developed								
21. PERCENT RATING DEVELOPED								
22. EFFICIENCY OF BOILER, FURNACE, AND GRATE								
23. EFFICIENCY OF PLANT WITH ECONOMISERS								
24. FINAL COST ANALYSIS:								
(a) Moisture								
(b) Volatile Matter								
(c) Fixed Carbon								
(d) Ash								
B. T. U. Per Lb. (as fired)								
25. Combustible in Ash %								

summary sheet in one color, yellow or blue, as the case may be, and the other sheets in black figures for the current period and red figures for the cumulative statistics. *(Ed. Note: These summary sheets are not shown in the reprinted article.)*

These reports go out each month as quickly as we can get them together for the preceding month. Ordinarily, they go out thirty or thirty-five days after the close of the month. It takes a good while to get them together, because they come from almost all over North America.

How Reports Are Used

The question may be raised as to what is done with these reports. We have a good many interesting discussions at our meeting of accountants. We have meetings of the cost accountants and engineers of the members two or three times a year. At these meetings methods of making reports and methods of using reports are most thoroughly discussed. We have had the question raised a good many times as to what is the use of all this after we have gone to the trouble and expense of preparing and sending out and getting back these reports. We are noticing, as time goes on, a most encouraging increase in the use of these reports and we are steadily getting additional companies to use our reports. Mind you, there is nothing compulsory about our work and never has been from the beginning of our Association. A company may be a member of the organization and may not contribute to these reports in any way, and in that case it will not get them. If it chooses to put its own accounting system on a standard basis so it has a common denominator, it then has the privilege of getting these reports if it wants to; but to repeat, there is no compulsion. As stated, we are getting an increasing number of companies who are participating in this exchange. We recently ran into a very interesting example; one of our men happened to go to a mill and stayed a couple of days and he wrote in about it. As the result of studies that have been started from these reports of ours, one well-known company is now saving $1.50 per ton on all the coal it is using, and there is a large amount of coal used at these mills. What it saves in one year would pay its dues to the organization for a long period of time. Staff meetings are held by some companies as soon as these reports are received, and the man whose costs of operating are above the line is called on the carpet and asked to tell why.

To sum up, we believe that every business man has the right to know all the essential facts in connection with the production and distribution of his product, but he has neither the moral nor the legal right, through agreement with his competitors, to endeavor to bring about an artificial condition beneficial to himself and hurtful to the public. That sums up as clearly as we can do it in our own case, our conception of how work of this kind must be carried on.

The cost accountant has a great function to perform and a great opportunity for service in the ascertainment of the economic facts essential to sound business and industry. On our part we have received a great deal of benefit from meetings of this organization individually. We are glad to be with you, you are helping us and we hope that occasionally we can help you.

(12) "Indirect Labor," February 15, 1924, Bulletin, Vol. 5, No. 11, Harry J. Ostlund, University of Minnesota

Indirect Labor [1]

Perhaps there is no other single item watched as carefully by a manufacturer as is labor. In many plants it is the largest single item; also in many cases it is the item least standardized. Its quality is not uniform, varying greatly from time to time and place to place, depending on the condition of the labor market; so that a day's work does not by any means represent the same thing at all times. Any means, therefore, by which a manufacturer can bring labor more fully under his administrative control is to be welcomed and tested for its merits.

Of all the labor control problems that a manager must face in his plant, perhaps that of adequate control of his indirect labor is the most perplexing. It appears from a general view of the situation as we find it in many manufacturing plants that one of the first things that is necessary is to get the problem out into the light where we can get a square look at it, and then to study its fundamentals with a view to discovering what we can of the general principles that may be applied. After that comes the specific, and not by any means always the easiest, part of the task, namely, that of applying these general principles to the actual complex of conditions that are to be found in the given case.

Meaning of Indirect Labor

Perhaps, however, we should attempt to define just what we mean by the terms direct labor and indirect labor. There are two bases for making the distinction between the terms. The first is what may be called the physical basis. That is, direct labor is that which is applied physically directly to the product itself either by hand or through the operation of a machine which is being used on the product. Indirect labor then becomes all that labor in a factory which is not physically applied directly to the product. This includes superintendents, foremen, clerical assistants, sweepers in productive departments, and all help of whatever sort in the auxiliary or service departments.

However, it is soon found that for cost purposes the above distinction is not wholly adequate, since there is much labor directly applied to the product, even in plants working on the order system, which, however, cannot be practically so charged. Instances of this sort are labor directly performed on

[1]This article is based on an address delivered before the Twin Cities Chapter of the National Association of Cost Accountants.

several short or small jobs, tasks requiring only a touch on each job on the part of its laborer, operations where the handling of the work is such that orders need not be identified as the work is performed. Here, though the labor may be physically direct, it becomes expedient to charge it indirectly. Hence there is the second basis for distinction between direct and indirect labor, namely, this: direct labor is that which is directly *charged* against specific lots or units of the product, while indirect labor is that which is not directly so charged. It will be perceived, therefore, that this is the only definition that is practicable for costing purposes since the other, important as it may be as a managerial distinction, cannot be expressed fully and practically in terms of costs. It remains to be stated, however, that the proportion of physically direct labor in any one plant that cannot be directly charged is probably usually small and of such a nature that its disposition will not be deeply hidden from view.

It is also understood that in this article we are dealing, unless mention is made to the contrary, only with indirect labor as carried on in connection with the productive functions of a business and excluding administrative and selling labor.

Indirect Labor Should Not Be Unproductive

We can now make one other statement concerning terminology. Sometimes direct and indirect labor are called respectively productive and non-productive labor; and in the minds of some the latter term has come to mean unproductive. So far as this use of terms may have led to erroneous concepts, it is unfortunate. But if the statements made earlier are true, namely that the development of industrial technique has led to a larger proportion of indirect labor in industry, then it would appear that indirect labor is perhaps really not so unproductive after all. In fact the increased use of machinery and the new administrative tools of management have resulted in making the net productiveness of the labor force, direct and indirect together, greater than when the percentage of direct labor was higher than it is now. Many a concern has found its net productivity per laborer increased as a result of no other change than the addition of some more indirect labor in the form of storekeeper, a planning department, cost clerks, internal transportation help,and others that might be mentioned, thus facilitating the work of the direct laborers or leaving them free to apply all of their time to their immediate tasks and relieving them of such other tasks as keeping their own time, looking after their own tools, getting their own supplies, and the like.

It is interesting to note that as the technique of production has been developed through the last century, indirect labor has come to play an increasingly important part in manufacture. The simpler methods of production in the past consisted almost entirely of labor applied directly to the product, while as machinery has come to play a more predominant part in industry, more and more of the former direct workers have been called upon to perform the various services that are necessary in order to facilitate the work of those who are directly employed upon the product. Furthermore, as a plant becomes more and more highly organized and specialization develops among its workers, the more necessary are the services of auxiliary departments for the maintenance of plant, handling of stores, accounting for time and production, inspection, and the like.

Normal Ratios Tend to Develop

It is true, however, that in any particular plant in which routines and methods have been pretty well established, there is a tendency for normal proportions to be established between direct labor and indirect labor. This observed fact has led many manufacturers to place a great deal of emphasis on the maintenance of the ratio, any departure, especially in the way of increased indirect labor, being regarded as unfavorable. But this significance should not be over emphasized as an indicator by itself. An increase in the proportion of indirect labor cost may be altogether favorable; especially is this true if in the case of direct labor working under a bonus system, the efficiency should be increased, when of course the added bonus would appear, under accounting methods used by most concerns, as an addition to the indirect labor cost. Then also as pointed out above any substantial improvement in processes or methods is likely to change the ratio by increasing indirect labor relatively. In other words, the fact that there is a change in the ratio of indirect labor to direct labor means very little if anything until the cause for that ratio be shown to determine whether the change is detrimental or beneficial.

On the other hand it is also true that under some conditions an increase in this ratio may represent a situation that should be remedied if possible. Particularly is this true when a plant is running below normal capacity. Direct labor is frequently the easiest to drop. Service departments have to be run anyway. Most of the clerical force and practically all of the supervision must be kept even under low capacity operation. All of this tends to increase the ratio of indirect labor to direct labor and it may in such cases become a fairly reliable index of inefficiency due to low capacity operation.

Indirect Labor Needs Careful Scrutiny

There are several reasons, however, why indirect labor should be given special attention by the plant manager. In the first place it does not stand out alone in the final reports as a separate item but appears as a part of that complex composite known as burden. Even when it does have a place in the departmental expense and burden reports, the item for each department frequently so lacks the element of homogeneity as to impair greatly its use as an index of efficient control.

In the second place indirect labor is largely unstandardized. That is to say in most cases there is no means of saying just what performance ought to be since often it is difficult to measure performance at all. An example of this is repair and maintenance labor working at odd jobs about the plant—perhaps no two jobs alike or performed under like conditions.

Growing out of these circumstances of lack of standardization and complexity of treatment there has resulted a condition for which management is largely to blame, namely, that almost the only attention given to indirect labor in many shops is to the aggregate rather than to the types of service it performs. Consequently, many indirect departments are woefully inefficient, in spite of the fact that management is trying to "hold down the percentage."

Forms That Indirect Labor May Take

Any service that the cost department can render in the control of indirect labor must be based upon the proper analysis of it and upon a recognition of the vast variety of different forms that it may take. Accepting the definition that indirect labor includes all labor that is not charged directly to individual units or lots of the product, we may include nearly all indirect labor in one of the following groups, some of which have already been incidentally mentioned.

There are two general forms of indirect labor charges. The first is where all the pay of the laborer for the given period is made an indirect labor charge, and the second is where the worker's pay for a given time is divided between direct and indirect costs.

Taking the first general class of indirect charges we have first foremen, time and dispatch clerks, sweepers, and other workers in manufacturing departments whose efforts are not applied directly to the product.

There is also labor applied directly to the product but applied in such a way as to make its direct charging impracticable, such as work on a series of small lots, or in departments where various lots or orders cannot profitably be distinguished as might happen in the dipping room of a paint shop where identity of orders makes little difference so long as the parts are dipped in the right tank. The same is true later while the goods are handled in the drying or baking ovens.

Then there is all labor in the various service or auxiliary departments of a plant, such as power, store room, planning department, general factory office and others.

In the case of plants using process systems all the labor is treated as indirect so far as concerns its manner of charging; that is to say, little attempt is made in analyzing departmental costs to distinguish between the different ways in which the labor is used.

Perhaps one of the most important of the indirect labor items to watch in many shops is that of idle time of laborers, direct and indirect. It is not always that work can be planned and expedited in such a way that no workman will ever have to wait for something to do. Delayed tools or materials, breakdowns, lack of instructions, and many other things frequently cause longer or shorter delays during which workmen, through no fault of their own, have to be idle. If such items are at all considerable, it is evident that they should be charged to a departmental idle time account so that they can be properly watched and analyzed for the purpose of study and possible elimination.

Then there are the numerous cases where a part of the total wage paid direct workers becomes an indirect labor charge. This is generally the situation under various bonus and premium plans of wage payment where it is found expedient to charge the product at a standard rate for labor and to charge the premium to the departmental burden account on the theory that the effect of the bonus is to reduce the burden cost per unit of the product, and that therefore it is properly an offset against this reduction.

Similar to the above is a group bonus paid in cases where it is difficult or impracticable to calculate individual bonuses. Such bonuses frequently apply to the foreman also.

Another element of labor cost chargeable to burden under some circumstances is extra pay for overtime on the part of direct workers. Without attempting to treat this case exhaustively, it may be said that if the overtime work is caused by a general rush of orders and if it is only temporary, the extra overtime pay can properly become a burden charge, whereas if overtime is worked in order to put out a particular rush order, the total cost of direct labor applied can very properly be charged to that order. In any case the final decision as to treatment of the charge would require a consideration of how other burden charges involved are to be treated, but this subject is a little beyond the scope of the present article.

Frequently, it becomes necessary to charge to burden a part of the wages of a worker who has been transferred temporarily from one department or line of work to another in which the rate of pay is lower than that drawn by the worker so transferred. It is frequently a question as to where this differential charge is to be placed, whether in the department whence the help came, the one to which it was transferred, or to the general factory burden. We need not refer to all the possible cases that might arise each requiring its own peculiar solution, any further than to say that under those circumstances where it is simply a matter of keeping laborers employed during a slack period the charge should be made to general overhead. When the transfer is due to a temporary but urgent demand from the department using the help, the charge can well be made to that department's overhead directly, while if the transfer is necessitated by some disorganization in the department where the workers belong, it should itself bear all the burden cost that is occasioned.

Often also a situation arises where new workers who will eventually go on a piece rate are guaranteed a minimum day rate. In those cases where the output of the worker is not sufficient at the piece rate to cover his guaranteed wage, it is customary to charge the difference to a burden account.

Other instances of indirect labor charges might easily be found, but these are sufficient to illustrate the varied phases of the problem and to indicate how inadequate must be the attempt to control indirect labor as if it were a homogeneous whole.

Control Paramount to Mere Costing

It must be clear by this time that the major problem of the plant manager, so far as his indirect labor is concerned, is that of its adequate control. This problem is paramount to that of mere costing. In fact it is the writer's opinion that if a good control system is established in the plant, reasonably correct unit costs will follow as a natural result, while a system that merely gives unit costs as its primary object does not necessarily provide an adequate means of managerial control.

We are thus confronted with the whole problem of standards of performance and records by means of which to check that performance.

As mentioned before, indirect labor does not readily lend itself to standardization of its performance. It is difficult to express it in terms of output. Examples of this difficulty are manifold. What definite unit standards of output can be assigned to the maintenance department, or to the stores department as to some of the clerical help, or to many foremen? It is next to impossible so far as individuals are concerned, and more particularly is this true in the small plant where division of labor and the consequent standardization of activities usually cannot be carried so far as they may be in the larger plants.

However, if individual standards cannot be set, sometimes group standards may be. The bases of these group standards may be either scientific, that is built on engineering calculations and time studies, or they may be experiential, that is, they may develop out of the general experience in the plant as indicated by its records compared from time to time. The latter are about the only means of building up standards of indirect expense at the command of the average plant.

Functional Classification Desirable

But any setting of group standards will necessitate the proper sort of grouping or departmentalization. Such grouping, therefore, should be done with the principle in mind of throwing together all sets of homogeneous or like activities and of not combining unlike activities. For instance, in a plant large enough to have several individuals occupied with the internal transportation, this forms a distinct type of activity which for the purpose of adequate control cannot well be split up and put under the several departmental foremen and be made a departmental cost, but which should be controlled and costed as a group, proper distribution being made to operating departments so far as possible on the basis of service rendered. Other instances are inspection and clerical work such as that of time clerks. While the work may have to be carried out in the operating departments and immediately, in some instances, under the supervision of the departmental foremen, the manner in which the work is done, the forms that are used and the disposition of the records that they construct should be controlled by one department of the factory office, under the comptroller if there is one, and the work should be costed separately to indicate just what this performance means to the management in the way of expense. Unless activities of a similar nature are thus grouped it must be evident that there can be adequate control of certain functions in the plant only with great difficulty. So far as possible departmentalization and costing should conform to the activities within the plant.

The illustrations indicate an attempt at what is generally known as functional classification of activities within the plant and the consequent attempt at a functional classification of accounts. A word of caution, however, is necessary at this point. Not all plants are large enough to permit of this clear cut classification of activities and consequently various adjustments must be made to keep operating and accounting systems as simple as possible. But in attempting this adaptation in the interests of simplicity at least one general principle ought to be kept in mind—every individual who has the administration of indirect labor under his control should be held fully responsible for its effective use and the records of the plant should show clearly just how well he meets that responsibility. This means that the classification of indirect labor accounts may have to be based upon the responsible supervision under which indirect laborers work rather than purely on the nature of the activities of the indirect laborers. However, there should always be an attempt to so organize the labor force that there will be a proper control of the labor and an adequate and sensible record of its performance.

Another caution might well be mentioned at this point. It often happens that an accountant or industrial engineer in installing a system for a plant keeps in mind more clearly established accounting and organization principles than he does the specific problems of the manufacturer whom he is supposed to serve. This is one of the factors that has resulted in very short life for many otherwise very good systems. They were perfect in isolation but useless in application; in fact many have proved an actual hindrance to efficiency. The point is that in accounting for indirect labor as well as for other burden costs, the classification and procedure should be made to conform to the situation actually prevailing in the plant.

The chart (see Figure 12-1) is intended merely to suggest a possible means of analyzing, in a functional way, the labor actually applied in the several operating and service departments. The totals obtained in the extreme right hand column are usually not necessary for purposes of burden distribution of costing but they may serve a very useful purpose in indicating the labor cost of the several functions in a plant. It is evident that it can readily be modified or expanded to meet the needs of any concern to which it applies at all. Also, it may be pointed out, supplies used can be analyzed in the same way if found expedient.

Figure 12-1

SUGGESTED TABULAR ANALYSIS FOR
CONTROL OF FACTORY LABOR

	SERVICE DEPARTMENTS							OPERATING DEPTS.				TOTAL
	Stores	Power	Tool Crib	Plant Maint.	Inspection	Factory Office		Dept. A	Dept. B	Dept. C		
Foremen and Assistants												
Time and Dispatch Clerks												
Genl. Deptl. Indirect Labor												
Cleaners, Sweepers, etc.												
Internal Transport												
Inspection												
Idle Time												
Direct Labor Bonus												
Total Indirect Labor												
Direct Labor												
Total Labor												

(13) "Methods of Supplying Cost Information to Foremen," June 1, 1924, Bulletin, Vol. 5, No. 18, Hugo Diemer, Director of Industrial Courses, LaSalle Extension University

Hugo Diemer, the author of this publication, has had a wide experience. He has been factory superintendent, production manager, and personnel superintendent, having served such companies as the National Motor Vehicle Co., the Goodman Manufacturing Co., and the Winchester Repeating Arms Co. He has been Professor of Mechanical Engineering and Industrial Engineering, and director of shops and laboratories at Michigan Agricultural College, the University of Kansas, and the Pennsylvania State College. During the war he served as Commanding Officer at the U. S. Cartridge Co. and later on the staff of the Commanding Officer at the Bethlehem Steel Co. At the present time he is Director of Industrial Courses for LaSalle Extension University, where he is also consulting Mechanical Engineer and adviser on management questions.

Methods of Supplying Cost Information to Foremen

The question may well be asked: To what extent are cost records actually brought to the attention of foremen at the present time? Our experience with over 1,000 foremen in 192 separate kinds of industry shows that in not over 10 per cent of the cases are cost records brought to the foreman's attention at all. In most of the smaller businesses, the management keeps cost data closely guarded and usually does not want the foreman to know what profit is being made. We recognize that it is very poor policy to do this, but we must look the facts in the face.

Most managers can be sold on the idea of the advantage of giving the foreman certain comparative cost data, even if they do not want to have him get total costs. Many managers feel that the foremen who are not completely sold on the idea of their being a part of the management will distribute cost information in the shop in such a way as to wreck the whole institution. This does not prove to be the case. However, if the fear exists, comparative cost data can still be given out in terms of percentages of increase or decrease. These percentages can be broken down by operations without disclosing the actual comparative figures. This procedure, of course, is advocated merely as a temporary expedient until such time as the management and foremen have complete confidence in each other and co-operate properly.

What Kind of Records May Safely Be Given to Foremen?

In most records that are in any sense of the word "modern" the following six classes of expenditures are found:

1. Direct labor

2. Direct material
3. Departmental overhead which is divided into
   (a) Departmental indirect labor
   (b) Departmental indirect material
   (c) Departmental service and rental charges. This group includes the items which it may fairly be assumed are controlled by foremen.
4. General shop overhead not controllable by departments.
5. Administrative and commercial overhead.
6. Sales expense.

Direct Labor

Foremen are usually irritated and justly so when cost records of direct labor are brought to them a considerable time after the labor has been performed and the question is asked "Why did this job take so long, or take so much time when it only took so long or cost so much on previous occasions?" The foreman's answer in such cases is always the statement that he cannot do anything with post-mortems, that the time to have taken this matter up was when the job was going through. One way to forestall this answer is to make it necessary for the foreman to initial or punch every work-ticket at the time it is turned in. If there has been any attempt at standardization, this work-ticket should contain for the information and guidance of the foreman and operative, data as to piece-rate, bonus or premium rate, time allowance, or predetermined estimate of time or direct-labor cost. Under this procedure, the foreman cannot side-step his responsibility for checking the actual performance against the standard and thus knowing why the job took too long.

Where there is a system of departmental dispatch boards on which each day's schedule of jobs ahead is posted by means of some visible index plan, it is the duty of a foreman to check up each operative's schedule for the day against the operative's progress from time to time during the day. Then he can readily see when a man is falling behind his schedule. The foreman's obvious duty in such cases is to discover the interferences and remove them, if possible.

In order to make such a dispatch board or visible index effective, it is necessary to schedule individual workmen and machines by separate days, and not merely to file jobs ahead in sequence. This latter procedure may be entirely satisfactory from a standpoint of central scheduling, but a foreman who is really controlling his production needs to make definite assignments of jobs to each man in advance of operations.

In order that a foreman may do his most effective work in preventing too much direct labor at the source, it is important that the work-ticket which he approves for the changing of jobs and the same ticket, or whatever other ticket may be used on the dispatch board, be designed in such a manner as to make it easy instead of difficult for the foreman to get just the information he needs. In this connection it should be borne in mind that the accounting type of mind adapts itself much more easily to the use of abbreviations in the form of symbols and numbers, than does the foreman's type of mind. In the long run, it pays to translate the symbols and numbers into a sufficient number of plain English words so that there will be no misunderstanding. For example, such information as the name of part and name of operation should be supplied for the purpose of more effective cost control by the foreman. Symbols and numbers should be used, however, for greater ease in sorting and classification of cost data.

Direct Material

The best way to help the foreman exercise cost control of direct material is to provide for every shop order that he gets, the accompanying material orders written in advance, with the proper numbers, symbols, and names inserted. In most cases, these material orders or store-room requisitions will be forwarded only to the foreman in the department which performs the first operation on the job. A further refinement, as some would term it, but a method which I would rather designate as a further check on material consumption, is the use of the "move material" slip, so-called. In many concerns the central stores department or the production department has control over inter-departmental movements of material. Where this is the case move material slips are written out in advance for all inter-departmental movements of material. Everything is filled out on these slips, excepting the number received, number completed, number rejected and number moved to next operation. These figures are left for the foreman to fill in. In this way, the foreman records his knowledge of and responsibility for any shortages, breakages or rejections. In a flow-type of industry, the move material ticket has its counterpart in the records of automatic scales, or other measuring devices.

Departmental Indirect Labor

The foreman should sign or punch all time-tickets or work-tickets of men engaged in performing indirect labor in his department. He should receive a resumé of the totals of these indirect labor orders for his department, covering every cost period. Having approved the tickets from which the resumé is made up, he has no alibi as to his responsibility. Here again, the kind of work should be stated in plain English as is the case also on the direct tickets as well as the proper symbol or number. In many cases, it will pay to have for each department a special indirect-labor ticket on the back of which are listed the numbers and definitions of all of the indirect-labor orders to be used in that department. The reason for this feature is that the assignment of work of this sort cannot pass through a central planning or production department, since it is usually made by the foreman himself and he, or his clerk, if he has one, usually fills in the face of this sort of work-ticket roughly in pencil.

Departmental Indirect Material

The same difficulties which make it impracticable for a central planning or production department to assign work to indirect labor apply also in the case of the authorization of the consumption of departmental indirect material. When the Cost Department sends each foreman a statement for the cost period, covering departmental indirect material costs, his attention should be called to anything that looks like extravagance in consumption of supplies, such as waste or too great breakage or too early discarding of drills, files, etc. The original papers filled out when these costs arose are usually clipped to such a statement.

Departmental Service and Rental Charges

The method employed in apportioning to each department its fair quota of heat, light and power charges, depreciation, taxes, insurance, etc., should be openly and clearly set forth, preferably in the statement of such costs itself. The statement can be printed in such a manner that all that need be entered for each department are certain figures indicating the percentage of the total figures or other basis on which that department is charged, such as square feet of floor space, cubic feet of space, etc. Here, again I advocate the use of plain English rather than symbols and numbers in preparing the statement. I know a case where a Personnel Manager began to investigate the expenses charged to his department under certain symbols. He noted that a certain symbol meant outside hospital expenses. He saw that from $2,000 to $5,000 a month was charged up against that symbol. On investigation he discovered that no accident had occurred which would have justified the expenses charged to this account. The Accounting Department referred the Personnel Manager to the Treasurer who told him that this account was simply a dumping place to conceal such expenses as bribery, detective service, etc. This sort of deception, while it might conceivably be practiced on a Personnel Superintendent without disastrous results, would be fatal to the continuance of any confidence in the Accounting Department, if practiced on a foreman.

Administrative and Commercial Overhead

It is not wise as a rule to inform the foremen about sales expenses without paving the way by a carefully prepared series of talks and charts, giving them fundamental instruction in general industrial economics and the specific economics of the industry in which they are working. They can scarcely be expected to acquire this information on their own initiative. On the other hand, if they are fully informed as to the nature of overhead, and the necessity for it, they gradually begin to assume the attitude and viewpoint of the business man. I recall how this change in attitude took place in a plant manufacturing shot-guns, where the direct labor represented about one-seventh of the selling price; material cost, about two-sevenths; and the total of shop overhead, administrative overhead, and sales expenses about four-sevenths. When the foremen were given figures as to the cost of catalogs, instruction books, packages, freight, interest on consigned goods, rentals or warehouses, traveling expenses, commissions, etc., in gross amounts and translated into percentages, their entire attitude and outlook changed.

Cost Accounts Versus Cost Records

Thus far, only the records of original entry which go to make up cost accounts have been discussed. If we use the term accounts in its technically correct meaning as consisting of debits and credits, we still have to consider the accounting aspect of cost records. It is only the rare and exceptional foreman who has studied bookkeeping and can be expected to make "head or tail" out of cost statements presented in accounting form.

There are certain cost accounts or features of cost accounts in accounting form, however, which when selected should be brought to the foreman's attention. These features are the following: 1. Raw materials in store-room; 2. Materials in progress; 3. Finished parts or groups of parts awaiting assembly; and 4. Comparison of money spent during a cost period and money received.

Taking the foregoing items separately, let us first consider the *raw materials* or other un-issued materials in the store-room. In some companies, the foreman has nothing to say with regard to the procurement of these materials. In other companies, his word or requisition is directly responsible for the procurement of such materials. In any event, his co-operative interest should be secured in holding down the investment in stores to a practical minimum, even though the majority of materials in the store-room may be allotted or apportioned to prospective production orders. A discussion by the Purchasing Agent and the head of the Stores Department or a conference between the Production Department and these officials, at which the leading foremen are present, in which the necessary time under existing conditions which elapses between the placing of orders and their delivery is made known, will help to keep down unnecessary investment in stores.

With regard to *materials in progress,* we will always find that certain foremen believe in making a great display of a large amount of material in their department, since it makes the workmen think there is lots of work ahead, and impresses other officials passing through the department with the industry and importance of that department. Here again, it is worth while to acquaint a foreman with the desirability of quick turn-over. Since we have developed a modern method of production control, there are many businesses which were satisfied ten years ago with one or one and one-half turnovers of their capital in a year, but today, however, are making three or four turnovers of their capital.

The old time foreman liked to look on the store-room and his own pile of partially-worked materials, as well, as an inexhaustible supply for all kinds of jobs which, without any definite planning or scheduling, he could assign to any workman who happened to run out of a job. This condition is incompatible with modern production methods and competition.

In an assembling industry, it is exceedingly important that the flow of *parts or group of parts awaiting assembly* be regulated in such a way as to make the most effective use of the assembler's time. Hence, it is important that a periodic check be made on this flow and its regulation. A capable Cost Department can devise reports that will furnish the basis for the necessary regulation.

There is hardly any business in which the seasonal fluctuations of income and expenditures do not play an important part. The foreman, Purchasing Agent, the Stores Department and the Sales Department can all render effective co-operation in reducing these fluctuations in order to make possible a minimum of borrowing and a maximum of cash discounts. This information in regard to the *comparison of money spent and received* during a period when put in graphical form, is readily understood and appreciated by the more intelligent type of foreman.

Characteristics of Foremen

Many foremen have risen from the ranks with very little formal schooling. Such men are apt to be skeptical regarding educational ventures of any kind. Their motto is "Practice makes perfect." As a class they do not realize that whenever they endeavor to find a reason for doing a certain thing — to get the "why" behind it — they are searching for theory. The dominant characteristics of any group of foremen are likely to be as follows:

1. They have mature minds.
2. They are inclined to scoff at theory.
3. They have well-established habits.
4. They are largely "self-made" men.
5. They are self-confident and of the "show me" type.
6. They are usually not entirely open-minded.

Figure 13-1

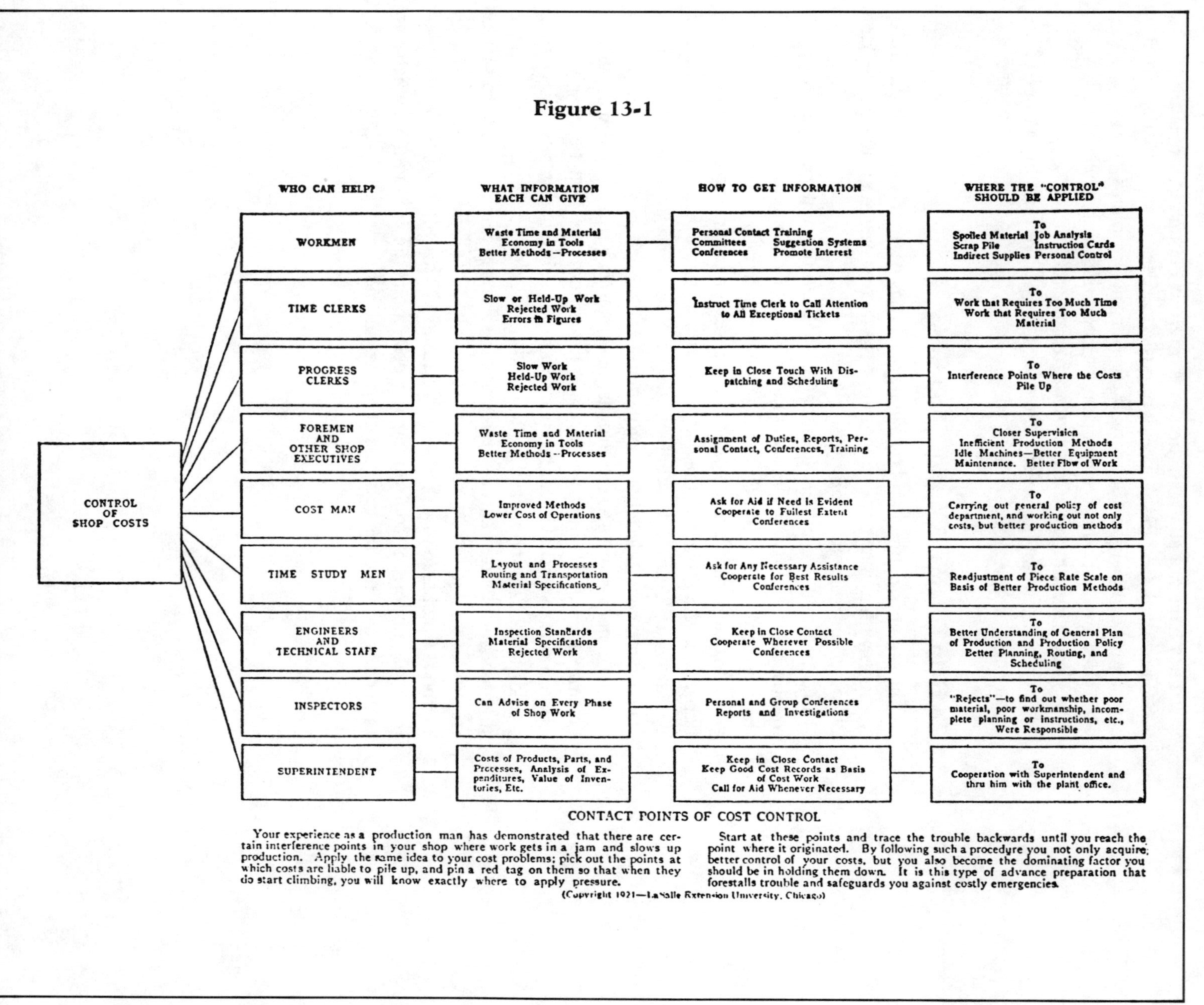
CONTROL OF SHOP COSTS
WHO CAN HELP?
WHAT INFORMATION EACH CAN GIVE
HOW TO GET INFORMATION
WHERE THE "CONTROL" SHOULD BE APPLIED
WORKMEN
Waste Time and Material Economy in Tools Better Methods—Processes
Personal Contact Training Committees Suggestion Systems Conferences Promote Interest
To Spoiled Material Job Analysis Scrap Pile Instruction Cards Indirect Supplies Personal Control
TIME CLERKS
Slow or Held-Up Work Rejected Work Errors in Figures
Instruct Time Clerk to Call Attention to All Exceptional Tickets
To Work that Requires Too Much Time Work that Requires Too Much Material
PROGRESS CLERKS
Slow Work Held-Up Work Rejected Work
Keep in Close Touch With Dispatching and Scheduling
To Interference Points Where the Costs Pile Up
FOREMEN AND OTHER SHOP EXECUTIVES
Waste Time and Material Economy in Tools Better Methods—Processes
Assignment of Duties, Reports, Personal Contact, Conferences, Training
To Closer Supervision Inefficient Production Methods Idle Machines—Better Equipment Maintenance. Better Flow of Work
COST MAN
Improved Methods Lower Cost of Operations
Ask for Aid if Need Is Evident Cooperate to Fullest Extent Conferences
To Carrying out general policy of cost department, and working out not only costs, but better production methods
TIME STUDY MEN
Layout and Processes Routing and Transportation Material Specifications
Ask for Any Necessary Assistance Cooperate for Best Results Conferences
To Readjustment of Piece Rate Scale on Basis of Better Production Methods
ENGINEERS AND TECHNICAL STAFF
Inspection Standards Material Specifications Rejected Work
Keep in Close Contact Cooperate Wherever Possible Conferences
To Better Understanding of General Plan of Production and Production Policy Better Planning, Routing, and Scheduling
INSPECTORS
Can Advise on Every Phase of Shop Work
Personal and Group Conferences Reports and Investigations
To "Rejects"—to find out whether poor material, poor workmanship, incomplete planning or instructions, etc., Were Responsible
SUPERINTENDENT
Costs of Products, Parts, and Processes, Analysis of Expenditures, Value of Inventories, Etc.
Keep in Close Contact Keep Good Cost Records as Basis of Cost Work Call for Aid Whenever Necessary
To Cooperation with Superintendent and thru him with the plant office.
CONTACT POINTS OF COST CONTROL
Your experience as a production man has demonstrated that there are certain interference points in your shop where work gets in a jam and slows up production. Apply the same idea to your cost problems; pick out the points at which costs are liable to pile up, and pin a red tag on them so that when they do start climbing, you will know exactly where to apply pressure.
Start at these points and trace the trouble backwards until you reach the point where it originated. By following such a procedure you not only acquire better control of your costs, but you also become the dominating factor you should be in holding them down. It is this type of advance preparation that forestalls trouble and safeguards you against costly emergencies.
(Copyright 1921—LaSalle Extension University, Chicago)

7. They have not analyzed their jobs carefully enough in some cases.
8. They think best in the face of opposition.
9. They keenly enjoy discussing their everyday problems.
10. They are cautious of encroachment upon their authority.
11. They have a high regard for the square deal.
12. They are willing to co-operate well if they have faith in the person in charge of any proposition.

To Help Foremen Control Shop Costs

The accompanying chart (see Figure 13-1) has been prepared for the use of foremen with a view to helping them help themselves in exercising the kind of cost control of which they are capable.

In conclusion it may be stated that it has been the writer's experience that in most cases, insufficient information as to costs is brought to the attention of the foreman. It is recommended that the foreman be systematically informed as to his departmental costs, covering direct labor, direct material and departmental overhead, the latter including departmental indirect labor, departmental indirect material and departmental service and rental charges. It is also recommended that the foreman be informed as to the periodic status of raw materials in the store-rooms, materials in process, finished parts or groups of parts awaiting assembly, and furthermore, that he be given an opportunity to discuss in conference cost reports supplied to him. I have tried to indicate the importance of understanding the characteristics of the average foreman and the necessity of presenting cost data to him in such form that he can understand it and be encouraged to use it in day-by-day control of costs by methods suitable to his capacity and authority. This whole question is one of the most important confronting the cost man, the solution of which can materially advance the progress of American industry.

(14) "Co-operation Between the Comptroller and the Engineer," November 15, 1924, Bulletin, Vol. 6, No. 6, Major J. W. Swaren

Publication Department Note

Events haven't happened in the life of the subject of this sketch. That is why after investigating the joys of working for many and varied concerns, he began consulting work in San Francisco, California, in 1909. His hobby was investigation for investors. He never achieved popularity with promoters. Perhaps this was occasioned by reason of the fact that no company, the purchase of whose stock he recommended has ever succumbed, or defaulted on its obligations.

In 1917 he joined up with the "big show" and after leaving the hospital in 1919 was Sales Manager for the Division Company of Dayton, Ohio, and New York Manager for the Merril Company of San Francisco.

But early in 1922, the Government couldn't collect enough income taxes so he was called into the Income Tax Unit as an engineer. Late in 1923, one of the Directors of this Association enticed him into private practice once more. And that is how it came about the Cleveland Chapter was told that the Engineer isn't such a bad chap after all.

Co-operation Between the Comptroller and the Engineer

For the fullest measure of co-operation between the comptroller and the engineer knowledge of the point of view of each on the part of the other is necessary. Let us consider somewhat the respective points of view of the comptroller and the engineer.

Accounts, obviously, are the bases of the work of the comptroller. And accounting is primarily historical. An event occurs, and it is recorded in the books of account by figures representing dollars and cents. From the records of what has happened, the comptroller endeavors to direct the financial relations of the company, and to forecast its financial future. This is the historical method.

But I am speaking to comptrollers and all of you are more familiar with this point of view than I.

It is my desire then to present to you the point of view of the engineer.

Engineering is based primarily on visualization. The training of the engineer is intended to acquaint him with the fundamental laws of nature and to enable him to reduce these to mathematical formulae, and by combinations, to visualize the project in hand. The engineer uses experience and records as a check against his visualization. And if his visualization stands the test of mathematical logic, he discards experience and proceeds on the bases of his computations. Here is encountered one point of contact between the comptroller and the engineer that requires a delicate touch to avoid friction. Suppose an appropriation is included in the budget for a construction job embodying advances into new or semi-explored territory of engineering and that it has been subjected to every theoretical and mathematical test. It may have been checked by the judgment of experience. But suppose the costs overrun. As to the reason it may be stated first that there are limits to the skill of artisans in interpreting the visualization of the engineer. Then there are limits to the stresses that may be withstood when materials are subjected to new and unusual conditions. The engineer finds excuses for his creation. The comptroller sees the overrun appropriation. Neither quite grasps the other's point of view as to the reasons for the overrun appropriation.

That one may gain an insight into the engineer's point of view, let us examine the method by which he approaches his task. Incidentally, it will disclose an important point of contact for co-operation — a co-operation that will save your company, and in fact, any company, money today, and more money in the future; and probably labor for both the comptroller's force and the engineering department.

Phases of Engineering Jobs

All engineering jobs, whether they be the conception and completion of a major project, such as a railway terminal, or a power plant, or merely a slight change in some operating method, comprise three distinct phases.

The first, and most important, is the assembling of all data pertinent to the task in contemplation. Please note the expression used — all data pertinent. This requires a rare perception of the essentials. It requires a sound knowledge of fundamental science and a consumate skill in coordination. And if the economics of the situation are to be clearly conserved, it requires access to accurate, distinct, and "engineeringly" intelligent cost records. With these factors in coordination, the decision, which is the termination of the first phase — is almost automatic. This phase is time consuming, and often gives rise to the thought that nothing is being accomplished.

The second phase, likewise second in importance, is the design of the project. This is a visualization almost in its entirety. From the decisions based on data accumulated is developed a visualization of the completed structure. This is reduced to concrete form by computation, and the results are drawings and specifications sufficient for the direction of the man who is actually to build the project. And far from the least of the tools used by the designer, are "engineeringly" intelligent cost records.

The third phase is the actual construction of the project. Here is required again a power of visualization so as to carry into materials of three dimensions and mass, the lines of the plans and the words of the specifications. And to the man in responsible charge, tools of the utmost importance are accurate and engineeringly intelligent cost records, both contemporaneous, of his daily progress, and retrospective, of other jobs, inclusive of similar operations.

Perhaps some curiosity has been aroused about the phrase "engineeringly intelligent cost records." By this is meant cost records identifying the major units in which the engineer thinks. Let me illustrate by an example, one intended to be purely illustrative, and not literal.

In the normal course of events at a certain factory it is necessary to build a fence. Its prime cost consists of labor and materials. These may be carried into the proper betterment account. The appropriate secondary costs are added and then a single journal entry carries the whole cost into plant account. A request from any department for the cost of that fence produces one item, the total cost. Some time afterward, it becomes necessary to run an overhead steam line into the factory yard. An estimate is being prepared. You are asked for the "costs" of the fence. And probably you see no connection between fences and steam lines as the total cost is sent down. Or if in one of those rare phases, with a little spare time, you segregate the total costs in secondary costs, labor and material. And the engineer makes a few remarks when he gets it, but vows that on the next job he'll have one of the draftsmen keep some costs that mean something. For he is thinking in operations. That fence required post holes. Digging these post holes is an operation. Each bent that is to carry the pipe line will require two holes of the same size as those post holes, and if the costs are available on the previous similar job, that is digging post holes for the fence, the estimate of the new job, building the steam line, can be made more accurately.

It is difficult to foresee just where certain items may be useful in determination of future work. Fortunately, most engineering work falls into a comparatively few basic functional operations. And the *engineeringly intelligent cost accounting* system provides that functional segregation. And it provides it today.

At the risk of repeating something all of you know, a cost accounting system on a construction job that doesn't give today's costs tonight isn't worth the paper consumed in its keeping as a tool for the engineer in charge. And it is mighty poor ammunition for the comptroller in a fight in the director's room.

Please do not think that I am advocating that cost forms should be prepared by the engineer. Quite the reverse. There is no need in my reminding you of the necessity for any form having to do with dollars and cents, tying into the balance sheet. I have seen a lot of cost forms prepared by engineers. I am not an accountant, but my guess is most of them couldn't have been tied into a balance sheet.

But, when you start to build a cost sheet, go to the engineer, and ask him what he wants on it. Your accounting skill should be able to give it to him.

It has been my experience that in very few concerns is it possible to go into the plant, lay one's hand on a piece of equipment and ask where it is in the balance sheet. It's in the plant account. But how did it get there? And is all of it there, or is too much of it there? I shall not stop to discuss this phase further, but shall summarize:

It is the duty of the comptroller to tie costs into the balance sheet through cost sheets. But it is the duty of the engineer to tie correct costs into the physical properties. And the two must co-ordinate to accomplish these objectives.

Property Records

Having examined at some length, the relative points of view of both the comptroller and the engineer and one specific point of contact, let us inquire what are other points of contact between the engineer and the comptroller. These are so many that only a few can be examined. My own experience has been largely with capital costs and only these will be discussed. Contacts in operating costs are just as plentiful and occur far more frequently as operation is continuous, while capital expenditure is intermittent.

Most capital contacts can be grouped under one general heading, namely, Property Records.

How many companies can tell the history and present location of every capital asset, from its acquisition to date, and its true balance sheet relation at all times? First of all let us see where accurate property records are of value.

Primarily, they are valuable, nay, indispensable, for the purpose of *operating costs.* Depreciation, obsolescence, and interest or investment are essential factors in any correct costing system.

What is *depreciation?* One definition is "An allowance for wear and tear, sufficient to return the cost of the asset during its normal life." And the setting up of a depreciation reserve results in a return of capital investment. But is that sufficient? To my mind, the nature of the industry is an important factor in the determination of depreciation reserve rates of accrual. Let me illustrate: One company buys a coal mine. It knows beyond any reasonable doubt that it has 1,000,000 tons of coal in the property. It is a developed property; i.e., there are working places and entries, but no equipment. It proceeds to build a hoist and tipple having an annual capacity of 100,000 tons. In ten years' time this equipment will remove the entire coal body. Now after ten years' use, this machinery will still have several years' life, but would it be salable? Probably not. Therefore, for the sake of simplicity, neglecting salvage value, for each year's operation, this company must include in its costs one-tenth of the cost of equipment, if the stockholders are to have returned their original investment. This can be done by charging one one-millionth of the cost to each ton of coal, or by charging off one-tenth of cost each year; or it may be done by sinking fund methods. The procedure is largely an accounting feature. But as an engineer interested in the protection of my clients, the stockholders, I want you, Mr. Comptroller, to return in some manner, the cost of that equipment.

Now let us turn to the manufacturer of mining machinery. Suppose he installs a new bay of machine tools and that it costs him $100,000. Determined by means to be discussed later, the life of this machinery likewise is ascertained to be 10 years. Do I want 10% returned each year? No. My clients at the end of 10 years are still making machinery. They expect to continue making machinery. What they want at that time is not $100,000 but a sum of money that will enable them to install another bay of machine tools capable of performing a like work as the tools just worn out. They want each year, 10% of the reproductive cost of their equipment. Will this be greater? Or will it be less? Will it be composed of the same items? Or will changes in the art require marked departures in the design? No one can foretell. But the engineer can tell you at the end of each fiscal period what the reproductive cost is. And for the following period, there should be included in the costs, one-tenth of this reproduction cost, plus or minus a balancing factor, so that with the amounts returned in the previous years, the proper reproductive fund is available at the end of the ten-year period. And this balancing factor cannot be determined by the engineer, or the comptroller, alone. Only by the closest co-operation between them can it be determined.

The amount of depreciation is fixed primarily by the life. Please note that life is the term used, and not *estimated* life. Your records tell you that the average life of a certain equipment has been so long. Now that is a definite fact—that has been. But is it safe to infer that the same type of equipment, or the same equipment if moved to other conditions, will deteriorate at the same rate?

When electrical energy was first offered for sale, it was sold by flat rates, because there were no practical meters for measuring it. But here was a point of contact between two conflicting interests. And accurate meters were soon available. But depreciation is an invisible reduction of value. No one thought seriously about it until recent years. But now there are available scientific instruments that will measure depreciation as accurately, and more quickly, than any electrical meter. I suppose all of you are more or less familiar with the Grand Trunk case, in Canada. Probably all of you feel that there are ample data on the wear of rails to render the computation of proper depreciation a mere matter of figures based on the date of installation and cost. Yet measurements of deterioration were taken on every mile of rail, and the deviation between the actual depreciation as measured, and as calculated, was very great.

The same condition exists in all industries. The engineer has available deterioration meters, if the accountant desires accurate measure to determine his costs. And the consulting engineer demands accurate costs, including reproductive return, in the interests of his clients, the security holders.

What I have just stated regarding depreciation is equally true of obsolescence. Its determination is more intricate, and much space in this article could be devoted to it. I shall content myself with stating that obsolescence must provide reproductive return to compensate for advancement of the industrial art.

The treatment of interest on investment is an accounting feature and any one of you is no doubt better able to discuss it than I. Many a concern would be in better health if its engineer had co-operated with the comptroller in regard to interest.

Other Uses of Property Records

It is difficult to determine the next most important use of accurate property records. It may be in connection with either taxation or insurance purposes. Whether taxes be a matter of Federal Income, State and Municipal or Estate taxes, accurate, provable, and intelligible property records are essential. The points of contact between engineer and comptroller in the matter of taxation are so many, and so important, that even those mostly concerned have scarcely scratched the surface of usefulness. Just to recount a few: We have prime valuation, invested capital, depreciation, depletion, capital losses, obsolescence, corroborative costs and investment, prime operating costs—in short, any schedule for any class of tax, having to do with investment or operation, can be strengthened by co-operation between comptroller and engineer.

It may be for insurance purposes. Here, the clear-cut differentiation between insurable and non-insurable values, saves many thousands of dollars in premiums. And accurate data as to depreciated value, reproductive value, and unexpired life, hasten the settlement of claims and assure correct recovery.

To the public service comptroller accurate data for use before regulatory bodies is of course, a prime essential. I shall not discuss this phase at all, but for the non-public utility shall group regulatory body affairs under *legal uses.*

This is the most spectacular, and far from least important of the value of accurate property records, and co-operation between engineer and comptroller. It is spectacular because it is usually unexpected, and being unexpected, requires prompt attention, which it generally gets until something else diverts the thought and time of the management, leaving the comptroller, engineer and counsel to work out the solution.

No company can foretell when it will be called before some regulatory or quasi-regulatory body. It may be only because of a refusal on the part of some taxing authority to accept schedules submitted after careful preparation on the part of the accounting forces. It may be a call to appear before the Federal

Trade Commission for some real or imagined infraction of the omnipotent act which gives it power. It may be a call to appear before the Interstate Commerce Commission, or state Public Utility Commission because of some phase of rate regulation; in short it may be a call to appear before any one of the more than 500 State and Federal agencies which seek to control the course of business. But in any case, where the question of physical, and on occasion, incorporeal property, is involved, both engineer and comptroller can co-operate with profit to all concerned.

None of these have to do with court proceedings which formerly were considered the chief province of the legal profession. But this is still another point of contact. Differences of opinion may easily arise between buyer and seller, between neighbors, and between parties of whom one side had no knowledge of the existence of the other until the issue is joined. No doubt each one of you has in mind some equally important point of contact not mentioned.

All of the above has had so much to do with records, that possibly you are beginning to think the engineer should usurp the function of the accounting forces and keep property records. That is far from the case. The point that I want to make is this: the engineer is an important factor in the design and construction of satisfactory records.

Let us examine for a moment the features which a satisfactory property record should reflect.

First, it must show accurately the complete history of the facilities. Since a facility has its inception in the design of the engineer and is constructed under his direction, he has a need for an accurate record of its physical life. And not the least important of historical data is the historical cost. In order that the engineer's future designs may be tempered by experience, it is imperative for the engineer that the historical cost be accurate, and "engineeringly" interpretable. Likewise, the comptroller demands accurate historical data in order that present investment value may be measured, and future expenditures be tempered by a knowledge of results as revealed by return on investment.

Property records should reflect past and present status from a value point of view for many and divergent purposes. This involves questions of deterioration, obsolescence, and reproductive costs. The determination of these factors is essentially an engineering function; the calculation and recording is essentially an accounting function. And it is highly desirable, almost imperative, that all the above enumerated uses be served by one and the same record. From an investment, from a legal, from an insurance point of view, both the engineer and the comptroller are essential to the design, construction and maintenance of a satisfactory record.

The question that automatically comes to mind at this time is—What assets should be treated in a property record? As a comptroller, you have funded debt and floating debt. An analogy could almost express the formula of property record content. The terms "fixed assets" and "floating assets" are frequently used. I like the term "floating asset" properly applied. But the term "fixed asset" is too limiting. It very properly is usually restricted to assets affixed directly or indirectly, to the real estate.

The most satisfactory method is to let the life of an asset, modified by its importance, determine its placement. Certain taxing and regulatory bodies have held that any asset which has a life of more than one year is a capital asset. To me this has always seemed more theoretical than practical. Many small hand tools have a life much longer than one year. Yet to call these capital assets individually is a costly expedient. These are being constantly replenished. Some last a few days, others as many years. Unquestionably then, a group inventory system is far more convenient, and for practical purposes, a sufficiently accurate method of capitalization. In certain branches of the chemical industry, on the other hand, expensive pieces of apparatus have lives materially less than one year. It would be equally absurd not to include such items in the property record.

So in each industry, the close co-operation of engineer and comptroller are essential to correct capital accounting and property records.

Phases of Property Records

It has been said that an engineering project passed through three phases, each successively of less importance. Let us examine the creation of a property record in the same light.

First, there is the assembling of data, and winnowing of the mass, to determine the pertinent facts. This means the correlation between what is customarily contained, and what is essential for a particular industry—and a particular concern which is paying the bill for such work. Such a study involves a knowledge of the industry, a perception of the legal restraints, and careful analysis of the particular case in hand. For some, the quantity production of Ford meets all requirements. For others, the stability and life and prestige of Packard is essential.

The second phase of property records is a proper design. In this connection a close co-operation between the engineer and the comptroller is required in order that the record may serve the fullest measure of purpose, and tie into the books. And it must be efficient. Any job that doesn't pay dividends isn't good engineering. No, I'll go one step farther and say it isn't engineering at all.

Needless to say, this problem of design may range all the way from quantity production to an accurate fitting of special conditions. No fixed rule can be promulgated.

And this leads to the third phase. How is a property record built? Two ways are available, and most records are a combination of the two. These are: (1) by reconstruction, and (2) by contemporaneous record.

Let us discuss the second method first. For sake of clearness, managerial and directorial responsibility have been and will be omitted throughout this entire discussion. The inception of a capital asset is in the province of the engineer. He prepares his estimates and sends these to a higher authority for approval. The comptroller is called upon for information as to funds and finance. If he is to have satisfactory accounts, he wants controlling records of these expenditures. And in controlled expenditures is the foundation of contemporaneous property records. Whatever you may call it, appropriation, authority for expenditure, or authorization, it should be the "original source" for the property record.

Taking up the first method, the establishing of a property record by reconstruction, presents an entirely different problem. There may have been no records of controlled expenditures. Records of all expenditures may be missing or unavoidable. Even the property the history of which is so essential for any one of a dozen reasons may be missing. But in any event, the foundation of a reconstructed property record is an appraisal.

Appraisals

Three words are virtually synonymous, namely: appraisal, appraisement, and valuation. The legal profession seems to favor the term "appraisement." But among engineers, the terms "appraisal" and "valuation" are usually employed. And a distinction is beginning to grow between these two. "Valuation" is more usually employed in connection with the determination of the value of some natural resource, but in any event, it is the placing of a value on an asset by personal opinion. Rarely is any scientific precaution taken to eliminate the personal equation. The professional reputation of the engineer is the prime basis of the valuation. "Appraisal" on the other hand denotes the scientific application to the assets, of prices and proven values as of specific dates, and then by use of determinative factors, reduction of this valuation to the required date. Every step of the process is traceable, and checkable, and the personal equation is eliminated as far as the cost of so doing is justified.

From a legal point of view, the work must be done by independent parties. Most regulatory bodies, including all Federal taxing and most State rate regulating bodies adhere rigidly to this rule.

The courts have emphasized this feature repeatedly.

Fortunately the leading cases are sufficiently long established to constitute satisfactory and easily accessible precedent. And Whitten in his "Valuation of Public Utilities" has made the legal phases readily accessible to the lay reader.

Both valuation and appraisal are based on accurate inventory. And an accurate inventory means the personal inspection of a competent lister. It may mean the measurement of deterioration as well. But under any condition it means a painstaking determination, item by item, of quantity, and frequently the quality, of every asset the presence of which is justified in the property record.

Appraisals are of two broad groupings: contemporaneous and retrospective.

Contemporaneous appraisals, as the name indicates, apply present day prices to the inventory items. These may, or may not, as occasion determines, be adjusted for deterioration.

Retrospective appraisals apply costs as of some specific date, other than the present, to the inventory items. Likewise, these may, or may not, as the occasion demands, be adjusted for deterioration.

Appraisals are of many classes, to fit the purpose in hand, or the limits of allowable time and cost. I will not endeavor to even mention the various types. But to give an idea of the scope, two will be described. The simplest is a mere pricing of the inventory. This is called a rate appraisal, as the most elementary form of inventory includes certain items of freight, cartage, and erection.

One of the more extensive is a reconstructed, compensated and adjusted retrospective appraisal. By "reconstructed" is meant the re-determination of costs based on the changes in the art. Thus a few years ago most building excavation was done by wagons and pick and shovel. Today it is done by tractors and trailers, or motor trucks, and steam shovels. The engineer who makes such an appraisal must study carefully the plans and specifications, reconstructing these, if necessary, and lay out his construction plant just as it would have been done on the date selected as the focal date.

By "compensated" is meant the adjustment necessary to provide for changes in value due to use. Thus the embankments of a canal settle, and to a certain extent improve with age. And while this improvement occurs, there is a paralleling deterioration, which must be considered. These two factors must be compensated.

By "adjusted" is meant the adjustment for change in value due to deterioration. Thus a structure may have been erected in 1910. In 1918 it is purchased by a certain group of interests. In 1924 these interests have a parting of ways. A value as of the date of purchase is desired. The inventory is priced as of the date of purchase. Then, based on such corroborative data as is obtainable, an adjustment of this value for the five years of life prior to the purchase is made.

The obtaining of corroborative data is a problem in itself, which I will not attempt to discuss. But it is my hope that these citations of points of contact have shown you a few of the many ways in which the comptroller and the engineer can join forces to the lessening of the labors of each, and the saving of many dollars to their employers — the investing public.

(15) "Standard Costs – Their Development and Use," March 2, 1925, Bulletin, Vol. 6, No. 13, F. Brugger, General Electric, Pittsfield

Publication Department Note

Mr. F. Brugger, the author of this article, is one of our "inherited" members. That is not a new class of membership but it is one growing out of the merging of the membership of another organization with that of the NACA. And that is what happened in this case. On February 13, 1923, the Albany Chapter of the Industrial Cost Association was merged with the Albany Chapter of the NACA and Mr. Brugger was one of the assets turned over by the Industrial Cost Association. In passing, it may be remarked that we are proud of our inheritance in this instance.

Mr. Brugger began his business career in December, 1903, when he became a clerk in the Payroll and Cost Department of the British-Thomson-Houston Company, Rugby, England. Some sixteen months later he entered the factory to get practical shop experience and worked in the pattern shop, winding department, assembly and test.

Leaving England in the early part of 1907 he came to this country and in March entered the employ as a student in the test of the General Electric Company at the Schenectady Works. A year later he secured a position in the accounting department of the General Electric Company, Pittsfield Works, where he was eventually placed in charge of factory accounts, expense statistics, taking inventories, and shop clerical systems. Since April, 1914, he has been supervisor of costs and has had charge of the cost department at the Pittsfield Works.

Standard Costs – Their Development and Use

In approaching the subject of standard or pre-determined costs, their development and use, let us first follow the successful business man's procedure in deciding to engage in the manufacture and marketing of a new article.

First, he considers the probable demand, then he estimates or obtains an estimate of the cost of manufacture, the cost of distribution, the amount of fixed investment and working capital necessary and the amount of net income required to make the venture a profitable one. After arriving at a satisfactory selling price in this manner, he again reviews his estimate of demand and if assured of the reasonableness of all these factors, he goes ahead with the enterprise. In other words, estimated or pre-determined costs form the very basis of his decision to risk his reputation and money in the new venture. Naturally, he is very much interested to know as soon as possible to what extent his estimates are met and it is the function of the cost accountant to so arrange the cost system that this information can be furnished as promptly as possible.

Although the illustration given refers to an entirely new business venture, the same line of reasoning is applicable to the every-day decisions of the management in the conduct of any going concern.

In the past the comparison of actual performances with standards was not recognized as being an essential part of a cost system and even today it is disregarded by many cost accountants. The blame for this condition is probably chargeable to the manufacturer more than to his accountant. The cost accountant *per se* is not generally qualified to set standards and there being no demand on the part of the management for cost information stated in comparison with standards, the accountant rather naturally contented himself with providing the customary information as to past happenings without reference to any preconceived idea of what should have been realized.

The "standard" method of cost accounting has been developed to meet the need for more constructive cost information than was provided under the older form.

A standard cost should be figured on the basis of an efficiency attainment reasonably possible in a factory operating at normal capacity.

Standard Material Costs

The quantity of material set for standard is the gross quantity estimated to be required after determining the kind and size of material best adapted for the manufacture of the part. This is ascertained by a study of the conditions under which material can be purchased (with due regard to variations in length, width, and thickness permissible under prevailing trade rules) and by a study of the manufacturing processes so as to determine the unavoidable loss of material incident to the manufacture, such as material lost in cutting, short ends, trimmings, etc.

The price of material set for standard may either be the average market value over a cycle of years or the market value at the date of the annual inventory, if, as I believe advisable, standards are revised at least once a year.

Standard Labor Costs

A standard direct labor cost represents the cost of the standard time required to perform the operation (as determined by careful time and motion studies) at the standard rate per hour, the latter representing, preferably, the going rate in the locality for the particular class of labor involved.

Standard Burden Rates

Standard burden rates are established for each department, production center, or machine group, the method adopted being dependent upon whichever of these is used as the unit for the purpose of controlling the expenses and distributing them to the product. The first step in the establishment of standard burden rates is to estimate the standard productive hour or producing payroll in the fiscal period when the plant is operated at normal, normal being defined as, for example, 80 per cent capacity. With this figure as the basis, standard allowances are set for all items of expense based on past experience and knowledge of the business. For the sake of control, expenses are grouped by main classes such as indirect labor, expense materials and supplies, power, heat and light, maintenance, depreciation, taxes, insurance and general assessment.

Separate sub-totals are determined for: (1) those expenses that are fixed in amount, irrespective of the volume of business; and (2) those that are expected to vary more or less consistently with the fluctuations of business. The ratio of the standard burden to the productive hours or producing payroll for the department, production center, or machine group, as the case may be, represents its standard burden rate.

Standard Cost Records

The principal records required to operate the standard cost system may conveniently be grouped as follows:

A. Standard cost data	Standard cost of parts Analysis of standard material and labor Standard burden statement Summary of standard cost of machines
B. Reports on actual performances	Material operation card Labor operation card
C. Statements and analysis for preparation of book	Production report Analysis of standard cost of shipments
D. Cost Ledger	Material inventory control account Material work in process account Labor work in process account Burden work in process account
E. Key statements for Executives	Summarized manufacturing statement Current cost of machines Adjusted cost of sales and profit and and loss statement Summarized manufacturing and efficiency statement Departmental efficiency statement

These records are illustrated in figures 15-1 to 15-4.

Standard Cost Data (See Figure 15-1)

The forms illustrated in the charts are designed to meet the requirements of a company manufacturing machinery.

A *Standard Cost of Parts* (Form A) is made out for each part to show:

1. The kind and size of material and the quantity established as standard to manufacture 100 pieces, the standard price and standard cost of the material.

2. The operations in sequence of performance, the standard labor costs thereof analyzed by departments and the total labor cost per 100 pieces.

Analysis of Standard Material and Labor (Form B) is the medium for the collection of the standard labor and material costs of the parts required for the manufacture of a complete machine as obtained from the Standard Cost

Figure 15-1

STANDARD COST DATA

CHART 1

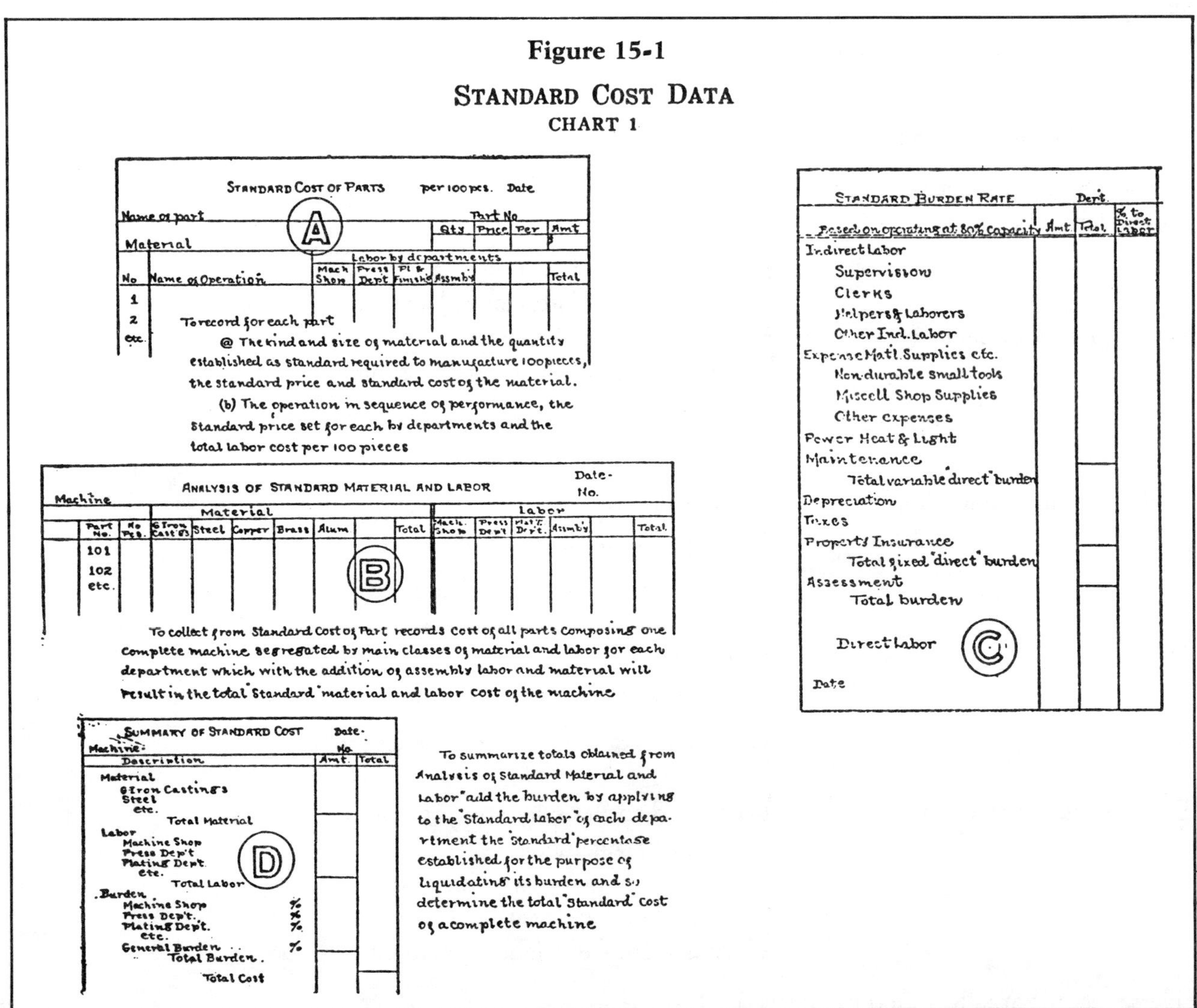

STANDARD COST OF PARTS per 100 pcs. Date

Name of part — Part No

Material — Qty | Price | Per | Amt

No	Name of Operation	Mach Shop	Press Dept	Pl & Finish'g	Assmb'y			Total
1								
2								
etc.								

Torecord for each part

@ The kind and size of material and the quantity established as standard required to manufacture 100 pieces, the standard price and standard cost of the material.

(b) The operation in sequence of performance, the standard price set for each by departments and the total labor cost per 100 pieces

ANALYSIS OF STANDARD MATERIAL AND LABOR — Date- No.

Machine

	Material								Labor					
Part No.	No Pcs.	G Iron Cast'gs	Steel	Copper	Brass	Alum		Total	Mach. Shop	Press Dep't	Plat'g Dep't.	Assmb'y		Total
101														
102														
etc.														

To collect from Standard Cost of Part records cost of all parts composing one complete machine segregated by main classes of material and labor for each department which with the addition of assembly labor and material will result in the total "Standard" material and labor cost of the machine

STANDARD BURDEN RATE — Dept.

Based on operating at 80% capacity	Amt.	Total	% to Direct Labor
Indirect Labor			
Supervision			
Clerks			
Helpers & Laborers			
Other Ind. Labor			
Expense Mat'l. Supplies etc.			
Non-durable small tools			
Miscell Shop Supplies			
Other expenses			
Power Heat & Light			
Maintenance			
Total variable "direct" burden			
Depreciation			
Taxes			
Property Insurance			
Total fixed "direct" burden			
Assessment			
Total burden			
Direct Labor			
Date			

SUMMARY OF STANDARD COST — Date- No.

Machine:

Description	Amt.	Total
Material		
G Iron Castings		
Steel		
etc.		
Total Material		
Labor		
Machine Shop		
Press Dep't		
Plating Dept.		
etc.		
Total Labor		
Burden		
Machine Shop %		
Press Dep't. %		
Plating Dept. %		
etc.		
General Burden %		
Total Burden.		
Total Cost		

To summarize totals obtained from Analysis of Standard Material and Labor" add the burden by applying to the "Standard Labor" of each department the "Standard" percentage established for the purpose of liquidating its burden and s. determine the total "Standard" cost of a complete machine of Parts record (Form A). On Form B the standard labor costs are analyzed by departments and the material costs by material classes. Standard assembling labor and material costs are added to the standard costs of the parts to obtain the total standard material and labor costs of the machine.

The *Standard Burden Rate Statement* (Form C) illustrates the manner in which the data required for the setting of the standard burden rate for each department or production center may be collected. The form is designed to show the standard allowances for each class of burden and sub-totals for "Variable direct" burden, "Fixed direct" burden and for the assessed charges over which the department head has little or no control.

As has already been pointed out, the standards shown on this statement are based on operating the plant efficiently at normal capacity. This basis is used in order to eliminate from the standard costs the element of burden due to idle equipment.

The *Summary of Standard Cost* (Form D) is designed to summarize the totals obtained from the Analysis of Standard Material and Labor, to add the burden by applying to the standard labor of each department the standard percentage established for the purpose of liquidating its burden and so to determine the total standard cost of a complete machine.

Reports on Actual Performance and Analysis for Preparation of Book Entries (See Figure 15-2)

Actual performance in regard to material consumption and labor expended is reported on Labor and Material Operation cards arranged for machine tabulation.

The *Labor Operation Card* (Form E) is designed to show:

1. Earnings of each employee for payroll and efficiency records.
2. Production record of parts.
3. Standard and actual hours and amounts for each part, class of product, and department.
4. Standard burden earned on standard time for each machine group and department.

From this information may be calculated the amount of variations from standards due: (1) to variation in the time consumed, and (2) to variations in labor rates.

The *Material Operation Card* (Form F) provides for recording the actual and standard quantities of material consumed. Both of these quantities are extended at the standard material price in order to determine the increase or decrease in cost due to variations from the standard material quantity.

The *Monthly Production Report* (Form G) is made up by departments and shows the production in the month by part numbers (as obtained from the

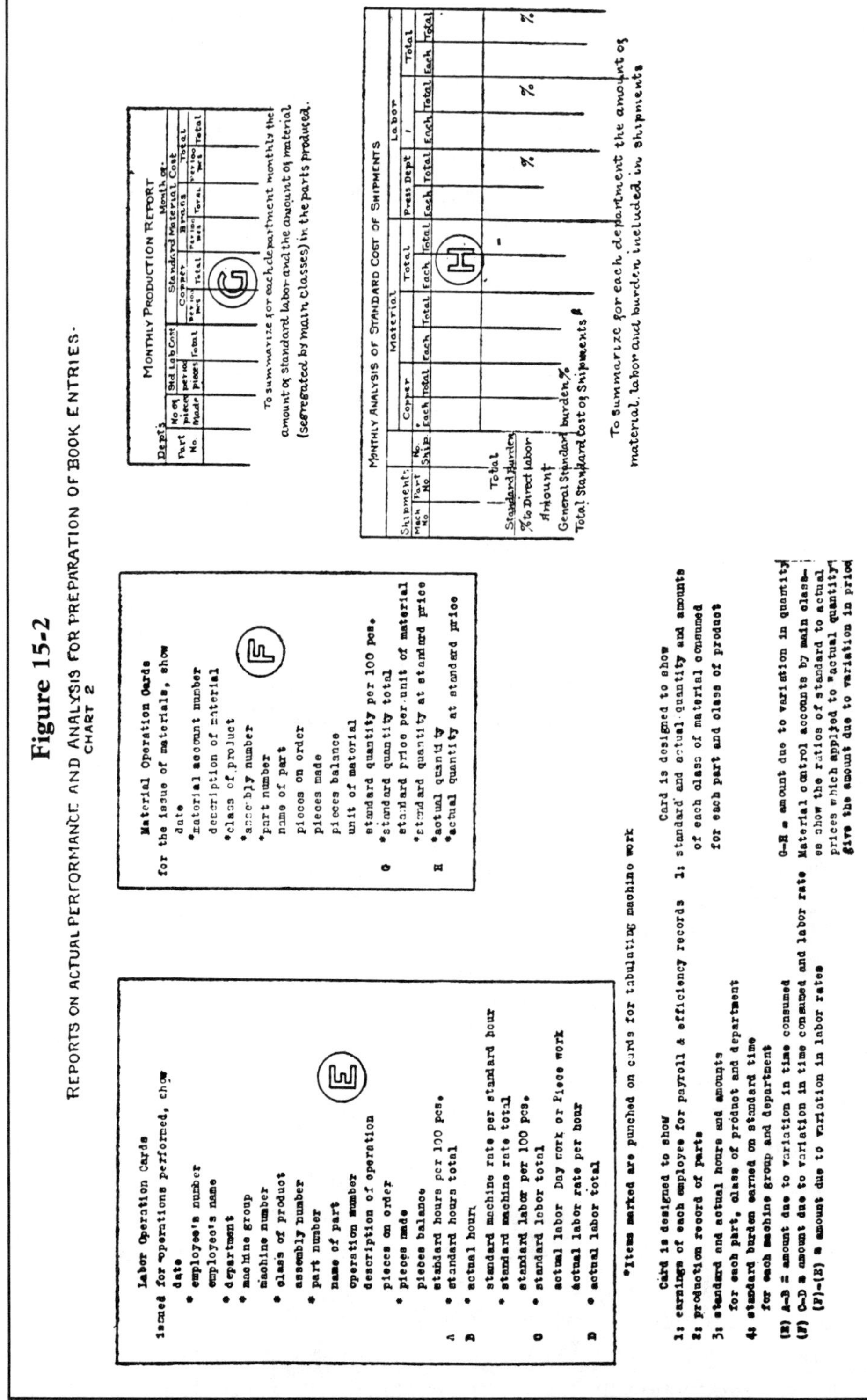
Figure 15-2
REPORTS ON ACTUAL PERFORMANCE AND ANALYSIS FOR PREPARATION OF BOOK ENTRIES-
CHART 2
Labor Operation Cards
issued for operations performed, show
date
* employee's number
employee's name
* department
* machine group
machine number
* class of product
assembly number
* part number
name of part
operation number
description of operation
pieces on order
* pieces made
pieces balance
standard hours per 100 pcs.
A * standard hours total
B * actual hours
standard machine rate per standard hour
* standard machine rate total
standard labor per 100 pcs.
C * standard labor total
actual labor Day work or Piece work
actual labor rate per hour
D * actual labor total
E
Material Operation Cards
for the issue of materials, show
date
*material account number
description of material
*class of product
*assembly number
*part number
name of part
pieces on order
pieces made
pieces balance
unit of material
standard quantity per 100 pcs.
G *standard quantity total
standard price per unit of material
*standard quantity at standard price
H *actual quantity
*actual quantity at standard price
F
MONTHLY PRODUCTION REPORT
Dept's
Month of
Part No.
No. of pieces Made
Std Lab Cost
per 100 pieces
Total
Standard Material Cost
Copper
Brass
Total
per 100 pcs
Total
G
To summarize for each department monthly the amount of standard labor and the amount of material (segregated by main classes) in the parts produced.
MONTHLY ANALYSIS OF STANDARD COST OF SHIPMENTS
Shipments
Mach No
Part No
No. Ship
Material
Copper
Total
Labor
Press Dept
Total
Each
Total
H
Total
Standard Burden
% to Direct labor
Amount
General Standard burden %
Total Standard Cost of Shipments
%
To summarize for each department the amount of material, labor and burden included in shipments
*Items marked are punched on cards for tabulating machine work
Card is designed to show
1: earnings of each employee for payroll & efficiency records
2: production record of parts
3: standard and actual hours and amounts for each part, class of product and department
4: standard burden earned on standard time for each machine group and department
(E) A-B = amount due to variation in time consumed
(F) C-D = amount due to variation in time consumed and labor rate
(F)-(E) = amount due to variation in labor rates
Card is designed to show
1: standard and actual quantity and amounts of each class of material consumed for each part and class of product
G-H = amount due to variation in quantity
Material control accounts by main classes show the ratios of standard to actual prices which applied to "actual quantity" give the amount due to variation in price

Labor Operations Cards) and the standard labor and material costs of this production obtained by extending the pieces made at the standard labor and burden costs as shown on the Standard Cost of Parts records (Form A).

The *Monthly Analysis of Standard Cost of Shipments* (Form H) shows the number of pieces shipped of each machine or part number, and the standard material and labor costs of these shipments, the former being analyzed by main material classes and the latter by departments. It also shows the standard burden cost of these shipments, also analyzed by departments. The totals obtained from this analysis are used to credit the finished stock account or the work in process account as will be shown later.

Cost Ledger (See Figure 15-3)

Standard and Actual costs are tied in with the books of account in the following manner:

Productive material is classified by accounts and in such detail that the fluctuations in market prices affect all items in the same class in approximately the same proportion. Invoices covering material and incoming freight, after being checked for correctness, are priced and extended at standard prices and distributed to the proper material classifications. Ledger accounts are maintained for each main class of raw material in the stores (Form I) with the total represented in the Inventory Control Account. These accounts are charged at "actual" as well as at "standard" cost with the inventory of raw material at the beginning and the purchases during the month. At the close of each month, the totals of the charges in the "actual" and "standard" columns are determined and the ratio of actual to standard charges figured. The material controlling accounts by main classes are credited in the "standard" column with amounts representing the actual quantities taken from Stores and extended at standard prices, as obtained from summaries of Material Operation Cards, Form F. The actual cost of the material withdrawn from stores is obtained by applying to its standard value the ratio of actual to standard shown on the debit side of the account. The accounts are then closed and the balances brought forward as representing the inventories at the beginning of the following month. The accounts deal with values only and are supplemented by stores records showing quantities for each size and kind of material and all other information required for the proper maintenance and control of materials. Stores records do not show values.

Material Work in Process Accounts (Form J) are also kept for each main class of material. They are charged with the inventories or balances of the accounts at the beginning of the month, the actual cost of material withdrawals during the month as shown on the credit side of the corresponding raw material control accounts and the standard costs of the material in the product as

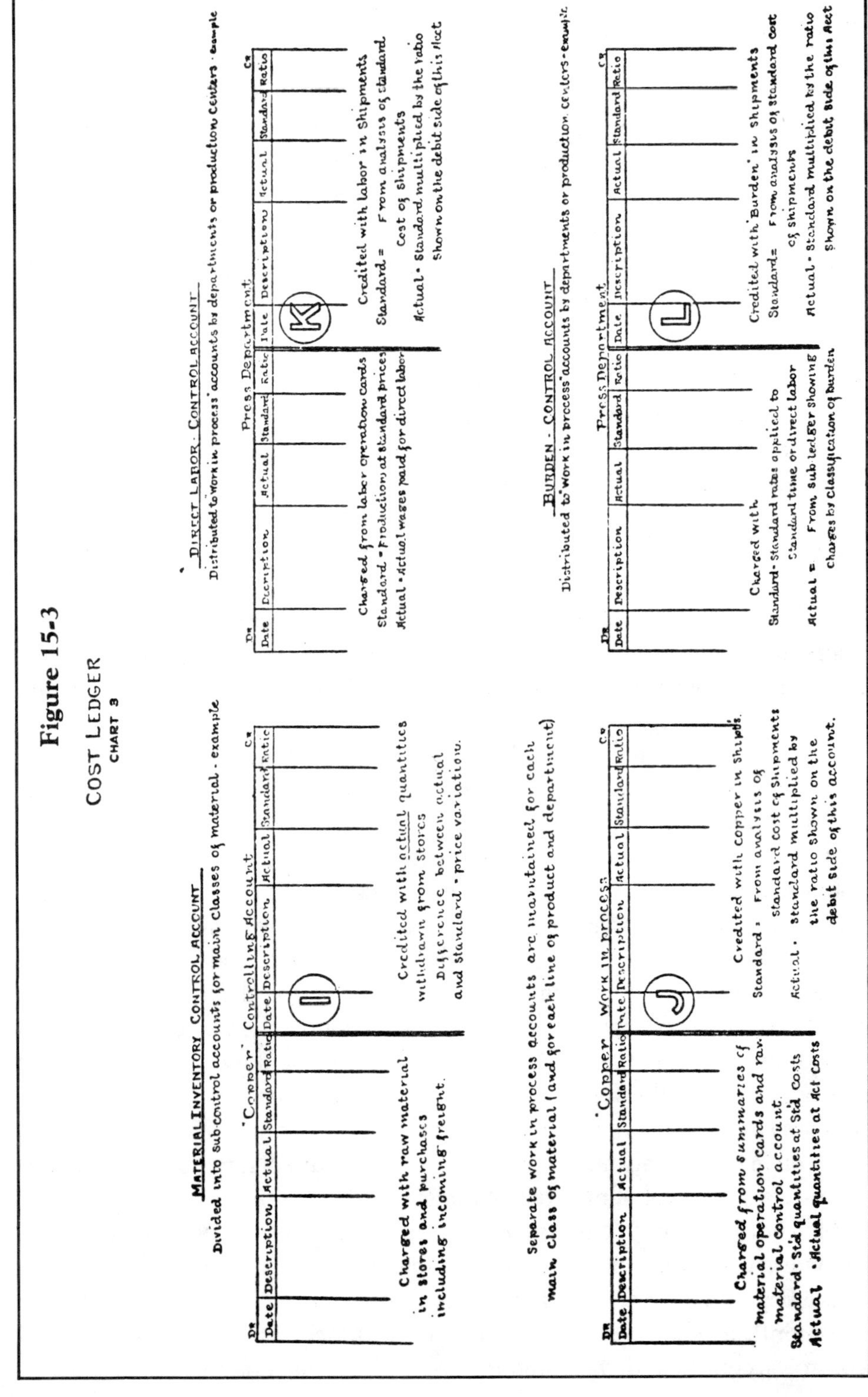
Figure 15-3
COST LEDGER
CHART 3
MATERIAL INVENTORY CONTROL ACCOUNT
Divided into sub-control accounts for main classes of material - example
Dr
"Copper" Controlling Account
Cr
Date | Description | Actual | Standard | Ratio | Date | Description | Actual | Standard | Ratio
I
Charged with raw material in stores and purchases including incoming freight.
Credited with actual quantities withdrawn from stores
Difference between actual and standard - price variation.
DIRECT LABOR - CONTROL ACCOUNT
Distributed to "work in process" accounts by departments or production centers - example
Dr
Press Department
Cr
Date | Description | Actual | Standard | Ratio | Date | Description | Actual | Standard | Ratio
K
Charged from labor operation cards
Standard - Production at standard prices
Actual - Actual wages paid for direct labor
Credited with labor in Shipments
Standard = From analysis of standard cost of shipments
Actual - Standard multiplied by the ratio shown on the debit side of this Acct
Separate work in process accounts are maintained for each main class of material (and for each line of product and department)
Dr
"Copper" Work in process
Cr
Date | Description | Actual | Standard | Ratio | Date | Description | Actual | Standard | Ratio
J
Charged from summaries of material operation cards and raw material control account.
Standard - Std quantities at Std Costs
Actual - Actual quantities at Act Costs
Credited with copper in Shipts.
Standard - From analysis of standard cost of shipments
Actual - Standard multiplied by the ratio shown on the debit side of this account.
BURDEN - CONTROL ACCOUNT
Distributed to "work in process" accounts by departments or production centers - example
Dr
Press Department
Cr
Date | Description | Actual | Standard | Ratio | Date | Description | Actual | Standard | Ratio
L
Charged with
Standard - Standard rates applied to standard time or direct labor
Actual = From sub ledger showing charges by classification of burden
Credited with "Burden" in Shipments
Standard = From analysis of standard cost of shipments
Actual - Standard multiplied by the ratio shown on the debit side of this Acct

obtained from summaries of Material Operation Cards, Form F. It will be noted that the differences between the standard and actual amounts credited to Raw Material Control Accounts represent variations in prices, whereas the differences between the standard and the actual amounts charged to the Work in Process accounts cover variations in quantities as well as prices. Material Work in Process accounts are credited in the "standard" column with the amount of standard material in shipments as obtained from the Monthly Analysis of Standard Cost of Shipments (Form H–Figure 15-2). They are credited in the "actual" column with amounts determined by applying to the standard value the ratio of actual to standard amount shown on the debit side of the accounts.

Direct Labor Control Accounts (Form K) and *Burden Control Accounts* (Form L) are maintained for each department or production center and handled similarly to the Material Work in Process accounts.

The Direct Labor Control accounts derive their charges from summaries of Labor Operation Cards, Form E. The Burden Control Accounts are charged in the "actual" column with the actual burden as determined from the burden ledger records and in the "standard" column with amounts calculated by applying the standard burden rates to the standard hours or amounts shown on the summaries of Labor Operation Cards, Form E. Credits to these accounts are determined from the Monthly Analysis of Standard Cost of Shipments, Form H, and ratios on the debit side of the respective accounts in precisely the same way as described in connection with the operation of the Material Work in Process accounts.

Key Statements for Executives (See Figure 15-4)

To indicate the character of periodic statements which under the standard cost system can be prepared for the executives for the purpose of control, a few sample forms are submitted.

The *Summarized Manufacturing Statement* (Form M) shows for each main class of material, for each department's direct labor and burden and for the general burden, the actual and standard cost, the ratio of the actual to standard, the increases or decreases over standard this month, last month and last year.

Current costs of individual machines can be compiled on a similar form.

The *Adjusted Cost of Sales and Profit and Loss Statement* (Form N) shows for each main class of material and for each department's labor and burden, the standard cost of shipments, the ratio of actual to standard costs and the adjusted cost of shipments which deducted from the amount billed gives the gross profits. Deducting the selling and administrative expenses from the latter gives the net profit for the month.

Figure 15-4

KEY STATEMENTS FOR·EXECUTIVES
CHART 4

SUMMARIZED MANUFACTURING STATEMENT

Month of. —

	This Month			Increases or Decr'e*		
	Ratio	Actual	Stand	This Mo	Last Mo	Last Yr
Material						
Grey Iron Castg's.						
Steel						
etc.-etc.						
Total Material						
Labor						
Machine Shop.						
Press Dep't						
Plating Dep't		M				
etc.-etc.						
Total Labor						
Burden						
Machine Shop						
Press Dep't.						
Plating Dep't						
etc.-etc.						
General Burden						
Total Burden						
Total Cost						
* Increases in Red						

Current costs of individual machines can be computed in similar form

ADJUSTED COST OF SALES AND PROFIT & LOSS STAMN'T.

Month of---

	Std Cost of Shipt's	Ratio Actual to Std	Adjusted Cost of Shipts.
Material			
Grey Iron Castings			
Steel			
etc.-etc.			
Total Material			
Labor			
Machine Shop			
Press Dep't			
Plating Dep't	N		
etc.-etc.-			
Total Labor			
Burden			
Machine Shop			
Press Dep't			
Plating Dep't			
etc.-etc.			
General Burden			
Total Burden			
Total Cost			
Amount Billed			
Gross Profit			
Selling & Administrative Exp			
Net Profit			

SUMMARIZED MANUFACTURING AND EFFICIENCY STATEMENT

Month of---

	St'd. Cost	Incr or Decr*		Actual Cost	Ratio Actual to St'd		
		Qty or Time	Prices or Rates		This Month	Last Month	Last Year
Material							
Grey Iron Castings							
Steel							
etc.-etc.							
Total Material							
Labor							
Machine Shop							
Press Dep't							
Plating Dep't							
etc. etc.							
Total Labor							
Burden							
Machine Shop							
Press Dept							
Plating Dep't							
etc.-etc.							
Total Prod Dep'ts Burden							
Burden - General							
Management							
Production Dep't							
Accounting-Cost-Pay Roll							
etc.-etc.							
Total General Burden							
Total Cost							
Variation in fixed burden due to idle equipment							
* Increase in red.							

Departmental efficiency statements are prepared along similar lines showing for each department in somewhat greater detail, particularly in regard to burden, the items over which the department has control to a major degree. General Burden is omitted from departmental statements but each non productive department is furnished with a statement showing comparison between the actual and standard cost of its operation.

The *Summarized Manufacturing and Efficiency Statement* (Form O) differs from the Summarized Manufacturing Statement (Form M) in that columns are added to the former to show the reasons for the increase or decrease in cost; i.e., whether the increase or decrease is due: (1) to quantity of material consumed or time taken; or (2) to changes in prices or rates of wages. It also separates burden into direct departmental burden and general burden and indicates the amount of fixed burden applicable to idle equipment.

Efficiency statements may be prepared along similar lines for each of the departments. Such statements might show labor segregated by machine groups and burden by main groups or even individual accounts. Departmental statements would show only items over which the department has control to a major degree. General burden would be omitted from such statements but the non-productive departments would be furnished with special statements showing comparisons of the actual and standard cost of the operation of their respective departments.

The number of statements required and the degree of details given therein depend, of course, on their practical value to the executives and the use made of them after they are compiled. As an indication of the refinements of information which could be furnished, if desired, it may be stated that it is perfectly possible to determine for each department or production center and for each class of product or even for each individual article:

1. Variations in fixed charges due to fluctuations in production caused by:
   a. Idle time
   b. Efficiency of operators
2. Variations in direct and indirect labor cost due to:
   a. Rates of wages
   b. Efficiency of operators
   c. Extra pay for overtime
3. Variations in Stores and Supplies due to:
   a. Price
   b. Consumption
4. Variations in power cost due to:
   a. Cost of producing power or price of purchased power
   b. Efficiency in use

Uses and Limitations of Standard Costs

The operation of a system of standard costs for a manufacturing plant having been described in some detail, it will be interesting to consider briefly the uses and limitations of standard costs in general. The logical procedure to follow in this connection would seem to be, first, to define the requirements of an efficient cost system, and second, to consider the system which has been described in relation to these requirements.

As the writer sees it the six prime requirements of an efficient cost system are as follows:

1. That it furnish actual current cost of sales, amount of sales billed and resulting profit for each product and class of product.
2. That it provide a means of ready conversion of existing to estimated future costs under current market conditions.
3. That it is adaptable to a ready analytical study of the detailed elements of cost.
4. That efficiency data are easily available.
5. That promptness in furnishing information is secured.
6. That its cost of operation must be consistent with benefits derived therefrom.

Whether or not accurate actual current costs can be prepared promptly and economically under the standard cost system depends, in the writer's judgment, upon the character of production and the nature of the product.

The standard cost plan seems best adapted for use in a plant manufacturing a rather limited number of standard articles in very large quantities requiring very few main classes of material. As the articles manufactured increase in number, as articles of special design for specific customers' requirements are introduced, and as the number of classified accounts for materials is increased, the standard cost system becomes less attractive from the standpoint of economy. This will be appreciated if it is remembered that each material control account can only contain such kinds and sizes of material as are affected by changes in market conditions to the same degree in relation to the standard price provided the plant manufactures more than one article using different kinds and sizes of materials or using the same kind and sizes of materials but in different relationships in regard to quantities. Furthermore, the accuracy and uniformity of the standards set become more and more important as the number of articles increases, because the final step in arriving at the so-called "actual" cost is the sum of a theoretical cost plus a pro-rating of the aggregate of variations in costs over the aggregate of the standard costs. If a plant manufacturing partly standard product in relatively large quantities and a considerable number of special articles in small quantities should adopt the standard cost system, the costs compiled are likely to be over-stated for the standard and under-stated for the special product. This is so because it may be safely assumed that the standards established for the standard product are more accurate than those for the special articles in connection with which less experience and data are available and for which time studies cannot be carried out to the same degree as for standard production in large quantities and also because special articles generally cost considerably more than we think they should.

Conversion of standard costs to estimated future costs under current market conditions can be effected readily and safely provided actual costs are not too far apart from the standard costs. Although standards set may or may not agree with actual past experience at the time they are established, care must be taken that standards are practical and attainable under normal manufacturing conditions, and that pressure brought to bear on the standard-setting and on the manufacturing departments, by the designer or even by the management in order to obtain a favorable cost, does not result in the promotion of the manufacture of one article to the detriment of all other articles. Large differences between standard and actual cost cast doubt on the accuracy of the standards and consequently there should be no hesitancy in changing standards as soon as investigation shows that revision is necessary.

Analytical study of detailed elements of cost is the very basis of a standard cost system. Consequently, the standard cost data are compiled in such a manner as to be of real value to executives, engineers, and designers in their endeavor to detect high spots and to introduce economies. Standard cost data, furthermore, are a useful tool for the operation of an efficient production system and form an excellent basis for efficiency reports.

It is one of the most important functions of a cost system to furnish the management with means of control. While some efficiency statistics can be prepared under practically any cost plan, the standard cost system is the only one under which it is possible to present to the executives each month for the previous month's operations a summarized comparison between actual performance and expectation which will show the difference classified by causes of the variations from standard. Under other cost systems, comparisons between actual and estimated costs can be and are prepared and summarized monthly – usually at the time of the completion of orders – but instead of presenting a statement reflecting the operating conditions and efficiencies of the various departments, we have only a summarized list of differences between estimated and actual costs with detailed explanations in aggravated cases and the results of operations over an indefinite period. In many instances, inefficiencies disclosed by such detailed statements occur months before they come to notice so that the value of a discussion of the particular items is rather limited and at its best the management is considering only the result of individual transactions instead of figures representing a composite picture of all transactions.

A further advantage of the standard cost system is that the standards, although subject to revision as conditions require, are uniform in principle for all time. As a result, the percentages of variation from standards as shown on the statements are truly comparable for different periods. This is much to be preferred to statements comparing merely actual costs obtained during different periods without indicating the degree of efficiency with which the manufacturing operations were carried on during the periods under consideration. It might be well, however, to mention at this point that standard cost data do not take the place of departmental burden budgets for varying volumes of business as a measure of control, because standards are set on the basis of normal capacity operation which is not attainable at all times. It is true that the variation statement shows the amount due to idle equipment, but it does not provide for comparison of actual performance with what should have been accomplished under existing production conditions.

In conclusion, it may be stated that no one system will fit all kinds of industries and operating conditions. To make a definite statement as to the exact circumstances under which the standard cost system could or could not be operated economically is a task which the writer does not feel competent to undertake. However, he is convinced that the standard cost system is sound in principle and worthy of careful study by all who earnestly endeavor to increase the value of cost accounting to the business world.

(16) "Various Wage-Systems in Relation to Factory Indirect Charges," Dec. 15, 1925, Bulletin, Vol. 7, No. 8, R. R. Thompson, McGill University

Editorial Department Note

The method of increasing the productive capacity of the factory is always an important problem and is oftentimes one very difficult of satisfactory solution. In this paper, the author presents the several methods of securing increased capacity, considers briefly their respective points of merit and demerit, and then passes on to a detailed examination of the relation of the various systems of wage payment to the problem of securing an increased factory output by this means.

The author, R. R. Thompson, is professor of accounting at McGill University, Montreal. He was educated at Wallasey Grammar School, served articles (5 yrs.) of apprenticeship to W. Griswood & Son, Chartered Accountants, Liverpool, England, 1905-1909 inclusive. He was admitted as an Associate Member of the Institute of Chartered Accountants of England and Wales, August, 1910, and continued in general practice with W. Griswood & Son until October, 1912. During this period he was lecturer in Accountancy for evening classes held under auspices of Liverpool & Widnes Municipalities, England. He became Treasury Auditor in British Civil Service under the National Insurance Scheme, November, 1912. Upon the outbreak of the war, August 4, 1914 he was mobilized as Second Lieutenant with the Fifth Argyll and Sutherland Highlanders serving in Gallipoli, Sinai Desert, and Palestine. He took up his duties at McGill University August, 1921; was admitted a member of the Association of Accountants in Montreal (Chartered Accountants) 1925.

He is a member of the Canadian Society of Cost Accountants and of the American Association of University Instructors in Accounting. This paper was delivered before the Montreal Chapter of the Canadian Society of Cost Accountants.

Various Wage-Systems in Relation to Factory Indirect Charges

If a manufacturing concern is faced with the problem of an extraordinary demand for its products beyond what its present equipment and methods are capable of supplying, it has four courses open. It may:

1. Buy elsewhere and re-sell
2. Enlarge its factory and increase its productive capacity
3. Work longer hours, that is, overtime, or possibly have two or three shifts of men
4. Produce more in the time already worked by giving its workmen an inducement, by means of a bonus or premium on their wages, to speed up production.

In deciding upon which course to pursue, the following considerations should first be taken into account:

1. If the first course is adopted, the concern loses all the profit that it could make by manufacturing more cheaply than it can buy.
2. The second course entails an outlay of capital in assets which will bring their own overhead charges. After the extraordinary demand has ceased these assets may be lying idle, earning nothing, and the standing overhead charges, such as obsolescence, decrepitude, insurance, caretaking, etc., are still running on. The capital invested is locked up and not available for other uses, and would, if raised on loan, be giving rise to an interest charge.
3. The third course entails no outlay of capital in fixed assets, and little or no increase in the standing indirect charges, such as obsolescence and decrepitude of buildings and machinery, insurance of these assets,etc. It will entail, however, an increase, proportional to the extra time worked, in those indirect charges which vary with the volume of production and constitute the fluctuating indirect charges, such as indirect labor, power, wear and tear of machinery, consumption of tools, spoiled work, and so on. This course may also entail a heavy increase in direct wages, because of overtime rates, unless extra men are taken on and unless different parties of them are worked in a series of shifts. If extra men are taken on, then, when slack times come, they will have to be discharged, and possibly there will be the extra expense of sending them to their homes.
4. If the fourth course is adopted this, too, results in no outlay of fixed capital and no increase in standing indirect charges. The fluctuating indirect charges will increase, but as a rule should not do so in anything like the same proportion as the production. The object of giving the bonus is to get the men to waste no time, to increase their skill and speed, and so to produce for the manufacturer more goods in proportion to the indirect factory charges than they have done hitherto.

Since the main thesis of my paper is the relation of various wage systems to this problem of production, we must now consider the principal varieties of wage-systems under which bonuses are paid for increased production, from two points of view, the workman's and the manufacturer's.

Viewing the matter from what is largely the workman's standpoint, we will see how his hourly remuneration rises in comparison with his increase in speed of production. By "hourly remuneration" I mean the total sum paid to the man per hour, including both regular wages and bonus. The manufacturer, also, must consider the matter from the workman's standpoint, because the latter will speed up in proportion, roughly, to the rate by which his hourly remuneration increases. As the workman speeds up, and saves time, which is used for further production, so does the manufacturer get more production for his indirect factory charges. To repeat, a quantity of the indirect charges, hitherto used up entirely for a certain quantity of production, is saved and is used for further production. But all depends on the rate up to which the men will speed, and that depends, in the end, mainly on the hourly remuneration.

Viewing the matter from what I will call the manufacturer's standpoint, we will consider the limit, up to which it will pay the manufacturer to give an extra bonus in order to save factory overhead or indirect charges, as they are variously called. Unless there are special circumstances, such as might exist in the case of a "rush" job, it will manifestly be worse than useless for a manufacturer to pay, for example, an extra 30 cents in hourly remuneration in order to save 25 cents an hour in factory overhead or indirect charges.

It is assumed, of course, that for the purposes of these comparisons all work turned out is of an equal standard. Obviously, a producer of spoiled goods can never be a cheap producer, however fast he may be. We must not confuse the issues.

We can divide all of these wage-systems into three main groups:

1. Those in which the employer shares in the working time or wages saved by the direct worker's increased speed, principally because the increased speed in production usually results in increased factory overhead, more power, etc., being consumed. If factory overhead remains at its ordinary rate the employer saves not only wages but factory overhead as well; and even if the factory overhead charges are running at a slightly greater rate, because of increased pressure, they are running for less time and a saving in expense will be made. Of these, the principal systems to be considered are the Halsey, Rowan, and Barth.

2. Those in which the employer saves nothing in wages, paying to the direct workmen and their helpers the full rate for the work done, whether it is done at normal rates of speed or more rapidly. These comprise the Ordinary Piece Rate System, and the Bedeaux Point System. Under the Ordinary Piece Rate, if the direct workman is below normal he is paid only for the work actually completed, while under the Bedeaux Point System he is paid the normal time rate.

3. Those in which the employer pays the direct worker the full rate for the work done, together with a bonus which, as the worker's speed increases, results in an increase in the hourly remuneration paid. This is done where the factory indirect charges are so heavy that it pays the employer to give the workman an extra bonus in order to save time. These systems are the Taylor Differential Piece-Rate, the Gantt, and the Emerson.

In all of the systems in these groups, except the Ordinary Piece-Rate System, the employer must be able to estimate before-hand the time which an average man working at normal rate will take for a job. That time is the standard time and gives the standard speed. Sometimes, it is called the previous average time, but by whatever name its use is the same. For a certain job a definite period of time is allotted. As the direct workman improves on this time, so does he get a bonus.

Under piece-rate systems, if the worker is below standard, his remuneration falls accordingly. Under the others, if he cannot reach a certain rate of production, he is usually changed to other work. After inspection of the graph (see Figure 16-1) you will note how expensive it is to employ workmen whose production is less than normal.

Now, the relative values of these various systems as incentives to increase production can be measured best by looking at them from the workman's standpoint. What will he be paid per hour for his work under the different systems? Quite apart from the nominal rate of pay, what will be his remuneration per hour? What will he get in dollars and cents?

In order to compare the different schemes, I have taken a job consisting of 120 pieces, which a first-class man working normally would complete in 120 hours. The hourly rate of pay, for the sake of simplicity, was taken at $1 per hour. The ordinary piece-rate would be $1 per piece. I will now direct your attention to the statement on page 232 which shows the hourly remuneration, under these various wage-systems, of direct workmen of various speed efficiencies. A man's speed efficiency is reckoned as follows:

$$\frac{\text{Standard Time}}{\text{Time Used}} \times 100.$$

Thus, a man who completes 120 pieces in 120 hours is 100% efficient in speed.

If a man completes 120 pieces in 150 hours his percentage of speed-efficiency is $\frac{120}{150} \times 100$ or 80.

If a man completes 120 pieces in 100 hours his percentage of speed-efficiency is $\frac{120}{100} \times 100$ or 120.

Next, I will direct your attention to the graph (see Figure 16-1) which shows the relative increases in hourly remuneration of men working at different speeds under the different wage-systems. Please note especially the diagonal line which marks the increase in speed-efficiency. All of the other lines must be considered in relation to this line.

We will now consider the main features of the various systems with the statement and the graph before us.

Figure 16-1

Graph to Show Relative Increases in Hourly Remuneration Under Various Wage-Systems by Workmen of Various Speed-Efficiencies.

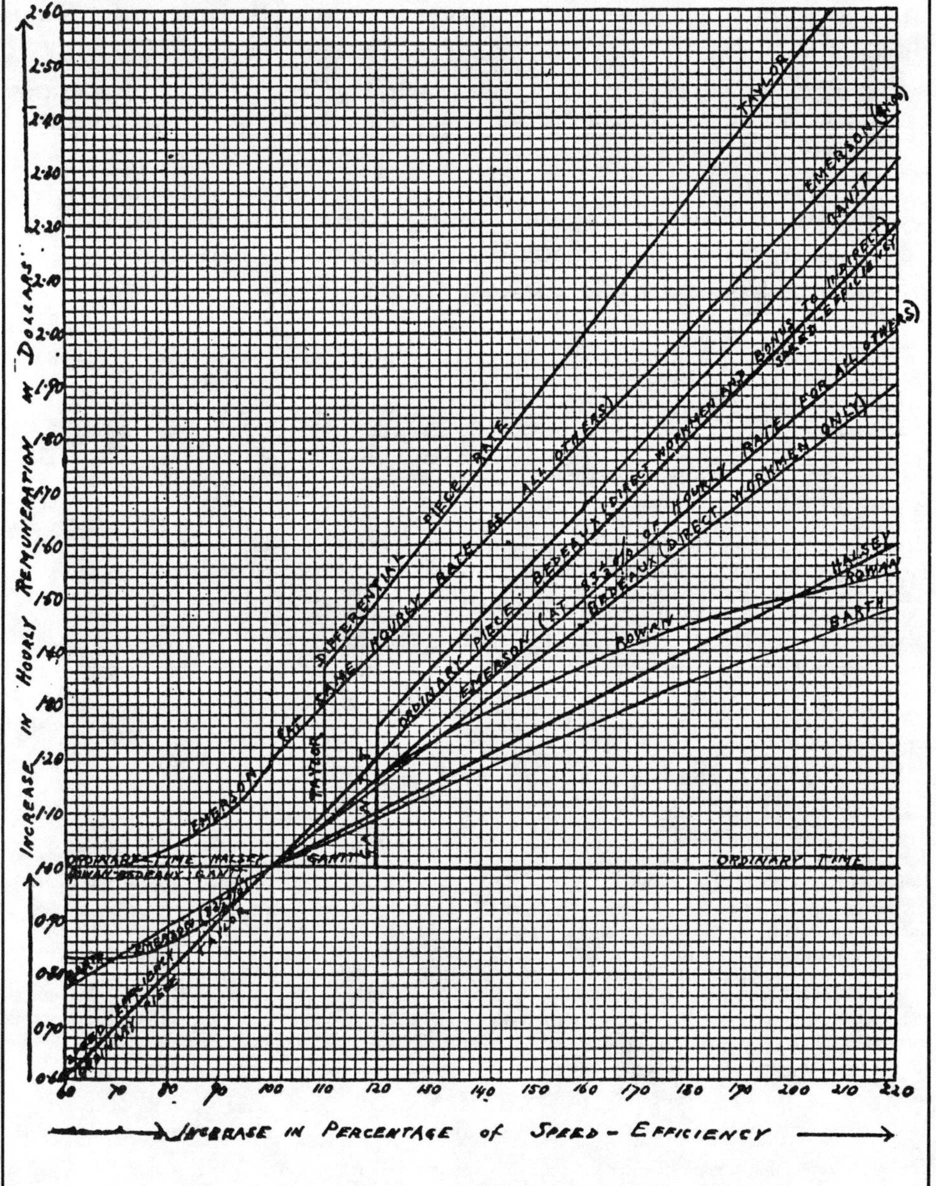

Halsey:

The workman is paid the ordinary hourly rate for the time worked, until he takes less than standard time. He is then paid the ordinary rate for the time worked, and gets as a bonus the ordinary rate for half of the time saved. You will note that, after 100% speed-efficiency has been passed, the hourly remuneration rises steadily and indefinitely—its line is quite straight—but that is nothing like in proportion to the increase in effort by the workman. For this reason, men will speed up to a point that does not cause them serious discomfort, but no further, as it is not worth while to them. Up to 200% speed-efficiency, that is to say for all practical purposes, it is the cheapest scheme to the employer, with the exception of the Barth. It is easy to introduce.

Statement to Show Total and Hourly Remunerations for a Job Received Under Various Wage-Systems by Workmen of Various Speed-Efficiencies.

Time Taken in Hours	181.82	171.42	150	133.3	120	109.09	100	92.3	85.7	80.
Percentage of Efficiency	66	70	80	90	100	110	120	130	140	150
Halsey:										
Total Remuneration	181.82	171.42	150	133.30	120	114.54	110	106.15	102.85	100
Hourly Remuneration	1.00	1.00	1.00	1.00	1.00	1.05	1.10	1.15	1.20	1.25
Rowan:										
Total Remuneration	181.82	171.42	150	133.30	120	119	116.66	113.60	110.20	106.66
Hourly Remuneration	1.00	1.00	1.00	1.00	1.00	1.09	1.16	1.23	1.28	1.33
Barth:										
Total Remuneration	147.71	143.42	134.20	126.47	120	114.41	109.54	105.24	101.41	97.98
Hourly Remuneration	.81	.83	.89	.95	1.00	1.05	1.09	1.14	1.18	1.22
Bedeaux:										
Total Remuneration	181.82	171.42	150	133.30	120	117.28	115	113.08	111.42	110
Hourly Remuneration	1.00	1.00	1.00	1.00	1.00	1.07	1.15	1.22	1.30	1.37
Taylor (25% Bonus at 110% Efficiency):										
Total Remuneration	120	120	120	120.	120	150	150	150	150	150
Hourly Remuneration	0.66	0.70	0.80	0.90	1.00	1.37	1.50	1.62	1.75	1.87
Gantt (Bonus of 20% commencing at 120% Efficiency):										
Total Remuneration	181.82	171.42	150	133.30	120	109.09	126	126	126	126
Hourly Remuneration	1.00	1.00	1.00	1.00	1.00	1.00	1.26	1.36	1.47	1.57
Emerson*:										
Total Remuneration	181.82	171.42	154.80	146.51	144	141.81	140	138.46	137.14	136
Hourly Remuneration	1.00	1.00	1.03	1.09	1.20	1.30	1.40	1.50	1.60	1.70

*If the rate of pay used under the Emerson System be 83⅓% of the rate used for all of the others, the hourly remuneration for the first-class man working at normal speed, that is, at 100% speed-efficiency, will be the same as under the other systems. If this had been done in the above statement the resultant figures would have been as follows:

Total Remuneration	†151.52	143.16	129.00	122.08	120.00	118.18	116.66	115.38	114.28	113.33
Hourly Remuneration	0.83⅓	0.83½	0.86	0.91	1.00	1.08⅓	1.16	1.25	1.33	1.41⅔

It will be noted that after 100% speed-efficiency has been reached, where $1.00 per hour is used, the increase in hourly remuneration per 10% of speed-efficiency is $0.100; whilst, where $0.83⅓ per hour is used the increase is $0.083.

Total remuneration for the job, and hourly remuneration are shown in dollars. Calculations are approximate.

Rowan:

In this, also, the workman is paid the ordinary hourly rate for the time worked until he exceeds 100% speed-efficiency.

His remuneration then is:

$$\text{Wages for Time Worked} + \left\{ \frac{\text{Time Saved}}{\text{Standard Time}} \times \text{Wages for Time Worked.} \right\}$$

As the time saved increases and with it the percentage that fixes the rate of bonus, so does the base, to which this percentage is applied, decrease. The result in the graph is a parabolic curve which becomes merged into and coincident with the $2.00 line at infinity. Thus, a man can never get twice the hourly rate. This system is very generous up to 150% speed efficiency, but after that rises more and more slowly. Again, the reward for an exceptional performance is so reduced that the workman will not speed up past a certain point. It is easy to obtain a substantial increase by only moderate exertions, whilst further exertions give the workman only a relatively much smaller increase. On the other hand, in a factory where experience does not help a great deal, it is difficult to estimate the proper Standard Time for jobs, and big mistakes may be made—usually in over-estimation. This system acts automatically. If a standard is fair it will be unusual for a man to do a job in less than ⅔ of Standard Time, that is with a speed-efficiency of 150%. If he does it in ½ or ⅓ of Standard Time, giving him 200% or 300% speed-efficiency, it will usually mean that a serious mistake has been made in over-estimating the Standard Time. This system saves the employer from serious loss in the event of an over-estimate of Standard Time. Some say that, if the employer's time estimates are very wide of the mark, he deserves to lose, and they condemn this system because they say that it is unfair to the extremely fast workman. Let them say that to the employer who wishes to speed-up production, and yet who has many practical difficulties to contend with, which will prevent him from correctly estimating the Standard Times during one or perhaps several accounting periods. If the Standard Time has been estimated with reasonable accuracy the workman will get a much more generous bonus under this scheme, than under the others in this group, unless he is a worker of most wonderful speed.

Barth:

Mr. Barth conceived his system from the Halsey. The remuneration in the Halsey System consists of the ordinary hourly rate for the arithmetical mean between the Time Worked and the Standard Time. Mr. Barth thought of these as two straight lines, but, instead of laying them side by side, he laid them at right angles, thought of the rectangle indicated, of a square equal in area, and then of the side of that square. He took the geometrical instead of the arithmetical mean. The result was the following formula for finding a man's total remuneration for a job:

$$\sqrt{\text{Standard Time} \times \text{Time Used}} \times \text{Ordinary Hourly Rate}$$

The Hourly Remuneration under this scheme =

$$\frac{\sqrt{\text{Standard Time} \times \text{Time Used}} \times \text{Ordinary Hourly Rate}}{\text{Time Used.}}$$

It will be noted that the Standard Time figure remains constant, while the Time Used figure decreases and occurs in both numerator and denominator. The result in the graph is a very flat parabolic curve—so flat as almost to be mistaken for a straight line after 180% speed-efficiency has been passed.

Its hourly remuneration line in the graph will not cross the Rowan line until after 255% speed-efficiency has been passed. It is therefore the most economical from the employer's standpoint. In order to put it into effect the workmen have to be supplied with slide-rules or computing diagrams.

All of the above systems save wages as well as indirect charges.

We will now consider the second group of systems.

Ordinary Piece Rate:

Men are paid according to production, whether great or small, although in some trades a minimum wage is guaranteed. The workman's hourly remuneration increases exactly in proportion to his speed-efficiency, and the two lines run coincidently in the graph.

Bedeaux Point System:

This saves no wages, as the employer pays away the whole of the standard wages for a job. If time is saved, he gives ¾ of the pay for it to the direct workmen; and ¼ is pooled for a bonus for the indirect workmen. This is done to insure co-operation between the two kinds of workmen. This system expresses all relationships in "points." A point represents the normal amount of work due for a minute. Normal production equals 60 points per hour. Up to this speed workmen are paid the normal rate per hour. Above it the bonus commences. If a workman produces 68 points in an hour, he receives credit for 60 + 6 points. Two points go into the pool for indirect labor. If pay is at the rate of $1 per hour, the rate per point is 1 ⅔ cents. In this case, after 100% speed-efficiency, the Hourly Remuneration line of the direct worker is straight, and, although it is much more generous than the Halsey, still it does not rise in proportion to the man's effort. The employer does not save, and, accordingly, the line for the direct-workers' Hourly Remuneration plus the bonus to the indirect workers runs coincidently with that for speed-efficiency.

Other Systems:

There is another system, which I will simply note here. Under it the direct workmen receive the ordinary hourly rate for ¾ of the time saved. The pay for the remaining quarter is pooled, and used to meet indirect charges, which are in excess of budget estimates. The amount not used in this manner is distributed among the direct workmen.

We will now consider the third group, that is, those systems under which an extra payment, over and above the ordinary hourly or piece rate, is made for the purpose of saving factory overhead.

Taylor Differential Piece-Rate:

Under this a minimum daily wage is not assured. Two piece-rates are used. One, the ordinary rate, is used for performances below the standard set. Another, 25% or 50% in excess of the ordinary, is used for men who attain a high standard of speed and better. In this case the standard has been taken at 110% of normal speed-efficiency. The bonus increase is taken at 25%. It will be noted that its hourly remuneration line runs coincidently with the Speed-Efficiency line, then takes a jump, and rises more rapidly than the speed-efficiency. In other words, as the workman's speed increases, the employer gradually pays more and more for the saving in factory indirect charges. The hourly remuneration increases at the rate of $\frac{125}{10 \times 100}$ of the ordinary hourly rate per 10% of Speed-Efficiency. If the bonus increase were 50%, the hourly remuneration would increase at the rate of $\frac{150}{10 \times 100}$ of the ordinary hourly rate per 10% of Speed-Efficiency.

Gantt:

This is similar to the Taylor, except that a daily wage is assured. Under this system the workman is paid by time until a high standard of speed is reached, after which, no matter what time he takes, he is paid for the Standard Time of the task, together with a bonus, usually from 20% to 50%. In the example, 20% has been taken.

It will be noted that between normal speed-efficiency and the Gantt set-standard for speed-efficiency the employer saves not only factory indirect charges but direct wages as well. After the set-standard has been reached, the line takes a jump and continues to rise more rapidly than the Speed-Efficiency line, but not so rapidly as the Taylor line. Under this, also, as the workman's speed increases, the employer gradually pays more and more for the saving in factory indirect charges.

Under this scheme a further bonus is given to foremen, when a given proportion of their men earn the bonus.

Emerson:

Under this system a daily wage is assured. A standard performance is a full and fair task. The standard time is the time taken by a first class man working at normal speed. In the graph it is the same as for the other systems, and is regarded as requiring 100% speed-efficiency. As soon as a workman exceeds 66 ⅔% of speed efficiency this is counted as 67%, and from there up to 100% he is paid the ordinary hourly rate for the time worked, together with a rapidly increasing bonus on the wages for the time worked. As soon as he passes the 100% point, he is paid the ordinary hourly rate for the time worked plus the time saved, together with a bonus of 20% on the time worked. The Emerson bonus rates as given by Kimball are as follows:

Emerson Bonus Rates

Efficiency per cent.	*Bonus per* $1.00 *wages*	*Efficiency per cent.*	*Bonus per* $1.00 *wages*
67	0.0001	85	0.0617
68	0.0004	86	0.0684
69	0.0011	87	0.0756
70	0.0022	87.5	0.0794
71	0.0037	88	0.0832
72	0.0055	89	0.0911
73	0.0076	90	0.0991
74	0.0102	91	0.1074
75	0.0131	92	0.1162
76	0.0164	93	0.1256
77	0.0199	94	0.1352
78	0.0238	95	0.1453
79	0.0280	96	0.1557
80	0.0327	97	0.1662
81	0.0378	98	0.1770
82	0.0433	99	0.1881
83	0.0492	100	0.2000
84	0.0553		

See *Principles of Industrial Organization* by Dexter S. Kimball (McGraw-Hill).

The bonus is calculated monthly, and not for individual jobs. This is done to prevent men from slackening off and taking the hourly wage for a while, so that they can make special spurts from time to time in order to earn big bonuses.

It will be noticed in the graph how the Emerson line for the same hourly rate as the others ($1.00) rises in an upward curve, which keeps getting steeper until 100% speed-efficiency is reached. After that it mounts in a straight line above and parallel to the speed-efficiency line. In other words, below 100% speed-efficiency the man's hourly remuneration increases more slowly than his increase in speed-efficiency, and then more rapidly. After the man's speed has exceeded 100% his hourly remuneration rises exactly in proportion to his increase in speed.

Where the $0.83 ⅓ per hour rate is used the line is similar in shape, but is below the ordinary time line until 100% speed-efficiency is reached, after which it rises, but not so rapidly as the man's speed-efficiency increases. In other words, after 100% has been passed, the employer saves, at an increasing rate, direct wages as well as factory indirect charges. However, it is apparent that any system, which entails the use of an hourly-rate less than the normal, will certainly meet with opposition from the workmen. Accordingly, I have regarded the Emerson as belonging to the third group of wage-systems.

We must now consider the question of the limit up to which it will pay the manufacturer to give an extra bonus in order to save factory indirect expense.

First of all I would emphasize how expensive it is to employ slow workmen, as against those who work at the normal rate. The excess cost in direct wages is shown in the graph proportionately as between the various systems, by the distances which the hourly remuneration lines are above the speed-efficiency line. It will be noted that the Emerson, using the normal hourly rate, is extremely expensive for all men below 100% speed-efficiency. If the factory indirect charges averaged $1 per productive hour, a line to show them would run coincidently with the ordinary time line. Probably, the indirect charges would show an increase after the 100% speed-efficiency has been exceeded, and the line would mount accordingly above the ordinary time line. Just at the moment, however, we are concerned with the men below 100% speed-efficiency, and you can judge their excess cost in factory indirect charges by the distance which its line—taking the ordinary time line to represent it—runs above the speed-efficiency line.

We will now turn our attention to the men above 100% speed-efficiency. Under the Halsey, Rowan, and Barth systems, as the speed of production increases, the manufacturer saves, not only factory indirect expenses, but direct wages as well. The proportions as between the systems are shown by the positions of the lines, the Barth being the cheapest. Accordingly, these systems will always pay, provided that the estimated allotted times are reasonably correct. Under the Gantt, also, he saves direct wages, when the workman is between 100% speed-efficiency and the standard set for the commencement of its bonus.

Under the Bedeaux and Ordinary Piece Rate he pays neither less nor more for work done, whether production increases or decreases, so that under these he will always save factory indirect charges by means of men who are above 100% in speed-efficiency. It is provided of course that the factory indirect charges will not show an utterly disproportionate rise because of consequent increased power and other expense.

Under the Taylor, Gantt, and Emerson, he pays the full estimated direct-wage cost of each job, and, in addition, an extra sum as soon as the workmen have reached a certain speed. The points at which the bonuses commence, and their relative increases are shown by their hourly remuneration lines in the graph. Under the Taylor he neither gains nor loses in direct wages until 100% speed-efficiency is reached. At that point this line jumps up and the system becomes the most expensive one, being increasingly so. For practical purposes the Gantt is the cheapest, as, although its line rises, the rise is very gradual.

Before any of these systems are introduced, careful consideration must be made in order to make certain that the manufacturer is not going to pay away more than he saves. A good margin, however, must be allowed, because it will seldom follow that the whole of the time saved is being fully utilized for further production. A margin must always be allowed for the changing over and fitting in of jobs.

To emphasize this we will consider a few simple cases, taking the figures set out in the statement above, and assuming that factory indirect charges are applied to the cost of the jobs on the productive-hour basis. Under the Taylor, if the rate for indirect charges is at $1.00 per productive hour:

At 120% *Speed-Efficiency,*

Saving in indirect charges = 20 hours or	$20.00
And the extra payment in wages to effect this saving =	30.00
Resulting in a loss for this job of	$10.00

At 150% *Speed-Efficiency,*

Saving in indirect charges = 40 hours or	$40.00
And the extra payment in wages =	30.00
Resulting in a saving for this job of	$10.00

If the rate per productive-hour were $2.70:

At 110% *Speed-Efficiency,*

Saving in indirect charges = 10.91 hours or	$29.45
And the extra payment in wages =	30.00
Resulting in a loss for this job of	00.55

At 120% *Speed-Efficiency,*

Saving indirect charges = 20 hours =	$54.00
And the extra payment in wages =	30.00
Resulting in a saving for this job of	$24.00

From this it will be seen that such a system, with such a percentage of bonus, would only pay at the lower speed-efficiencies if the rate per productive-hour were about 280% of the hourly rate of wages. As the speed increases so does the net saving on the job increase, but it is probable that the greater number of workmen will be of 150% speed efficiency and below.

Under the Gantt, if the rate per productive-hour were 30 cents:

At 120% *Speed-Efficiency,*

Saving in indirect charges = 20 hours or	$6.00
And the extra payment in wages =	6.00
Resulting in neither loss nor saving	......

At 130% *Speed-Efficiency,*

Saving in indirect charges = 27.70 hours or	$8.31
And the extra payment in wages =	6.00
Resulting in a saving for this job of	$2.31

From this it will be seen that the Gantt system, with the percentages given, will pay, if the rate per productive-hour is over 30% of the ordinary hourly rate for direct wages. Always, however, a margin must be left, and a relationship of at least the following be the rule before the system could be safely introduced: Productive-Hour Rate ÷ Ordinary Hourly-Wage = 32 ÷ 100.

Under the Emerson, using the normal hourly-rate of wages, the average speed-efficiency of all the workmen concerned must be over 100% or the system will result in heavy loss. If the rate per productive hour is $2.00:

At 110% *Speed-Efficiency,*

Saving in indirect charges = 10.91 hours or	$21.82
And the extra payment in wages =	21.81
Leaving the very small saving of	00.01

At 120% *Speed-Efficiency,*

Saving in indirect charges = 20 hours or	$40.00
And the extra payment in wages =	20.00
Leaving a saving of	$20.00

Accordingly, it will be seen that, if the average speed-efficiency of the workmen in a factory were expected to be only 110%, the ratio as between the productive-hour rate and the average ordinary hourly wage must be more than 2 to 1 or a loss will result. In other words if the average ordinary hourly wage be more than, say, 48% of the productive-hour rate, an introduction of the system would result in a loss. Theoretically, the limit could be put at 50%, but I have allowed a small margin of 2%; although this margin will be far too small in some cases. The probability of an increase in the indirect charge cost, because of increased consumption of power, etc., in consequence of increased production, must not be forgotten.

Furthermore, under any bonus or piece-work system the inspection of finished work must be very thorough, and the expense of the inspection will increase accordingly. Otherwise, bad work will slip through, and bad workmen are considerably more expensive than slow ones. When considering the loss that will accrue through bad or spoiled work, one has to take into account the total cost, i.e., direct material, direct labor, direct expense, and factory indirect charges, of bringing the work into its final condition before it was rejected, and also the total cost of turning it back into raw material, together with the cost of material wasted.

In conclusion, may I say that any wage-system must be studied from every standpoint before it is introduced into a concern, as once installed, it is difficult to change, unless it is changed for a system giving the work people a greater advantage. The following questions must be answered satisfactorily before any wage system is introduced:

1. Will it be possible to make good use of the time saved? It will be worse than useless to pay bonuses to get them to speed up and save time, and then be unable to make use of the time saved.

2. Is it going to give sufficient incentive to the workmen to get them to increase production to the required amount?

3. Is it going to cost more in the way of bonuses on direct wages and extra indirect charges for power, etc., than it will save in normal factory indirect charges? Among the extra charges must be considered the cost to run the system, which might be quite an item.

Generally speaking, where the increase in demand is not likely to be permanent, and so does not warrant a capital outlay in fixed assets which will be lying idle in slack times, and where factory indirect charges are heavy, a suitable bonus system will result in the necessary increase in production, without any great increase in charges for power, indirect labor, supplies, etc. This can be accomplished by inducing the workmen to lose not an atom of time, but to crowd every minute with its full quota of productive work.

(17) "Overhead in Economics and Accounting," April 15, 1926, Bulletin, Vol. 7, No. 6, T. H. Sanders, Professor of Accounting, Harvard University

Editorial Department Note

In the not far away past, to expect that an accountant would have a conception of the relation of general business principles and conditions to his work, would have been looked upon by accountants as expecting a qualification which had no relation to their work and by employers as a forlorn hope. How rapid in both cases the change in point of view has been is easily discernible by comparing the accounting literature of ten years ago with that of the present time. Then the emphasis was placed on technique, method, accuracy, and the proof of accuracy. "Letter" perfection was the goal. Now, when one finds himself in a gathering of accountants discussing professional matters, during at least eighty percent of the time, he is not conscious of the fact that these his associates are accountants; for it is the broad aspects of business policies which are receiving consideration, how the facts upon which these policies rest can best be secured and by what means proper executive supervision over operations may be secured and maintained.

Our present publication treats of some phases of these broader aspects of accounting in its business and economic relationships. The author, Thomas H. Sanders, is particularly well qualified to speak on this subject. Educated in England, with graduate work completed at Harvard, and with business and research experience both abroad and here, he is a close student of business. The paper was delivered before a recent meeting of the Cleveland Chapter of the NACA. Mr. Sanders is Associate Professor of Accounting in the Graduate School of Business Administration, Harvard University.

Overhead in Economics and Accounting

It is one of the commonplaces of economic discussions that modern business is now carried on through the agency of an enormous amount of plant and equipment as compared with that with which our forefathers operated, and that, arising out of the use of these fixed investments, business is loaded with heavy fixed charges which do not respond to fluctuations in output. Another outstanding fact is that the aggregate productive capacity of modern plants is greatly in excess of what the market can easily and regularly absorb. Nearly every firm is therefore at the point where a considerably increased business might be undertaken at a decreased cost per unit, if only a market could be found for that output.

Another fact of great importance which has to be faced is that this already heavy burden element will greatly increase in the future. It will increase not only in total amount but in the relative share of the total cost of any one article. This is to be expected in the course of our natural industrial progress, for that progress consists largely in providing workers with more and better equipment. The process will be still further hastened by the cutting off of the supply of cheap labor by means of a restricted immigration. Already we are being told that the demand for labor is exceeding the supply, and that labor costs are mounting as labor becomes more scarce. For society as a whole this represents progress, but for the individual firm it presents a problem of mounting costs which in many cases becomes acute. It means that labor will tend to become replaced by labor-saving equipment. Whenever labor costs rise to a point beyond which the market for that product will not go, the leaders in that industry have no option except to develop cheaper processes by the aid of labor-saving devices, or else get out of the industry.

Nor should this be regarded as an undesirable feature. As already stated, it is a mark of social and industrial progress. From the standpoint of the country as a whole, the people are prosperous in proportion to the per capita investment in plant and equipment which is placed at the service of the workers, though, on account of the temporary difficulties and hardships which are likely to arise with individual groups of workers at the time the changes are made, this larger aspect is frequently overlooked. It is particularly evident, however, to anyone who is familiar with other nations, less advanced economically than ourselves. A traveler, for example, in China, Japan or India is immediately struck by two outstanding facts; one is the scarcity and crudity of the equipment with which the natives of those countries work, and the other is the poverty of the people. The two facts are inseparably tied together, and our people should welcome increases and improvements in their manufacturing equipment, in spite of the temporary displacements of labor.

For the individual firm, however, the presence of this extensive investment in plant and equipment constitutes a constant and serious problem; in fact, it dominates business policy at many important points. The difficulties are still further augmented by the presence, in many industries, of peak loads at certain seasons necessitating an amount of equipment which at other periods of the year is largely idle. If this equipment could be permanently employed at full capacity both the individual business and the community would be better off. If it cannot be continuously employed the firm is still under the necessity of selling its product at a price which is sufficient to maintain the plant and equipment, or else it must go under. In every case the problem is a heavy one, so much so that writers among the economists are giving an increasing share of their attention to it.[1]

Before discussing this subject in greater detail, it will be well to differentiate in a broad way between the economic and the accounting concept of overhead.

[1] See "Economics of Overhead Costs," by J.M. Clark; University of Chicago Press.

It should first be stated that many of the disputes about the content of overhead arise from confusing the economic with the accounting definition of cost. Economists speaking of an industry as a whole, in its relation to society as a whole, define cost as including all sacrifices which the industry must undergo to supply its product to the market; in this sense, interest on all capital, and even the profits which must reward the entrepreneur for his efforts and risks, are costs incurred by the industry, which must be met by those who use the products of that industry. It is particularly important to weigh economic costs before actually embarking upon a business. When once capital has been invested in the fixed assets of a specific industry, however, accountants usually consider that they serve the best purpose by defining costs as the outlays made for production, thus enabling them to ascertain whether there is any residue from gross income to cover interest on invested capital and profits for the proprietors.

In order to do an increased business, however, it is ordinarily necessary for a firm either to cut prices or else to gain some preeminence in the market by an unusually successful product, or equally successful marketing policy. Often the successful firm will do both of these things, but it is difficult for the average firm to accomplish either of them. In terms of economics, the desirable thing would be that all industries would increase their outputs simultaneously; in this way the activities of one industry would create the market for the product of another industry. As the economists say, the supply of one kind of goods is the demand for another kind of goods.

General movements of this sort are, however, for practical purposes impossible to bring about, and the individual firm must go ahead and take its chances regardless as to whether firms in other lines of business make corresponding moves. It is therefore necessary to inquire what the individual firm may do to better its own position in these circumstances.

The most obvious measure for increasing the demand for a firm's products is to cut the prices, a policy which is often and successfully followed, but which needs extreme care and foresight. It would not be worth while to cut prices to the point where the net profit on the increased output was smaller than the net profit on the lesser output had hitherto been. Moreover, it is not profitable to reduce prices if it is simply going to result in demoralizing the market by making buyers hold off in the expectation of still further reductions. Here, again, what is needed is an all-round reduction in prices simultaneously, not only by competitors in the same line of business, but by other industries surrounding them. In this way those who sell to the industry would reduce its costs by quoting lower prices to it, while those who buy from the industry would help along the marketing of the product by reducing their prices in turn. Here again, however, such general arrangements are practically impossible, not to mention the fact that they are frowned upon by the law.

Ordinarily, therefore, decreased selling prices will be quoted by a firm not alone for the purpose of increasing its output under present conditions, but rather the lower prices will be quoted in conjunction with improved methods of manufacture which have actually reduced production costs. In other words, lower prices will be a result of better manufacturing and marketing methods more often than they will be merely a cause of increased output while business difficulties remain the same.

Another line of thought which has recently been argued is that the big industrial concerns should distribute more of their gross earnings to employees as wages, and thus increase the demand for their products, rather than add to their surplus, and use it for still further additions to plant. It has been seen that the fundamental difficulty is the inability of the market to absorb an increased production. The market can be enabled to do better, it is said, only if the general body of the people have larger incomes, and the general body of the people can have larger incomes only if wages are increased over a wide area.[2] This argument is without doubt fundamentally sound, but few firms are individually strong enough to take the initiative in such a course without receiving a good deal of collateral support, not only from other firms, but from other industries. In this connection, however, it is noteworthy that Henry Ford, with the usual courage of his convictions, has increased wages because, it is said, he believed that otherwise we might be approaching an era of declining trade. Few firms, however, have similar resources; nevertheless, this policy might well be considered by the more powerful businesses of the country.

This expression "discrimination" has been borrowed from Professor Clark's book, cited above. It does not for present purposes refer to unfair or illegal discriminations, such as the Interstate Commerce Commission had to suppress in the railroads years ago. It has reference to "charging what the traffic will bear" in the sense of making charges in proportion to the services rendered. Railroads, for instance, have their classifications of more and less valuable freight, which can be charged a different tariff. Electric companies and telephone companies may make lower charges for night services; the department stores may hold their January sales; and so on all along the line. The principle is that, at points where the utility of the product to the customer diminishes, or sales resistance increases, prices are lowered to meet what otherwise would be a greatly decreased demand. The principle is of very wide application; almost any business may make appeal to different classes of consumers at different price levels, the ultimate object being in all cases to find work for otherwise idle equipment.

[2]See "Profits," by Foster and Catchings; Houghton-Mifflin Company.

It is to be remembered that the objective in all these policies is to find the product which can absorb burden which at present is unabsorbed. That being so, the figures of the cost department must be relied upon to set the limits for these policies in various directions. In particular, they must establish the point at which prices are no longer high enough to make any contribution to the meeting of the burden charges. Such computations will require that the cost department shall make very careful distinctions between fixed charges and variable charges, and, among the latter, that they shall determine as closely as possible how greatly they vary with increases in output. Unless the cost department is able to supply definite information on these points, it is likely that some of the manoeuvering of the sales department will be carried on at a loss, and that the situation will be made worse instead of being improved. While, therefore, it is true that the problem is largely a sales problem, as regards determining what the response of the market is likely to be, yet it is not safe for the sales department to act without being constantly in touch with the cost department.

If it should transpire that, in spite of all these efforts, there appears to be a permanently idle capacity, it will be necessary for the directors to look for a correspondingly permanent remedy, in the shape of a new product. This new product obviously must be such that it can be manufactured by the idle equipment with a minimum of change or addition; and further, it should, so far as possible, be such that it can be marketed through approximately the same channels as the older products. An element of weakness is introduced if a secondary organization must be set up to handle the new product, thus dividing the interest and distracting the attention of the directors.

The situation also has a bearing upon the practice, now becoming common among cost accountants, of budgeting normal amounts of burden and from them of determining normal burden rates. It is seen that the definition of unabsorbed burden will depend almost wholly upon how these normal rates are set. The first thing necessary for a normal year in an ordinary business is that it shall earn a fair average return of net profit upon the capital investment in it; a year which does not give such a return should not be regarded as normal. The normal need not be the exact average of a number of years past; the average business will expect to grow, and the normal computed should take that fact into account. The volume of business which will meet the average expectations of the proprietors, and give them a normal profit, should also be used as the basis upon which to compute the burden rate. This will mean, if the burden expenses have been correctly estimated, that the total burden will be exactly absorbed in a normal year. It will mean, in any year, that an amount of burden will be charged against production, proportioned to the volume of business done. The balance of the burden account, representing overabsorbed or unabsorbed burden, will indicate where the business stands during that year as compared with a normal year.

It would appear that this first step, the estimating of a normal amount of burden expense, and the determining of a normal output upon which the burden should be distributed, is the most important step of all in the handling of burden. No other part of the burden computations is likely to influence the results drawn from the cost figures so greatly as this one factor.

Nevertheless, it is important, in many cases, to make a correct distribution of burden to the several departments. Where job, order, or lot costs are used, and where the different products engage the different departments for varying times and to varying extent, it makes an actual dollars and cents difference in the costs of the several products to make a correct departmental distribution, rather than to use a blanket rate for all products and all departments.

In the case of process costs, where a single product goes through the same series of processes, always by the same route, and in the same period of time, it might appear that it was unnecessary to bring down the overhead into departments; the total cost of a product will be unaffected thereby. But even in such cases, it is frequently found useful to show separately the costs of the various departments or sections of the processes, especially for two reasons; first, to keep a check upon the costs of the various departments from time to time, and second, to help direct research work undertaken for the purpose of improving or cheapening the processes. For the latter purpose the departmental costs will help to indicate where savings are most likely to be made.

In this connection it might be well also to mention the case of joint costs, where two or more products emerge from the same processes in such a way that no physical basis is available on which to cost them separately. If the second product is a true by-product, small in amount relatively to the main product, it may well be credited to the manufacturing account at what it will fetch in the market, leaving the rest of the manufacturing charges to fall upon the principal product. If both products are of considerable importance, so that it is hoped to make a profit on each, it becomes desirable to show a cost for each. In such cases it would seem to be in accord with economic principles to divide the total process cost between the two products in proportion to their subsequent selling values. It is for this sales value that manufacturing processes are undertaken, and if one product realizes more than the other product in the market, then more proportionately is the expenditure undertaken for the first product than for the second.

Some people object to this relating of costs to market values; they even assert that it is an abandonment of the true cost basis. The latter statement is not true at all; the amount which is apportioned is the total cost of the two products, and it cannot be said that any method of apportioning their total cost is an abandonment of the cost basis. The apportionment of the total cost on the basis of the selling prices to be realized seems to be in agreement with economic principles relating to that subject.

In discussing the question of the necessity and advantage of making a departmental distribution of overhead, it is necessary to make a distinction between purely departmental overhead, and items which are general to the entire plant, and must be apportioned on some arbitrary basis. There are many occasions when it is desirable to show the immediate departmental overhead, when it may be unnecessary to include therein any prorated items.

Considering again the case of job costs where different products spend different periods in the various departments, a prorating of general manufacturing items is necessary in order to get correct departmental totals, for the purpose of establishing departmental burden rates which will give accurate charges to the products.

With process costs the prorating of general charges seems less necessary. It has already been stated that departmental costs are shown in this case for the purpose of indicating the departmental efficiency, and for the purpose of pointing out where economies might possibly be effected by improved methods of manufacture. The matter of efficiency will in practice probably be covered by a series of departmental cost reports, and it has frequently been found that prorated items, included in such departmental reports, tend to diminish their usefulness rather than to increase it. Such prorated amounts are frequently not understood by the departmental foremen, who feel that in any case they are not responsible for these amounts, and can see no reason why such things should be called to their attention. In the matter of research work it is evidently sufficient to show the immediate costs of the department, without adding any arbitrary amounts by prorating.

In making such departmental reports it is more necessary to have a fairly definite idea as to how the cost figures should vary with changes in the amount of product handled, than it is to make prorations to the department on any particular basis. Many firms are giving thought to this question of the behaviour of overhead, and some of them have worked out charts showing how the cost per unit is likely to move with increased or decreased output.

Another case where prorating of items to departments is less necessary than some others, is where the physical or engineering processes and conditions of manufacture practically determine the costs. This idea is perhaps best illustrated by the assembly of Ford cars. With the product moving constantly at a cerain predetermined speed, and all operations regularly performed, each at a uniform speed, and a certain number of workmen employed along the route, this becomes practically a process cost. The cost per unit is the total cost of operating the process divided by the number of cars turned out during the period, and if the moving belt travels steadily at the same speed, there can be no variation in the cost of assembly operation. In all cases of this sort it is not necessary to make very detailed or frequent burden statements; the burden is predetermined and constant unless and until some change takes place in the method of operating. This, however, cannot be made to apply to all manufacturing plants, or even to the majority of plants. In a recently published article, Mr. Ford expressed his disapproval of private offices for foremen, of reports made on paper, and of clerical work generally within the factory. He stated that the business of the factory executives was to keep the tools in order, and not to read reports. This is true under the conditions described above, which he had in mind. It is true in all conditions that the business of the production executives is to produce; and cost reports or any other reports are useless unless they facilitate production. With varied products, however, and very much less opportunity for standardization than is possible in the case of manufacturing a Ford, it is frequently found desirable and necessary that the foremen and superintendents should be constantly advised of what is going on, and of the costs of operations, in order that attention may be called to special orders which for some reason are out of line. A plant making a great variety of products must use all the machinery of planning, routing, and scheduling its work, and of cost accounting to see that the various operations do not run away with more money than has been anticipated.

As a final remark on departmental distribution, it may be observed that if and when it is deemed desirable to distribute general overhead to departments, this task can be done with very much less trouble than would be supposed from hearing the protests of those who object to it. Moreover, when it has once been done the computations are good until some change in the general set-up of the factory takes place.

There remains only to determine the most accurate rate by which the burden of the department may be allocated to its product. It is not necessary here to enumerate the various methods in detail, but only to point out one or two features. It is probable that in many cases it makes very little difference as to which base is adopted for the computation of the rate; the same arithmetical result would be obtained from any one of several methods. In such case, of course, they will select the method which is easiest to operate in conjunction with their other cost accounting activities. Before this is done, however, the cost accountant should make a number of computations for the purpose of assuring himself that the basis he has selected really is as accurate as any other.

As a general rule a burden rate computed upon a time basis, that is, a labor hour or a machine hour, will be more accurate than a rate computed upon another basis, such as value. This is true for the reason that most of the burden items accrue on a time basis; depreciation, taxes, insurance, salaries of supervisors, and such like items are computed by the week, month, or year. Products should therefore be charged with these items in proportion to the time for which these products engage the services of the departments in which they are made. There has been some reluctance to use machine-hour rates, again under the impression that this is a complicated procedure. But where the machine is the principal agency in production, and labor is employed merely in feeding and tending the machine, the machine rate becomes the natural basis for charges to the product. Here again it may be stated that the difficulties of the computation have been greatly exaggerated. The same sort of rates is used to compute the real cost of operating furnaces in a brass foundry, and for similar units of plant.

One other question arises, and that is as to how often the burden rates should be changed. The answer to this question has been largely furnished by the discussion in the earlier parts of this paper. Burden rates will not be changed unless there is some permanent change in the cost conditions, caused either by some elements of cost being permanently changed, or else by a change in the method of manufacture itself. If it be agreed that one of the main purposes of cost accounting for burden is to show the extent of the variations from normal, then the burden rates will not be changed because of fluctuations in output; rather they will be used as a measure of the extent and direction of those fluctuations and their cost.

(18) "Question Box," 1926 Yearbook

Question Box

President Scovell was in the chair.

CHAIRMAN: What you have on these sheets, gentlemen, is what you and other members of the NACA said you wanted here. Away back in the winter I started to get an expression of opinion as to what you wanted to talk about at this session, and last week I digested the material, had the stencil cut, and here you have it.

Points to Be Debated

1. What are the best ways of accounting for the fixed charges on similar facilities acquired at different prices? Examples: (a) Two or more identical machines bought at different times and different prices. (b) Old model and new model machines for doing the same work. (c) Similar machines differing in size, but frequently used interchangeably.

2. Is it sound policy never to take orders below "normal cost"? If so, what, besides direct labor and material consumed on the order, should be reckoned into "normal cost" – particularly all of the normal burden? Or if not all, what part and that part determined on what principle or plan?

3. Is cost accounting generally more useful to business by determining costs of product (the finished article ready to sell) or costs of functions or factory services (e.g., steam costs, yard costs or sometimes a department cost)?

4.Should the cost department be part of the shop management (works department), or a subdivision of the accounting department?

5. Is the cost accountant often prevented from getting results because operating men do not understand accounting?

6. When should direct labor be combined with burden to make a composite rate? Are there any circumstances seeming to indicate such combination as convenient which may lead to unsuspected trouble?

7. When should experimental work be charged as selling expense? When as part of manufacturing burden? When, if ever, capitalized?

NOTE: On the following pages, the reader will find a carefully edited account of the session for the afternoon of Thursday, June 17. The session developed some widely diverse points of view, and some apparent diversities which, upon further analysis, proved not so real as they appeared. Under these circumstances, Mr. Scovell undertook, with the cooperation of the contributors, to revise and in many cases condense their remarks, so that the reader now has a connected story which undoubtedly reflects the views of the various speakers much more accurately than their extemporaneous remarks.

8. When should outlays for new tools be capitalized? Charged to the job on which first used? Charged to burden?

9. Should work in process be carried in the cost ledger separately as labor in process; material in process; burden in process? Why or why not?

10. When should depreciation (or total burden) be taken as a rate for unit of product (per barrel, per ton, per piece) rather than per month or per year?

11. When should group bonus be used?

12. Should set-up time be included in piece rate or be kept separate—particularly for the increase in factory efficiency?

13. When is it best to make a labor or payroll distribution daily, rather than by a weekly or longer payroll period?

14. What kinds of shop management details are handled best by a committee rather than by someone in authority giving orders?

15. Should normal burden be set: (a) by the best long-sustained experience of the plant, including ups and downs of sales demand; (b) by the best well-sustained operating efficiency; (c) by the best short spurt of operating excellence; (d) by some engineering or time study standard better than any operating experience?

16. What have you done this last year which has been most worth while: (a) to simplify or economize cost work; (b) to make cost results more vivid or effective for operating men—managers, superintendents, or foremen?

CHAIRMAN: I have said time and time again that I think the most important problem in cost accounting today has to do with normal costs, particularly normal burden, and there are two big questions on this sheet that have to do with normal burden, No. 2 and No. 15. I would like, first of all, to have some expression of opinion as to whether we should first talk about No. 2 or No. 15.

CHARLES VanZANDT, *Rex-Watson Corp., Canastota, N.Y.*: Mr. President, is not a definite understanding on question No. 15 necessary as a preliminary to an intelligent discussion of No. 2?

CHAIRMAN: If that is the way you feel about it, we will discuss No. 15 first.

Basis for Setting Normal Burden

CHAIRMAN: I take some satisfaction in the way that question 15 is worded. I tried to step the problem down by four stages from what I supposed would be the smallest denominator to what I thought would be the largest denominator of the burden fraction. You remember I have said over and over again that burden is always a fraction, in which the numerator is dollars and cents and the denominator is some expected output. To simplify our discussion, is there anybody who would be inclined to disagree with the idea that this statement does cover the whole range from the possible minimum to the possible maximum of a normal burden plan?[1] You might not agree that I have provided all the gradations in between, but shall we take that as a starting point, that we have here the top and bottom?

WILLIAM H. ALDEN, Jr., *Miller Lock Co., Philadelphia, Pa.*: Should we understand by the question that we are starting in with the agreement that it is safe to use a normal burden? That is, do you want to keep away from any argument on that one point, because if I were to start a discussion on this point, I should probably begin by questioning the desirability of using normal in place of actual burden in most instances.

CHAIRMAN: To answer your question, I was assuming that the whole cost accounting world had pretty universally come to the idea that we should use some kind of a normal burden. I think there might be a difference of opinion as to what you do with the remainder (unabsorbed or unearned burden). I mean if you have 100 possible units and you only function at the rate of 65, I think there is some possibility of a debate as to what you will do with the remaining unabsorbed 35 units; but I was assuming, as I said, that the whole cost accounting world has accepted the idea of trying to set a normal burden. Do you challenge that to begin with?

MR. ALDEN: The reason the cost accounting world has so generally come to the conclusion that the solution of the burden problem under conditions of low production is to use an estimated normal burden is because it is so obviously incorrect to charge all expenses into costs under such conditions, and in the absence of any other solution it has been thought that an estimated normal burden was the only way out.

As between charging all expenses into costs, regardless of the degree of productivity of the plant, and the use of an estimated normal burden for figuring costs, there can be no question but that the estimated burden method is much the better course to follow, but my contention is that there is still a better way; which is to analyze the items that go to make up burden expense, separating those elements which essentially fluctuate with production from those which are practically fixed. This is, of course, quite a problem but a fairly satisfactory solution can be reached.

There is no justification for relieving costs of any part of the fluctuating charges. Therefore, the problem resolves itself into simply taking out of burden

[1]If there is no attempt to use normal burden, and a plant spreads all its burden over the actual production from month to month, obviously some rates would greatly exceed normal even as defined in (a), but theoretically the rate would never be less than (d).

a proportion of the elements found to be fixed, corresponding to the degree of idleness of the plant, which in turn may easily be determined by figuring the percentage of idle machine hours as compared to the total number of machine hours under conditions of capacity operation. The difference between the total expense incurred and the expense of idleness as figured above is then the actual burden correctly chargeable to costs.

I agree that it is desirable to develop a standard burden, for the same reason that it is desirable to set up standard labor and material values, but I use these standards solely to determine ratios between standard and actual values, and fail to see that it is any more correct to use the standard burden figure as the value to be charged into costs than would be the case in connection with standard labor or standard material.

A more detailed explanation of the method of figuring idle facility expense used by me is given on page 115 of the 1924 Year Book of the NACA.

CHAIRMAN: Is the outstanding point of your philosophy that normal burden at full operation should be one thing, and normal burden at 85% something else, and normal burden at 70% something else?

MR. ALDEN: My standard burden is the same percentage of standard labor for a given machine group at all ranges of production, but this standard burden is used for comparative purposes only, just as I use standard labor and standard material as a means of analyzing actual values.

The burden to be charged into costs is arrived at by relieving total burden expense of that portion arising from the fixed charges of idle equipment.

This idle equipment expense arises from the very opposite of production and is no more a part of production cost than losses due to bad debts or to a fire.

CHAIRMAN: I thought you were starting out to disagree with our premise, but it now seems that you are simply restating our premise. Do you disagree with the concept I was taking for granted? Will you not make that plain?

MR. ALDEN: Possibly I misunderstand what you mean by normal burden. If I understand correctly what I have heard the last couple of days, the term normal burden means that burden which is going to be charged into costs. That is what I disagree with. In my experience I have seen what would be termed normal burden, by any basis I could calculate it, very considerably in error. That is, starting with normal burden based on past experience, I have seen the efficiency in regard to burden improved in one year's time to a point where the percentage of burden to direct labor was about 125%, whereas it has been up around 200%, even after charging off in each case a legitimate amount for the fixed charges on idle facilities. I do not see how you are going to take care of conditions of that kind, if you use a normal rate of burden in figuring costs.

CHAIRMAN: It seems to me that the comment you last made mingles two things, namely a change in burden conditions and a change in activity. To get this hypothesis straight, let us assume that burden conditions are well known and accurately defined, and the result is $1,000 of burden for a particular center. Let us assume, furthermore, to make our mental arithmetic easy, 1,000 units of production expected. That means $1.00 per unit of production. Now if we produce only 700 units, we have then absorbed 700 parts out of 1,000, and we have 300 parts out of 1,000 unabsorbed. When you say that the experience which reckons burden as $1,000 was an unsatisfactory guide, and that burden previously reckoned as $1,000 turns out to be $825, that is what I call mingling variations in burden experience with variations in activity. To set a normal burden rate we must assume a burden experience sufficiently well defined to be used. Obviously if we do better, if, for example, burden which we estimated at $1,000 turns out to be accomplished, shall I say, for $825, obviously the burden rate must be revised, and what was $1.00 per unit presently becomes 85¢. Having done that, if we still have 1,000 units of expected performance, and perform only 700 of them, we have 300 units of idleness at 85¢, instead of 300 units of idleness at $1.00. Have I separated your problem into two parts to your satisfaction, or will you try it again?

MR. ALDEN: Evidently I have not made it clear to the chairman that my differences in burden were after having taken into consideration the proportion of fixed charges that should be charged out for low production. After I get rid of these fixed charges I still find a considerable fluctuation in overhead. My feeling is that in many instances it is very unsafe to set up any standard as normal and use that, regardless of the actual change in efficiency in your factory. I do not believe you can hit very safe results in many instances. Sometimes, no doubt, you can, but it seems to me that you are taking a standard which at best cannot be more than an estimate, and using it as an actual, and I do not see how you can be sure that the unabsorbed burden arrived at in this way is really the amount represented by the cost of idle equipment as distinct from errors in figuring normal burden. I fail to see just how you tie that up.

FRANK L. SWEETSER, *Dutchess Mfg. Co., Poughkeepsie, N.Y.*: What would the gentleman suggest?

CHAIRMAN: What kind of business are you in?

MR. ALDEN: The manufacture of locks—The Miller Lock Works of the Yale & Towne Manufacturing Co.—and this procedure has given us results that are satisfactory to us, and it has shown us, we believe, the actual cost to us of our idle equipment (which has been charged to profit and loss).

CHAIRMAN: You absorb on production actually going on everything except fixed charges?

MR. ALDEN: Yes — everything but the proportion of fixed charges chargeable to idle equipment.

CHAIRMAN: A lot of things are not fixed — foremanship, supplies, etc. As to foremanship and other variable items, do you absorb them, no matter whether the production is big or little?

MR. ALDEN: Foremanship we consider practically fixed, and we charge a proportion of that to our fixed charges, except in so far as a foreman can be put on productive work. Of course, this is very complicated, and that is the reason I asked you whether you wanted to get into an argument on the question.

CHAIRMAN: In answer to your question, I do not see that we can get anything out of it today.

MR. VanZANDT: I think you will find that Mr. Alden agrees with us almost all the way. I do not think there will be much difference.

CHAIRMAN: Let us agree to go on with other items. Do you agree that (a), (b), (c), and (d), as I have them listed here, run the whole scale up and down, or do you want to put in any gradations other than (a), (b), (c) and (d)? Is there any other practical alternative except those four that I have suggested? Would anybody describe those four, or any one of those four, somewhat differently from what I have?

HENRY B. FERNALD, *Loomis, Jefferson & Fernald, New York City:* Mr. Chairman, I think some of us would conceive of the possibility of some combination of these factors you mention where we would not necessarily take (a), for example, "the best long sustained experience of the plant," as an absolute base to be applied, although that would be our primary consideration but we would rather merge to some extent (a) and (d), and as a result get our factor.

CHAIRMAN: Why do you jump from (a) to (d) — if you are going to pay any attention to (a) at all — when you have (b) and (c) on the way down? I can understand why a person would be interested in (a) or (d), but I must confess I cannot see why he would combine those two.

MR. FERNALD: The reason I mentioned (a) and (d) particularly is, that I think (a) may be modified by (d) whereas it seems to me that (a) and (b) are naturally antagonistic. In other words, we may take (a) as a base or (b), or (c), but I think that while we may intend to use (a), for example, as being our long sustained experience which will include ups and downs of sales demand, we may have had some change in engineering or operating practice which we feel should be taken into account. Accordingly while we are taking as a basic principle the long sustained experience, we must couple with that a knowledge of certain changes we have made, which will bring about a somewhat different result, and, therefore, we will take into account such changes as a modifying factor applying against our basic principle. Do I make that clear?

CHAIRMAN: Yes. In other words, what you said might be put this way: If during the period of a long sustained experience, item (a), we had been operating under the engineering conditions suggested by item (d), we would then have had (a) modified in the new engineering light of (d). In this connection, I wonder if it is clear to everybody that (d) is intended to refer to a standard determined by engineering methods (in this case chiefly time study) which indicates production at a higher rate than any experience.

MR. FERNALD: I would recognize the possibility of (a) or (b) being modified by (d), as giving a higher standard than any obtained in actual experience, but the point that I really intended to bring out was that instead of making a rule that we will use our actual past experience in every case, we should say that we will use past experience as a guide, but in each case subject to any modifications necessary to take into account present existing conditions and what we may reasonably expect in the future. I would further say that if we are intending to use (a) as representing our best long sustained experience, we should consider its possible modification not merely by reason of any changes in engineering conditions in the plant, but also its possible change by any commercial conditions which have already arisen, or which we expect to arise during the ensuing period. In this way we will modify (a) from a flat long sustained experience of the past to make it represent our best judgment of what will be our experience for a similar period in the future.

CHAIRMAN: I was going to say that by the same reasoning (d) would modify (a), (b), or (c) — any one of them. That is a good contribution.

JOHN M. SCANLON, *Hess-Bright Mfg. Co., Philadelphia, Pa.*: I believe any distribution of burden should be based on engineering studies made by the time study department. We recently had this done in our plant, and found it was necessary to take "unbalanced equipment" into consideration, as it may be possible that the department doing the initial operation is able to do 5,000 pieces of a given size, whereas a following department is able to turn out 15,000 pieces of the same size. The planning of production is based on studies made by the time study department, and the piece work rates are also based on the "time allowed" and "time used" set by the time study department for the different operations. If these studies are sufficiently accurate to plan production and form the basis of wage payments, it would seem that they should be used for the distribution of burden.

The results of the engineering study should be used, although they may be greater than that obtained by any past performance. Most plants are like individuals; they do not know what they are capable of doing until put to the test. Because a plant has not been able to obtain a certain production in the past, is no reason for its not securing a new standard in the future.

CHAIRMAN: Of course, gentlemen, there are many variables, but in my judgment this is very vital stuff in respect to cost accounting. You remember Mr. Kemp said to us last year in Detroit—I think I quote him correctly—that he was standing squarely on item (a). Of course, he or anybody else would have to make what allowance he could for changed engineering conditions, but he was plainly enough taking in the ups and downs of sales demand. There was no doubt about that at all.

MR. VanZANDT: Mr. Chairman, if you will bear with me for a moment, I think it would have been very valuable if you had told this convention something about the discussion on this very same point in Detroit. If you remember, both Mr. Kemp and myself advocated one view of normal volume of production. I think at that time you yourself summed up what might be described as normal volume of production in much better language than has been done in these questions, which I find confusing. At that time you summed up the three views that had been presented in this way: first, that the normal volume of production should be taken at practical capacity of the plant; at the other extreme is total cost divided by the actual product, and therefore high costs in dull periods and lower costs in active periods; the third view was that normal volume of production is a compromise between those two, and that is the view that Mr. Kemp and I argued.

CHAIRMAN: I thought Mr. Kemp was not on any middle ground at all. I thought he was on the ground of experience, including ups and downs of sales demand.

MR. VanZANDT: Unless I grossly misunderstand him, Mr. Kemp's normal production is a compromise between practical capacity and the average of past performances. It is very strongly in my mind because that is identically my own view, and I was so delighted to find that Mr. Kemp agreed with me 100% on the question.

CHAIRMAN: In other words, you claim that you and Mr. Kemp were in agreement in setting the denominator or the divisor for this burden fraction low, so that the burden rate would be relatively high.

MR. VanZANDT: Low is a comparative term.

CHAIRMAN: Yes, so the burden rate would be relatively high.

MR. VanZANDT: Relatively high, yes, if compared with rates based on practical capacity. We have, as I said a moment ago, two extremes; one of them the practical capacity of the plant, the other the actual current production; the third a compromise between those two extremes.

HARRY A. BULLIS, *Washburn-Crosby Co., Minneapolis, Minn.*: I believe that normal burden should be set by the most economical operating performance – the point of most efficient operation, where increasing economies cease and diminishing economies begin. This performance is the "exactly right gait" for the plant, and occurs when personnel, equipment, and materials are correlated in such a manner that operating costs are reduced to the minimum and profits for the entire organization increased to the maximum. This standard performance should be set by engineering studies using records of past experience as a basis for analysis and taking into consideration sales possibilities for the products. Using this method, the point may fall anywhere between (b) and (d).

MR. SWEETSER: Mr. Chairman, I would like to declare (d) to be absolutely right – with a full knowledge of what I am going into, and I would like somebody to fight about it. I think (d) is absolutely right and the only basis to take.

MR. VanZANDT: Mr. President, will you bear with me for a moment again? One of the speakers told us last night that the first thing we want to determine is "where we want to arrive," and it seems to me that before we tackle any one of these propositions, we should settle in our own minds the end that we want to reach. What do we want to accomplish? I believe that what we want to accomplish is to eliminate from the profit and loss statement any fluctuations in net earnings due to a difference in volume of production going through the plant. As I have said many times before, if normal rates are properly set, the profit and loss account should never be affected by any entries on account of unabsorbed or over-absorbed burden. If we could agree on that aim, I think we would have much less difficulty in arriving at an agreement as to what volume of production we should take as normal. Suppose we are keeping our books in the old-fashioned method, and not using any normal rate at all, i.e., putting 100% of current operating charges into our costs. Because of the variation in output and the corresponding variation in overhead from month to month and from year to year, we get extremely variable costs. Now what is the result of establishing normal rates? If we have done it with the idea of keeping unabsorbed or over-absorbed overhead out of the profit and loss statement, the result is to lessen the variations in cost, and if we are going to do that, to my mind, there is only one possible way to accomplish it, and that is to take as the normal volume of production a compromise figure between practical capacity, on the one hand, and on the other hand, the average demand for product over a period of time.

At this point the chairman wrote a table on the blackboard as follows:

Assuming a department with $1,000 of burden:

	Production	Burden per unit
(a)	700	1.43
(b)	860	1.16
(c)	930	1.08
(d)	1,000	1.00

CHAIRMAN: If you will look at the blackboard I will tell you what I had in mind when I prepared the classification (a), (b), (c), and (d). As a matter of convenience, we will say a year is "long sustained experience" (of course, you might argue that), and for (a) that the best year that this company ever maintained month after month was 700 units per period. (b) Under good operating condition, when the sales department kept them busy, they averaged 860 for a long period of time. (c) For about two weeks in that favorable period they maintained a pace of 930. Finally (d) the time study man says that, according to his calculations, they ought to produce 1,000 (these figures are per week, per day or whatever you please). Now, if we assume $1,000 for burden (which is, of course, arguable in the terms of Mr. Alden), we get a burden rate of $1.43, at 700 units, and we progress through these various stages until we get the (d) basis of $1.00. Assume a lot of 100 units going through, and assume material and direct labor are not subject to debate. On those 100 pieces shall we reckon $1.43 per unit for burden, or $1.00 per unit for burden, or something in between? Where would you strike your compromise, Mr. VanZandt? I suppose you would not put on as much as $1.43, and you would not be satisfied with as little as $1.00.

MR. VanZANDT: What does the 700 pieces represent with regard to capacity? Does it represent any definite figure?

CHAIRMAN: It represents the best run that this company has been able to maintain week in and week out for a year. There has been some idleness, some bad sales work, some kind of production difficulties, but that is the best long distance run they have had.

MR. VanZANDT: I would say, then, that that represents fairly accurately the average demand for the product. In that event the normal figure, according to my view, would be somewhere between (b) and (c); just exactly where I am unable to say, because I would have to know all the conditions of the company's past history, and have a pretty good estimate of what it is going to do in the immediate future before it would be possible to fix that point.

CHAIRMAN: I understood Mr. Sweetser to declare bluntly for (d).

MR. VanZANDT: The reason I seriously object to (d) is that the overhead rates then are too low, and they will never accumulate a reserve for unabsorbed overhead.

MR. SWEETSER: Gentlemen, what is the purpose of cost accounting? That is really the question we are debating, and from an executive point of view the purpose is not only to establish selling prices and not only to determine, perhaps, how the sales department is running, but it is fully as much to point the way to cost reductions in various factory and service departments. There are really three angles—(1) selling price; (2) asset value in inventory; and (3) how to use costs to improve the work of your organization. The best basis for pointing the way to cost reduction by your organization is the (d) basis. Assume that the quantity of 1,000 is scientifically determined by engineering practice, that will certainly make for a conservative inventory, and it will give something to shoot at that is worth while, and, gentlemen, we are facing at this time a competitive period when we want to know how low we can afford to go on selling prices. I think it is very important for the management to know where that danger line is. You can certainly add on to your lowest cost any factors necessary to cover idle capacity, or whatever else is desired. You do not have to have costs constructed in a particular way to make selling prices. The other features are more important.

MR. FERNALD: I would, now, emphasize what I spoke of before by saying that I think any one of the gradations (a), (b), and (c) should, perhaps, be subject to a modification, so that they should not be used flat. In other words, instead of saying that (a), (b), or (c) might be modified by (d), to say that (a), (b), or (c) should perhaps be modified in their use by the application to past experience of our best engineering judgment as to future expectancy.

CHAIRMAN: You are applying engineering judgment for revised conditions, not an engineering judgment to revise an experience; is that right?

MR. FERNALD: Yes, but I am saying that instead of making a rule that we will use past experience, we should use our best judgment for the future, based on past experience, but modified in every case to take into account present existing conditions and what we should reasonably expect in the future.

CHAIRMAN: To make our discussion easier, let us assume that the engineering conditions have not changed through a period of three years. We are doing the work now just the way we have done it for the three years. During that time the best the plant has been able to accomplish, even for a short spurt, is 930 units. A competent time study man comes in and says that there is a lag there still, that the work can be geared up to 1,000 units, and the foreman says, somewhat incredulously, "We have never done it. I think 930 is the best we can do." Mr. Sweetser, if I understood him, would say if the time study was competent and convincing, he would jack up the standard to 1,000; that is, increase the denominator and diminish the rate. Certainly Mr. VanZandt does not follow Mr. Sweetser up to the 1,000 at all. It is perfectly plain he stops somewhere between 930 and 700.

MR. VanZANDT: Mr. Chairman, I would like to call attention to the fact that Mr. Sweetser disagrees with me because he does not have the same aim. Recollect I said a few moments ago that the prime object I want to accomplish is to keep out of profit and loss all charges or credits on account of fluctuations in the volume of production. Now you will understand my idea very much better; at least, it will be much clearer, if I get the object of it over to you, that is, the principal object.

MR. SWEETSER: I object to your object entirely, Mr. VanZandt. My aim would be never to have any over-absorbed burden, unless the plant operates overtime.

MR. VanZANDT: The result would be that either through inefficiency or failure to sell the capacity of the plant, you would always be operating below your normal?

MR. SWEETSER: Yes.

MR. VanZANDT: That is what I believe is thoroughly wrong.

CHAIRMAN: There you have an issue joined just as sharply as anything could be. Mr. Sweetser said why he thought it was the thing to do. Do you want to add anything to that?

MR. VanZANDT: There is only one question I would like to ask. Have you had any trouble in selling the capacity of the plant?

MR. SWEETSER: Certainly. That is what I want to know.

MR. VanZANDT: There are some industries that always have capacity sold. When that is the situation, then all of this discussion has absolutely no point at all.

CHAIRMAN: Why do you object to that concept?

MR. VanZANDT: For the reason I gave you, Mr. Chairman, that I do not believe the profit and loss account should ever be affected by such entries. Normal production should be established at such a point that over a period of time (and by that I mean a period of years, not one year) unabsorbed overhead and over-absorbed overhead balance.

MR. SWEETSER: I think Mr. VanZandt's theory is absolutely untenable, because I do not believe we can project our figures accurately enough to keep some differential out of profit or loss. I have never seen a set-up that came out exactly right, and I do not believe anybody can do it. How would Mr. VanZandt answer that point?

Another point I would like to make is that what we want to know, is where we are falling down, and we want to know it very definitely so we can work with the organization. I believe that the accountant, or the treasurer, or the president, can better adjust himself on reading figures than can an organization of several thousand people. I want to sell the organization on a standard that is set up where it ought to be, so they will believe that it is a standard that can be lived up to; and it is much easier to adjust officials examining a profit and loss statement, than it is to adjust thousands of other people affected by this proposition.

CHAIRMAN: I suppose we must admit that a standard of 1,000 units, although determined by careful, competent time study often looks impossible to the practical men in the plant. They run along month after month and always have unearned burden, or, as you say, never over-earned burden. They then say to themselves, "The man on top is holding up in front of us, and to some extent holding us up to an impossible standard of performance. It is visionary, an unreal thing; it is not something we in our work-a-day performances can attain to. If only the manager would cut that down, and instead of setting the standards by this 'theoretical' time study, or because some man did make so-and-so for a forenoon, or perhaps for a day and a half—if he would modify the standard and get it down (for the purposes of this discussion to a 930 basis)—we would have to admit that we have done that two weeks in a stretch and we recognize that as an attainable thing; that looks to us like a human interpretation of this production problem." Do I not state pretty well a point of view which prevails in the shop?

MR. SWEETSER: Yes, but I think that point of view ought to be attacked.

Mr. Filene in Boston only expects 25% from any of his people. I find that whenever we have a real honest-to-goodness standard set up and have explained it to the people properly, and shown them how it can be done, it is surprising what actually we can get out of them. The human being reacts right if you go at it right. I will quote the president of our company last night on this principle. We do not do this thing cold; we do it in a very warm way. I think you all realized that when you listened to her. Tell the people what you have set as a standard and where it ought to be. I do not say it should be an impossible standard; it should not be, of course.

CHAIRMAN: I suppose a standard is always regarded as impossible until it has been worked out in practice.

A MEMBER: Did anyone ever set a piece work standard, after perhaps a month of study, that was not attacked by the most interested party in the shop? I never did. It is always attacked. Is it right? No, because they will go right out and beat it, sometimes 50% over your estimate.

MR. BULLIS: The standard should be fair both to the management and the workers. In the past, I believe that the people who have set standards have not always had the courage of their convictions, and that sometimes standards have been set too low. The method that I advocate of setting normal burden by the most economical and profitable operation would, in certain circumstances, make use of a standard performance which might seem too high to the workers. On the other hand, the use of such a standard performance, set by a competent engineer, would allow the executives to capitalize on the psychological fact that if a reasonable attainable standard is kept before a man and he knows that a record is being made of his progress toward that standard, he is going to do his utmost to reach it.

CHAIRMAN: I will take the liberty of giving this discussion a turn right at this point. Mr. VanZandt, if you will permit me, I will put your test aside for the moment. I do not say it should not be used; but I would like to have this discussion go on a basis somewhat different from your test.

MR. VanZANDT: May I make a point before you do that?

CHAIRMAN: Yes.

MR. VanZANDT: If I wanted that figure as Mr. Sweetser does, as a standard for the shop, to measure shop efficiency, or a mark for the shop to shoot at, I would agree with him 100%. We talk about normal as a standard. We have got off the question of normal production. Why do we say that normal and a standard are the same thing? They are totally different in my mind.

CHAIRMAN: That remark forces me to a little different comment from what

I had in mind when I started to talk. When I phrased this question when we had it up last year, and when I phrased it again this year, I had in mind that cost accounting has entirely got away from an idea that prevailed fifteen or twenty years ago, when we waited until the end of a production period to find out what the burden was and what the production had been, and then divided one by the other so that we would spread all the cost over all the product. Of course, that is going back to first principles, and I suppose everybody in this room will agree that for all practical purposes we have discarded that. Now what did we put in its place? Assuming for the moment standards of material and labor (which, of course, are sometimes debatable items) defined on any basis you please, to that you must add burden according to some plan. What is ordinarily called normal burden is a burden which can be sustained week after week and month after month. Mr. Sweetser introduces a policy and philosophy by saying, in substance, that he wants the burden figured as low as it can be on any logical basis. That is a perfectly fair paraphrase, and he nods his head in assent. Now somebody else says, "No, I cannot subscribe to any extreme or exacting view as that. I feel that I have practical uses for my costs in respect to inventory and shop efficiency and sales policy (the three things that Mr. Sweetser mentioned). I think those practical objects of mine are better attained if I modify this exacting standard of 1,000 and bring it down somewhere around 930 and 860." Now 930, mind you, according to my premise, was something the plant had done for a couple of weeks; 860 was something they had done for a long time when the sales department kept them busy. The 700 basis is simply 860 modified by the failure of the sales department to keep them busy. Now, personally, I feel this way about it: If I were the manager and saw two or three weeks (or any good, well-rounded period) that was hitting on the 930 basis, and then I looked at a period of six whole months when the shop had to admit that the sales department kept them busy, I would say to the shop, "Well, if you could hit 930 for two weeks, why could you not hit 930 for two months?" I feel between (c) and (b) that everybody who sympathizes with what I will call Mr. Sweetser's point of view, is going to insist on (c) as against (b). You would agree with that, would you not, Mr. Sweetser?

MR. SWEETSER: Yes.

CHAIRMAN: Now I would like to find out if there is anybody in this room who between (c) at 930 and (b) at 860 would put any emphasis on 860 as against 930, and why.

MR. FERNALD: I would, for this reason. I appreciate what Mr. Sweetser says, and if I were in what I imagine his position is, I would also be inclined toward his view, but it so happens that I am more concerned in looking at these costs from the viewpoint of people who are differently circumstanced—that is, not those who are directly concerned with the actual running of the business, but those who have money in the business and want to know what it is doing. Suppose a business is running on 60% capacity and I am asked to find what it costs to produce goods at that capacity. If I tell my people that to produce those goods it costs the same amount on 60% capacity that it does on 100% capacity, but that at 60% capacity there will be an unabsorbed burden which will eat up all their profits and show a loss on the business, they will not understand it or believe it is right. Or if those people have a statement of the costs which in effect says, "It costs so much per unit; we have sold so many units, we have an operating profit of so much per cent"—and I have to tell them that is simply on a basis of standard costs with a difference in unabsorbed burden, whereby the stated profit per unit is changed into an actual operating loss, they are apt to have the idea that the management is trying to misrepresent costs and fool the investor as to the actual profits from the business.

CHAIRMAN: Mr. Fernald, I think I will take the liberty of saying that that difficulty, which you describe so vividly and so accurately, is a difficulty in the education of the owners, and I think in today's discussion we must confine ourselves to the point of view of cost accountants and operators who do not have that particular mental disability. As a professional man, of course, I recognize your problem. I have been up against it; but let us lay that aside, and let us say we are within the group of those who do know and do understand and are willing, within such limits as Mr. Sweetser or Mr. VanZandt would agree, to work out the problem in the best way. We must argue the problem in the terms of cost accountants. We must narrow this discussion in order to get the point out. I am taking the liberty of doing that, if you do not object.

MR. FERNALD: I just want to say one more thing. I do not believe we can eliminate that point of view, because our industries are coming to be more generally owned by a large number of people, and if we attempt to go against their beliefs, which we must admit have a great deal of merit in them, we are not going to furnish accounting statements which will satisfy the business owners.

CHAIRMAN: For the operation of a steel mill, if the output is sufficiently uniform so that the cost per ton can be used, I will agree that we can get an answer in your terms which is useful to the management. It may be said when we produce 1,000 tons a week, or 930 or 860 tons a week, or 700 tons a week, the figures are like those on the board; but I assert with a great deal of confidence that such an interpretation of a varied industry breaks down, so that the resulting figures are useless. For a plant making a complicated industrial product, that line of reasoning, which you say must be respected, is not good for much except as a very narrow and crude index. Suppose a company is building washing machines, for example. In my opinion, you cannot argue that at 1,000 a week you can build these washing machines at a cost of $10 apiece (to lift the decimal point on the table) and if you build but 700 a week the cost would be $17.30. I think that argument with respect to washing machines is hardly worth stating, and I would undertake to educate the owner to the right reasoning.

MR. ALDEN: Right along that line, I would like to express my belief that the whole situation we are arguing about would be simplified very much if, instead of units of production, the number of hours of actual operation were taken as a standard. To make it simple, let us assume that there is one machine in a factory. If that machine is running the whole number of hours, I would say that the plant is running 100% capacity. Actually you have to discount that a certain amount to take care of break-downs and set-ups, etc. I use 80% of the possible hours of operation as my standard on which to figure my idle facilities, and also on which basis to figure my standard burdens.

CHAIRMAN: You call 80% an attainable performance, allowing for all human vagaries and weaknesses?

MR. ALDEN: Yes.

MR. SWEETSER: Do you not think an engineering standard is better than an 80% guess?

MR. ALDEN: Engineering studies combined with common sense should be the basis of the percentage decided upon in each case.

A. S. POHL, *Oneida Community, Ltd., Syracuse, N.Y.*: On a cost plus contract if you were trying to sell your burden rate, would you attempt to do it on (d) plan, or Mr. Sweetser's or Mr. VanZandt's or Mr. Fernald's?

CHAIRMAN: What kind of business are you in?

MR. POHL: Whether it is manufacturing some staple article for the government, or whether you are in the contracting business.

CHAIRMAN: When one says "cost plus," the suggestion immediately comes up in my mind of a contracting business, and that means organizing a particular job ranging from digging a cellar for a house to constructing the Delaware River bridge, and I take it there is a strong disposition in all such cases to take all outlays on the job as part of the cost of the job. We are dealing, it seems to me, with facts very different than this contracting experience.

J. F. STILES, JR., *Abbott Laboratories, Chicago, Ill.*: I want to ask, Mr. Chairman, if you were manufacturing specialty products for stock, which one of those four costs would you think was correct to submit to the man in charge of fixing the prices for a catalog, that is, the safest one?

CHAIRMAN: Well, I think that is a real question. I think, Mr. Stiles, if I were faced with that problem, I should pass over to the executive who was responsible for setting the selling prices, a cost figure that as to burden was somewhere between the 860 and the 930 basis; I would tell him as intelligently as I could how I had arrived at the figure. I would tell him what I thought the possibilities were of our competitor holding 930 when we did not hold it, but only occasionally got it. I would try to suggest to him what I thought the possibilities were of our competitor making an average that was 940, when we never got that at all. In such particulars I would tell him as intelligently as I could how I got the cost, and then I would let him put on what he, as a practical manager, thought was safe for the competitive market in the catalog. That is the way I think I would go at the problem, if I found a manager who really understood and did not have the difficulty which Mr. Fernald cites, (I think Mr. Fernald will agree that the man making the catalog and the man running the shop must have a common understanding). That is the way I would do it. Would you do it differently?[2]

MR. STILES: I have always kept a record of the cost of idle equipment. However, this is in memorandum only. We have tried to keep the costs we use for establishing the prices in our catalog as near the actual cost as possible. We refer only to the memorandum of the cost of idle equipment when we are figuring on special jobs, which are likely to be highly competitive.

CHAIRMAN: What you do, in substance, is to hit somewhere around my 920 or 910, and then say to the sales manager, "As we are running the plant, the best we have ever been able to do is something around 700. You must put a profit factor in these figures that recognizes all the loss between 910, which is a good attainable performance, and 700, which is what you fellows are selling."

MR. STILES: Suppose you did submit a figure between 860 and 930, and at the end of the year, or at the end of any accounting period you came below that point. You would, therefore, be forced to submit to the management an unabsorbed factory burden to be included in the operating statement. Would it not be up to the cost man and the catalog price fixer who had been called in to see that a sufficent factor was added to the price fixed?

[2]In correspondence after the convention Mr. VanZandt wrote: "I agree absolutely with the answer you made to Mr. Stiles, and on that basis, I do not know what you and I have been arguing about."

CHAIRMAN: If I were the man in the factory and you were the catalog price fixer, and the big boss called us in, if we knew our business, would we not say to him, "Mr. Boss, while you are objecting to the prices that we, as a factory man and a sales manager, have used, the X Company, we have good reason to believe, is hitting 940 right along?" Are we not duty bound to urge that possibility sharply upon his attention?

MR. STILES: That is very true; there is no question but what your competition would force you to do that. Nevertheless, I think you would find yourself in rather an embarrassing situation, if you are continually showing unabsorbed factory burden as a deduction from your operating statement.

CHAIRMAN: I would rather tend toward the extreme which Mr. Sweetser so gallantly espoused here. I would rather tend toward that extreme and risk the criticism which you speak of, Mr. Stiles, than I would to have the manager say, "You have got the price so high I cannot do anything in competition." I would rather go up the scale for production than down, and deal with the executive on that basis.

Should Orders Ever Be Taken Below Normal Cost?

CHAIRMAN: Let us turn to Mr. Stevenson's question, if you will, No. 2. Mr. Stevenson said at the Buffalo Regional Conference that he had pretty well come to the conclusion that people might just as well stand their ground and not cut prices, and then he undertook to define what he meant, and he defined it about as I have in No. 2, and I understand him to mean material, labor, and normal burden, and if we agree—just to put down some figure here—we have settled this problem, we will say, on the basis of 900, and we have got something like $1.11—that is our compromise figure. If I understood Mr. Stevenson, he would take the labor and material which had to be consumed in making the order and the burden $1.11—and, broadly speaking, he said that industry might just as well stand there and be done with it. That is pretty largely a matter of policy. What do you think about it, gentlemen? Were you there at the Buffalo Conference, Mr. VanZandt?

MR. VanZANDT: No.

CHAIRMAN: Who heard Mr. Stevenson at the Buffalo Conference?

MR. SWEETSER: I did.

CHAIRMAN: Do I represent him fairly, Mr. Sweetser?

MR. SWEETSER: Absolutely.

CHAIRMAN: I thought so. What about it, gentlemen?

G. H. FRIESEL, *United Engineering & Mfg. Co., Pittsburgh:* Industry as a whole would be in a better position if it could at all times sell its product at not less than a cost calculated on a normal basis of operation, but if any particular branch of industry is operating at only 30% or 50% of capacity, it is the tendency of the less successful concerns in the industry to sell at any price that will return the actual outlay necessary to manufacture the product plus whatever portion of the fixed or constant overhead that can be obtained. This condition exists particularly in the manufacture of a product that requires a large investment in plant and equipment per direct labor hour.

CHAIRMAN: In other words, you feel that what Mr. Stevenson announced is just as impossible as the enforcement of the prohibition law in Atlantic City. Is that right?

MR. FRIESEL: I do.

CHAIRMAN: Does anybody else want to comment on it?

MR. BULLIS: When the selling price includes the cost of the direct labor and material consumed on the order, it may be good business to take a certain amount of business below "normal cost," especially if taking this business keeps production up to the most economical and efficient performance, and the acceptance of the business does not depress the general price level. Take the factors of your problem, namely, burden expense $1,000, with an average normal burden rate of $1.11 computed on the basis of 900 units of production. If, in setting the figure 900, it was estimated that 100 would be below "normal cost" business, and that all the burden the traffic would allow on this business was 50¢, then the 100 units of below "normal cost business" would absorb $50 burden and leave $950 burden to be absorbed by the remaining 800 units at a rate of $1.19.

MR. ALDEN: The only proportion that you can legitimately cut and do business is the proportion of that $1.11 which is fixed, and that is not the entire amount of the burden. Certain elements of burden are fixed and others vary more or less in proportion to production. Assuming the fixed part of burden is 25¢, then if you accept a reduction of 10¢ on that $1.11 price, you can earn 15¢ of the fixed burden and help your company to that extent. If you make a reduction of more than 25¢, you are worse off with the business than if you did not get it.

CHAIRMAN: I think the difficulties of our discussion increase a great deal, when we consider fixed and variable items, although we must recognize that we have to face this phase of the matter in our daily work. Would you say, Mr. Alden, that you would expect to recover, not only labor and material, but all the burden which would be incurred because that order and others like it were taken; that is, a prime burden in the strictest sense of the word, or did you mean all the so-called variable burden according to normal experience?

MR. ALDEN: As nearly as I could figure it – of course, it is impossible to hit on an exact figure – if I could not get a variable burden which would not be incurred if I did not have that order, I certainly would not take the order, as I would then be out the difference between the amount received and the variable burden.

CHAIRMAN: I think you have to approach it as you do, but what actually happens is this: If 25¢ of that $1.11 represents interest on investment, taxes, insurance, and depreciation, which we will call for the purposes of this discussion fixed charges, then 86¢ represents variable burdens, heat, light and power, and foremanship. If you do not take the order you do not save all the 86¢, of course. Your argument goes all through the 25¢ and part way into the 86¢, of course.

MR. ALDEN: I am assuming that the 86¢ is really fluctuating in proportion to production. Then you will not have to spend the 86¢ if you do not take the order but you will have to spend the 25¢. Therefore the 25¢ is a dead loss if you do not take the business.

CHAIRMAN: You will have the 25¢, and unless you absolutely shut down, some part of the 86¢. It varies with production, does it not?

MR. ALDEN: There is an intermediate stage there that you cannot definitely fix, I agree with that.

MR. VanZANDT: You have taken a point here that, as nearly as I can see, approximates my idea. You have taken a compromise between two extremes for normal.

CHAIRMAN: I intended to ignore the 700 entirely. I mean my reasoning about it absolutely ignores this. I care nothing about this at all. At this point Mr. VanZandt placed two charts on the blackboard (see Figure 18-1).

MR. VanZANDT: These charts illustrate the result when operating with normal rates based on the idea I have recommended. Ideal conditions have been assumed. The first shows an accumulation in the reserve sufficient to carry through the depression, as illustrated by the production curve compared with normal. This condition permits the fixing of selling prices based on a normal cost at all times.

In actual practice it is always a condition of low production that induces the use of normal rates. In the accounting there is no alternative but to charge the unabsorbed burden to profit and loss until an upward swing results in over-absorbed burden. In fixing the selling prices there is perhaps a choice. The cost of unabsorbed burden may be added as a separate factor to the normal manufacturing cost before fixing the selling price, if it is possible to do so. Or the unabsorbed burden may be ignored, the selling price fixed on the normal cost and reliance placed on an intensive selling campaign to bring the volume up to normal.

H. E. HOWELL, *General Fire Extinguisher Co., Providence, R.I.*: Your question

Figure 18-1

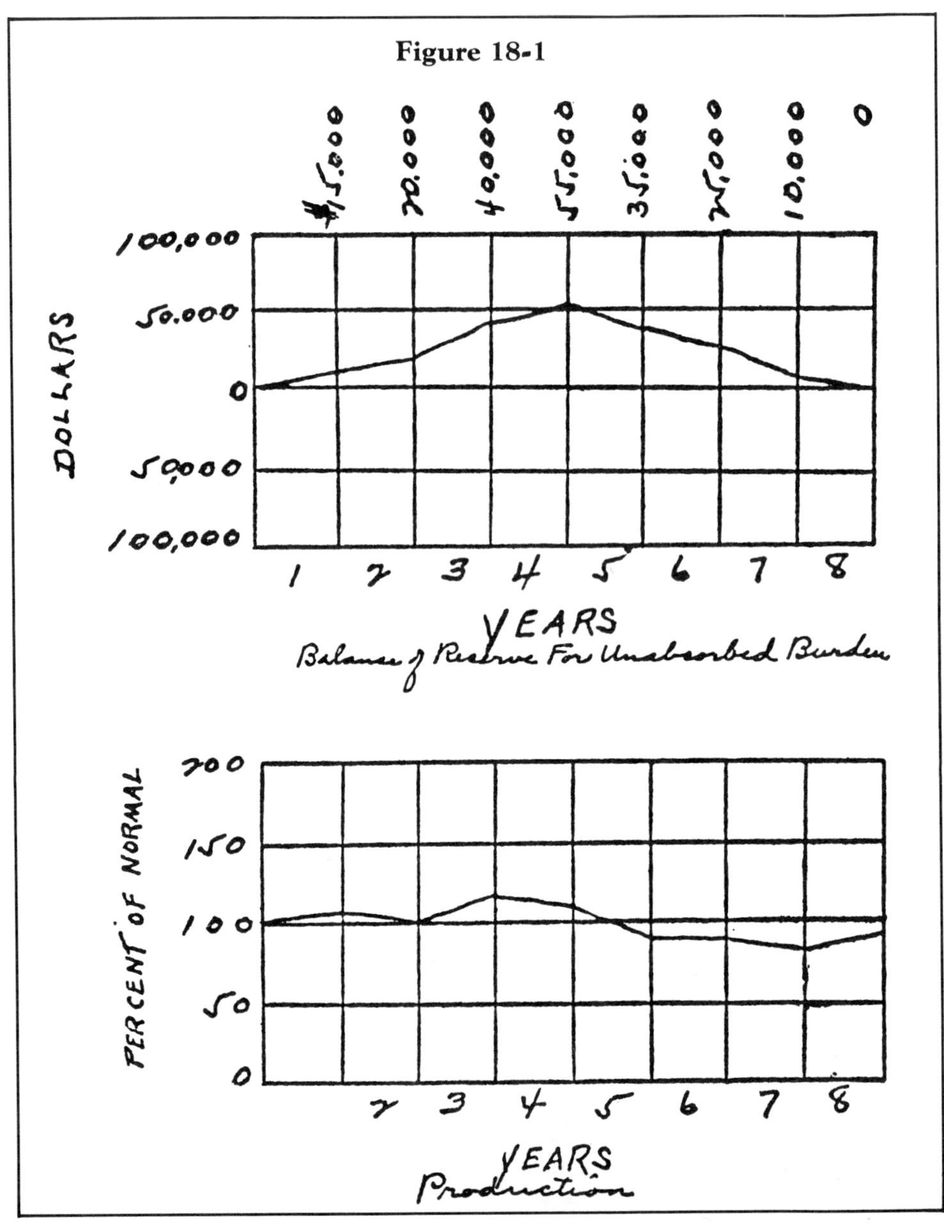

says, "Is it sound policy never to take orders below 'normal cost'?" Because it says "never," I want to cite a peculiar situation in one particular industry, and the practice which is now being followed for you gentlemen to give us your opinion on it. In a certain industry there is a price cutting war on at the present time. The selling prices are not based on cost or common sense, and until this situation corrects itself we are faced with the alternative of either shutting down plants or taking business at a price which we know will not cover the normal cost, as you call it. Is it not a fact that you have to protect a large intangible value not shown on the books, namely, good will and prestige derived from publicity, from warehouses and jobbing centers established and in strategic locations, and from having your name before the public? We have established a stop loss point, below which we will not sell. This we call expenditure cost, that is, everything we actually spend money for, such as material, labor, and electricity, power, light, and things like that. We figure that in the cost, but all these bookkeeping figures for depreciation and all that, we had to let slide. When we have a good year and prices go up, we will have to figure them in again.

CHAIRMAN: You are on the basis of taking the business if you can get a new dollar for an old one. And that is where you stop.

MR. HOWELL: Yes; as long as we can exchange a good dollar for one that has been spent. Of course, it is an unusual condition. The question says "never." I would say it is sound policy sometimes.

CHAIRMAN: I think if you are going to put a high value on "keeping your place in the sun," your battleline may have to go further into your pocketbook than what you said. I think you may have to sell the stuff for a time so you do not get a new dollar for an old one, if you have got yourself into that kind of a situation.

MR. HOWELL: I think that is the more practical way. We are talking very theoretically, but when we are actually faced with these things we have to throw a lot of accounting overboard.

To What Should Cost of Experimental Work Be Charged?

CHAIRMAN: What is next, gentlemen, out of the sixteen questions?

C. WALTER COAPMAN, *North East Electric Co., Rochester, N.Y.*: No. 7.

CHAIRMAN: What do you want to say about it, Mr. Coapman?

MR. COAPMAN: It seems to me that there is another question on experimental expense besides the ones you have enumerated. The paragraph now reads, "When should experimental work be charged as selling expense?

When as part of manufacturing burden? When, if ever, capitalized?" I think that experimental work is sometimes simply an allocation of profits. In other words, if a company is developing a new product and does not know what it is going to amount to, it is certainly not a part of selling expense, neither is it a part of manufacturing burden, and it probably is poor policy to set it up and capitalize it. It seems to me that such experimental work is simply a sort of appropriation from profits. There may be experimental work in connection with product that is purely a cost of manufacturing, but I think experimental work which is really development work for a new product is something entirely different; it is really an appropriation out of profits rather than part of selling expense or manufacturing burden.

CHAIRMAN: That is a very sound comment. Do you want to say, Mr. Coapman, since you started the discussion, what kind of experimental expense you think properly belongs in manufacturing burden?

MR. COAPMAN: Yes, I think experimental work, for instance, in change of design, in which you are trying out something new to see if it will be cheaper than your present design, either in actual machine work or in materials, or something like that, is a perfectly proper charge against manufacturing burden.

CHAIRMAN: You assume that a progressive management is always doing something of that sort?

MR. COAPMAN: Yes, all the time on their present product. In that case it is a part of manufacturing expense, because in the long run you are going to win out more times than you lose, and, therefore, it is a part of the cost in manufacturing that product.

CHAIRMAN: Expense of that kind is like that for maintaining a chemical laboratory for research. Under what circumstances should costs of experimental work be charged into selling expense?

G. E. BRENNAN, *Heikolz Mfg. Co., Rochester, N.Y.*: In the lithographing business we put an item of that nature, experimental work, into selling expense—making sketches and cuts, to get new business.

CHAIRMAN: Trying to get up something that will tickle the customer's fancy?

MR. BRENNAN: That is the idea.

MR. VanZANDT: How about capitalizing experimental expense? Does anybody think it ever should be capitalized?

MR. COAPMAN: I think it should be capitalized, if you are starting out with a new product in which you have very definite knowledge that there is a field for it, and you are going to spend a lot of money and you know it is going to come back to you.

CHAIRMAN: If we started out to make a new calculating machine, for example, we would capitalize everything we spent until the time we got the machine on the market?

MR. COAPMAN: That is the idea; then spread the preliminary cost over production.

MR. STILES: On what basis?

MR. COAPMAN: In the same way we spread special tools in our industry. We figure them as a separate item. We estimate how many we are going to make and we add so many cents per unit.

MR. VanZANDT: Suppose you do not make it?

MR. COAPMAN: In that case we lose. On the other hand, we may make more than we planned and if so there would be a profit. You are obliged to guess most of the time.

Cost Accomplishments of the Past Year

CHAIRMAN: What is the next question for discussion?

N. M. CARTMELL, *The Celluloid Co., Newark, N.J.*: No. 16.

CHAIRMAN: Here is a chance for those who are feeling generous to tell us something. Mr. Cartmell, what do you want to contribute?

MR. CARTMELL: I did one thing last year that was a little more interesting than anything else that I have done. We have the Bedeaux bonus plan out through the plant. Beginning last October, we have made similar time studies on all the work in the accounting department. The entire payroll, billing, tabulating, accounts receivable, cost of sales and inventory control sections have been time-studied, and those clerks are all on a bonus. I have in my payroll department seven clerks. The plant has about 1,500 employees, and those of you who know the Bedeaux bonus plan know that it is pretty complicated. We get operator efficiencies every day, department efficiencies every day, on every operator, in every department that is on bonus. Of the seven clerks in my payroll department only four are working on the payroll itself; two are working on these efficiencies. That is a decrease from eighteen people of about a year and a half ago.

CHAIRMAN: You accomplished your decrease chiefly by doing what?

MR. CARTMELL: First, the standardization of the work and finally the last part of it was done on the Bedeaux bonus plan. Of the eleven people cut out, about seven went as a result of making time studies of what they were doing—cutting out unnecessary operations and getting a standard on accomplishment which they should do. The other four were cut out as a result of the bonus plan itself.

CHAIRMAN: In other words, you applied what you would call shop methods to clerical work.

MR. CARTMELL: Yes and the errors did not increase in proportion to number of operations in handling time cards. For instance, my error percentage is about 1 to 4,000 handlings or operations, I think.

CHAIRMAN: I would like to ask anybody in this room whether they feel that errors tend to increase with speed. My feeling is that the speediest typists and the speediest operators maintain fully as high a score of accuracy as the slow ones. Does anyone disagree with that general idea? That is pertinent, of course, to Mr. Cartmell's comment.

MR. SWEETSER: Most anyone in the organization would disagree with you, but I do not.

CHAIRMAN: You mean to say that if you go back to your shop you would find workers down the line who would allege that errors increased with speed?

MR. SWEETSER: Yes.

MR. CARTMELL: My errors are somewhat less than before. Of course, we culled out the less efficient clerks and retained the best ones.

CHAIRMAN: The only point where my personal daily work touches that problem of accuracy, or otherwise, is in typewriting, and I am satisfied that our speediest operators are on the whole our most accurate ones.

MR. CARTMELL: That would be true in billing work, which, of course, is done on a comptometer and by typing. It has proven true that the slowest ones are the least accurate.

CHAIRMAN: Gentlemen, what other questions do you want to talk about? Does anybody want to make a further contribution on No. 16? Mr. Cartmell made a very significant one.

E. J. HANSEN, *Edison Electric Appliance Co., Chicago, Ill.*: Talking about bonus, our works manager started the first of this month with a bonus plan for servicing material returned to be repaired.

CHAIRMAN: What kind of business are you in?

MR. HANSEN: Electric heating devices – Hot Point Irons.

CHAIRMAN: And this is a bonus for your repairmen?

MR. HANSEN: Yes, sir.

CHAIRMAN: In other words, you found that the defects which these irons show when they come back from the user are so uniform that the workmen can put the irons into usable shape and you do not have to say what the trouble is?

MR. HANSEN: It is a standardized operation. It takes in the whole job, from taking the material from the receiving room to testing and packing it. We also have a bonus for men working on what we call cost reduction that has proved very satisfactory. We have men who just go about the shop trying to find ways and means of reducing cost, and giving them a bonus for what they get.

CHAIRMAN: That is a very, very different problem. It is just as interesting but it is very different. Can we not get a few more things like this out of No. 16?

MR. SWEETSER: I do not know whether this is worth while contributing; I suppose you are all doing this. We set up about six months ago standards on a production basis for each of the items in the overhead which the foremen in the plant can control, eliminating all others. We submitted the history over about three years to the foremen, of whom there were about forty-five in the group. They established standards of what they thought they should spend per 1,000 units for each item in their departments. We have been very much interested at the reaction. It was pretty hard at first, but every month the attitude improved. I will tell you one or two little interesting incidents. We saw one of our forewomen going around with a little 10¢ hammer. We said, "What is the hammer for?" "Well," she said, "I can drive nails myself and fix my own stuff. I do not need to have a carpenter and get charged for what I can do myself." Again a man in the pressing department had two idle pressing machines. They were items of considerable expense as they take up considerable space. He came to my office one day and said, "I want those two pressing machines removed from my room. I notice that I am being charged for floor space, interest on investment, and depreciation, and I do not need these machines. I can use that space to better advantage. Take them out." And so we did.

CHAIRMAN: That is a very significant example of intelligent reaction from shop foremen, and that is the kind of thing which I think burden ought to be made to mean. You notice that Mr. Sweetser is talking not only about variable burdens which the foreman, in the old language, "controlled," but about fixed charges which are assessed against his department.

MR. SWEETSER: At first we did not submit those fixed charges, but later found that plan an advantage.

CHAIRMAN: I have a feeling, gentlemen, that there is a great deal to what Mrs. Hull said last night. I have seen it, and my partners will back me up in it. Perhaps Mr. Fletcher who is here may want to say a word about that. It is a great thing for the people who are responsible for a business, whether owners or managers, to get that kind of a reaction. I know that Mr. Sweetser, having had that kind of reaction, felt that the foreman and the management at his plant were ever so much better together as a team after that kind of an incident. Life is like the little poem:

> "Who does not feel desire unending
> To solace through his daily strife
> With some mysterious blending,
> The weary drudgery of life?"

And that is one of the ways to do it.

F. R. FLETCHER, *Scovell, Wellington & Co., Boston, Mass.*: It seems to me that one of the greatest uses of costs is that when we know costs we are in a position to meet a market condition, if we need to do it. We are not sacrificing burden separately, or material or labor; we are simply using our judgment as to how much profit we will sacrifice, and it seems to me that a known cost is what we are all after, as accurate a cost as possible.

Carrying that a step further and with a little different angle from Mr. Scovell's thought, if we can give costs to salesmen, we can put each salesman into business for himself. We will sell him the company's goods at cost. He may work from a price list, with or without discretion to adjust those prices, but he knows the business that he is going after, and he knows the profits he is going to make. He has some idea of what his share in those profits is going to be.

A little while ago I had a conference with the sales manager of a concern where such a plan had been put into operation. One of his salesmen who covered a rather scattered territory came into the office one day and said, "I want less territory. I am jumping around all over this field and I find that I am spending an awful lot of time in traveling. I want less territory because I can make more money out of less territory." I believe that when costs are brought to the point where the salesmen are questioning, then we are coming to the point of real efficiency.

When Should Group Bonus Be Used?

CHAIRMAN: What is our next point for discussion?

MR. STILES: I should like to hear somebody say something about No. 11.

CHAIRMAN: Does not that mean that you would like to discuss it?

MR. STILES: I am perfectly willing. My own personal opinion is that a group bonus plan is the first step to an individual bonus system, and it is about the only satisfactory way that I have had of arriving at any such scheme.

CHAIRMAN: You would put group bonus ahead of individual bonus?

MR. STILES: Yes, that is in the order of installation. We have a group bonus now in several of our departments, viz., the shipping, tabulating, and billing departments, and in one manufacturing department.

CHAIRMAN: You can use it, I take it, only where the group has a common interest in the work.

MR. STILES: We do it that way in various groups of seven to twenty each.

CHAIRMAN: Does it work out so that if the group consists of, say seven people, somebody comes around and says, "No. 3 is too lazy"?

MR. STILES: That is really one of the benefits which we have received from it, because we keep individual personal efficiency records, and we can nearly always support any such statement or change the opinion of that person who makes those statements.

CHAIRMAN: What would you do if you had a group of seven, for example, and they were all but one speedy, high-strung chaps who were willing to work like the dickens, and No. 3, who had been there for a long time and deserved employment at the hands of your company, could not hold up the pace? Are you willing to keep him at work, after you admitted and he admitted that he could not hit it the way the other youngsters could in the group?

MR. STILES: Their personal salary usually takes care of that.

CHAIRMAN: Yes, but the group, the other fellows say, "This interferes with our getting our bonus." What do you do?

MR. STILES: I have had that very question, and my answer thus far has been: "This bonus scheme is getting toward an individual bonus scheme a little later."

CHAIRMAN: Would you say to this pushing energetic group, "This chap has been here a long time; he is older than you and you have got to carry him." Would you say that?

MR. STILES: Frankly I have said it.

CHAIRMAN: Frankly does it go?

MR. STILES: I have not had any serious objections to it. In fact, I have had one group of packers come and tell me that they would not think of having a change made because of that very reason, but I would like to know whether other folks feel the same way about a group bonus.

R. W. PEDEN, *Mueller Brass Co., Port Huron, Mich.*: I would like to submit our experience on the subject of the individual bonus versus the group bonus.

CHAIRMAN: What do you make?

MR. PEDEN: Brass goods.

CHAIRMAN: Plumbing goods?

MR. PEDEN: No, our company makes rods, tubing, castings, etc. About the first of January, 1922, we inaugurated a group bonus plan in one of our largest units. We were imbued with the idea that the entire organization should cooperate to increase the business of the department. We paid this bonus monthly, on the basis of the ratio between the output and the payroll of the department. At the end of about two years we were thoroughly convinced that it was not a very great success. We adopted instead an individual bonus plan, based on the Emerson curve of efficiency, using standard hour production rates on the individual machines, paying the men a bonus on their own individual efficiency as operators, and paying also a group bonus only when men were working on the same unit, or when their output was determined by the capacity of one machine.

CHAIRMAN: That is, where you had to rate two or more men together in order to rate them at all?

MR. PEDEN: Exactly. So, for example, we have one machine which is operated by seven men. Our production records throughout the year 1924 showed an average production of 19½ units per hour on that machine. We established a standard hour production rate of 24 units per hour which, if attained, gave these operators a weekly bonus of 20% in addition to their wages. During the entire year of 1925 they averaged 26 units per hour and so far in 1926 they have averaged 36 units per hour. Last month they averaged 37½ units per hour. They have actually attained a production in one particular hour of 60 units. I submit that as an actual evidence of the transcendent superiority of the individual bonus plan over any kind of group system.

J. M. SCANLON: I am particularly interested in having this question discussed, as our company has an individual bonus plan, but I understand the automobile companies (including the General Motors Company and the Packard Motor Car Company) have superseded the individual bonus plan with a group system. They say the group system works better, reduces clerical work, and instead of everyone working for himself, the employees now work for the benefit of the whole group. It is also claimed that as a result of the group system, the skilled workmen now assist those who are less efficient and teach them to work better and faster, as the workmen's earnings are affected by any inefficiency of the group.

It would seem to me, however, that the group bonus system would tend to do away with the individual efforts of the workmen and wherever possible the individual bonus system should be used.

MR. HANSEN: We have not been a supporter of the group bonus for the past three or four years, but now we have been going through the stage of changing every department over to the group bonus, and we subdivide some departments into lines, especially in the assembling lines, where we might assemble toasters, irons, or percolators individually. Our groups may be run anywheres from five to seven people. We run the foreman, assistant foreman, clerical help, truckers, inspectors, and die setters in the same group; but the inspectors are in a separate group. Due to the fact that we are changing design and appliances so frequently (because some of our devices only last on the market for two years before they are so changed you would not know them) we found that time study or piece work methods for individual operators required too much work, too many time study people, from clerical work all the way down the line, and we changed over to a full group bonus, which is paid once a month on the basis of saved hours between taken hours and allowed hours.

MR. BULLIS: I think group bonus is all right where it is not economical or satisfactory to give individual bonus. That is one thing the automobile companies have found in their assembling line; for instance, where it is impossible in a great many cases to tell how many pieces a man turns out. You have the same thing in the manufacture of electrical appliances just mentioned, where they admit that conditions are such that individual bonus is not practical on account of frequent changes in design. Group bonus must in the long run be made up of averages, the high man and the low man. Therefore, the man turning out the most work in a group bonus is either slowed down to the average of the group, or else he works fast on a particular operation and is penalized for the slow man somewhere else.

MR. STILES: We have a little individual record that is watched by the foremen, whereby the best men get the highest day rates. And another condition comes up within a department where some of the higher men go along and have helped, you might call it, the lower class help and they get them straightened out, show them how to do their operations so that their total bonus will come up.

CHAIRMAN: They get a special bonus, the high men?

MR. STILES: No, this day rate is higher than the average starting rate.

CHAIRMAN: It is recognized then?

MR. STILES: Yes, if we have a man starting at 40¢ an hour, the high man in that department may be getting as high as 50¢, 60¢, or 70¢ an hour.

MR. PEDEN: One more thought on that subject of group bonus. I think that any extra expense in timekeepers' wages is more than offset by the very great saving in the reduced cost per unit for burden which the individual bonus plan brings about. One reason why the group plan has been adopted so universally by the motor companies, I believe, is the fact of the assembling line. In other words, the production of the men is governed very largely by the speed of that assembling line. Now, in a manufacturing plant, such as ours, the production of the men is governed very largely by the capacity of their individual machines. Therefore, I believe the individual system is superior.

CHAIRMAN: What else do you want to say, gentlemen?

Other Topics

MR. STILES: Mr. Chairman, there are some very interesting questions here. I was wondering if we might not consider the suggestion of taking some unequivocal answers before we adjourn, just by way of voting on them.

CHAIRMAN: Where, for example?

MR. STILES: Well, I would like to see No. 5 and No. 4—(interrupted).

CHAIRMAN: Let us begin with No. 3. There are two things that cost accounting does: it reckons the cost of production, and it reckons internal or service costs to measure efficiency. They sometimes may be the same thing but they are sometimes different. Is the production cost or the service cost more important? Those who say production put up their hands. (8 responses.) Those who say service costs. (11 responses.)

Well now, No. 4 (reading question). Will those who would rather see the cost accounting done in the works department, please stand? (2 responses.) Those who would rather see it in the accounting department. (Balance of members.)

What about No. 5? "Is the cost accountant often prevented from getting results because operating men do not understand accounting?" How many think so? (16 responses) Those who think that is not much of a disability, stand up. (23 responses.)

I do not see how you can vote on No. 6. What else can you vote on here?

MR. STILES: No. 8.

CHAIRMAN: No, you have got to discuss that. You cannot vote on that. No. 12. "Should set-up time be included in piece rate or be kept separate—particularly for the increase in factory efficiency?" Those who would put it in as part of the piece work, stand up. (No response.) Those who would keep it separate, stand. (Unanimous response.)

Well, I do not see anything else to vote on here. Mr. Stiles, do you? I guess you people have had about all the cost convention you want. I think we had better stop and go home.

A MEMBER: I move we adjourn.

The motion was seconded; and the meeting adjourned.

(19) "Financial Control Policies of General Motors Corporation and Their Relationship to Cost Accounting," January 1, 1927, Bulletin, Vol. 8, No. 9, Albert Bradley, Assistant Treasurer, General Motors Corporation

Editorial Department Note

This paper is, in our opinion, a significant contribution to the literature dealing with accounting in its relations to financial management. It is a generally accepted dictum that unit cost of product decreases with volume of output. A necessary corollary is that selling price may therefore be cut without affecting the sum total of net profits. Starting with the idea that an industry should over a period of time earn a fair return on the capital investment, and with a standard volume of output, the author arrives at a selling price of product which will secure the fair economic return desired. Furthermore, he examines the problem as to what increase in volume of sales will be necessary to offset a given contemplated reduction in selling price, and the related problem as to what decrease in sales volume can be permitted without a further reduction of profit than would accrue from a cut in sales price resulting in a bare maintenance of former volume.

These are questions involving an examination of the whole fabric of cost accounting and a side excursion into the question as to the relation of interest on investment to costs and price policies. Treating, as the publication does, of the policies of one of the most romantic industries of modern times, it will receive a very careful reading by our membership.

The author, Albert Bradley, served for two years as works accountant for public utilities operated by the Stone and Webster Management Association after which he entered Dartmouth College in 1911 and was graduated a Bachelor of Science in 1915. He pursued graduate studies in the University of Michigan, where he received the degrees of Master of Arts, 1916, and Doctor of Philosophy in 1917, specializing in economics and finance. From 1917 to 1918, he was in the Air Service of the U.S. Army, during the first year specializing on distribution of overhead as applied to cost plus contracts. While in the Air Service of the Army, he became District Accounting Officer, Dayton District, and later District Accounting Officer, Detroit District.

He joined Comptroller's staff of General Motors Corporation in May, 1919, and was made Assistant Treasurer of the Corporation later in that year.

Mr. Bradley is a member of the Executive Committee of the American Management Association and has been actively interested in the financial aspects of management problems.

This paper was delivered before a recent meeting of the Detroit Chapter, National Association of Cost Accountants.

Financial Control Policies of General Motors Corporation and Their Relationship to Cost Accounting

Introduction

General Motors Is Primarily an Operating Concern. Before outlining the relationship to cost accounting of the financial control policies of General Motors, a few facts regarding this corporation may be of interest. General Motors is now primarily an operating concern engaged in the manufacture and sale of automobiles, their accessories and parts, and owning the plants, properties and other assets of its manufacturing operations, which are known as Divisions. Besides the Buick, Cadillac, Chevrolet, Oakland, Oldsmobile, and Pontiac passenger and commercial cars, the principal products of General Motors are accessories, parts and automobile bodies, which the accessory divisions sell not only to the car divisions of the General Motors family, but also to outside automotive and industrial concerns. A subsidiary of large and growing importance is the Delco-Light Company, makers of the Frigidaire Line of electric refrigerators for household and commercial use, and the world's leading manufacturer in this field. Through stock ownership General Motors owns a controlling interest in the Yellow Truck and Coach Manufacturing Company, and a number of other subsidiaries.

The products of the car divisions are marketed through some 20,000 dealers scattered all over the world, less than 4% of the total volume being sold at retail by the Corporation. The growth of General Motors has paralleled that of the automobile industry. In 1909, the Corporation produced and sold 25,000 cars, their sales value being $29,029,000. Within six years, that is, in 1915, sales had increased to 76,068 cars and trucks, valued at $94,424,000. In 1925, there were sold 835,902 cars and trucks, and net outside sales of the Corporation had reached a figure of $734,592,000, or eight times the volume at the end of the previous decade. For the nine months ended September 30, 1926, net outside sales were $830,000,000, or at the annual rate of over $1,100,000,000. The number of cars and trucks sold during this period was 996,321, or an indicated annual rate of over 1,300,000 vehicles. Total assets employed by the Corporation have increased from $18,381,000, at the end of 1909, to $915,000,000 at September 30, 1926. In short, total assets of General Motors Corporation are now approaching a billion dollars, and annual sales are running in excess of a billion dollars.

General Motors a Decentralized Organization. General Motors Corporation is operated as a decentralized organization. Each operating Division or Subsidiary is in principle entirely self-contained and is responsible for the successful design, manufacture, and sale of its product, subject to the general policies of the Corporation.

In order to co-ordinate the efforts of the various Divisions, and particularly to make available to each Division the experience of all members of the family, there are various inter-divisional relations committees which come together at frequent intervals. The names of these committees suggest their respective spheres. They are the General Technical, General Sales, General Purchasing, Operations, and Works Managers Committees. The members of these committees are the important executives from representative divisions, supplemented in certain instances by talent from the central organization. Thus it is seen that General Motors Corporation operates on the decentralized plan. Its fundamental policies are enunciated by the Executive and Finance Committees, and coordination is effected by the President and through the medium of inter-divisional relations committees.

The ideal of the Corporation is centralization of policy but decentralization of management, which means that the president of each of the constituent companies is allowed an altogether free hand in his company. He is expected to carry out the general policies of the Corporation, but the methods by which he does this are as personal to himself and as free from interference as if he were the head of an independent operation. This freedom of action on the part of managers is believed necessary in order to retain men of the calibre required. By this plan, the Corporation obtains all the advantages of personal, independent management—its initiative, its ability quickly to adapt its methods to changing conditions, and its close personal contact with its working force. By this means, also, are avoided many of the difficulties that arise when the size of a corporation becomes so great that no one man can possibly be wise enough, or wide-visioned enough, or have time enough really to be effective as its chief executive.

Financial Control Policies Serve Two General Purposes. Financial control policies of General Motors Corporation serve two general purposes: (1) The pricing of the product in a manner consistent with the fundamental policies of the Corporation as to return on investment; and (2) The maintenance of effective operating control through manufacturing schedules which are at all times in logical relationship to consumer demand. This requires not only the best possible estimates of the future volume of business, but also the maintenance of a healthy position in regard to: (a) Inventories carried by the Corporation and its dealers; and (b) Purchase commitments for materials made by the Corporation with its suppliers. The tool by means of which these policies are made effective is a comprehensive scheme of forecasting, combined with a systematic comparison of actual results with the forecast.

Financial Control Policies Made Effective Through Forecasting. The forecasting program of General Motors Corporation is nothing more than systematic planning applied to the conduct of its business, from the point of view of fundamental financial policies and of current operating control.

Systematic planning for the future, then, is the subject of this paper, with particular reference to the financial and economic aspects of the business, and their relationship, both direct and indirect, to the problems of the cost accountant.

Cost of Product

Let us first treat with certain broad aspects of the perennial problem of costs. It is, of course, axiomatic that the price of a product must reimburse the manufacturer not only for his direct outlays for labor and materials, but also for a proper portion of those costs which cannot be assigned directly to any particular unit or even class of product. As applied to the factory, these indirect expenses are usually referred to as "burden" or "overhead"; and as applied to the general administrative and sales organization, may be referred to as "commercial expense."

Factory Cost. The three elements of factory cost are usually referred to as: (1) Productive Labor – labor expended directly on the product – (2) Productive Materials – materials which enter into the composition of the final product – and, (3) Manufacturing Expense or Burden, consisting of so-called indirect labor – foremen, inspectors, material handling, etc. – indirect material, taxes, plant maintenance, light, heat and power, etc.

A correct accounting for productive labor and productive materials for many years has been the particular concern of the cost accountant, and the importance of this work as an aid to efficient operating management and in the control of inventories is well recognized. It is with certain aspects of indirect costs that this paper is principally concerned.

Manufacturing Ratios. For the typical automobile manufacturing plant, as opposed to an assembly plant, a fair segregation of factory cost into its three constituent elements is as follows:

1. Direct Materials	70%
2. Productive Labor	10
3. Burden or Overhead	20
TOTAL	100%

Manufacturing Expense. The general tendency is for manufacturing expense or burden to constitute an increasing portion of total factory cost. As industries develop, machine processes also develop, and the tendency is to substitute machine operations for hand operations. There results a decrease in total cost which may be caused by a decrease in labor cost per unit, which more than offsets the increase in burden cost per unit; or both labor and burden per unit may decrease. But in any event, the *percentage* which burden constitutes of total factory cost tends to increase.

Distribution of Overhead – Burden Center. It is, therefore, evident that factory burden or overhead as an element of factory cost is relatively more important than productive labor. Since the typical manufacturing establishment produces a variety of products, some of which involve a much greater relative use of machinery and other fixed investment in proportion to productive labor than others, and likewise are responsible for a larger portion of indirect costs such as depreciation, power, etc., cost accountants have for a number of years been actively engaged upon an analysis of factory conditions with a view to the development of methods for the logical apportionment of "burden" to the several classes of product. In the words of Hamilton Church written a score of years ago, "every dollar of charges must be burdened onto some item of work." The same writer outlined his views as to the method of analysis, in his admonition not to regard the shop as an organic whole, but rather to regard it as a collection of small "production centers," each differing from the other. By giving the fullest play to differences in responsibility for expense, instead of averaging conditions, cost finding has become much more scientific. For example, a typical manufacturing plant may have an over-all burden rate of 200 percent of productive labor, but this plant may consist of: Department A, with a preponderance of heavy machinery, with a burden rate of 300 percent of productive labor; Department B, with relatively little machinery, with a burden rate of only 100 percent of productive labor; and Department C, with a condition somewhat between the other two, with a burden rate of say 180 percent. Manifestly, if different products are made in these different departments, the application of an average burden rate for the entire plant in the calculation of costs will result in costs for products of Department A which are much too low, and of Department B, which are altogether too high. That industry is now keenly alive to the importance of burden distribution is evidenced by the large output, during the last few years, of books and magazine articles dealing with this subject.

Variance in Costs with Fluctuations in Volume. It may fairly be said that there is little or no lack of appreciation on the part of cost accountants of the importance of correctly accounting for direct labor and direct materials. The basic principles underlying the burden center idea are well understood, and perhaps a majority of industrial concerns now apply a series of burden rates rather than a general average rate in order more accurately to compute their costs. There is, of course, much difference of opinion as to the extent to which refinement in method of allocation and apportionment of expense shall be carried; and the cost accountant at all times must guard against advocating the compilation of such a mass of data that there would be required to man the cost department a personnel larger than that engaged in productive operations in the shop. With these matters of improved technique it is believed you cost accountants may safely be entrusted, and I will pass on to certain phases of the problem of variances in costs with changes in rate of operations which do not appear to have been given the recognition they deserve.

Costs of production and distribution per unit of product vary with fluctuation in volume, because of the fixed or non-variable nature of some of the expense items. Productive materials and productive labor may be considered costs which are 100 percent variable, since within reasonable limits the aggregate varies directly with volume, and the cost per unit of product therefore remains uniform.

Among the items which are classified as manufacturing expense or burden, there exist varying degrees of fluctuation with volume, owing to their greater or lesser degree of variability. Among the absolutely fixed items are such expenses as depreciation, taxes, etc., which may be referred to as 100 percent fixed, since within the limits of plant capacity the aggregate will not change, but the amount per unit of product will vary in inverse ratio to the output.

There is another group of items which may be classified as 100 percent variable, such as inspection, material handling, etc., the amount of which per unit of product is unaffected by volume. Between the classes of 100 percent fixed and 100 percent variable there is a large group of expense items which are partially variable, such as light, heat, power, salaries, etc. Lacking an exact means of determining the degree of variation, a practicable method is to approximate the condition by applying a variability factor calculated on the basis of past experience. To illustrate:

Standard Burden Rate. If the direct labor payroll is $100,000 for the accounting period, total manufacturing expense may aggregate $200,000 or 200 percent of direct labor. If the direct labor should amount to $150,000, manufacturing expense might increase to $275,000, or 133-1/3 percent of productive labor. On the other hand, if operations should decline to a point where productive labor is only $50,000, with proper control we should expect total manufacturing expense to decline to something like $125,000, or 250 percent of productive labor. Assuming that expenses have been properly controlled, the amount of non-variable expense indicated by these figures is $50,000, calculated as shown in Figure 19-1.

It is, of course, a fundamental principle that, in order to operate economically, and thereby be able to offer the greatest values to the public, factories should operate on as level a line of production as can reasonably be attained. Where there is a seasonal trend in the business, a level manufacturing curve means that finished product must be stored, a condition which is diametrically opposed to economical distribution, since the storing of the product produced in advance of consumers' requirements not only requires additional capital with its interest charge, but also expenses for insurance and other costs. There is also the danger, if sales do not come up to expectations, not only that the cost of carrying finished product may be unduly increased through prolonging the period of storage, but also that losses may result from the necessity of forced selling—i.e., distress merchandising of the excess stock at the end of the regular selling season.

As shown in Figure 19-2, there is a pronounced seasonal trend in the automobile business. It is the practice of the General Motors Corporation to adopt production schedules which are a compromise between economical manufacture requiring a level production, and economical distribution involving minimum stocks of finished products. The resultant production schedule is then one having seasonal characteristics, but without the radical changes indicated by the trend of sales to consumers. With such a production schedule, if total actual manufacturing expense is absorbed into actual costs

Figure 19-1

	Standard Volume	Above Standard	Below Standard
Various Volumes of Business under Observation, Prod. Labor.	$100,000	$150,000	$ 50,000
% of Standard Volume. . .	100%	150%	50%
Aggregate Mfg. Expense .	$200,000	$275,000	$125,000
If the Expenses Were Directly Proportionate to Volume, the Aggregate at the Indicated Volumes would be.	$200,000	$300,000	$100,000
The Difference Reflects the Non-Controllable Character of the Expenses . . .		$ 25,000	$ 25,000
If this Difference be Divided by the Percentage Variance from Standard Volume which is.		50%	50%
The Amount of Non-Controllable Expense is Indicated as.		$ 50,000	$ 50,000

each month, there would result variances in costs from month to month attributable to changes in rate of plant activity. Such cost figures are valueless for comparative purposes. They are also absolutely misleading as a guide in the determination of selling prices. For example, during a period of high volume, accounted costs would be low; while during periods of sub-normal volume, accounted costs would be high. It is, therefore, essential that there

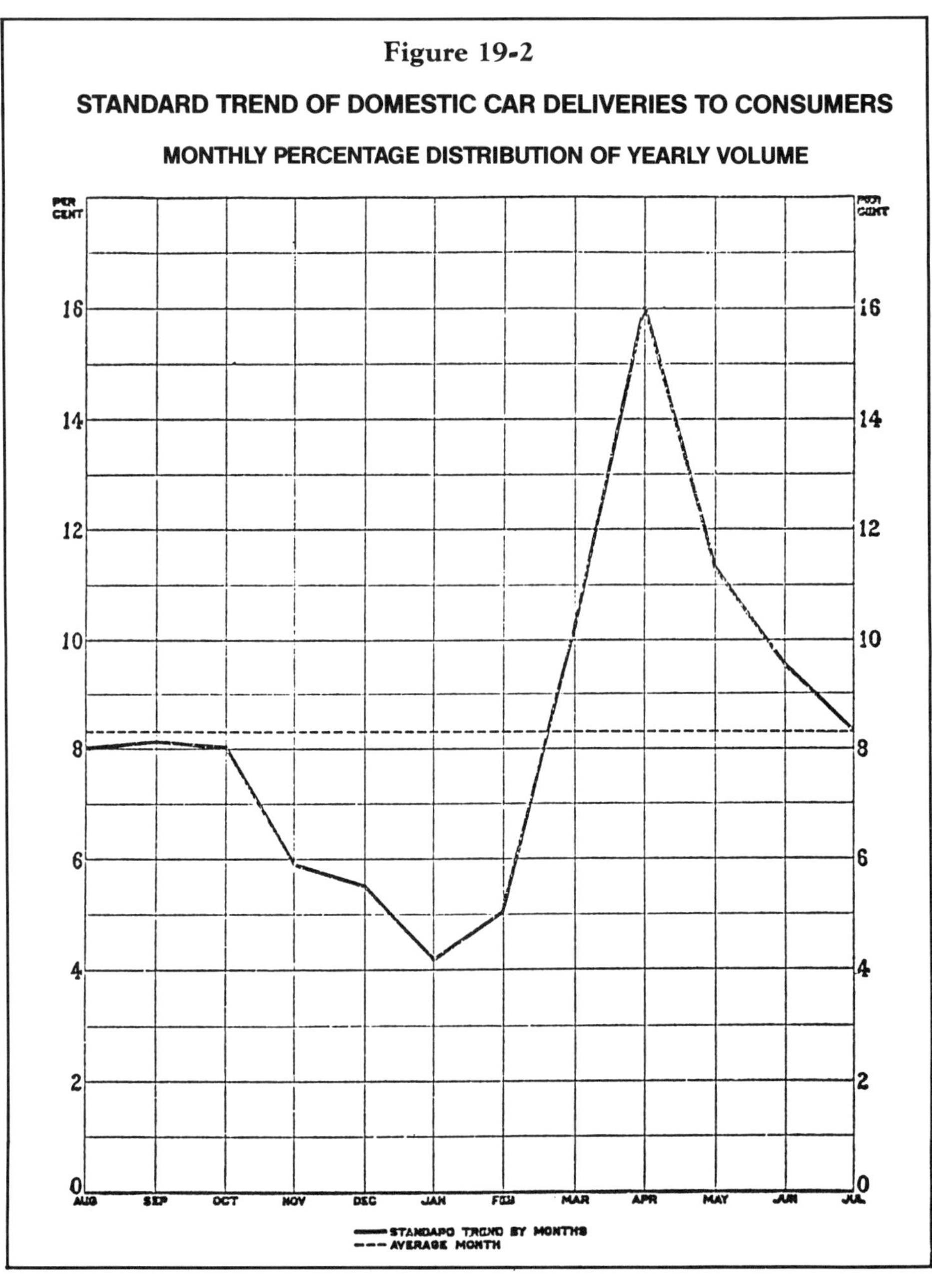

Figure 19-2

STANDARD TREND OF DOMESTIC CAR DELIVERIES TO CONSUMERS

MONTHLY PERCENTAGE DISTRIBUTION OF YEARLY VOLUME

be a definite method established whereby the effects of fluctuating volume upon overhead costs may be eliminated. The method followed by the General Motors Corporation is to develop standard burden rates for each "burden center," so that there will be included in costs a reasonable average allowance for manufacturing expense, with the result that at no time is there any change in costs due to changes in the rate of operations.

Standard Volume. The words "there will be included in costs a reasonable average allowance for manufacturing expense" are easily spoken. "Try and do it," many of you will say. It is first necessary to obtain an expression of the estimated normal average rate of plant operation.

Rate of plant operation is affected by such factors as: general business conditions; the extent of seasonal fluctuation in sales likely within years of large volume; policy with respect to seasonal accumulation of finished and/or semi-finished product for the purpose of leveling the production curve; the necessity or desirability of maintaining excess plant capacity for emergency use; and many other factors. Each of these factors should be carefully considered by a manufacturer in the determination of size of a new plant to be constructed, and before making additions to existing plants, in order that there may be a logical relationship between assumed normal average rate of plant operation and practical annual capacity. So far as practicable, the governing considerations should be applicable to the economic situation of the industry, rather than any abnormalities pertaining to a particular plant. The percentage accepted by General Motors Corporation as its policy in regard to the relationship between assumed normal rate of plant operation and practical annual capacity is referred to as standard volume.

Having determined the degree of variability of manufacturing expense, the estimated total expense at standard volume rate of operations can be established. A *standard burden rate* is then developed which represents the proper absorption of burden in costs at standard volume. In periods of low volume, the unabsorbed manufacturing expense is charged directly against profits as unabsorbed burden, while in periods of high volume, the overabsorbed manufacturing expense is credited to profits, as overabsorbed burden. By this generally accepted method, there is avoided the distortion of costs and inventory values which would result from spreading a fixed overhead over a fluctuating volume.

Commercial Expense. The usual practice of charging off commercial expenses from month to month eliminates the problem of overabsorption or underabsorption of expense made necessary in the case of manufacturing expense to avoid distortion to asset values in consequence of fluctuating volume. In the consideration of price to be established on the product, and in the preparation of estimated profit at various volumes, it is nevertheless important to analyze as to the variable and non-variable character of commercial expense and to determine the standard allowance for commercial expense. An analysis of commercial expenses along the lines suggested for manufacturing expenses can be made. Non-variable expense includes the principal administrative salaries, rents, etc. Salesmen's commissions typify 100 percent variable expense. Between these extremes comes the third class, expenses partially variable and partially non-variable, the amount of which increases or decreases with changes in volume, but not in direct proportion to those changes. This class includes such items as salesmen's and other salaries, traveling expense, etc., and the degree of variability can be determined for all practical purposes on the basis of past experience.

It is customary to allow for commercial expense as a given percentage of annual sales, and on this basis the *standard allowance* is the percentage which commercial expense constitutes of sales at standard volume rate of operations.

Return on Investment

So far we have dealt with factory costs and commercial expenses, which for the most part represent outlays by the manufacturer during the accounting period. An exception is depreciation of capital assets which have a greater length of life than the accounting period. To allow for this element of cost, there is usually included an allowance for depreciation in the overhead or burden rates used in compiling costs. Before an enterprise can be considered successful and worthy of continuation or expansion, however, there is still another element of cost which must be reckoned with. This is the cost of capital, including an allowance for profit.

Whether a business is large or small, there is a need of a policy in regard to the relation of capital investment to price of product, and the conditions under which additional capital is to be used to expand the business (either through retention of earnings instead of paying dividends, or from sale of capital securities). The governing considerations are rate of return on investment and the relationship of capacity to average and peak demands. In a small business where ownership and management are identical, the fundamental policy may never be formally expressed, but it will nevertheless be taken into account by the owner-manager in making up his mind whether or not to make any additions to his plant. In the typical large industry, however, where capital is supplied by a large number of stockholders, many of whom are not active in the management, and particularly where the operations are diversified and scattered, it is essential that machinery be established by which the fundamental considerations of pricing of product and expansion programs can be related to the established policies.

In dealing with cost of capital, the standard specifications of the usual accounting dissertation call for an answer to the question, "Is interest an element of cost?" As a general rule, writers amuse themselves by a treatise on whether or not interest should be included in the accounted costs, a question of accounting technique which serves usually to befog the issue.

The true basis for measuring the commercial success of any enterprise from the financial standpoint is the return on the capital employed in the business; since the stockholders will not be satisfied if a corporation builds and sells a million cars a year merely for the edification and amusement of the manufacturing and engineering departments. The stockholders themselves must also get a run for their money, and are entitled to distributions of profits in the form of dividends, with dividend requirements covered by a generous margin in the form of capital reinvested in the business through earnings retained.

Certain of these articles entitled, "Is interest a cost?" recall to mind the story of the commuter who told how each morning he had noticed a little fox terrier rush down to the railroad station barking and running after the train as it pulled out. As the engine speeded up, the terrier would fall behind and soon be lost to sight. It had occurred to the commuter to wonder what the dog would do with the train should he chance to catch it.

Return on investment is the basis of the policy in regard to the pricing of product, but it must be understood that the fundamental consideration is the average return over a protracted period of time, not the specific rate of return over any particular year or short period of time. This long-time rate of return on investment represents the official viewpoint as to the highest average rate of return which can be expected consistent with a healthy growth of the business, and may be referred to as the *economic* return attainable. The adjudged necessary rate of return on capital will vary as between separate lines of industry, as a result of differences in their economic situation; and within each industry there will be important differences in return on capital resulting primarily from the relatively greater efficiency of certain producers.

As outlined earlier in this paper, the fundamental policy in regard to pricing of product and expansion of the business necessitates an official viewpoint as to the normal average rate of plant operation. This relationship between assumed normal average rate of operation and practical annual capacity has been referred to as *standard volume,* and controls the rate of absorption of burden into costs.

The fundamental price policy is completely expressed in the conception of *standard volume* and *economic return* attainable. For example, if it is the accepted policy that *standard volume* represents 80 percent of practical annual capacity, and that an average of 20 percent per annum must be earned on the operating capital, it becomes possible to determine the *standard price* of a product; that is, that price, which with plants operating at 80 percent of capacity, will produce an annual return of 20 percent on the investment.

The calculation of standard prices of products necessitates the establishment of standards of capital requirement as well as expense factors, representative of the normal average operating condition, in terms of their respective ratios to annual sales or annual factory cost of production, according to whichever is the more direct relationship. Attention is called to the fact that the word "standard" as used in this connection represents the estimated normal average condition, not the goal of efficiency toward which operations are directed. A brief description of the development of standards of capital requirement follows:

Standard Fixed Investment Factor. The standard allowance for fixed investment is readily obtained, once standard volume and standard cost have been determined.

Standard Factor for Fixed Investment

Investment in Plant and Other Fixed Assets	$15,000,000
Practical Annual Capacity	50,000 units
Standard Volume, Percent of Practical Annual Capacity	80%
Standard Volume Equivalent	40,000 units
Factory Cost Per Unit at Standard Volume	$1,000
Annual Factory Cost of Production at Standard Volume	$40,000,000
Standard Factor for Fixed Investment	
(Ratio of Investment to Annual Factory Cost of Production) .	0.375

Working Capital Proportionate to Volume. The amount tied up in working capital items should be directly proportionate to the volume of business. For example, raw materials on hand should be in direct proportion to the manufacturing requirements—so many days' supply of this material, so many days' supply of that material, and so on—depending upon the condition and location of sources of supply, transportation conditions, etc. Work in process should be in direct proportion to the requirements of finished production, since it is dependent upon the length of time required for the material to pass from the raw to the finished state, and the amount of labor and other charges to be absorbed in the process. Finished product should be in direct proportion to sales requirements. Accounts receivable should be in direct proportion to sales, being dependent upon terms of payment and efficiency of collections. An illustration of the method of the determination of standard price appears in Figure 19-3.

There Is an Investment Center. Brief mention was made in an earlier part of this paper that continuous progress in scientific cost finding is being made through refinement in methods of distributing factory burden into costs, so as to reflect, as nearly as practicable, the actual expense involved departmentally, rather than to apply a general average burden rate to all departments. Proper distribution of burden departmentally is essential not only for the accurate costing of different products, but is also essential whenever there is occasion to compare the cost of manufacture of individual components or parts of a complete product with the prices at which similar units could be acquired elsewhere.

There is, however, an "investment center," just as truly as there is a burden center, and for industrial establishments manufacturing more than a single type of product, it will be found that responsibility for investment is not uniform. By giving fullest play to these differences in responsibility for investment, instead of averaging conditions, it will be found that the percentage which must be added to the total of manufacturing cost and commercial expense, in order to cover return on investment, varies widely as between different products.

Figure 19-3

ILLUSTRATION OF METHOD OF DEVELOPMENT OF STANDARD PRICE

	Normal Average Requirements		Standards of Capital Requirement	
	In Relation to	Turnover Per Year	Ratio to Sales Annual Basis	Ratio to Factory Cost Annual Basis
Cash	Sales	20 times	0.050	-
Drafts and Accounts Receivable.	Sales	10 times	0.100	-
Raw Material, and Work in Process	Factory Cost	6 times	-	0.16 2/3
Finished Product	Factory Cost	12 times	-	0.08 1/3
Gross Working Capital.			0.150	0.250
Fixed Investment			-	0.375
Total Investment			0.150	0.625
Economic Return Attainable - 20 Per Cent			-	-
Multiplying the Investment Ratio by this, the Necessary Net Profit Margin is Arrived at			0.030	0.125
Standard Allowance for Commercial Expenses, 7 Per Cent			0.070	-
Gross Margin Over Factory Cost.			0.100 a	0.125 b
Selling Price, as a Ratio to Factory Cost			$= \frac{1+b}{1-a} = \frac{1+0.125}{1-0.100} = 1.250$	
If Standard Cost			= $1.000	
Then Standard Price = $1.000 x 1.250			= $1.250	

In other words, there are different rates of capital turnover as applied to different products, and these varying rates of capital turnover should be an important factor in a consideration of prices to be established on different products. The importance of capital turnover is due to the fact that the annual capital turnover rate, multiplied by the profit margin percentage, determines the rate of return upon capital.

Responsibility for investment must be considered in calculating the standard price of each product as well as in calculating the over-all price for all products, since products with identical accounted costs may be responsible for investments which vary greatly. In the illustration given above, a uniform standard selling price of $1,250 was determined. Let us suppose, however, that this organization makes and sells two products, A and B, with equal manufacturing costs of $1,000 per unit, equal working capital requirements, and that 20,000 units of each product are produced. However, an analysis of fixed investment indicates that $10,000,000 is applicable to product A, while only $5,000,000 of fixed investment is applicable to product B. Each product must earn 20 percent on its investment in order to satisfy the standard condition. Figure 19-4 will illustrate the determination of the standard price for product A and product B.

It is to be noted that the accounted costs of these two products are identical, and that the difference in their standard prices results solely from the fact that a larger fixed investment is required for product A. An illustration is the case of an automobile company manufacturing its own open bodies, but purchasing closed bodies. For open cars there is an investment in body manufacturing facilities on which a return should be earned, while closed cars require no body plant investment by this manufacturer. From this analysis of investment, it becomes apparent that product A, which has the heavier fixed investment, should sell for $1,278, while product B should sell for only $1,222, in order to produce a return of 20 percent on the investment. Were both products sold for the composite average standard price of $1,250, then product A would not be bearing its share of the investment burden, while product B would be correspondingly over-priced.

In this illustration we have considered only a variance in the fixed investment factor, although, for a purchased body as compared with a manufactured body there would also be differences in inventory requirements. Variances in working capital requirements as between different products may be even more marked due to manufacturing methods, sales terms, merchandising policies, etc. Thus, to illustrate from the experience of General Motors Corporation, the inventory turnover rate of one line of products sold by a division of General Motors Corporation is six times a year, while inventory applicable to another line of products is turned over thirty times a year. In the latter case, the inventory investment required per dollar cost of sales is only one-fifth of that required in the case of the product with the slower turnover.

Just as there are differences in capital requirements as between different classes of product, so may the standard requirements for the same class of product require modification from time to time due to permanent changes in manufacturing processes, in location of sources of supply, more efficient scheduling and handling of materials, etc. Witness, for example, the improvement in Turnover of Productive Inventory (Total Inventory less Finished Product) of General Motors Corporation as a result of better control and more efficient manufacturing during the last six years. (See Figure 19-5.)[1] For the calendar year 1925 productive inventories were turned over 10.6 times, an increase of 50 percent over the best previous year, 1923, while for the twelve months ended September 30, 1926, productive inventories

Figure 19-4

VARIANCES IN STANDARD PRICE DUE TO VARIANCES IN RATES OF CAPITAL TURNOVER

Standards of Capital Requirements

	Product A		Product B		Total Product (A plus B)	
	Ratio to Sales Annual Basis	Ratio to Factory Cost Annual Basis	Ratio to Sales Annual Basis	Ratio to Factory Cost Annual Basis	Ratio to Sales Annual Basis	Ratio to Factory Cost Annual Basis
Gross Working Capital	0.150	0.250	0.150	0.250	0.150	0.250
Fixed Investment	-	0.500	-	0.250	-	0.375
Total Investment.	0.150	0.750	0.150	0.500	0.150	0.625
Economic Return Attainable - 20 Per Cent	-	-	-	-	-	-
Multiplying the Investment Ratio by this, the Necessary Net Profit Margin is Arrived at	0.030	0.150	0.030	0.100	0.030	0.125
Standard Allowance for Commercial Expenses, 7 Per Cent	0.070	-	0.070	-	0.070	-
Gross Margin Over Factory Cost. . . .	0.100 a	0.150 b	0.100 a	0.100 b	0.100 a	0.125 b
Selling Price, as a Ratio to Factory Cost $= \frac{1+b}{1-a} =$	$\frac{1.+0.150}{1.-0.100} = 1.278$		$\frac{1.+0.100}{1.-0.100} = 1.222$		$\frac{1.+0.125}{1.-0.100} = 1.250$	
If Standard Cost equals		$1,000		$1,000		$1,000
Then Standard Price equals		$1,278		$1,222		$1,250

[1]Turnover of Productive Inventory—The rate of turnover for the month at an annual rate is obtained by relating productive inventory investment at the beginning of the month to cost of finished production for the month multiplied by twelve. The yearly moving average turnover is obtained by dividing the cost of finished production for the twelve months period by the average production inventory investment during the period.

Figure 19-5

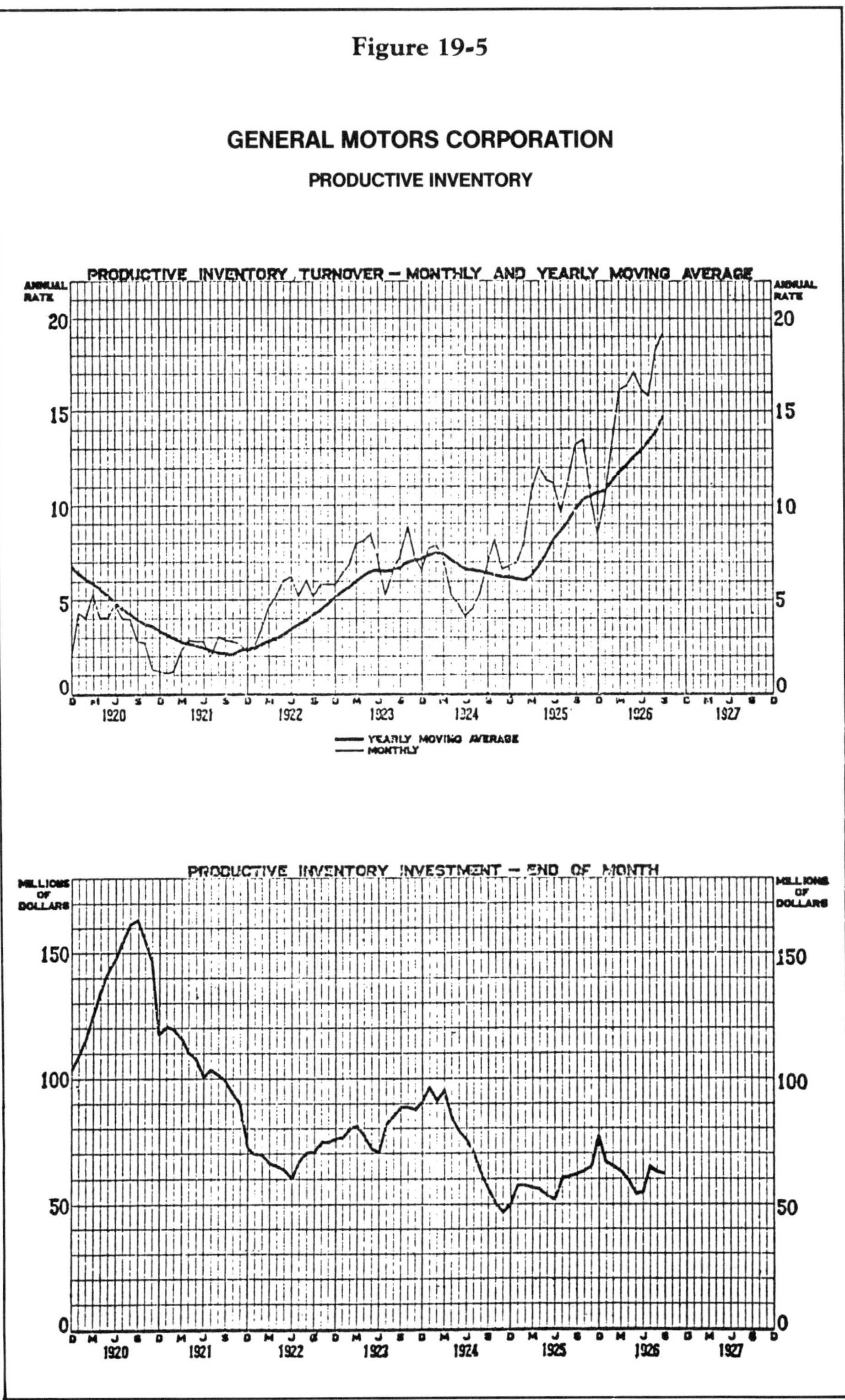
GENERAL MOTORS CORPORATION
PRODUCTIVE INVENTORY
PRODUCTIVE INVENTORY TURNOVER — MONTHLY AND YEARLY MOVING AVERAGE
ANNUAL RATE
20
15
10
5
0
1920
1921
1922
1923
1924
1925
1926
1927
YEARLY MOVING AVERAGE
MONTHLY
PRODUCTIVE INVENTORY INVESTMENT — END OF MONTH
MILLIONS OF DOLLARS
150
100
50
0
1920
1921
1922
1923
1924
1925
1926
1927

were turned over 14.7 times. Stating this another way—in 1923 with an average productive inventory investment of $81,655,000, cost of production amounted to $581,588,000, whereas for the twelve months ended September 30, 1926, cost of production increased 62 percent to $944,315,000 while average productive inventory investment declined to $63,171,000 or 23 percent less than in 1923.

Similarly, in the best previous year, 1923, total inventories, including finished product, were turned over 4.74 times. (See Figure 19-6.)[2] In 1925 this showing was improved to 6.3 times, while for the twelve months ended September 30, 1926, there was a still further improvement to 8.0 times. The importance of this improvement to the buyer of General Motors products may be appreciated from the following example: The total inventory investment for the twelve months ended September 30, 1926, would have averaged $182,490,000 if the turnover rate of 1923 (the best performance prior to 1925) had not been bettered, or an excess of $74,367,000 over the actual average investment. In other words, General Motors would have been compelled to charge $14,873,000 more for its product during this twelve-month period than was actually charged if prices had been established to yield say 20 percent on the operating capital required.

The effect of the improvement in inventory turnover is shown in another manner in Figure 19-7. In the calendar year 1922 Cost of Sales amounted to $372,907,000 and the average Total Inventory Investment to $106,337,000. In 1926 with practically the same average Inventory Investment it was possible to handle a volume of business represented by a Cost of Sales of $828,348,000.

Establishment of Capital and Expense Standards Means More Accurate Estimates. The analysis as to the degree of variability of manufacturing and commercial expenses with increases or decreases in volume of output, and the establishment of "standards" for the various investment items, makes it possible not only to develop "Standard Prices," but also to forecast, with much greater accuracy than otherwise would be possible, the capital requirements, profits, and return on capital at the different rates of operation which may result from seasonal conditions or from changes in the general business situation. Moreover, whenever it is necessary to calculate in advance the final effect on net profits of proposed increases or decreases in price, with their resulting changes in volume of output, consideration of the real economics of the

[2]Turnover of Total Inventory—The rate of turnover for the month at an annual rate is obtained by relating the total inventory investment at the beginning of the month to cost of sales for the month multiplied by twelve, after eliminating all inter-company sales. The yearly moving average turnover is obtained by dividing the cost of sales, after eliminating inter-company sales, for the twelve months period by the average total inventory investment during the period.

Figure 19-6

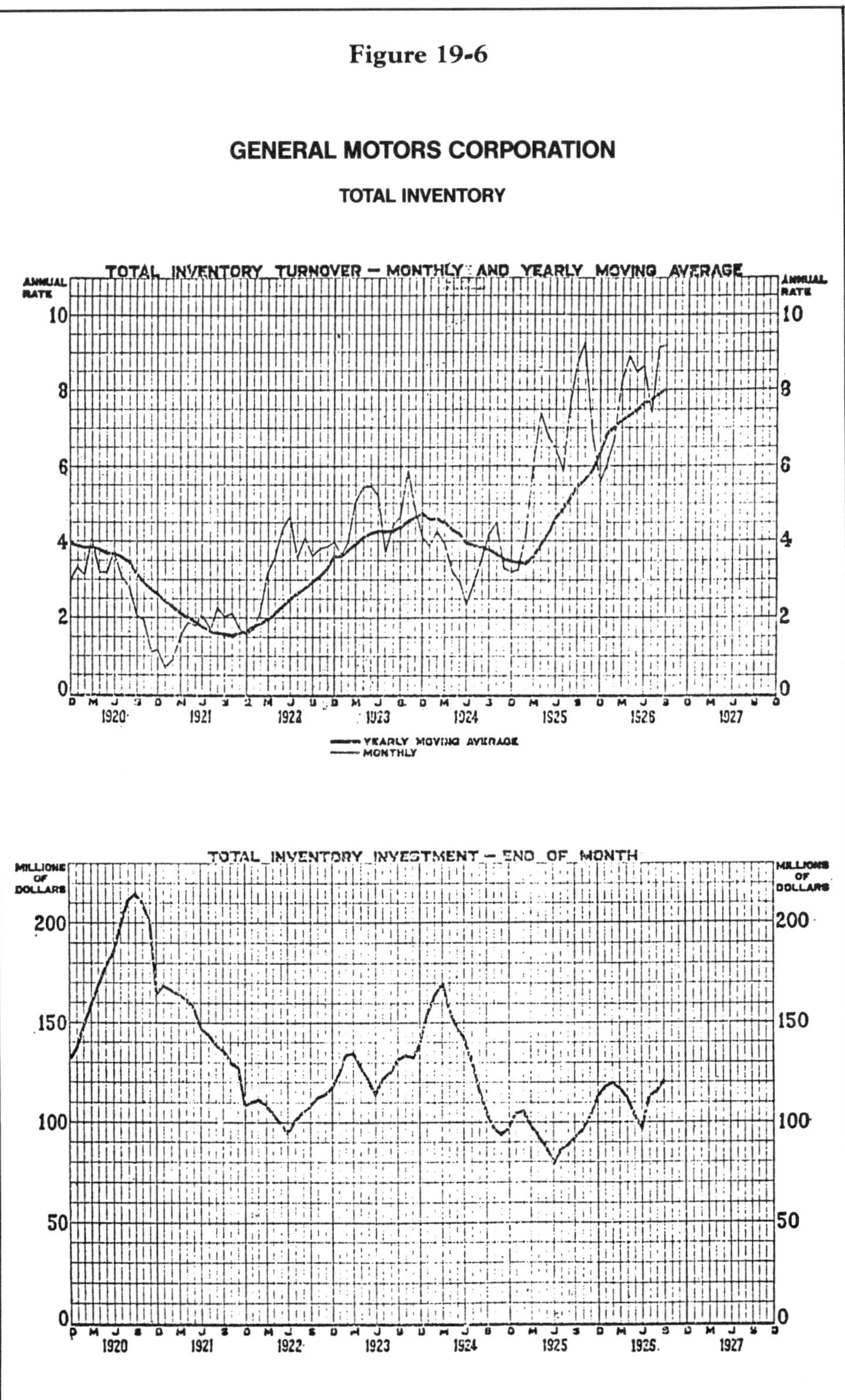
GENERAL MOTORS CORPORATION
TOTAL INVENTORY
TOTAL INVENTORY TURNOVER — MONTHLY AND YEARLY MOVING AVERAGE
ANNUAL RATE
1920
1921
1922
1923
1924
1925
1926
1927
YEARLY MOVING AVERAGE
MONTHLY
TOTAL INVENTORY INVESTMENT — END OF MONTH
MILLIONS OF DOLLARS

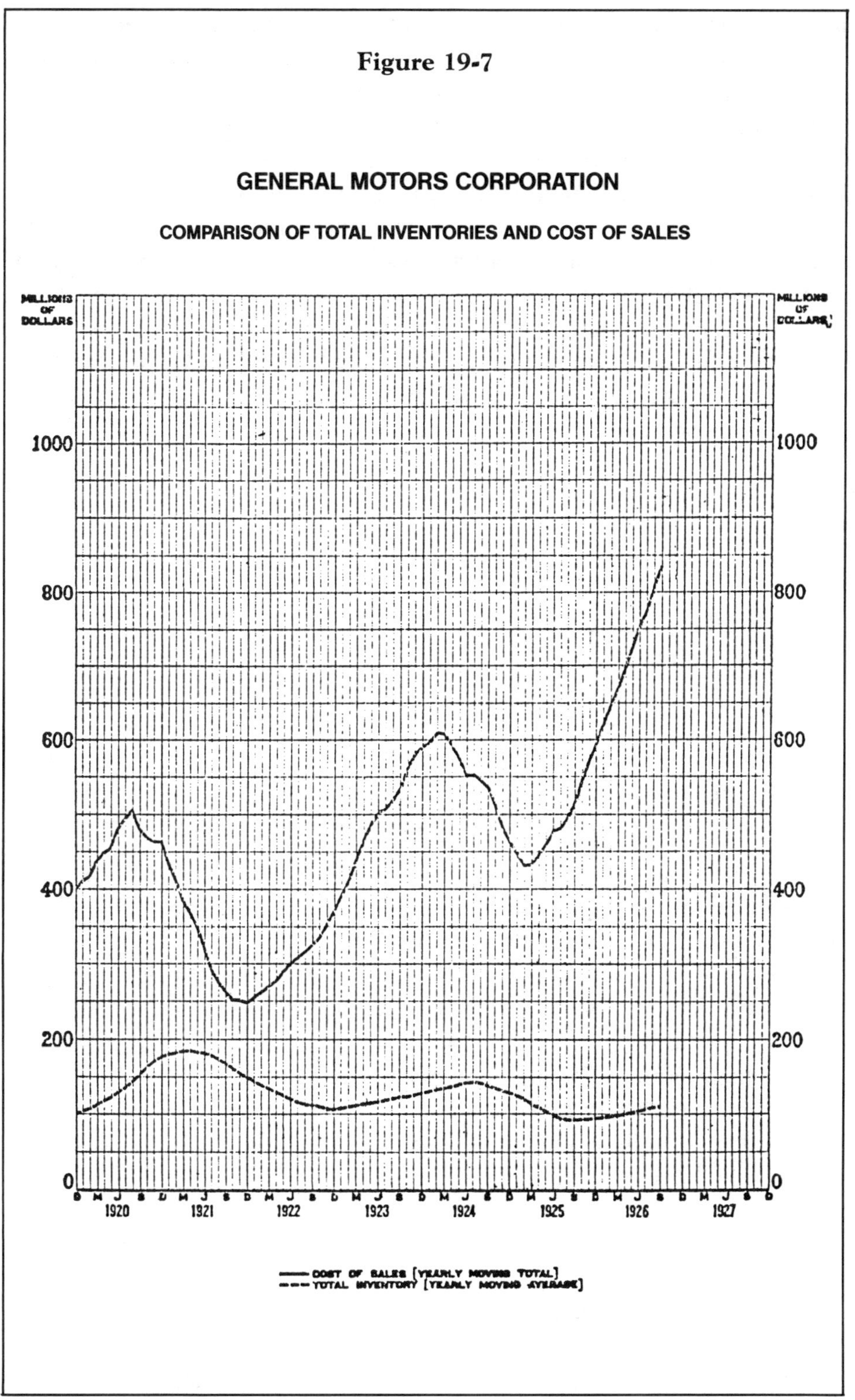
GENERAL MOTORS CORPORATION
COMPARISON OF TOTAL INVENTORIES AND COST OF SALES
MILLIONS OF DOLLARS
1000
800
600
400
200
0
1920
1921
1922
1923
1924
1925
1926
1927
COST OF SALES [YEARLY MOVING TOTAL]
TOTAL INVENTORY [YEARLY MOVING AVERAGE]

Figure 19-7

situation is facilitated by the availability of reliable basic data. For example, it may be desired to calculate the additional volume of business required to offset a contemplated reduction of five percent (5%) in price of product, without decreasing total net profits. For the typical automobile manufacturing establishment, an analysis of the fixed expense and profit position indicates that an increase of 34.28 percent in volume of business is required in order to offset a price reduction of five percent without the impairment of total profit, assuming that the necessary capacity is available. If the 34 percent increase in volume should necessitate additions to plant, or working capital in excess of normal average requirements, then an increase in volume in excess of 34 percent would be required in order to provide, after a five percent price reduction, a return on the additional capital employed and to maintain profits at the original level.

Case I.

Additional Sales Volume Required After 5% Reduction in List Price in Order to Yield Same Total Amount of Net Profit as Existed on Original Volume Before Price Reduction

	Total (a)	Per Unit (b)
1. *Volume Basis*	66,400	
2. Sales at Present Prices	$50,080,098	$754.22
3. Sales after 5% Reduction in Price	47,576,093	716.51
4. Net Profit at Present Price	5,100,467	76.81
5. Net Profit after 5% Reduction, present volume	2,596,462	39.10
6. Difference representing additional net profit required through added volume (Item 4-Item 5)	2,504,005	

Calculation of Additional Net Profit Resulting from Added Volume

	Total (a)	Per Unit (b)
7. Fixed Manufacturing Expense	$ 2,599,500	$ 39.15
8. Fixed Commercial Expense	2,108,033	31.75
9. Net Profit after 5% Reduction in (list) Price (Item 5b)	2,596,462	39.10
10. Additional profit resulting from each car of added volume		$110.00
11. Additional Volume Required to offset price reduction (Item 6 ÷ Item 10)	22,764 Cars	
11a. Additional Volume as percent of present volume (Item 1)	34.28%	

Case II.

Decrease in Sales Volume Permissible at Present Price Before Total Net Profits Are Reduced to an Amount Equivalent to Total Net Profits at Present Volume After a 5% Reduction in Price

	Total (a)	Per Unit (b)
12. Reduction in net profits with 5% reduction in list and no change in volume (Item 6 above)	$ 2,504,005	

Calculation of Decrease in Profits Resulting from Reduction in Volume

13. Fixed Manufacturing Expense	$ 2,599,500	$ 39.15
14. Fixed Commercial Expense	2,108,033	31.75
15. Net Profit at present price (Item 4)	5,100,467	76.81
16. Decrease in Profits resulting from each car of reduced volume		$147.71
17. Decrease in Sales Volume Permissible (Item 12 ÷ Item 16)	16,952 Cars	
18. Percent Decrease in Sales Volume Permissible (Item 17 ÷ Item 1)	25.53%	
Note: To offset each 1% Reduction in Price the Volume at present price can be reduced	5.10%	

Similarly, this analysis indicates that a decline of 25.53 percent in volume of business at present prices can be suffered before profits are reduced to a figure as low as they would be if present volume were sustained at the expense of a five percent reduction in prices.

It is believed that these figures are typical of the automobile industry today, and they are of unusual significance. Perhaps the outstanding economic achievement of the automobile manufacturer during the last twenty years has been his ability to cut costs, and to widen his market through reduced selling prices. Successful companies have been able to increase total profits as a result of the much larger volume sold at lower prices, and no theory could have been more sound throughout the period of rapid growth of the industry. How rapid that growth has been is indicated by the table on page 306.

Only ten years ago, in 1916, annual production first exceeded a million cars and trucks. Four years later this record had been doubled, for the year 1920 saw the production of 2,205,197 cars and trucks. Within the short space of three years, the record has again been doubled, for production in 1923 exceeded 4,000,000 vehicles. For the four-year period 1923-1926 inclusive (with the last quarter of 1926 estimated) annual production has *averaged* about 4,100,000 cars and trucks. The poorest of these four years, 1924, fell below the average only ten percent. The indication for 1926 is a new record of about 4,600,000 vehicles, but this record is not more than 12 percent above the four-year average. It seems evident, therefore, that the automotive industry cannot expect in the future the tremendous annual rates of increase realized in the years prior to 1924. The expectation is rather that of a healthy growth in line with the increase in population and wealth of the country, and the further development of the export market.

There is a vital message in these figures showing that the present economic position of the typical automobile manufacturer required an increase of 34 percent in sales volume to offset a modest price reduction of 5 percent, whereas no such increase as 34 percent is possible for the industry. It is possible, although not at all likely, that a small manufacturer, say with an annual volume of 6,640 cars, might be able to gain an added volume of 34 percent or 2,276 cars as a result of a price reduction of 5 percent, and thereby not suffer an actual reduction in aggregate profits. It seems extremely doubtful, however, that even a 5 percent reduction in price of itself would prove a sufficient stimulus to attract 34 percent more business. A 5 percent price reduction by the manufacturer would reduce the delivered price of the average car only about $45, or 4.6 percent of the average delivered price of $970. The percentage reduction in delivered price is less than the percentage reduction by the manufacturer by reason of the fact that he cannot reduce the freight delivery cost. For a manufacturer with an annual production of 66,400 cars, the required 34 percent increase in volume would be 22,764 cars, a tremendous gain. For the industry as a whole, the necessary annual increase of 34 percent, or approximately 1,400,000 cars a year, would be entirely out of the question. Apparently, therefore, we have reached or are fast approaching the point for the industry where lowered prices cannot attract business in volume sufficient to compensate for the reduced profit margin per car.

Annual Production of Motor Vehicles
Total Cars and Trucks

Year	Number	Year	Number
[3]1899	4,192	1915	892,618
1903	11,000	1916	1,617,708
[3]1904	22,830	[4]1917	1,868,949
1905	25,000	[4]1918	1,153,638
1906	34,000	1919	1,974,016
1907	44,000	[5]1920	2,205,197
1908	65,000	[5]1921	1,661,550
[3]1909	130,986	[5]1922	2,659,064
1910	187,000	1923	4,095,000
1911	210,000	1924	3,640,000
1912	378,000	1925	4,336,000
1913	485,000	[6]1926	4,600,000
[3]1914	569,054		

[3]From U. S. Census reports. 1899 for fiscal year ended June 30, 1900.

[4]Production figures compiled by Automotive Products Section, War Industries Board, from sworn statements by manufacturers.

[5]Figures include production of plants located in Canada, making motor vehicles of U. S. design.

[6]Estimated, based on 9 months production of 3,675,692.

Summary

To recapitulate: the fundamental price policy of a corporation, once formulated, is completely expressed in the conception of *standard volume* (relationship of estimated long-time average rate of plant operation to practical annual capacity, which rate of operation controls the absorption of burden into costs) and expected long-time average rate of return on investment. An analysis of investment along lines of responsibility, together with accounted costs, makes it possible to establish standard cost and capital factors which in turn permit the expression of the fundamental policy in terms of price of product, i.e., standard price. While prices cannot be established on the basis of any formula alone, and no definite rule for establishing prices can be rigidly adhered to, the determination of standard prices affords a means of gauging proposed and actual prices, profits and return on capital in terms of the fundamental price policy, and the extent of necessary departures due to competition and other practical considerations; and submits the policy itself to the test of experience.

The development of industry usually is accomplished by an increase in fixed investment, which results from the further adaptation of labor-saving machinery, and from the tendency of the industrial unit to become a more complete manufacturer. Total cost may decrease, but the proportion of selling price necessary to cover indirect expense and return on investment tends to increase. The problem of equitably distributing over different products both indirect costs and the profit margin necessary to provide return on the capital employed is, therefore, one of increasing importance, and its solution is facilitated by the periodic development of standard prices, based upon standards of capital requirement and of manufacturing and commercial expense.

Stability of prices is a condition under which industry prospers. The cost accountant is in a position to present information that is an essential part of an appraisal of the real economic situation of his own company, and thereby to act as a safeguard against action fundamentally unsound. In proportion to the accomplishment of this purpose will the cost accountant contribute to intelligent competition and consequent stability within his own industry, a condition which will contribute toward improvement in the economic well-being of the country.

(20) "The Group Bonus and Labor Standards," April 15, 1927, Bulletin, Vol. 8, No. 16, E. H. Tingley, Secretary, National Association of Foremen

Editorial Department Note

As evidenced by the inquiries coming to the editor's desk, there is a good deal of active interest in the group bonus method of paying labor. The outstanding achievement of management in its relation to labor today has been and is its ability to secure a spirit of co-operation which has enabled management to cut cost of production and at the same time increase the pay envelope to labor. The group bonus incentive wage plan is a good example of the way this is being accomplished. The current publication deals with this subject in a practical way.

The author, Mr. E. H. Tingley, after being graduated from Cornell University with the degree of Mechanical Engineer, worked for the Westinghouse Electric and Manufacturing Company at East Pittsburgh. During the war he spent over three years in the Ordnance Department. For the past seven he has been connected with the Delco Light Company, Dayton, Ohio, having been in charge of the factory budgetary control work, and also in an executive capacity in the Works Manager's office.

He is co-author with Thomas B. Fordham of the book entitled "Organization and Budgetary Control in Manufacturing." For the past two years Mr. Tingley has developed the Foremen's Magazine *and since the first of the year has devoted his full time as editor of this magazine. He is also secretary of the National Association of Foremen.*

This talk was given before a recent meeting of the Chicago Chapter, National Association of Cost Accountants.

The Group Bonus and Labor Standards

In fixing labor standards—this word, standard, is almost a misnomer—I think we are in a world today where standards are changing. What is today a standard may not be so tomorrow. But nevertheless we have to have some standards to measure things by. We have to have standards both in business and in our ordinary life.

I want to go back a little in the history of setting labor standards. For the purposes of this discussion I am going to limit the subject to a consideration of direct labor. That is the standard you put in your costs. Your indirect labor, as we know it, comes later on in the discussion of overhead items or burden.

In fixing these standards, Mr. Frederick W. Taylor, back in 1881, saw the need of finding a better way of doing things than to go back through all the records to see how long it took a man to do a certain operation. So he decided to use a stop watch. He tried it for two years before he told anybody it was a new method. Then he experimented another fourteen years before he announced it to the public. It was in Detroit in 1895 that he spoke for the first time of using a stop watch and of taking time studies of operations. Again in 1903 he published a contribution on this subject, and by that time the manufacturers began to pay a little attention to the idea which had sprung from Mr. Taylor back at the Midvale Steel Co. in Philadelphia. I think we can feel today that time study is being used in the majority of industries that have any standards at all for setting their labor rates.

At first many mistakes were made in setting time standards. There was no conception in these standards of methods or equipment. We took what we had and made time studies on the things we had. There was no assurance of a steady flow of material to the worker. You cannot set a standard and expect men to work half an hour, and then wait around for more work and expect to hold them to your piecework rate. Usually time studies were taken secretly. Men hid behind boxes and peeped around to see what the fellow was doing. They had a watch and they pressed it secretly. Some had a glass cage, and a man would sit in it and telephone the operations to a man in the office, who kept the time. All those things seem ludicrous today, but they had their place then, which was mainly to get this time study made, but they failed in the big thing of not getting the cooperation of the worker. Today we find that we must have the cooperation of the man who is going to do this work day in and day out. Those earlier methods have been discarded and we use today the method of calling the worker into a conference and working with him.

Any task entails three elements: (1) What implements we are going to use, and whether we have the tools and machinery to do it with; (2) How it is done; you want to know whether the man is doing it in a certain way and how efficiently he is operating; and (3) The length of time required for the operation. In our discussion this evening we are going to treat mainly this third element, the length of time. That is the most important thing. We expect the tools to be in good working order. We expect to have a good method, and we expect that there will be a minimum expenditure of time and energy on a given task, and I think you accountants can demand that of the shop man, to see that he does plan his work, his machinery and his methods to take a minimum of time and minimum expenditure of time and energy.

We appreciate fully that the setting of a real standard may depend upon the standards of your equipment and your materials. I am just leading up to the problems of concerns who do not take this into account when they try to set time standards in a hurry. You must go back into your materials and machinery before you can set any standards which your cost accountant can use over a month of time. In reality that is motion study, and I think the men in the shop do not fully appreciate the matter. The time study man can teach the foreman and the shopmen in general, chiefly because he has time to study these operations. He has time to see the waste motion. He has time to see the fatiguing postures the men have to be in. He is watching all those matters. The foreman says, "Here's the job. I want it out by noon."

The thing we are trying to do is to see the thing in its broad viewpoint. Time study has as its objects: (1) The determination of possible improvements in equipment and conditions, (2) Improvement in actual methods of doing the work, which, as I said, is very important—I was at Richmond, Indiana, the other day, watching some girls in a factory making overalls and khaki uniforms. We were watching girls sewing on buttons. I said, "What is this woman working so hard for?" She was really working harder than we would want to. The foreman said, "I tried to break her of the habit, but she can't get any results unless she works that way." She did not consume any effort but she would make her arms go and everything in time. She was probably too old to change. We find the factory does need a very careful checkup of methods of doing the work—and, (3) A determination of the unit time the task should be finished in. Time study should be constructive and have as its object the establishment of a fair and equitable rate at which the work should be done. This object is reached only after each act has been carefully analyzed, made convenient and as easy as possible for the operator, and all unnecessary work eliminated.

I think we are a bit prone in the factory to accept certain operations as "father did them," and we do things that way because we feel that is the custom. I believe we need to get this question before us from a cost standpoint, to feel we are justified in going to the factory man and saying we believe he can do the task better than in the past.

The fundamental principle is that the greatest gain comes to the employer only when the employee gains also, and when the responsibility for this gain is equally divided between management and the men. It must not be all on management or all on the men. We feel we should divide it equally. Of course management has to provide tools, equipment, and material. We believe that, if we thoroughly acquaint our workers in the shop with the objects and aims of time study, of setting labor standards, we are going to get farther than if we just say, "We are operating under this method, and here is the price." We in the Delco Light Co. have recently got out a little book on the group bonus wage incentive plan. It is a very readable book, with large type, and a man can read it at home with his glasses on. It tells him what he is going to do, and how he can calculate his earnings and know every day what he has earned, and how much money he can count on taking home at the end of the week. This serves the purpose of acquainting the man with what we have in mind and what he should have in mind.

Mr. Taylor, at the start, dealt entirely with piecework. He took his operations on a piecework basis. It has developed into various other operation studies, and today we have one of the leading types in the group bonus method of wage payment. I felt it would be advantageous if I could tell you more about it. I want to bring out some points as to how we have operated it in our factory and what it does for us in getting a standard labor cost.

A group bonus is a wage incentive plan which rewards groups of men in proportion to the achievement of their combined effort. That is a really good definition. I want to repeat it, because certain phrases have a very great significance. A group bonus is a wage incentive plan which rewards groups of men — not individuals, but groups of men — in proportion — the more they work the more they get — to the achievement of their combined effort — not the achievement of their individual effort, but of their combined effort. That is really a new idea. It is quite different from the piecework plan of "every man for himself and the devil take the company." We are trying to bring out this new method of cooperation whereby the workman will consider the company along with increased earnings, and will not lose sight of doing good to the public and everybody concerned.

The group bonus method was put into practice in 1918, and is now used in about twenty of the General Motors plants, and many others. There is no patent on it, and those of you who are interested in it can get a copy of this little book. Here is how the plan operates.

We take a group of operators, such as assembly workers, who can be arranged along a bench or group of machines. It is a matter of grouping certain operations which can be done more or less consecutively. We take a standard time for each operation, or each man, and combine them into the assembly operation. We add these together and allow a certain time allowance for contingencies, such as personal service, temporary absences from the machines to get new tools, or getting new supplies like screws, etc. These allowances are made in order to establish a fair, standard time for the complete operation.

When we hire a man we establish a base rate, depending upon his ability and efficiency. This base rate is guaranteed per hour. Some men get 45c., 48c., and 50c., and we pay our group leaders 2 cents more an hour. That gives him anywhere from $2.00 to $3.00 a week for taking the responsibility of being a group leader. The rates are thus set based on the men's ability. This base rate is set according to living conditions in the city. We take for granted that Chicago may have higher wages in general than, possibly, Dayton; or Detroit may pay more than Kalamazoo, etc.; but the base rate depends on the living conditions of the local city. You also set it on the basis of the usual earnings men get in the industry. You understand the conditions in your city, and you set the base rate in proportion to what is a good, fair earning for help.

You can also set it on the cost which you desire. That is very important on a standard cost basis. You can set your base rate so your cost can be predetermined – and I will discuss that in a few minutes.

The standard time is the amount of time required by the average competent workman to do the operation repeatedly and at a fair rate of speed. We say the time required by the "average man" to do it "repeatedly, at a fair rate of speed." We take a group, an average group, and give them the benefit of this group efficiency. In figuring the group's efficiency, we have an efficiency composed of credits offset by debits. A group's credit is the number of good pieces that come off the end of the line, multiplied by your standard time allowed. If you have allowed half an hour for each unit, and they do 100 units, they have 50 hours to their credit. The debits are the actual time consumed by the group in doing the work. If you have a 9-hour day, and you have 5 men, and they finish 100 pieces in a day, they have 45 hours debited. But they have 50 hours credits. Dividing one by the other, you get their efficiency. That efficiency determines how much bonus they will receive, based on their rate of earnings. An illustration will show how this works out. Suppose we have a man working 50 hours a week as a leader and getting 52 cents an hour. He gets $26 for his base rate earnings. Another man works 41 hours. He was sick one day, and he was only getting 50 cents an hour. That nets him $20.50 for his base earnings. They have made a group credit of 125% efficiency. Turning to the table, we find that 125% efficiency gives them 50% bonus on their base earnings. Therefore the first man, who earned $26 base earnings would get $13 bonus, making a total of $39. He would have more because he worked longer than the one who put in 41 hours and who therefore, gets $10.25 bonus making a total of $30.75. The leader earns a little more also because his bonus is based on the 2 cents an hour more.

It is interesting to note that the efficiency listed in this bonus table pays 1% at only 75% efficiency; so you see the efficiency table is determined from long experience on the basis that men are expected to make at least 100% efficiency. You pay 10% bonus at 90% efficiency; 20% bonus at 100%; and 50% at 125% efficiency; and so on. This table gives you a constant unit cost at all efficiencies over 100%. Whether a man makes 175% efficiency, your unit cost is just the same. I can prove it to you if you want to take the time. At 90% efficiency your cost increases 1.8%. So you see when you get below 100%, you study your base rate tables to see if the men cannot make 100%. At 80% efficiency your cost increases 8.3% and at 70% it is about 18%. So you see management watches the fellows who are making below 100%. Bear in mind also that the men in the group watch it, too. So you see changing your base rates is one method of changing your cost. Your efficiency does not make any difference above 100%. The men may do well and your standard labor cost is constant. You are safe if the men are working at above 100% efficiency, as long as you do not change your base rate. The earnings have nothing to do with your cost. That seems a little odd at first, but I am talking labor efficiency. If you take into account that you are getting double production, your actual overhead is really half. If you are getting more bonus for the men, you are getting a really better actual overhead. You turn these savings over into over-absorbed burden and still keep your cost the same way.

To re-state the situation, the earnings the man makes can be first set by the base rate; and, secondly, by the standard time, which is so set that he should operate with at least 100% efficiency. You may have to work that out with a time study man, so you can be sure the men can do that. We have had some startling results on that basis. We went into a group making certain parts, and we immediately cut 25% off the labor cost. The men said it could not be done. So far we have practically cut the cost 48% over the old piecework rate. Of course we have eliminated some of the men, and got them to work more efficiently. It has given us a lower cost and given the men more money.

We have a third thing that earnings are set by. The group's ability and willingness to work. That is a big item in the situation. That also entered into piecework. If a man did not work, he did not earn anything, but the company still had an interest in keeping up production. Here, we get an incentive, for the man's earnings increase because the group is able to work and wants to work.

If you would like to know what the cost of a certain article will be, you can predetermine your cost as soon as you have your standard time set. In a way we accept our standard time as standard until we change it by engineering changes, whether in the design of the product, the amount of material used, etc. But if you are not changing these things, your standard time is standard. You can take your standard time and multiply it by the man's base rate. Suppose we take the group of men earning 45c., 48c., 50c., and 52c., depending on the man's ability, his efficiency, and the kind of operation he is doing. There may be 100 men in the group. There are places for the older men, places for the younger men, places for the slower fellows and the quick fellows. It is not necessary that there be but one kind of men in the row or group. The group is what we are getting at; we are getting group efficiency and group interest in the work. So we take the standard time, multiply it by the average base rate of the group, and add 20% efficiency. We add 20% bonus to get a total 100% efficiency. It works out very nicely in that way.

Under the group bonus plan, fixed costs are secured and incentives are given to the men. I am talking labor now. Do not confuse this with any other saving you may make. Under the group bonus we do secure a lot of savings. Indirect labor operations that used to be in the overhead are now placed in the direct group, and this direct group often eliminates that from indirect operations. Men will do things they used to have a janitor do. They do it themselves and get along very nicely. We have had some other men walk back and feed the line and go down to the end and take them off.

Group bonus tends to give an even flow of materials and better assembly methods. You cost accountants are directly interested in that proposition, because if you can get an even flow of materials and better assembly, you can interest the management in talking about lower costs. We also get a simple and more accurate factory time-keeping system. At the end of each day each group turns in a report of the number of pieces made, and we can quickly figure their efficiency. The next morning at 9:00 o'clock we have determined the group's efficiency and the man knows what his earnings are. We can go out the next morning and see whether this group fell down or kept up to standard costs. If the group efficiency fell below 100% the unit cost increased.

First we get a simple and more accurate factory cost system, and next an accurate, simple check for all productive and many non-productive operations.

In my office today we are computing a budget for next year, both for the entire year and for several months ahead. It is not our usual practice to purchase goods beyond four months in advance. We also make our budget for the present month and three months to come, because we have a firm belief, as all sane business men have, that the world is changing and conditions change. I remember very well we had a speaker come to college, and he said, "Go as far as you can see, and then see how far you can go." The same principle is applied in our budget. We are going as far as we can see, and then we will be able to see how far we can go.

The next result of the group bonus plan is a reduction of defective workmanship. In my first statement I said we paid only on the good ones that come off the assembly line. They do not put defective stuff through; they catch things; they will not use them, and that saves the company a lot. We had some departments that ran 18% to 20% in re-operation. Group production came into our picture the last year, and we have eliminated this question of re-operation in a marked degree.

High production per man hour. That is absolutely shown. We must take an interest in making this an incentive that will get out production at a high rate per man hour. We also get low unit cost, and we get high hourly earnings for the men. Offhand it sometimes seems that the men's earnings are larger than necessary. When we get high production per hour and low unit cost, we will make more money because as a whole we are getting more production, lower costs, lower overhead and better efficiency, and lots of things you cannot measure, such as cooperation and a better spirit in the whole organization, because the man realizes the unit at the end of the line will have to be good or he will not be paid for it. Therefore he has a keen interest in seeing what he makes is all right.

Then we have a spirit of cooperation, or teamwork, which reduces labor turn-over. I was asked tonight whether the elimination of a man here and there in the groups does not make for labor turn-over? We do not eliminate men by letting them go out of the organization; we may take them out of one group and put them in some other operation. I am not one of those who advocate that labor turn-over in itself is an evil. We are so close to the Kentucky hills, and we get many men who lack technical education and ability and who cannot do the work. There are some men who have so called wooden heads. Some other men have stone heads, and we are prone sometimes to give a stone-headed job to a wooden-headed man and wonder why he cannot do it. But our group bonus does reduce labor turn-over, from the standpoint that the men are better satisfied on their jobs.

Another thing which appeals to us who are working with foremen, from an executive standpoint, is that it relieves the foreman of planning to keep the men busy. They keep themselves busy. We do not have to do so much planning, because it is the leader's job to get a flow of work sufficient to make at least 100% and maintain the standard labor cost.

Another thing we get is the development of leadership and we need it badly. In my work with the National Association of Foremen, we know there is a big demand for good foremen and a real dearth of them. We can train a man, and soon he is a leader of twenty-five, and he often develops into a good foreman, and perhaps a good job superintendent or department superintendent. Management can watch the efficiencies and take care of the two extremes. If you set a rate and the men earn a bonus which is off, your standard time is wrong. You must watch the lower end, below 100% efficiency so you know whether they are making it. If those men are falling down, there is something wrong. If your man is not a leader, you have made a mistake in appointing him. He has not the ability to set the pace, and you must make a change in leadership. Our men are taking care of hundreds of men in departments when heretofore they were busy taking care of fifty or sixty.

From management's standpoint, you men will say, where are you going to make a saving if your standard costs do not change? You will find out you can make a saving by reducing your standard time, by new methods and new efficiencies. You can go in with new equipment and re-study your operation. We often find the men do the changing. They see the time is out of line and they will say, "This is all wrong and we would like to have a new study, so we will get a good day's work." You have a chance to get your saving there. But you can also change your base rate. Suppose, as many of our business prophets prognosticate, next year is going to be a bad year. You can go into your factory and say to the men that conditions are such that costs must be cut to meet competition. You take two cents off the base rate. Each man just makes $2 or $3 less a week. You have changed your cost, and have done it by cutting the base rate. We tried that on an operation in our own plant. We had some car builders—the men who made these beautiful mahogany hand-tooled cars which the steel cars of today have largely superseded. Those men had to earn 2 cents more an hour than the average carpenter should. We set their base rate at 55c., and we set the painters who sprayed on the paint at 50c., so we had to have an adjustment. We had a meeting and got all the group leaders in. We sold them on the idea. We cut all the rates to 48c. and 50c. and the group leaders to 52c. We were able to hold our costs by setting the base rates at a point where they would let us. We find good workmen coming to our plant; they are making good earnings and they know we have a good layout. We are getting the whole factory group lined up on so many hundred per day. We are getting factory cooperation we did not get before on piecework. A man could come in and get a good price and he wanted to keep the job himself. We found the other day on an old job we issued enough production orders to cover 250,000 to get 100,000 good pieces. What happened to them? Those fellows turned in the old production cards and did not do the work. Then they went back and claimed the card was lost, so we paid them 2½ times on all piecework. We can pay for the total product turned out, and our machinery fellows who did the job ten days ago get paid when it comes off the line. They feel we are interested in these operations and they are interested in us, and we get a factory spirit of cooperation; we get good work.

I might mention briefly that we are getting through the foremen and the so-called job foremen a better conception of what cost is all about. I think we have done that through getting the standard cost idea to them. This group bonus has interested them all the way down the line as to what is cost anyway, why we must have a profit, why we want to keep a cost standard. We have adopted as a slogan this year, "A Better Product at a Lower Cost." That takes into account the question of quality, and if the men do not get paid for poor stuff, they are working for quality every minute of the day.

We have taken that up in our *Foremen's Magazine,* which I would like to take the liberty of mentioning to you. I do not like to advertise what we are doing. Our *Foremen's Magazine* is attaining the size of a regular magazine these days. We are ending our third year, and are reaching about 6500 foremen in 29 states. We are running an article on time study, and we are trying to present this problem of costs. We need an article on the selling phase of the problem, what the salesman has to know. He must know production, and all this problem of costs. If lower costs can be had, the product is easier to sell out in the field. If we can make a better product, it is easier to sell out in the field. We get all those phases of the problem and are trying to bring them to the foreman and to sell him on the necessity of knowing all about business.

I think you men could go home and start off some of this group bonus, start something of this kind in your own shop. You probably already have time studies; you have information on hand for each operation. If you can see your way clear to creating a group, take one little group and try that out. Show them how they can make more on the group basis. They will like it, and soon the rest of the fellows will say, "Why can't we have some of this group business, it is simple enough." You probably have some firms in Chicago using it. I know the automobile field in Michigan is full of it. You are perfectly welcome to come to our factory and we will show you all about it. Talk to the men who are operating under it; and you can go back to your people and say, "Our factory can certainly save money by creating a standard labor cost."

I think Mr. Camman, who spoke last month, talked in somewhat general terms, and I have tried to bring you something in detail so you will see the need of standard labor costs.

I would like to summarize some of the things necessary if you want standard labor costs. You need a simple method of figuring the bonus. So many methods have fallen down because the men cannot figure their earnings. Some of these bonus propositions that pay the men at the end of the year are too far away. The men say, "Suppose the company does make any money —why should I worry about a bonus after January 1st?" The men want something they can figure and take home. Some of the plants do not stop the machines during the noon hour, so the men can work. One man will operate a group of machines, and they take turns having lunch and keeping the machines going.

Secondly, we need a simple way of figuring costs. You know this old historical cost method—I hate to ask how many are using it. Under it you figure on what happened several months ago. Someone mislaid the books and you cannot figure the bonus, and you go back and tell the office last July it cost $28. Under our method, we can tell you pretty close.

Group bonus permits us to add up the group costs, and we can have costs every week if desired. This can be accomplished rather easily because group costs are figured daily.

Then we need in our standard cost some way to coordinate the various abilities of men. Life is full of varieties. I said to some one here tonight that there is not a man here whose face I would recognize as having seen before; you are all strangers to me. We all have different mental talents and we are of various types. Industry must make use of them.

We also need an incentive for increased earnings. It must not be all on the factory side. Everybody has to benefit. The men feel an interest, and the company benefits also. We get it in turn-over; decreased labor in actual labor cost; it shows in overhead and better efficiency, and all these intangible things. We get elimination of waste, which you men as accountants deplore so much, when you see it. How you men do "kick" about this idle time, when you see three men standing around the tool crib waiting for tools. I used to listen to altercations between the factory cost department and the factory production man, and I got it from both sides.

I understand from your chairman that it is customary to throw the meeting open to discussion. I will be very glad to answer any questions.

Discussion

President Wilson: Mr. Tingley has given us all a great deal to think about. Maybe I am the worst cost accountant in the room, but I know he has given me lots of things to ask about. However, it is my job to give you people a chance to ask these questions first. Is there anybody who would like to get further details from Mr. Tingley?

Question: I would like to ask Mr. Tingley how far in his organization he carries this plan. In our particular organization we have been running the group bonus plan for something like seven years. I wonder if he has had any success with everybody on it.

Mr. Tingley: We are operating about 93% group bonus of the labor that could be put on the group bonus. We have not tried to include our foremen in our group. We still have certain operations which eventually we hope to put in the line of production. We have taken the man who took care of the stock and brought him in, and the man who fed the wooden parts on the truck. The man who fills the tank of the car that takes them away is in this group. We do not expect our inspectors to be in the group bonus; they must be kept out of the group.

Question: Our plan is just a trifle different. As I understand Mr. Tingley, you must have time studies on which to base your standards. In other words, there are places where you cannot measure activities but you can measure results. We include every foreman in our bonus plan because we make the result responsible for the job. We take those groups who have traffic departments. You regulate your traffic conditions and keep the traffic cost as low as possible. Consequently if you find out the results you want that department to accomplish, you can set up standards. In other words, if we tried to cut our traffic department down, the chances are we should increase our traffic costs considerably. The way we set the plan up, it does not make any difference whether we put on 20 men or take 10 off. We have to take every department, even the inspection department and other office groups from start to finish. I think if Mr. Tingley is going to stay in town I would like very much to have him visit us. I think we can get a lot of good from each other. I am going to try to visit his plant next week for an entirely different reason.

Question: I am sure these men would like to know how you standardize your cost department.

President Wilson: We are talking about labor tonight, and there is no labor in the cost department. It is not very often that a cost accountant gets a factory superintendent with a chance to cross-question him.

Mr. Hansen: What do you do about estimating a job prior to going into the bonus?

Mr. Tingley: We have an estimating department that I had the honor to start. We began that on the basis of our old time studies. We studied operations by blue prints and cost cards. Everything in our factory is estimated before it goes into production. We have another thing for which we use this estimating department. They tell us what they think the factory should be able to do; they say they should get the cost at a certain figure; the factory is supposed somehow to meet it. You might say the estimating men are not practical men, but they are. They are time study men, men who have had experience in knowing what they are talking about. We estimate all our products and we have departments now checking actuals and estimates; we take those costs and break them down. We go to the superintendent and tell him we think this thing is costing too much; we tell the foremen and superintendent they are not meeting the estimated cost. How do you know? We have broken it down into operations. He calls the time study man and says either the time is wrong or something is wrong with the equipment. Our estimated costs have been surprisingly accurate in comparison with what the actual cost should be. We estimate these things before every operation. Now with the group bonus we have figures on our cards, we keep a set of cards, and we are able to take these and go back and estimate anything offering a similar operation. There are lots of men who have new ideas, and there are a lot of those things we are trying out. We take them into the estimating department and estimate the cost. The estimating department is always busy. It is an important function in our work because it gives us a standard of what the factory can do. You can do that if you have good tools, if you keep them in good shape and operate efficiently and have a constant flow of materials.

Question: You say 98% of your workers are working under the bonus plan?

Mr. Tingley: In one plant.

Question: I would like to know what class of labor you found it was not suited for.

Mr. Tingley: The men who repair machinery, the men in the carpenter shop who put up partitions, etc., and the painters who keep the place up to date. The janitors are in some of the groups and the men who used to be called "truckers" are in the groups; but some of these operators, like the repair men, etc., have to be in a department by themselves. They maintain equipment, and sometimes the job will take a day and sometimes half an hour. They do not figure in our groups.

I like the idea of your traffic and office departments, and I believe some of these departments which have the problem of bringing in so much material every day can be put on. The traffic department's job is to bring in enough to keep that line going. Some day we can possibly include the tool repair men. In our automatic department we have a repair man in the group. He is interested in keeping those machines in top-notch order, therefore he is sharing in the group. We have had to reduce our overhead rates because the group bonus has taken lots of this overhead away.

Question: In starting with the group bonus, do you pay for each unit produced by each particular group until you have the entire plant on the group plan?

Mr. Tingley: If we had assembly work for 100 men, we would take the first operation and pay them for what they do. Then we pass it on to the men who put the side panels on. We pay the men who hang the doors. Then the painters are in a group.

Take a little group that you can sell it to. Begin with a small group. Let them make a door, for instance, and pay for the completed door. You will soon find they are sold on it and it is no trouble to sell a second group.

Question: Suppose after you got the group started it was necessary to put in a new man. Was the group penalized by putting in the new man?

Mr. Tingley: The first three days the company pays the man an instruction allowance. His pay is not debited against the group. The last three days of the week he is in the group and has to be carried by the group. If he does not make good they have the privilege of referring him back to the department. Sometimes they think they need him, and after things are started they find they do not need him.

Question: How do you handle inspectors?

Mr. Tingley: Entirely on an hourly rate.

Question: How do they average?

Mr. Tingley: They do not make as much. It does not take a highly skilled man to do that.

Question: Can you explain how you handle the group bonus in a department where you have 8, 10, or 12 separate assemblies?

Mr. Tingley: It is not a panacea for every operation, but you will be surprised how far you can go. There will be some departments that cannot be put on.

Take the department retreating certain parts. They cannot be paid by the number of units going out. Of course you have to group types of machines. You cannot have automatic machines grouped with lathes. We try to group machines by operations where the men can help each other. You have to use discretion and you cannot expect to solve all your problems in every department.

Question: As to defective work, do the men have to repair their own defective work at their own expense? Is that taken from the group and all repaired at once, or do the men take turns leaving the group and retreating defectives?

Mr. Tingley: Suppose we have some defective material and the men have laid it aside because it is defective. They finish up what they can. The floor is full. They finish, and go back and repair this defective workmanship, and clean up the ones they set off the track. They re-operate them and bring them through. In the automatic department the man gets them from the screw machines and re-operates them. Sometimes two or three men will jump in. They will clean up the defective work and shoot it through. It all depends on the operation whether anyone in the group can go back and put it through.

Question: Do you find men staying out of the group and working on their old time, or do you find them more willing to get the guaranteed time rate?

Mr. Tingley: Their time is charged to the group. If it is defective material, we do not penalize the men; we give them new parts. They go back to the department that made them. If it has been worked on the machines, they repair them.

We have this problem too. We try to group girls, especially types of girls that can work together. We may have three different groups of efficiency. Here is the slower group, here is the middle group, and here are the speedy ones. A girl who can beat the gang does not work, but put her up against some 98% girls and they all work better.

Question: With reference to the attitude of union labor, what has union labor to say with reference to this perfect freedom of management as to how many shall be in a group, or what the base rates shall be, whether it shall be decreased, or whether the men shall be dropped?

Mr. Tingley: Dayton is a non-union town, and I probably am not qualified to say what the attitude is in other cities. I can see no reason why it has not been successful in Flint. I think you will find the union man wants to make as much money as anybody else. The labor unions have had their troubles; they have had poor leadership. Management has had poor leadership. But I think we can feel safe in saying that when a union man can earn all he can get, he is not complaining about the wages. We are not limiting the men in the group. We say the standard time is half an hour; make all you can. The men know it is a reasonable figure and they are willing to work that way. The incentive increases much faster. The harder they work, the bigger the bonus they make. Of course, Dayton being a non-union town, we have had no discussion along that line. I am not qualified to speak of the attitude of union labor, but because it is operating in a large number of factories all over the country, they must be running into the union question.

Comment: I might give you our experience in our tool room. We tackled that department one of the last, for the simple reason we realized we were dealing with about 80% union men. We put them on the bonus. They objected to it very strongly. At the end of the first month we paid them the bonus. They refused to take it. We refused to take it back. At the close of the following month there was not one of these men who came in to offer to return his bonus pay.

Question: I should like your opinion as to the feasibility of applying a group bonus plan to a factory or manufacturing plant where you have a seasonal production, and a large force to take care of the seasonal production.

Mr. Tingley: Do you keep this entire force through the seasonal slump by means of a reduction of the hours of labor, or what do you do?

Question: We practically close down certain places after the season is closed. It means that in some places we have a large force, numbering several hundred, which only works for six to eight weeks or three months. Would it be possible in that position to adopt such a plan? Do you happen to know whether any concern similarly situated is doing it?

Mr. Tingley: Our Frigidaire production is very much seasonal. Our biggest peak comes in May and June. We have to reduce the hours of labor, taking off Saturday morning, to hold the organization as long as we can in the fall. But we do it this way. If we have parallel operations, we can keep one group going and cut down another. We cut down to one group and keep it through the winter season. If you have to have 300 men part of the time and only 100 during the balance, you can keep the 100 and keep them going so you will have a nucleus when you spread out. You might have to make some allowance for education if the skilled men stay in the group and educate the new help. The automobile plants have seasonal business. They lay off men, and go back again and build up their organization.

Question: We have the problem in certain places where we close down the plant entirely, except for the maintenance help, and the next season we may import an entirely new force. We have been considering the bonus group plan, but we have never found it practical. I was wondering if you had found anyone who was able to make it work.

Mr. Tingley: I cannot answer that.

Question: Have you seen in your organization, or any organization, the same group of men employed on alternating positions during the day? For instance, some groups of men may handle six or eight departments, due to the job being a small one. We transfer men from group to group. We find some of our painters can paint almost anything. We have to take men off one operation and transfer them to another. Of course it takes a little time to learn the operations, and you do not put a wooden-headed man on a steel-headed job. You have a flying squad.

Mr. Tingley: I think one of the strongest points in the group bonus plan is the very flexibility you are talking about. As long as the man is in the particular group you are not using a dozen time tickets to take care of his time.

Question: Does the bonus work as well in time of curtailed production? When you are laying them off one day, or working short hours, do you find the men will work as well?

Mr. Tingley: We leave the standard time and the base rate alone. The men feel the work is not so urgent, and they do not make as many units per hour, but if you have a certain schedule you hold them to it. There will be a little falling off, because they recognize there is no need of rushing. We find it better to cut the number of days down and the men will make a week's pay in five days. The men will slow up a little bit. If we have to slow up a little of course it cuts their earnings, but your standard cost has not changed any.

Question: If you have a condition where you have over-estimated your sales volume and you have greater production capacity, would you not have to keep production down in line with sales, and the man would figure he would be the loser at the end of the week?

Mr. Tingley: We are giving the men an incentive well above 100%. Your cost remains the same whether he works at 150%, 125%, or 100%. He is the loser in his pay. You do not have to worry about your cost from the competitive standpoint. They get their wages, but the closer they get to 100%, the smaller the bonus.

Just as the automobile concerns, we like to stabilize production, but we feel that we want to hold our organization together, because to us a skilled group of men is worth just as much as interest on a lot of money tied up. When we want production, these men will work overtime and they are right at hand because you have taken care of them over the winter season. We have carried them through the winter season, and they know it. I do not know how far we could go without having to shut things off. If you go through Ford's plant today, he is running about 50% of his equipment; but when he is rushing he is running every day and night. They have not changed their standards, the rest of the stuff is standing still.

Question: I wonder if it would take more time experts than workers to figure out what a man had coming.

Mr. Tingley: If we set a standard time for a style, and if they make one style this time and another the next time, you add them all together and get your total group credits. The total time spent gives you their efficiency. We have a great many units in one group, but we pay by the number of units that come off the end of the track. From the efficiency standards we know if we can keep the men on one style of thing all day they can make better time. They have the same problem in making shoe lasts; the styles change. The men have to set the machines up and tear them down. You have to make some allowances for the time taken in setting up and changing over.

Question: The problem I have in mind concerns, say, a production of 250 pieces with 100 different styles.

Mr. Tingley: You must have a job shop. I am afraid it would vary too much, unless you found a way to build up that stock and let the men run a couple of hours. I do not know how it is going to work as efficiently as where you have standardized materials and standardized processes.

Question: How do you handle the problem of lost time on account of shortage of materials? Do you have any complaint from the men?

Mr. Tingley: We have to pay the day rate during that period. That is penalized on the purchasing department or material control. The men lose their bonus, but we have to pay them the day rate during the time they are standing idle. The other day they were taking up some concrete and shoved the drill through our cable line. The plant shut down that morning and we sent the men home. Of course the men were penalized, and the colored man went back to work and said, "What hit me?" I do think there is an injustice to labor in a case like that. They have to be sent home because we cannot give them employment. I think we are coming to this status where some day we are going to guarantee the men certain wages if they will give an honest day's work. If the company cannot do it, it is a penalization of management if they are not efficient enough to keep up a certain guaranty for the men; because when a man gets married, and assumes obligations, he cannot let the family wait for a couple of days when he is not getting paid. You will find that in industry as a whole, as I see it and as we are working in our national association, that is one of the fundamental things, stabilization of employment and profit in industry. Those two things must go together.

Mr. Stiles: Do you keep records strictly on process costs in your cost department, or do you have any job costs at all?

Mr. Tingley: Our cost department relies a great deal for operations on service parts that go just so far, on the estimating department. They estimate the cost and tell you what it is half way through the operation on certain assemblies that we have no group cards for. We are getting mostly into group costs. With certain things like the cylinder block, we have a group of machines and we know how much the cylinder costs. You have the cost on your pistons, and on your automatic punch. You still have some operations on which you do not have group costs. We can take the standard time set by the time study man on that operation, make a certain allowance, multiply it by the standard rate, and add 20%. We do not have it in the cost department as they used to have it on the old piece rate. We know what the cost is, and we can figure it on any group, because there is the efficiency, and there is your standard time. We do not need any cost by detailed operations any more. We still have some piecework operations in the factory. We have those problems that you can adjust in your factory, and you probably will never get away from them until you are paying for the complete unit, and the foreman gets a bonus and the inspector gets a bonus. That will come some day.

Question: Is your time study man furnished with a copy of the estimates?

Mr. Tingley: The copy is available, but not in their files. You should go on the basis that nothing is perfect. Before they O.K. a cost on a group basis, they consult the estimating department to see if it is where it should be. If it is below, it is fine: if above, they go back and see where they have made too much allowance and where they can reduce an operation or eliminate it entirely.

Question: Speaking of obsolete parts, what effect does some radical change in design have on the men who made the individual parts? For instance, you said a short time ago that material moved through in 15 days from raw material into finished product. Naturally you would have some parts ahead of the assembly operation. I do not know whether it has occurred in your work, but there are radical changes which make some of those parts obsolete before they reach the assembly department. What do you pay back to the men as a bonus for the parts that do not reach the finished product?

Mr. Tingley: We do not put the change in until the stock is balanced. Any parts left over are scrapped. We draw that out on a scrap ticket and it is charged to scrap account. We make some new ones and bring them through. There are times when we have obsolete parts. You can just write them off and nobody knows the difference. On some sheets of material you save four inches off the edge, thinking you can use it—four inches, and nobody wants it. We have to have some adjustment on it. When a change goes through we try to balance our stock; we know it is going to come through and we will begin a new style on a certain date. We dispose of the old style through the good salesmen we have on the outside.

Question: Are time studies any different from what they would be if you were setting up piecework rates?

Mr. Tingley: Our group bonus has demanded a standardization of equipment and better assembling and manufacturing methods. Therefore we are able to get as good a time study and not allow as much lost time. The machines are in order, the material flows through to the next man and he pushes it along. Therefore our allowances do not have to be any greater; in fact, I think they are closer than when you allowed for a lot of contingencies which the men found a way to use. We have very much the same time study except that we add it all together, and allow a certain percent of time for sickness and delays. We have an idea of what the cost should be and what the men ought to earn. It makes your bookkeeping simpler than to have allowances and have to keep writing them off.

President Wilson: It is getting near the hour when some of us suburbanites have to catch our train, and I do not want to hold this meeting formally too long. We have the room as long as we want it. We will continue this informally as long as anybody wants to stay.

Before closing our formal program this evening, I would like to introduce to you a former member, an officer of the New York chapter, and one of the deans of standard cost accounting, Mr. G. Charter Harrison.

Mr. Harrison: I certainly have enjoyed hearing Mr. Tingley's most interesting talk this evening. I have always claimed that the closer the factory gets to perfection, the less cost accounting it requires. The absolutely 100% ideal factory would practically need no cost accounting at all. Everything would be standard, and we would figure standard costs, and that would be all there would be to it. The group bonus plan which Mr. Tingley has so admirably described to my mind is a tremendous advance toward this business of eliminating the cost accountant. I think some of us can see the wonderful possibilities of this plan, considered from the cost angle, in eliminating the necessity of keeping track of individual operations.

I was particularly interested in the constant price feature of the plan which Mr. Tingley described, because in so many of these systems the cost fluctuates and gets us into all kinds of trouble with standard costs, whereas with Mr. Tingley's plan, for 100% and over of efficiency your costs are absolutely constant.

I do not want to take much of your time this evening, because, as the president has said, the hour is late; but I would like to mention one feature of Mr. Tingley's plan which appealed to me very much, and that was the facility with which you can get daily efficiency reports. The cost accountant should be able to tell the superintendent tomorrow exactly where he was inefficient yesterday. I think this group bonus plan is founded on sound psychology. I think it is absolutely in line with our modern trend toward cooperation. It makes the work in the factory somewhat similar to the teamwork we get in a football game.

There is one thing I would like to ask Mr. Tingley, and that is, with all these savings (I am building a house, and I am interested), when are we going to get the price of Frigidaires down?

Mr. Tingley: You will notice that we cut the price recently. We are hoping to pass on all those savings to the consumer, and I think we have done very well with the fine quality which we have in it.

President Wilson: Mr. Harrison tells us we are working ourselves out of a job. I know he is absolutely sincere, because the thing that brought him out from New York was to become sales manager of a radio corporation. I have often wondered why he ever passed up accounting to go into the sales end of the game. Now I know; he saw the handwriting on the wall.

Are there any more things we would like to talk over in an informal way? Do not take seriously what I said about quitting. There are a lot more interesting phases of this subject, and discussion is welcome.

Question: Suppose you have an assembly order and the setting up of machines requires four or five different operations. In the manufacture of metal weights an order comes through for 1,500 for one job. They are different weights, but the assembly takes the same time. How would you pool your business system on those?

Mr. Tingley: In our automatic screw machine departments we have classified such setting up of machines in group time. That is not necessary in the condition you state where the men are obliged to change the machines frequently for different weights. That probably could still be kept in your overhead, and let the group on the assembly line have the benefit of group efficiency. If you tried to make allowances and set new rates, you would not get efficiency. Probably you could have duplicate machines, so you could be doing other things and the group still working. We have lots of such things that have been done sometimes in the evening.

That goes into overhead, but during the day the group is running at top speed.

Mr. Bennett: Being a great believer in plant visits, I would like to have the gentlemen invite us.

Mr. Scott: You are welcome to come to our plant at any time.

President Wilson: Mr. Woodbury, have you anything to bring up on this?

Mr. Woodbury: My question has already been asked. I have been trying to get our men interested in group bonus since I left General Motors. We have several hundred different styles and sizes of pencils. It is a problem.

Mr. Tingley: You want to talk to Mr. Hoover and see if you cannot get him to reduce the styles of pencils.

I want to thank you men for making this discussion so lively. I came here with the impression that I would give you a very poor talk, and the matter would be over in forty minutes. I have enjoyed it more than I can say. I am certainly glad I was invited up here.

(21) "Cost Accounting Practice with Special Reference to Machine Hour Rate," June 1, 1927, Bulletin, Vol. 8, No. 19, Clinton H. Scovell, formerly Senior Partner, Scovell, Wellington & Company

Editorial Department Note

Those members of our Association who were privileged to attend the "Quiz" sessions at recent Annual Conventions have a lasting and refreshing memory of Clinton H. Scovell, the man and his attitude towards his profession. More than anything he loved those discussions that dealt with practical problems of cost accounting and their solution. The "give and take," to discover the soundness of principle in an argument, was a source of personal delight to him as well as an inspiration to others.

Mr. Scovell was a pioneer in the field of cost accounting, particularly in the analysis and development of manufacturing burden. The accompanying reprint of an address which he delivered in 1913 illustrates his conception at that time of the importance of cost accounting as an aid to management; while the reprint of a letter which he wrote in January, 1926, and included in this memorial booklet, expresses his opinion of the present-day use and further trend of cost accounting. In this letter, written nearly thirteen years later, he reiterates the importance of cost information as a guide to management, which he had expounded so vigorously and had been called upon to defend so strenuously before the Machine Tool Builders. He also points out many of the advances that have been made in industry during these years, and largely so because of the use of the information in this manner.

Mr. Scovell was born in Manchester, N.H., July 15, 1876. After obtaining the A.B. and M.A. degrees at Harvard, he was employed in accounting work by the Great Northern Railroad and United States Smelting, Refining and Mining Company from 1904 to 1906.

In public accountancy he was with Gunn, Richards and Company, New York, during 1907 and 1908 and with Harvey S. Chase & Company, Boston, during 1909 and 1910.

In December, 1910, he organized Clinton H. Scovell & Company the name of which in October, 1916, was changed to Scovell, Wellington & Company. At the time of his death, December 31, 1926, he was senior partner of the firm which now has offices in Boston, New York, Chicago, Philadelphia, Cleveland, Springfield, Mass., Syracuse, Kansas City, Mo., and San Francisco.

One of its charter members and since its formation a director in the National Association of Cost Accountants, Mr. Scovell was its president in 1925-6, and gave unsparingly of his time and effort in the promotion of its welfare. A man of high personal and professional ideals, though often misunderstood and misjudged, he was an indefatigable worker and has left a measurable impress on his profession and, in a more intimate way, on the wide circle of his acquaintance.

Cost Accounting Practice with Special Reference to Machine Hour Rate[1]

There is more reason now than at any other time for many years why American manufacturers should consider most carefully the problems of finance and management in connection with their business undertakings. Facing the prospect of increased foreign competition in some lines and the tendency towards higher wages which inevitably follows the increased cost of living, and especially the increased cost of food which makes up such an important part of workingmen's expenses, manufacturers are necessarily interested in any ways or means to make their industrial operations more efficient.

Many things contribute to the efficiency of shop management. When a business is small, its success usually depends on the ability, foresight, and good judgment of one or two energetic men. As the business grows, methods and system must more and more take the place of the manager's personal oversight, and consequently the need increases for accounting, sound in principle and simple in operation.

Under the influence of the new science of management, there has been a constant study in the last few years of manufacturing methods, operating standards, cutting speeds, etc., which has resulted many times in such marked increases of production that the management may be sure that an improvement has been made, even if it does not know exactly *how much* saving has been effected.

It has been clearly established, however, that the cheapening of manufacturing operations which is brought about by a better operating practice is frequently secured at a considerably increased cost for office force, planning departments, helpers, supervision, and other indirect labor, sometimes wrongly called non-productive. As a result the practical problem for the manufacturer is to compare the lessened direct cost for labor and equipment with the increased cost for the other factors. This he can do only when he has an adequate cost accounting practice.

It is my purpose to point out the essentials of a cost system for a machine shop or a manufacturing plant where the operating conditions are similar, with especial reference to the theory and practice of a machine hour rate. I expect to show you that this is an intensely practical matter and that it has an important bearing on the sales policy and the general management of your business.

[1]An address delivered before the annual convention of the National Association of Machine Tool Builders, Hotel Astor, New York, October 22, 1913, and now reprinted through their courtesy.

Classify Expense Properly – Distribute It Correctly. Good cost accounting depends on the correct application of a few well understood principles. The first of these is to have the direct charges from the original sources, that is, pay-roll and material distributions, correctly classified between direct and indirect costs, and then to determine how the indirect, or so-called non-productive charges, may be identified with the product.

Any cost accounting practice worthy of the name should record accurately the direct labor costs. In a machine shop, or under similar conditions, this direct labor cost should be applied with precision to each job going through the shop. *Very little cost accounting practice, however, has attained any similar precision for distributing the indirect charges for equipment, referred to hereafter in this article as burden.*

What Is Burden? As the difficult and important part of cost accounting is to determine how a correct distribution of burden may be accomplished, it is clearly worth while to consider briefly the elements of burden.

It is a tedious and expensive undertaking to build and equip a new plant and to complete the cycle of manufacture from design to finished product; and there is much to gain in the way of a clear understanding of costs, if we trace out this development step by step, taking careful note of the elements of the problems as we proceed.

When a new industry is to be established, the directors first buy a parcel of land suitable for the location of the proposed shop. If the purchase price is $40,000 the new enterprise has at once absorbed capital that should earn about $2,000 to the ordinary, prudent investor, who takes no manufacturing or trading risks. A site as costly as this is probably situated in or near a city, so that it will be subject to taxes of $500 or $600.

Shop buildings are next erected at a cost, let us say, of $200,000 more. This outlay of capital, like the investment in land, involves an annual interest charge (of some $10,000), and under present laws, an annual penalty of some thousands of dollars more for taxes. But, unlike land, the buildings will require constant repairs. Even then they are subject to a slow but certain deterioration and obsolescence that must be met by a charge for depreciation. To protect the investment, the owners must pay insurance and provide watchmen. To make the buildings usable, they must be heated and lighted, supplied with water and fresh air, and regularly cleaned. The striking thing about these charges is that they all go on without abatement, unless the shop is shut down, dark and cold, and even then the principal charges – interest, taxes, insurance, repairs, and depreciation – abate scarcely at all.

All this expense has been incurred by the management to provide suitable areas for the intended manufacturing process. If there are five or six sub-divisions, each one may occupy an entire small building, or all or part of a floor in a larger building. Whatever the details, each department (if we may use that overworked word) uses so many hundred square feet of floor space and must carry its proportionate share of the land and building charges already described.

Within a department there may be one or more different operations, such as, milling, grinding, boring, turning, planing, fitting, and assembling. The equipment in each case represents an investment of capital; it requires the payment of taxes and insurance; it suffers depreciation (even more rapid than the building); and it incurs charges for power, repairs, and such indirect items as superintendence, inspection, and helpers' services. If the shop shuts down, the power may be shut off and the foreman dismissed; but so long as it runs, however short handed or however inefficiently, these charges do not change materially; and the fundamentals of interest, taxes, insurance, etc., (with the possible exception of repairs) are not one whit less.

All that has been described so far is overhead expense, more properly termed *burden*, and does not include any labor applied directly to the product (like the operative who is working at a lathe or boring mill).

This great accumulation of burden *represents manufacturing capacity.* Each department, and each separate machine tool has a known annual burden. Its cost per hour is determined by dividing the total burden by the hours in the working schedule, and the shorter the schedule, the greater the hourly cost.

Having completed the buildings and installed the equipment, the management is ready to begin manufacturing operations. As the several parts of the machine progress from rough castings or forgings to finished pieces ready for the assembling floor, their value has increased as they have absorbed the successive increments of direct or productive labor and of the burden appertaining to the production centers through which they have passed.

Cost Accounting and Production Control. Before illustrating the practical application of this theory, I want to point out that good cost accounting is a help to efficient management, not only as it traces and records values but also as it may be made a powerful agent for production control. From my experience in professional service for industrial plants, I emphasize more and more the practical value of this second aspect of the work.

It follows, therefore, that the first step in planning a cost accounting practice for a machine shop is to consider by whom and how authority to manufacture shall be exercised. It is simple enough to order ten castings from a given pattern which has already been made, but as you all know, the production of a machine tool involves orders for castings of many different patterns and sizes, bar stock for forgings, etc., and these material orders are all very simple in comparison with the complex schedule of machine operations which are required to produce the finished parts. You all recognize how important it is that parts should be made in quantities that are economical and that the different pieces required should be ready together on the assembly floor. It is, therefore, of the utmost importance to make effective plans to initiate and control the production so that these results may be accomplished. The management will then have a definite schedule of manufacturing operation on which costs may be determined by orders, by lots, by individual parts—with as much or as little detail as may be necessary.

What Constitutes an Adequate Cost Practice. Returning now to the subject of specific costs, the first step is to provide such labor records, preferably with good automatic time stamps, as will make possible the necessary distinction between direct and indirect operations, and the exact time devoted to each lot of material or each expense order.

The next step is to compute the burden correctly for each department, including interest, taxes, insurance and depreciation on the buildings and equipment, and the additional charges for power, supervision and repairs. In many industrial plants "manufacturing expense" includes only part of these charges. The first cost of manufacturing is plant investment—land and buildings. No management using a rented plant would think of omitting rent from overhead charges. When the manufacturer becomes also a landlord, as when the plant is owned by the manufacturing company, what sound reason can possibly be given for omitting from burden the charges which the management incurs in lieu of rent?

The equipment presents a slightly different problem. Very few manufacturers operate with rented equipment; if they do, there is rent to pay, as an unavoidable burden on the manufacturing operations. When the equipment is owned, the maintenance charges are equally unavoidable. The manufacturer must get interest on his investment before he has in any sense a profit, and he must bear the expense of taxes, insurance, depreciation, and repairs. Although these elements of cost may be neglected or not stated, they are, nevertheless, taking their proper share, or more, of what is figured without them as gross profits.

The weakness of many cost systems is that important elements of indirect cost are thrown together in a "general expense" account, concealing the leaks and wastes that reduce efficiency and curtail profits. Many manufacturers have no doubt been satisfied to handle burden in vague and general terms because they did not know any better way to dispose of it.

It may be stated confidently that under ordinary machine shop conditions, no accurate distribution of burden can be accomplished, and therefore no accurate costs determined, by spreading burden over all the work done in the shop as a percentage of the cost of direct labor. In the shop proper, with its widely varying equipment of machine tools, distribution on the basis of a man-hour rate is not very much better, although, as I shall point out later, that plan works very well for fitters and assembly men.

To secure a correct burden distribution it is only necessary to prove, by analysis, the elements of which burden is composed and then to consider how all this overhead is actually applied to the product.

Attention Should be Fixed on the Production Center. At this point we encounter another mistaken tradition of "departmentalized costs." To define burden correctly in each department is good as far as it goes, but it does not go very far, especially in a machine shop. *The attention of the manager and the cost accountant ought to be fixed on the individual production center,* usually a power machine. Recent developments under the actual shop conditions show that *the correct burden* for a machine tool *may vary from less than ten percent to over three hundred percent of a machinist's wages.* The widely accepted method of charging burden to costs on the value of productive labor makes no distinction between the mechanic at the bench, whose work has practically no burden except supervision, and the operator using a costly machine, which involves heavy charges for maintenance, power, and repairs.

Fallacy of Average Rates. Face this situation squarely and the fallacy of an average rate is exploded forever. Instead we recognize as many elements of burden as possible, and while it is not necessary or desirable to apply these elements separately to the cost of each job, it is from every point of view desirable to identify the burden with the production centers through which it is charged to the jobs. For machine tools, under this plan, there is a charge to each job for the use of a tool as specific and as definite as the charge for the wages of the mechanic who operates the tool.

Bench Hands and Assembling Crews. The work of bench hands and mechanics on the erecting floor must be accompanied by a burden charge which obviously is not literally a machine hour rate. The burden rate for bench equipment differs not at all in principle from the rates for the machine tools. If, as is usually the case, the mechanics at the bench work under substantially uniform conditions, a uniform rate may be made at so much per hour for the use of the accommodations which they require for their work. In a large shop the bench rate might be different in different departments. Since it is uniform for all mechanics who work at the bench, it is practically a man-hour rate. It must be borne in mind, however, *that it is a rate for the use of equipment only,* unless indeed the circumstances make it convenient to merge the cost of supervision with the cost of equipment.

The erecting hands in a shop present a problem of a different kind. Their work usually requires a considerable area, and important charges for crane service and supervision. To speak of this work in terms which have long been familiar in cost accounting practice, the erecting floor may be considered as a department whose burden is to be distributed with reference to the work performed by the mechanics employed in the department. Probably the best way to distribute this burden is on a man-hour rate derived by dividing the total annual burden by the number of man-hours for the department.

General Burden. There are other charges connected with the management of a machine shop or manufacturing plant which are not necessarily well expressed through an hourly equipment rate. Such are charges for the drafting room, the bookkeeping, cost accounting, supervision, liability insurance, and general charges of management not specifically and directly connected with the maintenance and operation of machinery. These are charges which in a small shop should be applied in a fairly uniform way over all the employees in the establishment, preferably on a man-hour basis. This charge would be known as general burden, and since it would be uniform, it may be applied to the cost of each job, against which hours of mechanics' time have already been recorded, with very little additional work.

Why Scientific Machine Rates are Important. The successful operation of a scientific machine rate is the most important development that has occurred in cost accounting practice in a generation. As these rates may be applied to the cost of jobs, the charge for burden which hitherto has been the difficult and uncertain part of cost accounting will be as accurate as the charge for direct labor. Furthermore, the use of equipment rates, in effect *a precision method* for the important part of overhead expense or burden, requires no more work in a cost office than the application of a rate which contains only part of these charges.

There are two good reasons for saying that a scientific machine rate is a development of tremendous importance in cost accounting practice. The first is that referred to in the opening paragraph of this article, namely that it is essential when scientific management is introduced that there should be an *exact* measure of the saving which is effected by it. The literature on this subject has not thus far made a sufficient recognition of the very important fact that if an operative reduces the time on a given job from ten to seven hours, for example, he has not only saved three hours at his wage rate, but also three hours of the rate for the machine tool which he has used, and three hours of general burden. As will appear from the table annexed to this article (Figure 21-1), these overhead costs are frequently more important than the direct wage which has already received so much attention.

Cost accounting practice, moreover, which analyzes burden charges as described in the foregoing paragraphs would naturally make a very precise account of the increases in overhead expense of any kind. In some cases in connection with the introduction of scientific management, these increases would be in a particular department, and would operate to increase the burden which would be disposed of as a machine hour rate for the tools in that department. Usually, however, the additional charges would operate to increase the general burden, which is one of the most important and at the same time, one of the most elusive elements of manufacturing cost.

A Measure of Loss Due to Slack Production and Inefficient Operation. The second reason for attaching so much importance to a *scientific machine rate* is that it *makes possible an accurate measure of the loss due to slack production or interrupted operation.* This is perhaps more important than the improved accuracy of cost records referred to above. When the board of directors is gathered at the end of the year, or once in six months, to learn about the results of the period under review, they do not often consider such detailed matters as the cost of individual orders. On the other hand, they are always interested in any explanation which the manager has to make about losses that are due to curtailment of manufacturing operations.

The directors at such times would value more than anything else a clear statement showing *how much* their company had lost on this account, especially if the details of the statement could be readily understood and readily proved by an analysis of the operating conditions. The big problems, in regard to manufacturing, which the directors have to settle are those involved in the effort to make an efficient use of plant and equipment, especially if they are asked to decide on new additions to meet a probable volume of business. The new plant means an added investment, and it is of the utmost importance that the accounts should subsequently show to what extent this investment was utilized.

It is essential to distinguish clearly between losses or gains on machines actually made and sold, and losses due to slack production or inefficient use of equipment.

It must be borne in mind that the finished product has *absorbed only the burden of the equipment actually used in its manufacture.* It has not absorbed the burden of unused equipment or idle machinery. If the plant includes a foundry and the management decides to purchase castings, the idle foundry has contributed nothing to the product. It is obviously unfair to charge into the cost of goods the burden charges on the automatic machinery that may be idle because the management is buying and not making machine screws. If only three-quarters of the lathes run, the idle remainder have not helped machine parts actually manufactured, and although the plant may go into bankruptcy if it cannot utilize its equipment, the *cost of the work actually done is not greater on that account.*

The burden on idle machinery is no more a part of the cost of manufacture (unless due to enforced seasonal variations) than the burden on a shop owned by another corporation. When there is a proper distribution and application of expense burden, only the burden is charged to cost which represents the equipment utilized in manufacture, and burden not applied remains as a balance to be charged direct to the loss and gain account at the end of the month, six months, or a year. (See Figure 21-1.)

This is readily accomplished through the means of burden accounts which collect by a very simple bookkeeping practice all of the charges in a given class, and receive credits as burden rates of the same kind as charged to the cost of product going through the works. The unearned burden in some cases may indicate an error which is to be corrected by using a more accurate rate in a subsequent period, but when proper records have been established, *the unearned burden is a clear loss,* and the balances of the burden accounts should be transferred directly to the profit and loss account.

I have sometimes referred to the manufacture of powder to illustrate this point. As a matter of safety the company builds small scattered plants, rather than bringing together one great manufacturing unit. If their production is to be curtailed they may shut down plants Nos. 2, 8 or 10 as the case may be. No one would contend that the cost of making powder in plant No. 3 is any greater because plants Nos. 2, 8 and 10 are shut down. A director of the

Figure 21-1

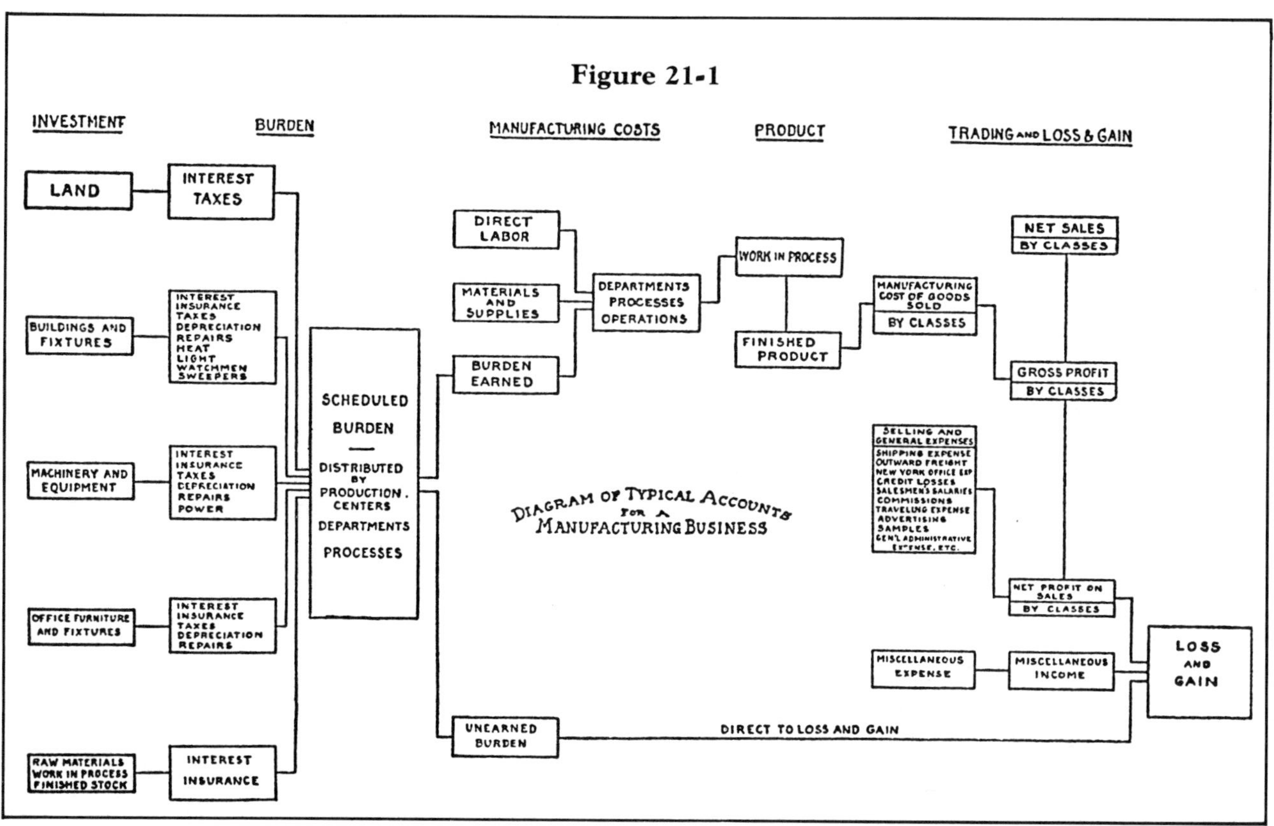

Powder Company would be interested to see whether the plants as a whole run profitably, and whether they individually make a product that will sell at a profit. The corporation as a whole must suffer the losses due to idle plants.

Now that theory is just as applicable to the separate units of your plants. If you have twenty lathes in one department, you may run thirteen and shut down the other seven. You can keep out of the current cost the burden pertaining to the seven that are shut down just as easily as the Powder Company can keep the operation of the three idle powder plants out of the cost of those that operate.

Effect on Sales Policy. If the distinction is maintained between losses or gains on goods made and sold, and losses due to restricted output, the management will consider sales policies in a much more certain way than is possible when the facts are obscured in the haze of average costs, calculated on varying volumes of product. In respect to burden it is frequently true that costs figured as averages vary beyond all hope of comparison as the volume of output goes up or down.

When a cost accounting practice is maintained that distinguishes carefully between prime costs for material and labor (which vary almost directly with the volume) and overhead charges or burden, the managers can see exactly in times of slack production at what price they can take any work that is offered and get something to carry the burden of the shop, in addition to the direct cost of labor and material. This, it must be admitted, is to some extent a matter of policy, for it may be better to hold a price and restrict output, rather than break the market by quoting prices that will give temporarily a little additional profit.

A Measure of Manufacturing Efficiency. Whatever the effect on sales policy, good cost accounting, including correct burden distribution, is a matter of enduring importance from the point of view of manufacturing. Changes in volume may completely obscure gains or losses in efficiency, and render comparative costs of similar jobs impossible from season to season, solely because of the variations in the amount of business done. Exact costs, comparable under all conditions, are not to be secured unless the burden charged to production is only that appertaining to the equipment that is actually at work.

From the manager's point of view, the significant fact is that the burden, which is proposed to apply through a series of equipment rates, is not appreciably less when the operating schedule of the plant is reduced. It is true that power charges may be slightly less, but the fixed charges for building space, interest, insurance, taxes, depreciation, and in some circumstances for repairs also, are no less when the machines are idle. *The manager of a machine shop cannot make a greater mistake in figuring costs than to charge a higher burden in any form whatsoever for the operation of part of his equipment, because the rest of it is temporarily idle, or a higher rate for a smaller labor force because the plant is working on part time. These differences which have always attracted the attention of observing managers are almost entirely clear loss or waste, and should be recognized as such and charged directly to the profit and loss account.*

A Practical Example. The practical manager who regards these ideas as too theoretical will do well to inspect the following list which shows the results of working out a machine hour rate for direct operating burden in a plant operating about one hundred and fifty machines.

Number of Machines		Rates in Cents	Number of Machines		Rates in Cents
6	@	1.5	12	@	7.0
4	"	2.0	12	"	8.0
9	"	2.5	7	"	8.7
4	"	3.0	4	"	9.0
6	"	4.0	3	"	9.5
2	"	5.0	10	"	10.0
4	"	6.0	3	"	11.0
10	"	6.6	13	"	12.0
2	"	13.0	3	"	24
2	"	14	2	"	25
11	"	15	1	"	26
1	"	17	1	"	29
3	"	18	2	"	30
1	"	19	1	"	47
1	"	20	1	"	52
1	"	22	1	"	76
4	"	23			

If one is disposed to criticise the minute division that has been made, such as having rates at 8¢, 8.7¢, 9¢, 9.5¢, and 10¢, it should be borne in mind that there is practically no more work in the cost accounting department in using five rates instead of two. Moreover, if an effort is made to combine some of these rates, it is exceedingly hard to say which rates should be raised and which should be lowered. If five rates like those mentioned above should be brought together, some of the rates would be at least 15% out of the way. Such an error is altogether too large to be tolerated unnecessarily, when one is seeking for really accurate costs.

At the plant where these rates are in force the burden for erecting hands, including the charges for floor space, crane service and supervision, was *five times the rate for bench hands.* In addition to these rates every employee participates in general burden which includes superintendence, managers, drafting, cost accounting, and all general charges, except those connected with selling expenses.

Inaccuracy of the Old Methods. The results which have been secured in working out these machine rates need only be stated to a practical man to show the violent inaccuracy which there must have been in cost accounting when overhead charges were applied as a percentage of productive labor, or even on a uniform man-hour basis. The following figures will supply a vivid illustration of the inaccuracy of the old method:

Job No. 1		*Job No. 2*	
5 hours labor @ 28¢	= $1.40	5 hours labor @ 28¢	= $1.40
5 hours burden on the average plan @ 30¢	= 1.50	5 hours burden on the average plan @ 30¢	= 1.50
Total cost	= $2.90	Total cost	= $2.90

At the same wage rate the two jobs show the same cost because they took the same time, although job No. 1 may have used a machine worth 3¢ per hour and job No. 2 a machine worth 24¢ per hour, or even one worth 50¢ per hour or more. Under these conditions, and assuming a general burden rate of 10¢ per hour, the true cost of these two jobs was as follows:

Job No. 1		*Job No. 2*	
5 hours labor @ 28¢	= $1.40	5 hours labor @ 28¢	= $1.40
5 hours machine rate @ 3¢	= .15	5 hours machine rate @ 24¢	= 1.20
5 hours general burden @ 10¢	= .50	5 hours general burden @ 10¢	= .50
Total cost	= $2.05	Total cost	= $3.10

This is a very conservative comparison. If job No. 2 required a machine worth 60¢ per hour, the cost would have been $1.40 + $3.00 + $.50 = $4.90. The percentage on labor method, or a straight man-hour rate in the shop, would show that these three jobs had the same cost, although as a matter of fact in the second case the cost was 151% and in the third case 239% greater than the first.

Perhaps the best thing that can be said about cost accounting practice by machine hour methods is that it does not require any more work than any of the older methods that have been well developed as a means for taking out costs. At the plant from which the above illustration is drawn, it is not expected that there will be any increase in the cost accounting force for the operation of the plan as outlined. Of course, if a plant with an under-developed cost practice, or none at all, starts to make improvements in a wholesale way, it must expect to increase the overhead charges. If this increase is wisely planned, it is sure to be a money making expenditure.

Mass Production and Automatic Machines. As noted earlier in this article, there are some conditions, of course, under which a machine rate cannot be used to distribute burden, *but the underlying principle of collecting all burden charges for each production center is sound, whatever method may be used for distribution.* Some operations can best use a process rate, which includes labor and accessory supplies as well as burden. This method is particularly applicable to mass production, or any work that is not made on successive and clearly distinguished manufacturing orders. The application of overhead charges, however, can be made through a process rate strictly in accordance with approved principles of burden distribution.

Automatic or semi-automatic machines present a troublesome problem of burden distribution, especially as the burden is usually far more important than the labor as an element of manufacturing cost. This problem has been handled at a plant operating several hundred automatic machines by a plan of efficiency charts, which provide for charging to the job the cost of the effective operation of the machine. Cost accounts under this plan measure with great precision the loss due to slack production or careless attention from the operator.

Conclusion. There are still some managers who do not realize the importance of a good cost and accounting practice, but the knowledge it supplies is undoubtedly a valuable business asset, as well as a powerful aid to efficient management. The best possible evidence for this statement is that progressive and successful manufacturing enterprises are making liberal expenditures for work of this character.

The present day trend of business is undoubtedly in the direction of a more exact and scientific knowledge of every important detail. Success by rule of thumb, or from energy and enthusiasm alone, is becoming more and more impossible. "The man who knows and knows that he knows" is the man who wins.

After concluding the paper, Mr. Scovell said: "If any of you gentlemen would like to ask questions or put in some counter-fire, if it is consistent with the custom of your Convention, I shall be very glad to have you do so."

Discussion

PRESIDENT BULLARD: Mr. Scovell has given us a very interesting paper, and I thank him on behalf of the Convention. He has also suggested that we cross-examine him on this subject. I know that he would welcome any discussion that you wish to bring up; so you can be quite free with your remarks or questions. We have plenty of time at our disposal for this purpose.

MR. GEORGE I. ALDEN, *Norton Grinding Co., Worcester, Mass.*: I suppose that one object of cost accounting is adjusting the selling price of your goods.

Of course where you do a jobbing business this matter of keeping the burden on the separate machines is quite an important one; but what do you do with the unearned burden? You say that the unearned burden of the machine goes in with the cost of the product. What do you do with the unearned burden in fixing the selling price of your product is one question I would like to ask. Another object, it seems to me, of a cost accounting system, is to learn where your losses are and to try and keep up the efficiency of each one of your departments; but if you are simply manufacturing a product like lathes, planers, or shapers, a knowledge of all these details of the cost in each department and the unearned burden would not affect your profits at the end of the year, unless the details help you to get your cost less and manage your factory better. Of course if you are doing a jobbing business it is quite unfair to charge one man the same price for work on a large, expensive machine as you charge another man for work which does not require as expensive a machine. But I think so far as the cost system is of value, it must be so in helping you to reduce your real cost, which to my mind is its principal object. Another of its objects is to enable you to fix your prices so that you will know what your profits are.

I want to say in regard to the matter of charging interest, I know there is quite a difference in practice in regard to charging interest on your original investment as a part of your cost. It seems to me that there are two ways of looking at that. I presume that the way the matter was presented in the paper is correct—I think it is, in a sense. I did not hear anything said about where dividends come in in this cost accounting; but we have all got to acknowledge that under the system recommended when we get any dividends or so-called profits they will be absolutely over and above the interest on the investment. Dividends are not something to pay you interest on your investment, but they are "velvet" so to speak. I suppose a socialist might object to that view of it, but I do not object to it.

MR. SCOVELL: I think the relation of the cost of manufacture to the selling price is the very crux of the whole problem. If your production is rather slack, the profit is not very large, and the apparent costs according to the old method are distressingly high. That is usually due to a trade condition which would not give you any warrant for making a corresponding boost in the price of your product; in other words, you are perfectly sure that you cannot load on to your customer any cost of the inefficiency of your own plant. You have to sell your machines in competition with all other competing manufacturers and you have to make a price which represents in the long run efficient manufacture. Under such circumstances you will want to know the real manufacturing cost as accurately as possible. If an order comes along for twenty machines of a certain type, you want to know how much additional expense you will incur to manufacture them, so that you may wisely decide to take the order or leave it.

When you start that order through the shop it means purchases of castings, unless you have your own foundry, and it involves from one to a dozen machine operations on each part; and what you want, gentlemen, is the actual cost. Most manufacturers measure out the labor cost with considerable accuracy, and if you can calculate the burden for the equipment used and the proper burden rate for the men at the bench and on the assembly floor, you may figure out the total cost just as definitely as the amounts you pay for wages. If you are so unfortunate, notwithstanding this hypothetical order of twenty machines, that you do not have your shop filled up, you have a burden of unused machines, and I think you should charge that burden direct to profit and loss. It has no relation whatever to the cost of the product manufactured. In other words, the unearned burden has nothing to do with fixing the cost of the product sold.

MR. ALDEN: What do you do with the unearned burden?

MR. SCOVELL: Charge it off to profit and loss.

MR. ALDEN: What relation does that bear to the price at which you sell your machines?

MR. SCOVELL: I do not see that it has any.

MR. ALDEN: Then you might have an unearned burden at the end of the year which would put you out of business?

MR. SCOVELL: The cost accounting should be so arranged that the unearned burden is known for each department of the business, and as frequently, at least, as once a month. The efficient utilization of the equipment, you will agree, is one of the important aspects of good management. Another point in shop practice which needs to be carefully considered is to see that each operation is done as economically as possible. Among other things, this means putting the work on the proper machine tool, and exact comparisons of this kind cannot be made unless the burden belonging to the respective tools is accurately known and taken into account in comparison with the respective labor costs, in considering one machine or another for the work. In this way, a correct cost accounting practice is an important help to more efficient work and therefore to reduced costs in the shop.

MR. ALDEN: I agree that if you want to call the cost one thing or another you may. But if you have other expenses, they must come in somewhere before you can intelligently tell for what to sell your product. You spoke of machines lying idle which would mean an unearned burden. I think there are a good many machine builders that are getting a little unearned burden at the present time. But this is not a question of today or tomorrow but largely a question year after year which tells what the product really costs. It is all very easy to say that at the end of the year you are to charge off an unearned burden to profit and loss, but is there going to be anything to balance it at the end of the year? I do not think it makes any difference what each machine does or what the burden of each machine is; all you want to know really is the total. That is all you care for unless this other information can help you manufacture more cheaply. All this segregation of burden is beautiful enough, is very correct and all right, but it seems to me that a great deal of it is of no use, if at the end of the year you are simply going to charge it to profit and loss. It is of no use unless it helps you to manufacture the product more cheaply and keep your shop full. The machine tool business, as I see the way it now runs, has to carry an unearned burden a good deal of the time, and we want to know how we can meet it in some way when we have it. Charging it to profit and loss is all well enough in the accounting, but that is a mere matter of bookkeeping.

There is one thing helpful to me to keep in mind in connection with the profits in dull times. I try to know about how much productive labor I have got to carry in the shop that the product of this productive labor may bring enough to pay expenses. When I get below that amount of productive labor I know that I am losing money. When I keep above that amount I am pretty sure that I will sell the product some time and that I will not be a loser. So that while it is all right to keep this accounting system, I think regarding unearned burden you have to know about what it is going to average, or you will not know how much you may have to charge to profit and loss at the end of the year.

MR. SCOVELL: I see there is a practical aspect of this matter of which I did not make sufficient recognition. If you conceive of your industry as one that is inevitably subject to such variations, you have to fix the price of your machines high enough so that the margin of profit between cost, as I have defined it, and the selling price will give you a surplus out of which the bad experience and unearned burden of your succeeding years can be provided for. It is necessary to qualify my remark that the unearned burden had nothing to do with fixing the prices of the machine with this perfectly obvious explanation, otherwise I will not do justice to the questioner or myself.

Reference was made to dividends, and my explanation is that interest on investment should be charged into cost and credited to the current profit and loss account, and is available for dividends unless there are offsetting charges from other sources (*e.g.* product sold at a loss or unearned burden). It is essential to distinguish between the real burden used in making the product and the unearned burden due to idle equipment. When you get into a sharply competitive market it seems to me that that is the only practical theory to go on, so that you may know at just what price you can afford to take an order.

Perhaps you may say you do not care to enter into that kind of competition, but even if you do not get enough on an order to carry all the burden which belongs to it, it may be desirable to take that order if you can get back all the direct labor and material cost which you must pay out of pocket to make it, and part of the burden, which otherwise goes on absolutely unutilized. Do I make that point perfectly clear? It seems to me that is of tremendous practical importance.

My questioner made another reference for which I thank him. Experience shows over and over again that when the bookkeeping according to the usual plan shows an apparent rising burden as production falls off, it is recognized as an unhealthy tendency, but it is not human nature for you to get after that condition and make the plans to correct it with any where near the energy you would if your accounting showed exactly *how much* the loss was from month to month. Nothing brings that home so definitely as dollars and cents figures representing the manufacturing capacity that you do not use.

Reference was also made to the value of a cost system in helping a management learn where the losses are and reduce the real costs in the shops. In that respect a good cost system is like a recording instrument which reports facts for the guidance of those in charge. The cost reports should cover the right kind of information, and it is especially important that it all should be very promptly available. When a cost accounting practice meets these two tests, the active manager will naturally use it extensively to secure the greater economy of production which you are all aiming at.

MR. ALDEN: When you have found this $13,400 burden, just what do you do? I mean of what advantage is the knowledge?

MR. SCOVELL: Under such circumstances you are a good deal like the man who has consulted a physician and is advised that he must get more sleep or must move to another climate. It is a practical matter. It is not for your physician to tell you how you are to go about getting more sleep, or just what plan you can adopt to move to Colorado; that is for your family and yourself to consider. So it is here when the accountant is calling shop matters to your attention, especially when you get the information every month; it is up to you as a practical business man to decide what you should do.

MR. ALDEN: It seems to me that your cost system is the answer, that it will tell you pretty nearly so that you can go right to the source where the loss seems to be the greatest, and try to remedy it. But the separation of the items does not appeal to me as of any particular value except to call attention to the aggregate loss; but the whole cost system itself enables you to keep track each and every month of where the cost of this or that part of the work is rising.

MR. SCOVELL: When you say that the separation does not appeal to you I am reminded of a murder trial now going on in Massachusetts. The victim is said to have died from arsenical poisoning. How are the jury to know that, or how many grains of arsenic were found in the man's stomach unless they have recourse to some laboratory method to ascertain it? So you must rely on laboratory methods in order to determine the facts.

PRESIDENT BULLARD: Some two or three years ago, in discussing this same problem with a prominent machine tool manufacturer, he told me that he had created a reserve fund to take care of this unearned burden. During the good times he had an overhead charge, which we will call one hundred percent normally; but he said that he applied an extra ten or fifteen percent regularly on his product during the prosperous times when his plant was running at full capacity, and from it set aside a reserve which enabled him to absorb the unearned burden during the dull times.

Now this seemed to me to be a very wise provision. The only difficulty that I see in applying it would be that it would increase our price ten or fifteen percent during the good times, and it is a question whether our product would stand it, whether the market would absorb our product at the increased price. But it is a matter of averages in the machine tool business, and we must in some way provide during the prosperous times which we sometimes have for the inevitable dull times which are coming; and our profits would have to be sufficient during the good times to do it.

As I understand it, Mr. Scovell's method of overcoming our difficulties by his cost system is simply to point out to us our weakness through so keeping the cost that we can intelligently create a sufficient reserve during the good times when it is possible to do it in order that, when the dull times come, we can have the reserve to fall back on and feel that we can absorb our unearned burden thereby. This reserve would be in the profit and loss account whether you had kept a record of it or not. It would be desirable, I would say, to know that it is there. Now what is to put it there? It seems to me that the only answer is increased prices during the good times.

Is there any further discussion of this subject?

MR. R.S. REED, *Francis Reed Co., Worcester, Mass.*: You spoke of increasing the price perhaps fifteen percent during good times?

PRESIDENT BULLARD: That was merely a suggestion, not an absolute figure.

MR. REED: In case you do that would it then follow that you would establish a lower price when business was dull?

PRESIDENT BULLARD: The increased price might permit of that when it was necessary.

MR. REED: Is that a question of business policy?

PRESIDENT BULLARD: It is not a question of policy, it is a question of accounting. As I see it, increasing the price during good times would not necessarily mean to decrease the price in dull times. It would merely mean that by increasing the price we would create a reserve which we could draw on during dull times. There is no justification in dull times for reduction of prices so far as cost is concerned.

MR. THAYER: There are a number of machines that might be put through not necessarily at a profit but in order to take up part of the overhead charges. How to maintain your organization during dull periods is a pretty important question in a large plant. Sometimes a considerable proportion of the labor is maintained at an actual loss, simply to hold it. It would be interesting to know about how much we could afford to pay or how much we were actually paying for maintaining that labor.

MR. SCOVELL: The remark that the gentleman has just made suggests something else. I notice that some of you are advertising to your prospective customers that they can save money by using this or that machine which you make. How can your customers intelligently make a comparison between your machine and any other unless they are to go at it in just about the way that I have described?

A MEMBER: Suppose that a certain manufacturer makes a hundred machines one year, and in the following year business is such that he sells just about one hundred machines. How would that affect the cost of those machines inasmuch as they were not manufactured within the year when they were sold?

MR. SCOVELL: That is an accounting problem. As I see it there is no profit on those one hundred machines until they have been actually sold. I should fix my attention on the year in which they were made in order to determine their cost, and the unearned burden, if there was any, in the shop during that period. I should not be interested at all (in so far as cost of those machines was concerned) in the cost of the shop during the period in which they were sold. If you fill up a factory with finished machines they would be taken in stock at their cost. In the following year you may make a profit by a favorable sale of machines built the previous year and carried over, with or without profitable operation of the year which is then current. In other words, you have one hundred machines made in 1912 carried over into 1913, and you sell them at a profit. That is profit which belongs to 1913; but it is not related to the shop operation in 1913. If, as a question of manufacturing policy to keep up shop organization in 1912, you thought it wise to make this product ahead, let us hope your judgment has been justified in 1913. But you have a new problem as to what you will do with the shop in 1913.

MR. E.T. HENDEE, *Joseph T. Ryerson & Son, Chicago, Ill.*: I notice that on your diagram you show an interest charge on the investment covering buildings, machinery, fixtures, etc., as part of the burden. It has always been our custom to charge, in addition to that, interest on the money used in carrying on the business, that is to say interest on outstanding accounts, stock, etc., and it would seem to me that this charge could be considered just as legitimate as would interest on the building investment.

MR. SCOVELL: I agree with you.

MR. HENDEE: You didn't say that.

MR. SCOVELL: As I tried to have some reasonable limits to my paper, I did not discuss the cost of selling. You may be in a trade where your terms are thirty days; with another man the terms in vogue are ninety days. The beef wholesalers collect once a week, and a restaurant every meal. Now a business which collects once a week is different from a business which carries a line of credit for ninety days, and one of the items of cost of the ninety day business is undoubtedly the capital tied up in the outstanding accounts, but this is not a manufacturing cost. If you have in stock one hundred machines that cost you one hundred dollars apiece, then you have $10,000 tied up in finished stock. If you carry a similar amount of stock in finished parts, that is also one of the costs of doing your business, and you should make a charge accordingly against the selling expenses.

MR. E.R. NORRIS, *Westinghouse E. & M. Co., Pittsburgh, Pa.*: I would like to ask the gentleman a question. During slack time, time of depression, when you have a great many machines idle, possibly machines doing a similar class of work but with different overhead—for instance, one machine with an overhead of one dollar and another with an overhead of fifty cents—would you recommend using the cheap machine and letting the high-priced overhead machine stand idle? In other words, it might be possible to do the work in less time on the high-priced machine which would naturally carry a larger overhead, but it would be better to use the machine with less overhead from a cost standpoint; now which would you use?

MR. SCOVELL: That is a decidedly practical question. It is a great deal like choosing an automobile for a trip on Sunday afternoon, whether you are going to use one that you bought at a bargain for $1,250, or another that cost you $4,000. Theoretically, it costs you more to run a higher priced machine; but if you have both machines idle it is a practical shop problem. The actual running time required for the job should decide the question as to whether you would use one or the other. The choice might become unimportant from the point of view of cost, it might be altogether a question of expediency. You might be whitewashing that part of the shop and would not want to work over the tool.

MR. JAMES N. HEALD, *Heald Machine Co., Worcester, Mass.*: Probably the answer to that, in the case of regular manufacturing where you didn't have to guess quickly, would be arrived at by adding the direct labor cost to the overhead burden which comes on that machine. For instance, the machine having the lower burden might be an older type of machine that would increase the number of hours of labor required so that the cost would be higher than with the machine with the more expensive rate, but which would cut the time considerably owing to its increased efficiency. The true answer is the sum of those two elements, in any case.

With regard to the remarks made by my friend, Mr. Alden, who opened the discussion in regard to the selling price as compared to the cost, I am inclined to think that while the cost system is the basis, the selling price may not be related so very closely to the cost. Of course we all know that there are lots of elements besides manufacturing cost to be considered. There is a good deal of money spent in selling, for advertising, direct representation, commissions to dealers, and traveling expenses, all of which have a great deal to do with fixing upon the selling prices.

Then the progressiveness of a concern makes a difference. If you are pushing direct representation with demonstrators and taking large space in the trade papers, the selling cost must be affected correspondingly.

Furthermore, if you are determined to be in the lead and to make continuous advances and improvements in your product, bring out new designs and add new lines, and still wish to pay your bills and earn dividends, you have got to have your selling price high enough to allow for this. The selling price is therefore made up of a large number of elements. I think the gentleman who opened the discussion desired to make the point that it did not particularly matter to him whether he had an exact division between the earned burden and the unearned burden provided he knew what it was costing him during the year to produce the goods, and he was interested in getting the selling price high enough to be sure that those expense charges were all paid. But the writer of the paper desires to show that this division becomes valuable in correctly showing the true amount of use of any given kind of equipment during a certain period, and if, for instance, there should be a flurry in the lathe department so that apparently more lathes are needed, it is mighty convenient to be able to look back and see that for a long time there have been many of them standing idle, so that a little overtime work or some similar temporary scheme would care for the present need, and the purchase of additional machines is really unnecessary.

Therefore a correct and scientific balancing-up of equipment is made easy, which is an essential feature of efficient and economical management.

MR. SCOVELL: I appreciate very much, gentlemen, the interest you have shown in this subject. I am pleased that so many have taken part in the discussion.

(22) "The Profit Element," September 15, 1927, Bulletin, Vol. 9, No. 2, James H. Rand, Jr., President, Remington Rand Company

Editorial Department Note

We are indeed fortunate in being able to present in this issue a paper by one of the business leaders of the country, in which stands out prominently the basic simplicity and saneness of the philosophy on which rest his policies of business management. To find combined in one man a grasp of the broad economic principles on which the business structure of the country rests, an ability to interpret present economic conditions from the data available, and a genius to apply those principles in the management of a business enterprise is most unusual. Our readers will be interested in seeing verified some of the predictions made in this paper about six months ago.

The author, James H. Rand, Jr., is one of those outstanding captains of American industry who has accomplished much in a comparatively short time. Although he is the executive head of Rand Kardex Bureau, a world wide organization selling more than forty million dollars worth of business management equipment every year, Mr. Rand has attained his great success before the age of forty.

Graduating from Harvard in 1908, where he had shown his aggressive character by winning his place on the varsity football team, Mr. Rand plunged into his father's business, the Rand Company, and soon won his way to the position of sales manager. In 1916 he decided to form his own organization and, borrowing $10,000, he created the American Kardex Company.

Ten years later the two concerns were merged, under the direction of Mr. Rand, placing him at the head of a ten million dollar corporation. Then followed, within an incredibly brief period, the consolidation with Index Visible, Library Bureau, Safe-Cabinet, Baker-Vawter, and Remington Typewriter, the present company being known as the Remington Rand Company.

Mr. Rand has shown exceptional capacities for organization and leadership. His abilities are many sided. He is still regarded as the star salesman of the company. He has introduced many labor-saving practices into the production of his products and invented the major features contained in Kardex.

Mr. Rand was able to build up his original company, after repaying its first loan, entirely from the earnings of the company. He has demonstrated an exceptional grasp of sound finance. Not only is he able to see a big vision of future possibilities, but he can set to work to make that vision materialize.

Democratic and approachable, Mr. Rand knows how to retain the good will of everyone he meets and still conserve his time and physical energies for the major tasks at hand. He is well regarded locally as he is nationally, serving on the board of directors of the Marine Trust Company of Buffalo and the First Trust Company, Tonawanda.

This Official Publication is the stenographic report of a talk given by Mr. Rand before one of the Spring meetings of the Buffalo Chapter, NACA, of which he himself is a member.

The Profit Element

Andrew Carnegie was the first cost accountant that ever entered into business in America. He was a Scotchman and he made a most excellent cost accountant; he had a sharp pencil. He always employed Scotch assistants in financial matters wherever he could, and also throughout the shop. To give an example of how thrifty those assistants of Andrew's were, I will tell you a story that he used to tell about one of those Scotch foremen, who was walking down the street and a friend accosted him and said, "Say, Aleck, do you know that your wife was in a railroad accident?"

Aleck replied, "No, was she?"

His friend said, "Yes, I saw it in the paper."

Then Aleck asked, "Have you a paper?"

His friend replied, "Why, no. There is a newsboy; you can buy one from him and find out whether she was seriously injured."

Then Aleck said, "I guess I will wait until the 5 o'clock edition and then I can get the baseball news, too."

Sometimes the big inside news of American financial history is not printed and is little known; but Andrew Carnegie knew his costs to the point where he was not afraid to compete with the giants of industry in those days. His contemporaries, although larger than he, did not understand costs and were largely in the hands of financiers, such as J. P. Morgan, the elder, who were good lawyers and administrators, but not practical cost accountants.

When the United States Steel Corporation was formed, in the early days, it comprised about 70% of all of the then known steel companies. About this time Andrew Carnegie had made sufficient money so that he was ready to retire, and he made a proposition to the United States Steel Corporation—or rather, they asked him to make them a proposition—to sell out for $250,000,000. Mr. Morgan and some of his contemporaries talked with him and they threw up their hands. They said, "$250,000,000? Why, that is outrageous! We would never think of paying you that much money." Whereupon Andrew Carnegie said, "Very well, gentlemen, the deal is off."

A few years later they decided that it was necessary for them to annex Andrew Carnegie's low-cost operating unit to their corporation, the United States Steel Corporation; and Charlie Schwab, J. P. Morgan and a man named Gage sat in Mr. Morgan's living-room from 5 o'clock in the evening until 7 o'clock the next morning, sweating blood and trying to decide whether they could get along without Mr. Carnegie's low-cost producing units; and just as the day was dawning, Mr. Morgan turned to Charlie Schwab and said, "Charlie, go over and see how much you can buy Carnegie's steel business for. I have come to the conclusion that we have got to have it. His costs are too low."

Mr. Schwab then went over and talked to Mr. Carnegie and came back and said, "$500,000,000 is the price, and not a cent less."

They sweat blood for a few more hours and finally Mr. Morgan said, "Go over and pay it." So they went over and closed the deal.

Now, I maintain that the lack of knowledge of operating costs on the part of J. P. Morgan and the United States Steel Corporation cost the Steel Corporation $250,000,000 in three years' time. Ignorance of costs, gentlemen—think of it—$250,000,000 in three years' time.

So the cost man has come into his own, and from that day until this, costs and cost analysis have steadily come to the front.

Twenty years ago costs and cost men and cost departments were looked upon as something up to date, something to be adopted by large institutions that had a sufficient surplus to go into the work of compiling interesting statistics, which statistics were promptly filed away.

Ten years ago we found that cost departments were becoming very generally used and were commencing to have an effect upon many selling methods. Today the cost department of the average business is looked upon as a right arm of first importance in management. Without the cost department today 90% of our businesses would be out of existence; they would not be able to live.

John H. Patterson once called a meeting of his executives for the purpose of analyzing their troubles. They were having sharp reductions in income and profit. Their income was all right, but their profits were very narrow and they could not understand it; so he called a general meeting of the executives to discover, if he could, what the trouble was; and at that meeting he called upon the executives, one by one, to suggest ways and means of immediately cutting down the costs of operation. He went around the room and they all had their say. Finally he came to Hugh Chalmers, who was then Sales Manager, and Mr. Chalmers said, "Mr. Patterson, if you will pardon my reference to another department I will tell you where we can save $100,000 a year without even affecting our business adversely in the slightest degree."

Mr. Patterson asked, "What department is that?"

Mr. Chalmers replied, "Up on the top floor of our administration building there is a whole floor full of clerks that have been there for several years. I believe it is known as the cost department, where all of our manufacturing costs are analyzed. The whole top floor is full of clerks and calculating machines and red tape. If anybody in this room—sales managers, production managers, engineers, the office manager, treasurer, vice-president, or you, Mr. Patterson—can show where any use of those figures has been made in effecting lower manufacturing costs or lower selling costs, or has ever had any influence in changing our prices upward or downward, then I will withdraw my suggestion; but I defy anybody in this room to show where that department has been used to advantage at any time during the past twelve months."

Mr. Patterson asked the question, "Can anyone in the room show where it has been used to advantage or mention any case where those figures have had a beneficial effect upon the business?"

Not one suggestion was forthcoming according to the report. Whereupon the department was promptly abolished at a saving of $100,000 a year; and I say that that department should have been abolished, and any department should be abolished which can be abolished without detriment to the business.

Today the National Cash Register Company has built up a cost department which is second to none, and which is used day in and day out, month in and month out, to check their selling prices; not only their manufacturing and operating costs, but their selling costs, their advertising costs; and every department of the business is checked against certain standards which have been set up. That department is actually a vital force in the business and is having a very commendable effect. It is now a very indispensable department, although, as it was formerly, it was just a bunch of red tape, which should have been wiped out.

And so I am coming to one of my major premises in this talk, and that is that in order to insure the element of profit in business it is first necessary to see that your work — that is, the work of the cost men, of the cost department — is actively applied to the conduct of the business.

Now, if I might make a general criticism from my observation of cost men, I might say that they have been too diffident and too silent about the things that they know. The day is coming — in fact, it is here now — when it is time for the cost man to speak out what he knows; for him to make a noise, and make a loud noise, because he has in his grasp the figures which are going to largely control the policies of his company.

You will be interested to know what effect cost analysis has had upon our business. We manufacture one article, which we call our leader, and which is of prime importance; that is, the visible card record cabinet, known as Kardex equipment. In these recent mergers we have sought not to spread-eagle — not to spread out and take in a diversified line of equipment — but rather to put ourselves in a position where we can more quickly become of benefit to business at large through the general distribution of a superior article to displace an inferior article.

When I say it is superior, I mean that it is superior from the standpoint of the user as compared with what has been used heretofore; and it is superior from the standpoint of the manufacturer because it is a specialty and not a staple commodity. As manufacturers we found ourselves in the temporary position — perhaps in a permanent position — of manufacturing facilities for a wide, diversified line of equipment used by banks, offices, and factories.

What made it possible for us to merge, with a fair degree of certainty as to the outcome, was the analyses of these lines of business by our cost department for the purpose of finding out, not so much how good they were, how efficient these plants were, as far as manufacture was concerned, but rather to find out how inefficient they were, how many barnacles they had accumulated over a period of forty or fifty years, which nobody had taken the time or trouble to prune off, and to tabulate what could be done when our standards of operating costs were applied to those other businesses. And I want to tell you that the result was amazing. We found, for example — I say "we"; I class myself as one of the cost men because I put a large amount of my time on that analysis — our cost department found in one company we took over that 90% of the profit they had formerly been making was dissipated on high manufacturing costs, due to a variety of different practices, one of which was the making of a too widely diversified line of equipment — not enough standardization so they could get quantity production on any one of their models. We also found another case where more than half of the profit of the company — it was doing millions of dollars in volume — was produced by three articles that represented less than 25% of the total volume. Think of it! Less than 25% of the volume was producing the majority of the profit of that company.

I have often been asked if, in merging companies, in standardizing the products, eliminating and simplifying some of them, it would not be necessary to take a drastic cut in the total volume, and my answer has always been, "If a drastic cut in total volume results, let it come." We do not want to build volume that means no profit; and one of the first fundamentals of a successful business is that it must earn a profit so as to pay dividends to its stockholders. We have found that one article manufactured by one of our companies to a volume of $800,000 per year was causing us a loss of $32,400 per year. I ask you whether it were better to continue that volume of $800,000 or cut it off? Cut it off, of course.

The cost department of the future, then, is going to have more effect upon the profits of the business and upon the general management of business than any other single department. That is a broad statement, but I am going to qualify it by saying that those of you who are cost men, those of you who are treasurers, comptrollers, sales managers, and production managers will probably agree with me when I say that the work of cost analysis has justified itself in production and should be extended to distribution. And, gentlemen, in my opinion the major portion of the work of the cost department of the future is going to be in applying recognized principles of cost analysis to sales expenses, for there is the greatest evil in present-day industry, the high cost, the extravagant, outrageous cost, of distribution.

I recently attended a meeting of the National Association of Office Appliance Manufacturers, in Cleveland, and when I made the statement that the cost of selling was eating up the vitals of American business, every man in the room apparently agreed with me, and many of them came around afterwards and wanted to know if I could give them some of our experience as to just how they could cut down that high cost of selling.

Now, to get into technicalities for a little while, let me tell you one of the fallacies of business today as far as the cost of selling is concerned. Many institutions are now figuring their cost of selling in terms of the dollars and cents which they receive for their product directly from the middle man. I want to say that, in my opinion, is a radically wrong method. The cost of selling should be figured in terms of the price paid by the ultimate consumer. I can tell you of two instances where those two policies have clashed in our business. The Library Bureau had made a practice of selling through their own distributing organization, their branches and their own salesmen. They had a selling cost of approximately 37%. The Globe-Wernicke[1] Company, of Cincinnati, had always made a practice of selling, except in a few cities, through dealer distribution, and still do, at a selling cost of 3%, 3%, mind you! Which is the most efficient of those two methods of distribution? You would say, naturally, that the Globe-Wernicke policy of 3% was the more efficient; but it was the least efficient from our standpoint because they granted off the list price of their goods a discount of about 45% to 50%, depending upon the class of goods which they sold to the dealer. I hope I am not talking out of school now, but there are no secrets in our business any more. Now, you add to that discount of 45% to 50% the 3% and you have a selling cost of from 48% to 53%, as compared with the 37% of the Library Bureau, and you find that their selling costs are higher.

Now, I maintain that unless cost men can reduce the high cost of distribution and of selling, in the next few years — and it has got to be done quickly — we are facing a radical change in business, a new era in distribution. You are likely to wake up some morning and find that the world has changed in that its major products are being sold by your competitors direct from the factory to consumer instead of through the usual jobber, middle man, dealers, and the leeches on the profits all the way down the line to the ultimate consumer.

I have nothing against dealers at all, but I do believe that in order to avoid a radical disturbance in the next few years it is going to be necessary for us to

[1]Since this paper was delivered the Globe-Wernicke Co. has resumed its orginal separate status.

cut the cost of selling. You men have got to figure out how that can be done, in co-operation with your sales departments.

I might say that we are on the verge of a test, in our own business, where, in the next few weeks, a commodity will be offered direct to the consumers from our factory, and where all intervening sales costs are eliminated. We always go by tests, and if that test is successful we may add another article to it, and then another, until who knows but what we may do all of our business direct. But those things must be given careful consideration, because right now we are facing — and many of you are aware of it — a period of the fiercest competition that the world has ever known. I say that advisedly, and I am in pretty close touch with some of the biggest interests — financial and industrial — and also voice their sentiments. We are on the eve of a period of the fiercest competition that the world has ever known. I do not want to preach my own gospel — you know that I believe in the economical operation of big business; that united we stand and divided we fall, when it comes to competition and excessive operating costs; and that through mergers great economies can be effected — but I say that it is necessary for big business in the prime phases of industry to get together and trim their sales costs, either through mergers or through united co-operative action of some kind; and for this reason. On the other side of the water — in England, France, and Germany — right at this minute there are being formed cyclops of industry, giants of commerce. They are springing up on all hands and a great many of them through the aid of American capital. Those countries today are preparing for a trade war such as the world has never known. It means their life blood and they are bound and determined to get back their pre-war supremacy in foreign trade, in order to compete with the now existent large corporations in the United States, and in order to supersede, in foreign fields, the smaller corporations of the United States. They are forming these gigantic corporations with literally billions of dollars of capital back of them and, from the operating viewpoint, with the very minimum of operating costs, because Germany, Austria, Czecho-Slovakia and France are away ahead of the United States when it comes to cost analysis. I know what I am talking about because we have had a plant for five years in Germany and we have done business through forty or fifty branch offices, selling systems and methods of control to German business houses; and we have our fingers on the pulse of German capital. They are away ahead of us now on those things. Add to that, further economies in the cost of operation through combinations of capital, through the adoption of the American Henry Ford policy of straight-line production and progressive assembly, and you have something to contend with. Now, I say that our prosperity will be at stake unless we either get together or co-operate with other institutions in our line of business, in order to compete with foreign fields.

Now, mind you, the difference between prosperity and normalcy in the United States is only 20%. The fluctuations of the volume of sales of corporations represented in this room in good times, as compared with a period of depression, will average about 20%. That 20% represents almost identically the proportion of foreign trade to domestic trade of our exports of American institutions as compared with their domestic sales volume.

Now, it makes no difference whether you are engaged in foreign trade or whether someone else is engaged in foreign trade, that 20% has got to be shipped into foreign countries in order to give us an outlet for the surplus that exists in the United States today: Therefore, I say that our prosperity is at stake unless corporations put themselves in a position where they can compete in the markets of the world.

For our own company we adopted a policy, several years ago, of going over into Germany because we expected the Germans to compete with us in American markets and we wanted to start from scratch at the crack of the gun, to build up an organization in Germany, so that if anyone in Germany started to manufacture our line of goods we could have an organization that was already larger than theirs, and with lower manufacturing costs, to ship over into the United States products of our manufacture on exactly the same wage scale and production basis as they would be operating on, and they would have nothing on us when it came to producing for the United States, as well as for South America and other foreign countries.

I say that we are coming to a period of intense competition. Perhaps next year, or in 1928, you will realize more fully what I have to say. I am not a pessimist and I am not unduly, I hope, an optimist on business. I believe we are going to have a healthy condition and a period of continued prosperity. What I mean by "prosperity" and what you mean by "prosperity" may be two entirely separate things; but I am convinced that Americans are sufficiently resourceful — and the kind of talk I am handing out tonight is being handed out not only here, but all over the United States, in various ways and by various individuals, because, after all, business men throughout the United States come pretty close to talking the same language — I believe that the resourcefulness of American business men is going to cause them to rise to the occasion, so that industry will be on a basis where we can compete.

Now, in this period of intense competition you are going to see — and you are seeing it already in American business — a narrowing margin of profit. Prices of commodities are actually going to tend lower. The purchasing power of the dollar, which varies almost inversely in proportion to the variation in commodity price levels, will gradually rise. In this period of low prices I predict — and I predict this within the next eight months — that you will see the price of one of the most important commodities with which we have to deal, i.e., money, reduced. We have at the present time $4,500,000,000 in gold in our reserves in the United States; and with the exception of one month in 1924 that is the highest level of gold supply that we have ever known. I predict that that commodity known as money is going down with the other commodities in price because of an abundance of supply; and you will see, in the next eight or ten months, another reduction in the Federal Reserve rediscount rate, which is now at 3½%; you will see the prices of bonds—I am talking about first-class gilt-edged widows' and orphans' securities—on a basis of the old-time interest rates of 3½%, 3¾% and 4% as compared with 4½%, 4¾% and 5%, as at the present time.

Now, those conditions, I want to point out, in the light of American industrial and financial history, are the very conditions that are necessary for a prolonged period of prosperity; and I am one of those who believe that we are in for a prolonged period of prosperity that will last for several years. I am not worrying about this year or next year or the following year, barring minor ups and downs. I want to say that it is up to you, the kind of language that you talk, and the kind of ideas that you spread, to maintain a healthy and optimistic attitude so long as there are no clouds on the horizon; and I, for one, am unable to pick out any clouds on the business horizon at the present time. It is a pretty generally recognized fact that the psychologic factor in business atmosphere is responsible for the extent of about 40% for good business; that the economic factor is responsible for not over 60% of prosperity. Now, if that is true, and the economic factor is sound, do not take my word for it, but listen to men like Mellon, Hoover, Charles Mitchell, Elbert Gary and all of the rest of them, who cannot afford to risk their reputation on wild statements as to financial conditions. Put them down as sound unless you know they are not; and if any man here knows of anything that indicates breakers ahead, I wish he would tell me before he leaves this room, because I do not see any. Therefore, there remains that psychologic factor, which is a 40% factor. That is the thing we have got to look out for.

There are some astounding things that I cannot help but mention in passing. According to statistics collected by the government, of 298,000 major industries, 119,000, or 40%, showed not only no profit, but an aggregate loss in the last 12 months of $2,000,000,000. Now, that is an astounding fact; but it is due, in my opinion, to the very absence of the thing which we are seeking to introduce into business, viz.: a proper application and consideration of costs and cost analyses. There is no excuse for any business failing to make a profit or to liquidate in a solvent condition.

When the Pilgrims came over in the Mayflower they did not engage, upon landing, in a poker game, where some of them made money and the others had to starve. No. They all went into business and did serious, hard work;

and they produced a living, not for one, but for all of them; and their community was prosperous although they had to use a make-shift for a medium of exchange. The industrial world today is simply a magnification of this little colony in Plymouth, and there is no reason why we should not all prosper and make money; at least, we can liquidate in a solvent condition if we follow one of the immutable laws which I am going to state, namely that we should limit our commitments to the amount of money which we take in from the sale of our product. Now, I want to state that as a cardinal principle of our business, and one which can be applied to a peanut stand or to United States Steel—After you have developed a working basis and hypothesis upon which to base your procedure, there is no reason why any corporation should not continue to operate at a profit—and a cash profit at that—or liquidate in a solvent condition. By way of proof I want to say that there is no business in the world that can go on spending or making commitments for more, in total dollars, than the cash which they take in over an extended period. In other words, if, year after year, we are going to make money in business, year after year we will have to show total commitments, which afterwards take the form of wages and so forth, amounting to less than the cash which we take in during the corresponding period. You cannot let your commitments exceed your cash receipts; if you do, somebody has to put up the cash or you have got to get out.

If, therefore, you cannot do that—and everybody admits that fact—why try it? And if you are not going to try it, why, then, not conform? If you have been operating on a profitable basis in the last two years, analyze and find out how much you spend for manufacturing, how much for sales and subdivide that—how much you spend for advertising and how much for administrative expenses. After you have found out how much you spend, then take your cash receipts for a quarter or six months' period and deduct, first, the amount of profit that you are sure you made, and appropriate the balance for other purposes. Now, in our business we will take off at least 10%. We are not satisfied to manufacture and stand the risk of doing business at less than 10% profit. If we take off 10% and our cash collections are, we will say, $1,000,000 for one period, then during the ensuing period we have 90%, or $900,000, to spend for all purposes in the business. We take that $900,000 and we hand it to the various department managers—the sales manager, production manager, engineer and so forth—to appropriate as per his own ideas, which he has tabulated, with the aid of the cost department—the cost department always has its hand in it—and then his problem is to operate his department within his appropriation, and his efficiency is gauged largely by the results which he secures in the application of the funds made available to him through that budget. In the case of the advertising manager, for example, it would be just as much a sin for him to spend too little out of his appropriation as to spend too much, or exceed the allowance, because advertising is one of the main factors in getting new business. It is the life blood of the sales function. Now, all of the departments are charged with the responsibility of keeping within their appropriations, so that if they all spend up to their limit, they have spent a total of not exceeding $900,000, and we have something left. What does it amount to? $100,000, or 10% on the volume of the cash that came in. And what is that to be used for? That is to be used 50% for dividends and 50% for building up the business, in the way of additions to plant and so forth, if we need them. If we do not, it is there in the way of a reserve. I believe that that policy is being followed by a great many corporations; and whether you know it or not, if your corporation is making money, it is following, in the last analysis, that program; and it is better to follow it consciously and intentionally than unintentionally. Now, if your cash collections drop off, you are going to shrink your appropriations accordingly; but you will always be keeping your commitments within your receipts, and you will be liquidating in a solvent condition. You cannot become financially embarrassed so long as you follow that plan. The reason I say "commitments" is because if you start tabulating your accounts payable — your invoices and so forth — you are doing something that a large rubber company tried to do and found it would not work. They tabulated the damage after the invoices came in, and that is like locking the door after the horse has been stolen, because when an invoice comes in, it must be paid; and they found that their commitments were on an aggregate larger than their balance; and they found themselves in the hands of the bankers. You must limit your commitments at the time they are made and not at the time the invoices are received.

In conclusion, I want to ask you to do something for the good of American business: try to be optimistic in your conversation. So long as there are no breakers on the surface and there are no clouds on the horizon, do the right and the square thing by business. And, mind you, if you find a man who is pessimistic and who says that things are all going wrong, you tell him point blank, "Do not speculate on the stock market and you will be all right. Get back to work and come down to earth." In other words, gentlemen, nail the pessimist in his tracks and spread this gospel of optimism, which takes care of the 40% factor of prosperity.

Now, I say to you men who are cost accountants and you men who are treasurers, and all of you who are interested in reducing the cost to make, the cost to sell, and the cost to administer, more power to you in your work; you are doing the thing that is necessary to put American industry where it belongs, to put it in position where it can compete. And do not try to economize on costs by taking the pruning knife to the payroll. That is not the place to start. The place to start is up at the top. Start with the president, if you will, and come down; and you will find more chances to economize among those who are holding down soft jobs at the top than you will with the men who are actually producing the goods. Go over the non-productive workers in the organization. Apply the test of indispensability to every job, and where you find that a man and his job are not indispensable, ask yourself, "What would happen if this man should drop dead?" And if you find that the business would go along without interruption to volume, to efficiency and to profit by the elimination, let him go off that job and let him go to work where he will become a productive worker. I say that industry is top heavy and it is time for us to start pruning; but let us start at the top. Wherever you find an opportunity to cut expenses, do not forget to make a noise about it and do not hesitate to speak up and call the attention of the management to those opportunities, because if you keep silent, your company is going to suffer and in the long run you are going to suffer yourself.

And so, in conclusion, I will say again that I am very glad to belong to this association, which has such a commendable purpose. I believe that the cost man is going to be a top-notcher; that the future presidents of corporations are going to be a sort of a combination of lawyer, cost accountant, and sales manager. Now, that does not mean that a production manager cannot also be a president; for the cost accountant factor is the most important factor in the making up of the manager. Referring again to J. P. Morgan and his lack of knowledge of the application of the principles of cost accounting to the Carnegie Steel Company, which cost him $250,000,000, do not let any of us make the same mistake of underestimating the importance of cost analysis. If we follow along the principles for which your association was organized, I say that this organization and all of the other associations which are being built up in various parts of the country, are going to have a powerful influence in business and are going to take not only the risk out of competition, but they are going to put more joy into living our business lives.

(23) "The Accountant's Relation to the Budgetary Program," 1927 Yearbook, James O. McKinsey, J. O. McKinsey & Company

The Accountant's Relation to the Budgetary Program

I have been asked to talk to you this morning on the relation of the accountant to the budgetary program. In order to discuss the subject intelligently, it is necessary to have clearly in mind what budgets are. As I think of budgets, and as I think the accountant should think of them, they are a statement of future accounts expressed in terms of units of responsibility. The accounts record what has happened prior to the beginning of the budget period; the budget shows what we expect the accounts will show has happened at the end of the budget period.

It is essential that the budgets be made in such form that they will present a statement of future accounts, for otherwise it is difficult, if not impossible, to make comparisons between the estimated and actual results, and unless such comparisons are made it is impossible to judge whether the budget has been carried out efficiently. The budget should be expressed in units of responsibility because responsibility must be placed upon specific individuals in the organization for the preparation and carrying out of budgets. In the final analysis, control of activities is effected through individuals.

From this point of view, it is our problem to consider the relation of the accountant to the preparation and operation of budgets. The first essential in the preparation of an effective budget is the procuring of adequate information for use as a basis of forecasting results. The information needed for this purpose is of two kinds: First, information as to past results which is obtained from the accounting records. Every budget prepared should be based upon past results and the accountant should be the member of the organization who is most competent to collect, present, analyze, and interpret such information. Consequently, the first responsibility of the accountant with reference to the budgetary program is the collection, presentation, analysis, and interpretation of the information concerning past results which is needed as a basis for the budgetary program.

But it is extremely dangerous to use information concerning past results alone, or to use such information too literally. It is unfortunate that in many cases business firms make their budgets by simply adding an arbitrary percentage to the past results. For example, mercantile and manufacturing firms frequently prepare statements of their past sales, add 10% or 15% to these and present the result as a sales budget. I think it should be apparent to you that such a statement is not a budget. It is merely a mathematical computation. It doesn't require ability or ingenuity to make a budget of that type and such a budget is frequently dangerous rather than helpful. I think it worth while to discuss briefly some of the factors to be considered when interpreting past results as a basis of making budgets and to indicate in what way the accountant can be helpful in the consideration of these factors.

It should be apparent that the factors to be considered vary greatly from business to business and from time to time in the same business. All I can do here is to point out some of the factors which have been found to be important in different types of industries and let you draw such conclusions as you can from these specific illustrations. One of the first problems which should be considered when a sales budget which shows an increase in sales is being prepared is, What will be the probable effect of such an increase on the sales price of the product? In other words, is it possible to get the desired increase in sales volume without decreasing the sales price of the product?

Our Chairman, Mr. Andersen, stated that it is probable that during the next few years we shall have falling prices. I believe that many people who have given careful study to forecasting future business conditions agree with him. Because of this condition we must give careful attention to the effect of an increasing volume upon sales prices, for it will probably be difficult in most lines of industry to maintain the sales prices even if no growth in volume is sought. It is apparent that the effect of an increase in volume on price depends to a considerable extent on the volume which a company sells. In a small company which is not an important factor in its line of industry, it may be possible to take advantage of specific opportunities to increase the sales volume and not affect the market price at all, but when a large company whose volume is an important factor in determining the price in an industry, attempts to increase its volume 10 or 15 or 20%, a very detrimental effect upon the price will usually result. In fact, in some lines of industry, the whole market structure would be disrupted.

I can think of a company with whose operations I am intimately acquainted which could not possibly consider seeking an increase of 15% in its sales volume during any specific period, for to do this would disrupt the market to such an extent that it would affect all members of the industry. If a company decides that it cannot obtain the volume it desires at the present sales price, it is then necessary to decide whether it is desirable to secure the increase in volume at a smaller sales price. In given lines of industry, the problem of setting sales prices is one of the most important factors in the preparation of the budgetary program.

We frequently discuss the coordination of sales and production, and in this discussion we often forget that in many lines of industry the real point of coordination between sales and production is the price at which the product is to be sold. In many cases, we should think of coordination between sales and production as a matter of pricing policy before we think of it in terms of total quantities to be sold and total quantities to be produced. It is, of course, commonplace knowledge that if a lower price produces a greater sales volume, this in turn makes possible a greater production volume which under normal conditions should produce a decrease in unit cost. This may also produce a greater turnover and the savings in unit cost and the greater profit made by the rapid turnover may produce a larger profit than will a smaller volume at a higher price.

This problem of coordinating sales price, unit cost and velocity of turnover is simple to state but often difficult to solve, and I am sorry to say, that in many cases it is a problem to which executives and accountants have given far too little attention. In very few industries where I have worked, have I found anything like adequate consideration given to the effect of the sales price upon the volume that can be sold, upon the unit cost of the product and upon the turnover of the product. I venture that in the next few years, the accountant will find it necessary to give very earnest consideration to the pricing policies of his company. Many times the establishment of prices is left primarily to the sales department. The sales department is likely to take the cost figures, add a margin which it would like to obtain and then modify this according to competitive prices. In many cases, the accountant's advice is not asked with reference to the price set. It is my opinion, that the accountant with his knowledge of past results and with his ability for analytical work should play an important part in the establishment of sales prices. He is probably the only member of the organization who is able to see all the factors which should be considered in the establishment of prices.

Another important factor in the preparation of budgets to which the accountant should direct his attention is the relation of the sales program to the production program from the point of view of economical production—in other words, whether the sales program provides for a well-balanced production program. This does not merely involve considering whether the production department can produce more or less than the sales department plans to sell, although this is an important question. It also involves whether the sales program calls for the production of the products which the production department can produce most economically. In many lines of industry, it is not possible to have the machinery entirely flexible so that machines may be shifted easily and quickly from the manufacture of one product to another. Even if machines can be so shifted, the process involves considerable expense.

The typical sales department does not understand production problems and in many cases it does not realize the effect on production cost of a shift in sales emphasis from one product to another. It is true that the production department, in so far as possible, should be a service department and should attempt to produce the products which can be sold most profitably. It is equally true, that when a company has invested its capital in machinery and equipment, the sales department should become a service department to the extent that it should attempt to market profitably, products which can be produced most economically with the existing equipment.

In considering these problems, the accountant with his knowledge of costs and with his ability to analyze results should be able to give constructive advice concerning the coordination of the sales program with a well-balanced economical production program.

Another important factor to be considered in the preparation of a budget is the organization of the sales program so that the maximum amount of sales can be obtained with the least amount of cost. This brings us to a consideration of the whole question of market analysis.

When we plan to secure an increase in sales volume, we are immediately confronted with the question, In what lines of products and which territories should the increase be obtained? The typical sales executive is an optimist. He is a man of the dynamic type. He is a man who thinks that if a goal is set up in the form of a certain volume, the most important thing to do is to pep up the sales force and to send it out to get that volume. The typical sales executive is not a man who carefully analyzes markets, marshalls the facts and decides where he can obtain the greatest volume of business with the least sales resistance. In present competitive conditions, if business organizations are to continue to grow, it is necessary, when planning an increase in the sales volume, to consider to whom their products should be sold, where these customers are and the best method of reaching them. To do this requires a careful analysis of the market to ascertain the sales outlets and the method of reaching these outlets. It is necessary to find the type of people who buy each of the products which the business sells, where these people are located, what competition exists in that locality, and the best method of reaching these particular people.

This is a problem of sufficient importance and complexity to be a challenge to the thought of any of us. It is the field to which the accountant may well direct his attention with confidence that he may render a distinct service. You may say that such work is out of the field of the accountant. I can only reply, that in my opinion there will be no limit to the field of the accountant of the future. The accountant should be the eyes and ears of the chief executive. He should be the one who is responsible for analyzing all the problems of the business and his field should be wherever the capital of the company is invested. It should be his responsibility to see that the activities of the company, wherever they may be and whatever they may be, are in harmony with the policies of the business. The accountant who does not conceive his job in this light will never be able to take the place he should in the budgetary program. He must recognize that when figures on past results and information on future results have been collected, it is his job to call to the attention of the chief executive and the major executives of the business any tendency, any factors or any information which should influence them in making decisions. He is the man who should be best qualified to analyze, interpret and advise with reference to the facts under consideration. In the past many accountants have felt that their task was completed when they had made up statements which presented past results in what they considered a satisfactory form. The accountant who so conceives his responsibility is to me much like the man who, with his wife, spent a couple of days in an American plan hotel in one of our large cities. At the time of departure at the end of two days, he was informed by the clerk that he owed $50. In answer to his question of why he owed so much, the clerk explained that he owed $25 for the use of the room for two days and $25 for the meals of himself and wife. The gentleman explained that he and his wife had not eaten at the hotel but had eaten in a neighborhood restaurant. To this the clerk replied, "That is immaterial for this is an American plan hotel. We provide the food for you to eat and if you don't eat it, that isn't our fault." The man handed the clerk $25. The clerk insisted that he owed $50. The man then replied, "I am giving you only $25 for I am charging you $25 for kissing my wife." The clerk replied that he hadn't kissed the gentleman's wife, to which the gentleman replied, "That isn't my fault. She was here to be kissed if you wanted to do so."

From my point of view, many accountants work on the American plan. They prepare elaborate statements and present them to executives with the thought that they have given them to the executives to use if they want to and it isn't their fault if they mean little or nothing to the executives. What I am trying to emphasize is that the task of the accountant only begins when the executive's report is made. His major duty is to interpret these reports to the executive and to assist him in formulating policies based on them.

Another problem to which serious consideration must be given in the preparation of the budgetary program is the personnel of the organization. Some companies seek to expand so rapidly that it is impossible to develop the organization with sufficient rapidity to handle the problems of the company efficiently. One of the very important problems which faces any company planning a rapid growth is whether or not its organization is qualified to administer the enlarged business — in other words, whether the executives of the business can grow in ability as rapidly as it is planned to increase the volume of sales and production. Many times a sales manager may be very efficient when he is supervising the sales of a company with sales of $5,000,000 a year, but may be quite inefficient in administering the sales activities of the company if the sales volume increases in a very short period to $20,000,000 or $30,000,000 a year. Some companies have recognized this difficulty and have purposely restricted their growth so that their organization may keep pace with their volume of business.

I am rash enough to assert that the accountant can render service in the study of this problem. Since he is constantly studying the activities of all the departments of the business, he should be able to obtain a knowledge of the abilities and deficiencies in the organization because, after all, the results of the activities of all the employees are reflected in the accounts, and if the accountant has his records set up in the right form so that he can see the results of the activities of each of the departments, he has an opportunity to judge the abilities of executives responsible for these activities. It is true that the accountant must use judgment in offering criticisms in reference to executives, but he should recognize that his is the responsibility of presenting to the chief executive information which will enable him to judge the abilities of his subordinates.

I might discuss with you a number of other factors which should be considered in preparing your budget program but I think the illustrations I have given are sufficient to indicate the nature of the problems. If we assume that the factors mentioned as well as many others which should be considered have been given proper consideration, and that a budget has been prepared as a result of this consideration, the next problem is to ascertain whether the budgetary program is being properly executed.

To do this it is necessary to have at least monthly and sometimes weekly comparisons between the actual and the estimated results. It is necessary that the executives be presented a picture which will show how near they have come to doing what they planned, when the budgets were prepared and approved. It is the function of the accountant to prepare statements which will give this information for it is important that we do not have two kinds of statements prepared, one showing the actual results and the other the estimated results.

It is important that the accounting reports be revised at the time budgets are installed so that each accounting report presented to an executive will show a comparison between the actual and estimated results. If two sets of statements are presented to the executive at different times, he will give more attention to the one received first. If very shortly after the end of the month the accountant can lay on the desk of the executive a statement which shows him what each unit of the business under his jurisdiction has done, and what they planned to do, then the executive has a report which enables him to judge the efficiency of the executives in carrying out the budget program.

No matter how carefully the budget program has been prepared, there will always be some variation between the estimated and actual results. As a consequence the accountant's responsibility is not over when he has prepared a statement showing a comparison between actual and the estimated results. It is his responsibility to prepare an analysis which will point out the reasons for these variations so that the executives may know whether the variations are justified, and if they are not justified, who is responsible for the variation. Once a month there should go to the chief executive as well as the other executives of the business, a picture showing a comprehensive comparison of actual and estimated results and a comprehensive analysis of the variation.

If this is to be the accountant's work, he must not be too sensitive to criticism, for invariably he will offend the sensibilities of some of his associates and will be criticized for explanations which he offers. Moreover, the analysis prepared by the accountant will not always be entirely correct and sometimes he will find that he must retract some statements. But the accountant who has properly established himself in the organization and has fully won the confidence of his superior officer will have little difficulty, if he uses ordinary judgment in preparing his analysis and making his recommendations. The accountant who never presents an analysis until he is absolutely sure that he has made no errors, will present so few analyses that he will be of little value to the executives of the business. He should present his reports and suggestions in the spirit of helpfulness and cooperation.

He should present his report as soon as possible after the end of the budget period. One of the reasons that reports of this kind are sometimes not considered seriously by the executives is that so much time has intervened between the end of the period and the receipt of the reports, that the information provided therein is ancient history. The typical executive, by some means or other, forms an opinion as to results very soon after the end of the period. Whether a formal report is presented to him or not, he has an idea in his own mind as to what the results are, and if he obtains this information from his subordinates before the accounting reports are submitted, it is likely that he will not give the reports as much attention as he should. It is also true that if reports are submitted for one period near the close of the next period, there may be a tendency on the part of the executive to wait to see what will happen in the current period. For example, if he received a report on the 25th of July giving him the results of the operations for June, there will be a tendency on his part to wait until he obtains the results for July.

If the budget reports are to be of the value which they should, the accounting procedure must be speeded up so that reports showing a comparison between actual and estimated results can be submitted very shortly after the close of each period. There are a number of problems involved in speeding up the accounting procedure, but the progress made by many companies has been almost unbelievable and the accountant will frequently find it is possible to make more progress than he originally believed possible.

The third function of the accountant with reference to the budgetary program is responsibility for the formulation of the budgetary procedure. The accountant is responsible for preparing the procedure for the maintenance of the accounting records, and if the budgets are to be considered as statements of future accounts, it would seem logical that he should be the one responsible for preparing the budget procedure.

A clear distinction should be made between the responsibility for the budget program, which in the final analysis should rest on the chief executive, and the responsibility for the procedure by which the program is carried out, which should rest on the accountant. I know that in many companies this responsibility is not placed on the accountant. One reason for this is that in some organizations the accountant does not have the point of view on budgets which we have taken this morning. In some cases it is impossible to sell the budget idea, in the fullest sense, to the accountant. Although I strongly believe that the accountant should be responsible for the budgetary procedure, I have often found it necessary to advise clients to place this responsibility on someone else in the organization because the accountant would not function properly in this capacity. If the accountant sees the objectives of the budgetary program, and has the tact and executive ability which are needed to supervise the budgetary procedure, the responsibility for this procedure should be placed on him. He should be responsible for preparing the procedure and issuing instructions to the various units with reference to the preparation of the various budgets, for collecting the estimates submitted by the various units of the company, summarizing and analyzing these various budgets, and finally preparing a summarized report for the use of the chief executive or preferably for the use of the budget committee composed of the chief executive and his major assistants. The accountant should be secretary of this committee. In this capacity he should be in charge of all the technical procedure involved in the preparation and use of budgets.

To summarize, I have tried to show how the accountant may be of service to the budgetary program in three ways:

(1) By assisting in the collection, analysis, and interpretation of the data which are necessary for the preparation of a budget.

(2) As the agent through whom the monthly reports are made which show a comparison between the actual and the estimated and in the interpretation of these differences and submission of recommendations with reference to them.

(3) In the preparation and enforcement of the budgetary procedure.

If the accountant can thus conceive of the function of the budget, and if he can sell the budget idea to his associates, he should occupy an important place in the budgetary program, and in the fullfillment of his responsibility to this program he should have an opportunity to become one of the most important executives in the organization. His work in connection with the budgets is not only interesting but it is a continuous and ever-changing work. An organization can never make its program so perfect that there will not be numerous important problems involved in the preparation and carrying out of the budget. It will never be possible to have a perfect budget and because of this, many important problems will always be involved in budgetary work.

Although it is impossible to prepare a perfect budget, and even to formulate a perfect budgetary procedure, may I leave with you this final thought: Isn't it better to plan and think ahead even if the plan is only approximately accurate rather than not to plan at all? Isn't it in this field of planning that the accountant can render one of his most important services to management?

(24) "The Use of a Thirteen-Month Calendar," 1928 Yearbook, M.B. Folsom, Eastman Kodak Company

M. B. Folsom is a graduate of the University of Georgia and of the Harvard Graduate School of Business Administration. He has had twelve years' experience with the Eastman Kodak Company where he has held the positions of Statistician and Office Manager, and is at present Assistant to the Chairman of the Board.

The Use of a Thirteen-Month Calendar

Defects of Present Calendar

There are many defects in the present twelve-month calendar, but, considered from the business point of view, the two principal defects are: (1) the variation in the number of days in the month, and (2) the fact that the month is not a multiple of the week. There is a variation of 11% between the length of February in ordinary years and the length of a 31-day month. There may be a variation of 19% in the number of working days in a month — between 21 days and 25 days. A variation of this extent in a unit which is used as a base for the great majority of reports compiled in business is obviously a serious defect.

There is another factor which complicates it further. In most lines of industry and commerce the individual days of the week are not of the same value. The best illustration is that of a factory which works only half-days on Saturday. Comparisons between months of five Saturdays and months of four Saturdays are obviously inaccurate. If production in a certain plant were uniform throughout the year 1927, the monthly output in March would show an increase of 19% over February, April output report would show a decline of 6% from March, and the May report a decline of 8% from March. If no adjustments were made for these variations, the plant manager would obtain a false impression of the state of his business.

Take the hotel business as another illustration: Thursday is the best day of the week for the hotel business, the average receipts on Thursday equaling 18% of the receipts of the week, while Sunday receipts are only 7%, and Saturday receipts 10% of the receipts of the week. This variation in the number of the days in the month and the difference in the value of the days of the week causes quite a fluctuation in the value of the months of any one year and also in the value of corresponding months of different years. Using 1926 as an illustration: If January were considered as 100, February would have a value of 93.5, March a value of 106.5, April 102, May 100, etc. If the hotel manager made no adjustment for these variations, he would get a wrong conception of the course of his business. He would probably make allowance for February, but it is doubtful whether he would make allowance between March and May, for instance. If no allowance were made and if his business were uniform during the year, he would get the impression from the monthly report that the business had declined 6% from March to May and that it had increased 14% from February to March.

The second defect is that there may be four weeks or five weeks in a month. All accountants are familiar with the split-payroll difficulty and with the erratic course of the burden and cost statements owing to the fact that some months have five paydays and others only four paydays. This variation in the number of paydays upsets comparisons not only between months of the same year but also between corresponding months of consecutive years, because the month does not always have the same number of paydays in different years.

It is obvious from the few illustrations which have been given that, if adjustments were not made for the variations in the number of days and the number of weeks in a month, all monthly reports would be misleading, and inaccurate comparisons would be obtained. If adjustments are made, additional clerical help is required.

Several methods have been used by accountants to overcome these defects in the present calendar, the two principal ones being: (1) the use of four-week and five-week months, and (2) the use of thirteen periods of four weeks each. A study of these two plans indicates that the latter method has more advantages and fewer disadvantages than the former. In this paper it is planned to describe the experience of concerns who have been using the thirteen-period calendar for their internal records.

Thirteen-Period Calendar

Under this plan the year is divided into thirteen periods of four weeks each, each period consisting of 28 days. Except for holidays, the periods are of the same length and are, therefore, comparable without adjustment. Thirteen months of twenty-eight days account for 364 days, leaving one day over in ordinary years and two days over in leap years. Thirteen is not divisible by four, hence thirteen periods cannot be grouped into quarters having an even number of whole periods. Many concerns, nevertheless, have adopted the thirteen-period calendar for their records and accounts and some concerns have used this calendar for over thirty years.

Survey of Forty-eight Concerns Using the Thirteen-Period Calendar

In order to find out the experience of these concerns with this calendar, the advantages and disadvantages which they found, and the methods which they used in overcoming obstacles, a questionnaire was sent to a list of over sixty concerns using this calendar of whom we had record. Replies were received from forty-eight concerns.

Some of the concerns from whom information was received are as follows:

Carter's Ink Company, Boston, Mass.
C. G. Conn, Ltd., Elkhart, Ind.
Crocker-McElwain & Chemical Paper Mfg. Co., Holyoke, Mass.
Eastman Kodak Co., Rochester, N. Y.
Fiberloid Corporation, Indian Orchard, Mass.
Robert H. Foerderer, Inc., Philadelphia, Pa.
Fuller Brush Company, Hartford, Conn.
Graton & Knight Mfg. Co., Worcester, Mass.
Hearst Publications, Inc., San Francisco, Calif.
Jewel Tea Company, Chicago, Ill.
Kendall Mills, Walpole, Mass.
Loews, Incorporated, New York City
Lukens Steel Company, Coatesville, Pa.
McCallum Hosiery Company, Northampton, Mass.
Rome Brass & Copper Company, Rome, N. Y.
Sauquoit Silk Mfg. Company, Philadelphia, Pa.
Southworth Company, Mittineague, Mass.
United Press, New York City
Western Clock Company, La Salle, Ill.

Two companies have used this method of handling their accounts and records for over thirty years, the Western Clock Company, and R. H. Foerderer, Inc.

Method of Handling the Extra Day

Each ordinary year has one extra day beyond thirteen months of twenty-eight days and leap year has two extra days. There are two methods of taking care of these extra days. The first method, which is used by the majority of firms, is the plan of letting these days accumulate and inserting an extra week in the thirteenth period every five or six years. This means that in the fifth or sixth year the thirteenth period will not be comparable with the other periods, and allowance will have to be made for this in comparative statements. This method has an advantage in that the period would always begin with the same day of the week and always end with the same day of the week. Upon inauguration of the calendar a concern can select any day it chooses for beginning the period.

The other method is to include the extra day, or two extra days in leap year, in the last period, so that the thirteenth period of this year, for instance, if the first period began on January 1, 1928, would end with regular calendar month, December 31, 1928. The 1929 work calendar would then begin the same as the regular calendar, on January 1. This method has the advantage of starting the work calendar on the same date as the regular calendar. The thirteenth period would not be exactly comparable with the other periods under this method, but there would be a difference of only 1/28 in ordinary years and 1/14 in leap years, which should not upset comparisons very much. It has another disadvantage in that corresponding periods of different years begin on different days of the week.

Of thirty-eight companies replying to this question, twenty-two use the method of accumulating the extra day for five or six years then adding the extra week, and sixteen use the method of including the extra day in the first or last period of each year.

Method of Handling Quarterly Closings and Reports

In the thirteen-period calendar the quarter consists of three periods plus one week, the half-year consists of six periods plus two weeks, and three-quarters consists of nine periods and three weeks. This is one of the chief objections which has been raised against the use of a thirteen-period calendar. Over half of the companies who replied to this question stated that they had done away with quarterly closings and reports entirely, finding them unnecessary. The general practice among these concerns is to issue cumulative reports by periods, having a report, say, of the second period, the third period, the first four periods, etc., getting comparisons with the corresponding periods of different years. If it is necessary to compare the first three periods with the second three periods, this can easily be done, whether this length of time exactly corresponds with the quarters under the regular calendar or not.

The other practice is to have three quarters of three periods each and one quarter of four periods. The nature of the business determines in which quarter of the year the extra period will be included. Most of the companies reporting use the first three quarters of three periods each and the last quarter of four periods. In other companies the second or third and in one company the first quarter has the extra period. In a seasonal business it often happens that the sales in four periods during the slack time of the year would not exceed the sales in three periods during the busy part of the year. In such a business there is then practically no disadvantage in having the extra period included in one of the quarters.

Four of the concerns reporting close their books according to the quarters under the regular calendar. This practice, of course, involves an extra closing and an additional report, but in some cases the quarterly reports may be issued in place of monthly reports.

There is a tendency, however, for concerns using this type of calendar to do away with quarterly reports entirely, and many of those who are using the second method indicate that the number of quarterly reports has been considerably reduced, as they were found to be unnecessary.

Extent of Use Within the Individual Concern

1. Accounts Receivable and Statements to the Trade. Most of the companies send their statements to the trade according to the regular calendar. Some companies stated that they tried sending statements by periods, but it was confusing to the trade, who were using the regular calendar, and consequently they have gone back to the regular calendar. Two concerns have been able to send their statements out according to the periods without causing any difficulty to the trade.

Some concerns stated that, while they were sending their statements out to the trade according to the regular calendar, they closed their accounts receivable ledgers according to the period basis. Their accounts were cumulative and statements would be taken off at the end of the regular calendar month.

2. Handling Accounts Payable. Of thirty-nine companies who replied definitely to this question, ten use the periods in paying accounts payable, and twenty-nine pay according to the regular calendar month. The larger proportion using the regular calendar is accounted for by the difficulty of getting the concerns from whom the materials, supplies, and services are bought to render statements according to the periods used by the individual concern. The ten concerns who are paying their bills according to the thirteen-period calendar have in many cases made arrangements with their vendors to send statements according to their period dates. Several of them have made arrangements with their banks, supplying the banks with the closing dates of their periods, and statements are rendered on these dates and not at the end of the month.

3. Internal Records and Accounts for Both Office and Factory. In answer to the question, "Do you use the Calendar for all internal records, statements, and accounts for both office and factory?" thirty-four out of a total of forty-three answered "Yes." The others said they did with a few exceptions. In some cases the general books were excluded, in some the customers' accounts receivable were closed according to the regular calendar, some companies use it for cost accounting only, and other companies are using it only in their factory and not for the executive offices.

From the replies received on this question, it seems to be the general practice to use the thirteen-period calendar for all the internal records including the general books. Of course, if all the advantages are to be obtained, the application should be universal within the company. Those companies who use it in the factory only will undoubtedly encounter difficulty and confusion from the use of the two systems, because they will have some statements on the thirteen-period basis and some on the regular calendar basis. If the plan is advantageous for the factory, there seems to be little reason why it would not also be advantageous for compiling sales records and the many other records necessary for the administrative end of the business.

Payment of Salaried Employees

Most of the concerns reporting pay the salaried employees thirteen times a year. There seems to have been little difficulty experienced in putting these employees on the thirteen-period basis, and in many cases the employees were glad to have their pay thirteen times a year instead of twelve. It simplifies the costs, of course, if the salaried employees are on the same basis as the other costs.

Difficulty in Introducing the Plan

In answer to the question, "Did you experience any difficulty in introducing the calendar?" thirty-six companies replied "No." Two companies replied "Little if any." Two companies stated that there was slight resistance within the organization owing to the change in a long-established custom, but this was soon overcome and the people who objected were soon convinced of the advantages. There seems, therefore, to have been very little difficulty experienced in introducing the calendar.

Difficulty will be experienced during the first year in which the thirteen-period calendar is introduced in making comparisons between that year and the preceding year when the statements and reports were compiled on a twelve-month basis. Fairly accurate comparisons can be made between the periods of one year and the corresponding months of previous years, but for more accurate comparisons especially for the periods near the middle of the year it may be necessary to convert previous years to the thirteen-period basis. Of course, the comparisons between the weekly reports of the two years would not be upset nor would the cumulative reports.

Advantages

The outstanding advantage of the thirteen-period calendar is that all months are comparable without any adjustment being necessary for the unequal number of days or the unequal number of weeks as found in the ordinary twelve-month calendar. In the replies to the questionnaire the great majority of the companies gave "Facilitates comparisons as all periods are comparable" as the outstanding advantage. The advantages of "more accurate cost and production records," "elimination of split payrolls," "assisting budgeting," "having every closing on the same day," "having the end of the week coincide with the end of the period," and "the more effective planning of clerical work in closing the books owing to more efficient scheduling" are among the advantages most commonly listed by the companies. The following extracts are taken from some of the replies received and indicate concisely the advantages which these companies have obtained from the thirteen-period calendar.

Western Clock Company

In establishing a thirteen-month calendar in 1892, the Western Clock Company took a long step forward towards establishing time standardization. In our production, sales, cost, budgeting, timekeeping, etc., the thirteen-month method of accounting has proved invaluable over and over again. The twenty-eight-day month allows for flexibility of accounting. Each month is made up of exactly four weeks, and holidays excepted, the total number of days never varies. Each month is constant, invariable, uniform.

The Fiberloid Company

There are people who assume that a change to four-week periods will cause considerable work and confusion at the time it is established. There is absolutely no foundation to this feeling. From an accounting point of view it is simple. Merely specify the date of closing the several books of original entry and make the postings to the general ledger. The trial balance will automatically give the results of the period, and the financial statements prepared from the trial balance will, of course, reveal the same conditions.

Fuller Brush Company

Working as we do on a weekly basis it is much simpler to build up our months or, as we call them, periods, by making them multiples of weeks. With the more even flow of orders from the field and without the difficulty of having extra orders on account of split weeks, we find it a much more simple matter to regulate our warehouses and from there all the way down to our factory production.

Another advantage of the period plan in connection with our office work is the fact that we can schedule our routine on a weekly basis. All the work goes through on a regular schedule and at the end of the period there are no split weeks to handle.

All in all, we feel that the thirteen-period calendar plan has been of distinct advantage to us and that it is one of those things which tends to make business simpler and more effective.

Crocker-McElwain Company

The advantages from the standpoint of accounting and statistical comparisons are very many and we have ceased to recognize any disadvantages in the scheme if, in fact, we ever imagined any of importance.

Graton & Knight Company From a business point of view, I know of no real objection to the thirteen-period calendar. Having used it in our business for over ten years, I venture to state that no real objections could be found to its universal use.

The success which the Graton & Knight Company has had with this "natural" or thirteen-period calendar enthuses us to wholeheartedly recommend it to others.

Southworth Company The advantage of the period system is that you can keep your costs much more accurately, and you can make comparative statements more easily. We believe the matter of the cost system is the most important as it is always difficult to close the books at the end of the month when it comes in the middle of the week, as there are always adjustments to be made, payroll, etc.

Eastern Manufacturing Co. Comparable figures on all reports and statistics. More efficient planning of clerical help in closing books, due to definite scheduling of work. Clear cut distribution of wages by weeks, not requiring division of weekly payroll between two months. Facilitates building up all accounting records covering reserves, fixed charges, accrued terms, etc.

Robert H. Foerderer, Inc. The chief advantage is that it keeps all things in line with the payroll.

Liberty Paper Company Gives a more concise follow-up on sales and purchases. Also found it very satisfactory for Budget Work.

Kendall Mills, Inc. Even division of the year.
More accurate comparative figures.
Elimination of necessity for splitting payrolls, accruals, etc.

Rome Brass & Copper Company Having equal periods for comparison of results shown by all departments both as to production cost, profit, or loss, etc.

C. G. Conn, Ltd. Uniform periods in comparisons of sales, collections, etc. Elimination of necessity of splitting factory costs to conform to twelve-month calendar.

Universal Boring Machine Co. Makes closing easier at end of period instead of end of month, because of even number of days and even number of weeks, period always closes on Saturday.

The Carter's Ink Company We established the thirteen-month calendar primarily for our cost accounting records and in connection with the installation of a perpetual inventory system. This obviates the splitting of payrolls which in many cases are not accurate. Every closing takes place on a Saturday and is a complete record in itself.

Disadvantages

Fifteen of the companies who replied stated that there were no disadvantages. Thirteen companies stated that there were none except that their accounts to the trade and from the trade had to be kept on the twelve-month basis, and they had to follow the rest of the world on certain operations. Other disadvantages mentioned were the inability to divide thirteen into four equal periods, the additional clerical work involved with thirteen periods instead of twelve, and the addition of an extra week every five or six years.

The following is quoted from the several replies indicating the nature of the disadvantages which have been experienced:

Not commonly used, which requires all contact with customers and vendors on twelve-month calendar. Interest on bank deposits, call loans, and like investments credited to account twelve times per year, which results in the Income Sheet showing no such income during one period. *Champion-International Co.*

More closings per year. More clerical work. Comparisons with other companies difficult. One period each year, no bills paid and discount feature abnormal. Shoe business seasonal. *Louis A. Crossett Co.*

The only practical disadvantage comes in sending out customers' statements monthly rather than periodically. *Eastern Mfg. Co.*

Have experienced none of any consequence. Probably involves a little additional expense in clerical work due to the one extra closing of books. *The Sanymetal Products Co.*

No disadvantage whatever, except harmonizing our thirteen-period year with the twelve-month year in dealing with our customers and suppliers. This disadvantage is very slight indeed, and would disappear of course with uniform adoption. *The Root Company*

Balance must be proved with Control accounts for Accounts Receivable and Accounts Payable at the end of each month in addition to the ending of the periods. *Pooley Company*

Once in about every five years we have a five-week period which causes some little inconvenience in making periodical comparison. *Tasty Baking Company*

Inability to divide the thirteen periods into four equal quarters. Lack of uniformity in period endings in comparing statements with concerns using twelve monthly periods. *Loew's Incorporated*

Other concerns send their statements at the end of the month instead of at the end of period. *Universal Boring Machine Co.*

We have yet to learn of any disadvantage that may be chargeable to the use of the thirteen-month calendar. It has been employed very satisfactorily for ten years and surely in that length of time if there had been disadvantages they would have shown up by this time. *The Carter's Ink Co.*

Jewel Tea Co., Inc. We are obliged to keep separate records for the periodic distribution of rent, taxes, insurance, etc. With the universal adoption of the thirteen-period calendar, these objections would be eliminated.

It is evident from the experience of these companies that practically the only disadvantage experienced is in connection with having two calendars. All of these disadvantages would disappear should the thirteen-period calendar be adopted universally. It is surprising to note that only two companies mention the disadvantage of the inability to divide thirteen into four equal periods. Only three mentioned that there was additional clerical work involved, and two of these stated that the advantages far outweighed the additional clerical work involved.

The experience of these companies who have actually used the thirteen-period calendar would, therefore, indicate that the universal adoption of the thirteen-period calendar would be a distinct advantage to the business world in general and would involve only slight disadvantages, if any.

The International Fixed Calendar

Last year the National Association of Cost Accountants went on record endorsing the International Fixed Calendar. The following is quoted from a letter received from Dr. S. C. McLeod, Secretary:

At a meeting of the Board of Directors of the National Association of Cost Accountants held on Thursday, April 21, 1927, the question of Calendar Reform was considered. Every member of the Board present expressed himself individually as being in favor of the proposed reform of the calendar into thirteen months, and a resolution to this effect was adopted.

Our Board is strongly in favor of this movement. We would be glad of the opportunity to contribute toward its accomplishment, but we believe that it ought to be organized on the broadest possible basis and in such a way as to remove any possibility of its being exploited by any individual for his personal profit.

The International Fixed Calendar consists of thirteen periods of twenty-eight days each, the thirteenth month to be inserted between June and July. The extra day in ordinary years is taken care of by inserting a day between Saturday, December 28, and Sunday, January 1, dating it December 29 but giving it no weekday name. This would be considered either as an extra Sabbath or an extra holiday. Such a day would also be inserted in leap years as June 29 between Saturday, June 28, and Sunday, July 1. In this way the objection of having to add an extra period every six or seven years, as experienced by several concerns, would be overcome. The period would always start with Sunday, the first, and end with Saturday, the twenty-eighth.

A referendum was conducted by Mr. George Eastman, an advocate of this calendar, in 1927, to a thousand typical business men and leaders in other fields of work last year. Of the 600 replies which he received, over 90% were in favor of the International Fixed Calendar.

It seems pretty well established that the business world in general would look with favor upon the universal adoption of the thirteen-period calendar. The actual practice of concerns who are using the thirteen-period work calendar in their business, especially those who have used it for many years (some over thirty years) is conclusive evidence of the advantages which such a calendar would have to business. Practically all the disadvantages which these concerns have experienced would be overcome if this calendar were adopted universally.

In addition to the advantages from the business point of view there would be a number of other advantages if the International Fixed Calendar were adopted universally. For instance, it is part of the plan to have all holidays on Monday. While this would be of great benefit to business concerns because they would not be forced to close their plants in the middle of the week, which is rather expensive, it would also be a tremendous benefit to people at large, especially to the working people, to have holidays in conjunction with week-ends. It would also be advantageous to every one in home affairs, and to housewives, in particular, to have exactly four weeks in every month, enabling them to budget their expenses on the same basis as their income. They would not have the difficulty now experienced of having some months of only four pay days with which to meet their monthly bills. Another feature of the plan is that provision is made for a fixed Easter — the second Sunday in April; the churches seemed to be in favor of this plan.

Present Status of Movement

It may be of interest to those who favor this calendar to know that there has been distinct progress in the last few years toward its universal adoption. The League of Nations recently asked each country to set up a national committee to look into the question of calendar simplification. The Pan-American Congress at the recent meeting in Havana unanimously endorsed the League's invitation and asked the members to have such a committee appointed. The League presented the matter to the Secretary of State, Mr. Kellogg, and a national committee is now being formed in this country under the chairmanship of Mr. George Eastman. The committee will be composed of government officials and representative men and women from business, religion, and many other fields. The personnel will be announced very soon. A number of associations in this country have set up committees to study calendar simplification, and it is believed that considerable progress will be made within the next year. It is hoped that the plan will be universally adopted on January 1, 1933.

In many respects the simplification of the calendar can be compared to the introduction of standard time. In 1879 Sir Sanford Fleming, builder of the Canadian Pacific Railway, experienced such difficulty with the different kinds of time in use in the United States and Canada that he conceived the idea of standard time. In New York City there were six different clock times in use. Chicago had seven varieties. Most other cities varied. In spite of the public confusion and business waste which such a condition forced upon the nation it was argued and widely believed that local noon-times would never be changed. By 1884 the sentiment in favor of standard time was so universal that President Arthur called an international conference. Two years later standard time was adopted by all the leading nations with but one exception. Today that international standard time is in use and has developed great public convenience throughout the world. It is so universal that most people have forgotten that any other time ever existed.

The League of Nations is the logical organization to coordinate the work being done in various countries toward the simplification of the calendar. As soon as the national committees find out the sentiment in their respective countries, an international conference will probably be called by the League of Nations. The conference will decide the plan which should be adopted and the date on which it should take effect. All that will be required then will be to have the necessary legislation adopted by the various countries.

(25) "Incentives in Distribution," 1929 Yearbook, Frederick D. Hess, Manager, Sales and Advertising, Cooperative Foundry Company

Frederick D. Hess obtained his Bachelor of Science Degree from Northwestern University School of Commerce, being primarily interested in marketing work. Following his graduation, he held positions of sales manager and sales research manager for several companies, prior to his connection in 1928 with the Cooperative Foundry Company as Director of Sales and Advertising. He is a member of the Society of Industrial Engineers, Advertising Club, Sales Managers Club, and a life member of his college fraternity, and the Commerce Club of his University.

Incentives in Distribution

Your job as accountants is not complete when you have designed a nice system, drawn up some beautiful forms and have synchronized the whole thing into a set of accounts, because as I see it, "our job is to move merchandise at a profit," and, therefore, we need your help in analyzing the weak spots in distribution with a view of increasing our net profits.

After all, your accounts, books and most of your statements are only photographs of past events, whereas, we need you as financial advisers in our efforts to move merchandise not yet sold; and merchandise is moved mainly because of the incentive, or "motive power" inherent in the merchandise, or accompanying it on the path from the factory to the final consumer.

In this travel, we find as a general rule, three distinct groups to be influenced, and need, therefore, an incentive "chain" with three links:

One for executives, and key men, inside the organization; another, incentives for distributors, including wholesalers, jobbers, dealers and sales agents; and the third, which is almost the most important now, incentives for consumers.

In other words, where we formerly introduced some incentive plan for salesmen only, in order to move goods, nowadays we are forced by mass distribution, chain store methods, and other modern marketing tendencies, to create new incentives. And note how American industry is changing steadily from incentive methods for the personnel to methods for the distributor, then finally to incentives direct to the final consumer — over the heads of the ones previously mentioned. All in an effort to establish more or less automatic demands, and thus, in a way, eliminate incentives altogether, at least, as formerly used.

Now let us classify and discuss the most important incentives according to the following sub-divisions:

1. Incentives for the sales personnel in the company.

2. Incentives for distributors.
3. Incentives for consumers.

And in each case I shall sub-divide the subject, as far as possible, into financial incentives and non-financial incentives.

Incentives for the Distribution Executives Inside the Organization

Formerly the sales incentives to this group of personnel consisted of salaries, with an occasional commission, bonus, or prize, for special campaigns. Such methods were, of course, too weak to get more than the average results. Company after company is finding out that its executives and key men need more powerful stimulants in order to exert their utmost, and, furthermore, that some of the same tonics have to be applied to their assistants in order to get the best results.

Financial Incentives

Commission Plan

You heard yesterday a very fine address on incentive plans in the National Cash Register Company selling direct. Such a plan is fine and is wonderful for a company of this type; but more companies distribute the other way, that is, through a middleman. Therefore, such a plan as described yesterday is not sufficient, and is usually subject to changes and improvements.

Point Plan for Branch Managers

At the Stromberg-Carlson Co. in Rochester, such a plan is in operation and has been used successfully for several years. Branch managers have been set a certain standard as:

Quota of Volume for the year, equals	40%
Average profit for the year, equals	30%
Average expenses for the year, equals	30%
Total	100%

The method of computation of earnings is expressed by the equation:

$$\left(\frac{\text{Volume Sold} \times 40\%}{\text{Quota Volume}}\right) + \left(\frac{\text{Actual Profit} \times 30\%}{\text{Quota Profit}}\right) +$$
$$\left(\frac{\text{Standard Expenses} \times 30\%}{\text{Actual Expenses}}\right) \times \text{Salary Rate Per Week} =$$

Total Income per week (Branch Manager for example.)
(Income per week) × 52 = Yearly Income.

This works very well, and, of course, the main benefit from such a plan is that in order to set up standards, the company had to tell the branch managers, key men and salesmen, what items were profitable and what items are not. As a consequence, the entire level of profit has been raised through that simple plan.

Salary plus a Bonus Plan, Based on Net Profits of Company

The successful executive and sales bonus plan of the Leeds & Northrup Co., of Philadelphia, manufacturers of electrical measuring apparatus, will work where you cannot establish bonus or incentive plans based on the efficiency of the individual branch or unit.

The reason for such a plan is that one sales engineer might sell a certain equipment to the production department of a company in Oklahoma; another sales engineer of the same company might have to call on the purchasing department in Chicago, whereas, a third sales engineer of the same company might have to call on the chief engineer in New York. The entire sales force, therefore, has to work together and accept a bonus based on net profits of the entire company.

Profit-sharing Plan Based on Sales Unit Standard

Such a plan is in successful operation, according to A. S. Rodgers, President, in the White Sewing Machine Co., Cleveland,Ohio, with 125 branches. Here certain standards are set up as, for example, profits per sale per unit, for amount collected per open account, and for percentage of accounts collected. Then the branch managers are given a profit-sharing of a certain per cent of salary for each $1.00 increase in unit profits above standard, another per cent of salary for increases in collections above standard, and again a different graduated scale of per cents of salary for increases in open accounts above standard. Of course, such a plan has its limitations in that you can stay only within a certain standard with that plan.

A Split Profit-Sharing Plan

Such a plan is in use by the Walworth Co., Boston, Mass., selling to jobbers, dealers and also direct. Therefore, the branch executives get a bonus, 50% of which comes from the profits of their own individual branches, and the other 50% from the profits of the company as a whole. The bonus is said to run anywhere from 10% to 25% of salaries of the executives.

Combination Plans Used in One Company

Several plans are, according to F. E. Ketchum, President, in use by the Graybar Electric Co., Inc., a sales not a manufacturing organization. This distributing organization consists of nineteen main "houses," each having under its supervision from one to eight branches (47 branch offices).

The executives constituting the "house committee" – house manager, sales manager, service manager and credit manager – enjoy one bonus plan based on net profits of the house. The branch executives and sub-executives, correspondents, accountants, promotion men, etc., called the "office committee," enjoy a bonus plan based on saving over and above standard ratios between gross profits and expenses under their control. For example, if 1%

is saved, they get 2% bonus, based on salaries. Certain "general office" executives, President and Vice-presidents, form the "general department committee" and receive a bonus based on a certain percentage of net profits of the company.

In all of these plans the salary is, of course, the main basis, but room is left for the judgment and decision of department heads. Results are published monthly.

Stock Profit-sharing Plan

Such a stock profit-sharing plan is in use at the present time at the Dennison Mfg. Co., Framingham, Mass. The annual distribution of extra remuneration is in the form of stock with a cash dividend on stock holdings. This is really the main difference between this plan and the previous ones. However, it is worthy of note that two distinct plans are being used with this company, viz., the "employees' industrial partnership plan" and also the "managerial industrial partnership plan."

Since the first one concerns the general rank and file employees only, I shall confine my remarks to the latter. According to "Some Dennison Plans and Practices," the official publication of the Dennison Company, the executives and sub-executives share in the net profits of the company, five years of service being the prerequisite for partnership. In 1927 some 37,899 shares of stock were distributed (par value $10.00) to a total number of 413 managerial partners.

Deferred Stock Bonus Plan

Such a plan is in use at the present time by the DuPont Co., where executives are not paid a bonus in cash immediately, but in deferred stock, along the lines of the plan of General Motors, which you all know about, since it has received so much publicity since its initiation.

Note also that at DuPont's they use a class "A" stock bonus for any employee for conspicuous service, distributed regardless of company earnings, whereas class "B" stock bonus, is distributed to "selected" executives, according to net profits of the company.

In all the profit-sharing plans in use today, comparatively little effort or success has been made with a more accurate rating scale as a means of a more exact payment of the efforts of individuals. I believe that the only company which has succeeded to some extent along this line is the Dennison Mfg. Co.

I fully believe that here is a field which is wide open for accountants, as well as other managerial executives, to perfect. We all need your help to set up more definite standards so that earnings of executives can be made more accurate. We need more job analysis, and we need more unlimited earning scales, so that we can get every executive on his toes, and to exert his utmost. I agree with Mr. Jordan that we will be benefited thereby. So far, I think, we have not even scratched the surface when it comes to developing a real honest-to-goodness effective profit-sharing plan, which will make an executive feel more like a co-partner of a business enterprise. There is an unlimited field for accountants.

Let me call your attention to a statement published not long ago by Charles M. Schwab: "Let us make the salary not $10,000.00, but $3,000.00. In addition to that, I will give you a percentage on all you save in manufacturing costs, based on an average of $1.50 per ton for putting the material into pig iron. If you cut the cost to $1.45, I will give you 1% of the amount saved; if to $1.35, 2%, and so on. Thus you may be able to earn for yourself not $10,000.00, but $25,000.00, or $75,000.00, and more. You devote yourself to cutting costs and making money for the company and the company will play fairly with you. In that way you will, in effect, determine your own salary every year."

History of Profit-Sharing Plans

While at the present time probably only 10% of American executives are on a special compensation or profit-sharing plan, it is safe to say that such plans will increase rapidly during the next few years. You will note the constantly increasing growth of such plans from the following:

The term "profit-sharing" was, according to Mr. Boris Emmett (Bulletin of U. S. A. Bureau of Labor No. 208) clearly defined, by the International Co-operative Congress, Paris, France, in 1889 as:

"An agreement freely entered into by which the employees received a share, *fixed in advance, of the profits.*"

Profit-sharing plans have long been in operation in Europe, but have not been successful nor popular in this country up to the present century, prior to 1915. It is said that (according to Forster and Dietel, Princeton University, "Employee Stock Ownership in U. S. A.") the total number of plans in operation up to that time did not exceed sixty, the Illinois Central Railway Co. plan being one of the few shining examples.

After the year 1900 such leading companies as the Pittsburgh Coal Company, National Biscuit Co., Firestone Tire & Rubber Co., U. S. Steel Corporation, Proctor & Gamble Co., began to share profits with employees through transfer of stock. With this remarkable start, and with the still more remarkable growth of sales of stock of public utilities, profit-sharing plans have been in favor ever since.

Such other large companies as DuPont, the International Harvester Co., and Dennison Mfg. Co., set the pace before and during the World War. With the taste of Liberty Bonds, the American public took more freely to profit-sharing plans, and since 1923 such prominent companies as the Radio Corporation of America, the Standard Oil Co. of New York, Bethlehem Steel

Corporation, the General Motors Corporation, the United Cigar Stores, the Great Atlantic & Pacific Tea Co., etc. started similar plans.

That, and the phenomenal growth of chain stores—with profit-sharing plans for chain store managers—gave considerable additional momentum to the steadily increasing growth of these plans.

But we must here make a sharp distinction between "employees' stock purchase plans" and "executive profit-sharing." The great majority of employees' stock purchase plans have nothing whatsoever to do with executive profit-sharing. In fact, when Professor Balderston, of the University of Pennsylvania, recently investigated 141 American plans, he found only 65 that included "executive" profit-sharing. Nevertheless, the total number of companies working on such a plan is rapidly growing. So much for the financial incentives for executives.

Non-Financial Incentives for Distribution Executives

The foregoing financial incentives, of course, are extremely important because they seem to appeal to every type of executive imaginable, yet the non-financial incentives at times may be equally effective and very often much less expensive.

To develop and use non-financial incentive plans, there must be a definite promotion and organization scheme, preferably in connection with job analysis. Here the chain stores organizations are certainly setting the pace for the rest of us. They are doing everything they can to use job analysis, and analysis of every single branch, in order to pay their managers as efficiently as possible, according to individual ability. For example, the W. T. Grant Co., uses not only master record cards of key men, but inspectors also visit each store periodically for checking purposes. Furthermore, managers report on assistants according to a regular rating scale; in fact, every single department is recorded as to sales, actual against quota, turnover, mark-down and mark-up, inventory, etc., so that each branch may be compensated very closely in accordance with its own standard. Branch managers and assistants are promoted according to their standing and ability and this is a most powerful incentive.

In addition to such non-financial promotion plans, I might mention, in order to clarify this subject, that on an average, the chain groceries pay salaries from $20.00 to $35.00 per week, with percentage on gross sales ranging from one-half to two or more per cent, besides prizes for sales of special products.

Drug chain stores pay generally a straight salary, although some chains pay an annual bonus and others a P. M. on all goods or novelties that yield more than the average profit. The Liggett Co. is said to pay a straight salary, plus a share in the *increase* in the *net profits* of each individual store over the previous year, besides cash prize contests.

In the five and ten-cent field, the average is a straight salary plus a per cent of the net profits of the store — the one exception to such a rule is the J. C. Penney Co., each of whose store managers, as you know, has a one-third interest in the store he operates. Note also that the United Cigar Stores Co. which at one time paid commissions on sales, now is said to work on a straight salary basis.

I believe, however, that in the ordinary company, we need more organization charts and definite promotion plans, so that every executive may know just what is ahead of him. It is human nature to want recognition; we all like to see our accomplishments appreciated and recognized officially. We all like to feel that we are being promoted. Money isn't everything. Responsibility, power, titles, rank, and privileges count.

Let me also call your attention to some very important changes going on at present. If you have studied incentives as I have for the last five, ten or more years, you will note that there are certain changes taking place periodically. When we have a "seller's market" there is one kind of payment; then most companies put their entire force, including executives, on a straight salary basis, simply because the increase in sales and profits is due to *business conditions,* and not to personal effort. On the other hand, when there is a "buyer's" market, then executives and key men are put on a commission basis, if possible, or salary and bonus, to make the executives exert their utmost to get sales and increased profits.

But the biggest movement, the big change that is taking place just now, is the change from straight salary, to a profit-sharing plan of some sort. And if you are planning to install some profit-sharing plan, may I caution you regarding several points?

There is a general tendency to under-estimate the importance of the human element and to over-emphasize the mechanical features, such as forms, systems, methods, and I believe that that is why we do not get maximum results.

Furthermore, incentives depend very often on two things; inside working conditions and outside conditions.

A good example of the first came to my attention just a couple of days ago, when a good friend of mine, a sales executive, prominent in his field, turned down an offer of four times his present income, simply because he did not like to work with certain executives in the other company. He did not believe in their policies, and he could not see where he would get any chance to progress under their direction. So you see, inside conditions have a great deal to do with the carrying out of an incentive plan.

Then, again, outside conditions have a great deal of influence. For example, suppose you set up a commission plan, or profit-sharing plan, for your executives. Suppose you all get busy. Suppose you stir up the sales organization to a high pitch of activity and double your sales in a month by over-loading your dealers. Is that worth while? Does that pay?

Unless you also provide your distributors with similar incentives, although they might buy and be quite enthusiastic, as they sometimes are, still they might not move the merchandise when there is no demand. Does that pay? Not unless you have a third, and final, incentive for your consumers, so that you get what Mr. Freeman said in his speech, a few minutes ago — "a pull from one side and a push from the other." And how to get the "pull" from the consumer side, I shall explain when we discuss "Incentives for Customers."

Incentives for Distributors

Financial Incentives

Discount — Open or Secret

In the old days all the incentives we had for dealers were discounts. But discounts today have lost their flavor; and discounts might sometimes increase your sales, but not increase your net profits.

I know, for example, of a company making gas appliances. This company decided a short while ago to change over to distributors and jobbers. To do that they had to offer, of course, an unusual discount because this was the only way in which they could break in. Their sales grew wonderfully and everybody felt happy; but when the controller came around with the profit and loss statement, that presented a different side of the story. The discounts to jobbers had been so large that they cut into profits.

What good was that incentive plan?

Quantity Bonus

Such incentives are used very frequently, for example, in the cosmetic trade, where often, with every one dozen of shaving cream or face powder, one unit may be given the dealer free of charge, as a special inducement. That is nothing more nor less than price-cutting. It will work temporarily in certain trades, but I do not think it is a sound incentive.

Profit-Sharing Plans By Manufacturers

This is, of course, one of the more modern and important developments now used successfully by several leading dealers and manufacturers.

The Union Tobacco Co. has a plan which makes jobbers and retailers stockholders in the company. The demand for such a plan came from the tobacco jobbers and retailers themselves, no doubt on account of the small markup. This company then set aside only 300,000 shares of common stock to carry out the plan. For the jobber it was decided that for every $1,000.00 worth of cigarettes, at wholesale price, bought and paid for, he would be granted a credit of $30.00 worth of stock; or one share of stock per $1,000.00 worth of cigarettes.

For the retailer, a warrant for the proper fractional share of stock was packed in each carton of 10 packages. The dealer buying $300.00 worth of goods, received one share of stock through the redemption of these warrants.

The Postum Co. of New York has another type of plan in which the following standards are set up:

1. Guarantee of quality.
2. Guarantee of prices.
3. Guarantee of sales.
4. Guarantee of proper turnover of stock, based on acceptance of purchase plans presented by sales representatives.
5. Guarantee of a single price basis to all customers in the same freight zone.

This plan, as you know, is based on an increase in purchases by the average store, as follows: "If the total gain in a year is 10% to 15%, an extra profit dividend is distributed on the basis of 1% of the total net purchases of the year previous, after deducting 2% cash discount. If the gain is 15% to 20%, a profit dividend of 1½% is given; and if the gain is 20% and over, an extra profit dividend of 2% is given. Note that all stores are expected to stock all Postum goods."

The Van Heusen plan provides the following:

1. If a dealer in 1929 purchases 25% more collars than in 1928, 10% of such increased purchases only, is paid as a cash bonus.
2. If a dealer's 1929 purchases are more than 15%, but less than 25% of 1928 net, 7 1/2% of such increase is paid in cash.
3. If 1929 net purchases are 1% or more, but less than 15% increase over 1928 net, a cash bonus of 5% of such increase is paid.

Such bonus plans, based on increases of dealers' sales, may not, after all, increase the sales, due to the fact that there is no reward for the sales person selling the collars.

A still newer plan is the 50-50 investment plan, such as the one used by the May Oil Burner Corporation, Baltimore, Md. To be eligible for participation, a dealer must have completed a sales quota for a year, or the six months prior to purchasing. Then he may subscribe for one share of May common stock, for each May Oil Burner sold by him during that period. This stock is to be paid for over a period of three years. During the first year the company will contribute one-half of the payments for that year. The second year the company will set aside a part of its earnings, which it is contemplated will equal in each year at least one-half of that year's payment of the subscription price of the stock.

Whether such a plan, or the plans previously mentioned above, eventually leads into a situation where the distributors may own the parent company, or the parent company may own the distributors, I shall leave to your own imagination, as well as judgement.

Jobbers' Profit-sharing Plan

Such a plan was in use until a short time ago by the Electric Hose & Rubber Co., Wilmington, Del. It consisted in deducting from net profits for a certain year, a sum equal to 10% of par value of outstanding capital stock. Of the profits remaining 25% was used for profit-sharing with employees, and another 25% was set aside for customers. Distributions to customers were made in the proportion that the total net profits from each customer's business for the year was to the aggregate total net profit made on all such customers' business.

The plan was somewhat successful for four years, but was dropped because, evidently, many jobbers used the profit-sharing plan as an argument to get lower prices from competitors. It was found also somewhat impractical to divide customers into groups, and to share profits with some and not with others. Finally the company found that comparatively few jobbers co-operated wholeheartedly with this company regarding such modern profit-sharing plans.

In talking about financial incentives for distributors, let us not forget another important fact. You can pay your distributors, managers and executives, as much money, and as heavy an incentive as you please or as you can afford, but often in the final analysis, the dealers' clerks are the ones to influence. They can make or break your sales; they are your representatives before the final consumers, and if you do not enthuse them and give them the same courteous and intelligent treatment you give your own sales force, they may kill your extensive sales campaign.

In many trades, premiums or prizes are given to clerks, either by dealers or manufacturers, as well as free entertainment, instruction and education, visits to the factory, gifts, souvenirs, etc., from time to time. They have many items to sell, and require especially intensive cultivation and instruction in the specific selling points of your product.

Non-Financial Incentives for Distributors

Exclusive Territorial Arrangement

This incentive you all know so well, that it needs no explanation.

Special Consignment, or Warehouse Facilities

I believe you are all familiar with this point also. In one company a short while ago, the addition of some warehouses, strategically located, almost doubled sales, due to the simple fact that dealers then felt more inclined to place orders with the company when they could get quick service and delivery. Such incentive plans need no proof of their practicability.

Concentration Plan

Such a concentration plan is sponsored by Wilson Bros., Chicago. Its outcome is very problematical. It is too new and has not had proper time for a conclusive test.

Consumers' Demand – Actual or Promised

This interesting and intangible incentive is frequently as valuable as all of the previously mentioned put together; not only when working on a prospective dealer campaign, but also with old dealers. Consumer demand is often created by national or local advertising, by high quality of the product, by special uses, by unusual features and selling points. Such created incentives and established demands, practically guarantee re-sale of products. That is why this is such an attractive incentive for distributors. One of the best proofs of this is, that the chain stores recently have begun to handle nationally advertised goods, a method which is said everywhere to be a phenomenal success.

Regarding promised demand, note that in a certain company manufacturing brushing lacquer, a strong local advertising campaign was laid out for the metropolitan city of New York, and almost a thousand new dealers were secured in less than a year as a result.

Again, it seems to make little difference whether we take the cost of certain incentives and add them to the cost of the product, or deduct them from the discount to distributors. For example, the Gillette safety razor blades are sold at an extremely low markup, perhaps a few cents for a small package, and yet dealers accept them readily on account of a steady demand, and sales keep on increasing.

Merchandising Helps

These consist of all supplementary incentives to stimulate demand and to move merchandise such as:

Free samples for distribution.

Advertising allowances – or sharing of local advertising expenditures.

Re-sale crews (used, for example, by Hoover Vacuum Cleaner Co.).

Manufacturers or jobbers Service Bureaus (such as, National Cash Register Co.; and Hibbard, Spencer, Bartlett Co.).

Special exhibits, fairs, style shows, etc.

Traveling demonstrators, or at times, salesmen demonstrating.

The usual helps, such as window display, direct mail advertising, etc.

Unusual Selling Features, Actual or Created

The best way to illustrate this is to give you an example. In one company manufacturing ladies' underwear, there was found a lack of demand on the dealers' part and, as a result, constantly diminishing sales and net profits. After a careful analysis, a slightly different product was designed, a French name was secured from a French designer by payment of a few thousand francs, was played up in local advertising and proved so popular that sales were doubled in less than eight months.

Good Will, As An Incentive

In this connection, I should also like to call your attention to the importance played by the term "good will," either inherent or created. Note, for example, that it is said that the Graybar Electric Co. spent last year over one million dollars to advertise its name, to establish good will and to create a demand for its products, now distributed under the new name. It is believed that such an incentive of a million dollars is well spent and will prove a profitable investment.

Concluding this section on Incentives for Distributors, may I draw your attention to the modern changes. One of these changes is important. It is a change, or a "shift" from applying incentives to the personnel of the organization, to applying the same or similar incentives, or applying the same amount of money in different incentives directly to distributors. Again, may I illustrate, by stating the case of a manufacturer of cosmetics, who, the last few years, gradually has called all of his salesmen off the road, and has spent approximately the same amount of money on creating national demand (by national and local advertising), and on discount and price reductions to his distributors, all with the result that his sales have been steadily increasing at a lower cost, and with increased profits.

Regardless of the threat of syndicates, mergers and chain organizations, and similar modern merchandising methods, no doubt caused, in part, by the possible reductions in distribution costs, I believe that we are going to see more such remarkable changes in incentive methods in the near future than we have in the past, perhaps due to the more intense competition we have today which makes us analyze every penny spent for distribution.

Mutual Incentives

In discussing chains and mergers, permit me to digress for a moment, by calling your attention to the distribution incentive plan inaugurated in 1928 by the Beechnut Packing Co., and the United Cigar Stores Co. According to this plan, the United obtained some fifty thousand shares of common stock at about $50.00 per share, in consideration of which, it is said, it practically guaranteed to promote the sales of the Beechnut confection in United stores. And within a short time, the manufacturers of Life-Savers, Beechnut's competitors, made a deal of the same nature with a similar organization. The main reason for this arrangement was, evidently, control of distribution and to provide for a mutual incentive between manufacturer and distributor. Note that, theoretically, Beechnut could have secured $750,000.00 more from bankers for this stock. The question remains, could they have spent this amount of money with better results in national advertising for the benefit of all of their outlets, than they did by receiving the guarantee of automatic demand in some three thousand stores of the United? No doubt, there was a powerful incentive for such a distribution plan, or it would not have been consummated.

Incentives for Consumers

Financial

While your distributors may be enthusiastic about your products, you still have to provide some important incentives for your consumers to move merchandise at a profit. Many ask me, "How can you give an incentive to consumers? It isn't being done."

It is, and I am going to give you a number of such methods.

The Club and Bonus, or Premium Plan

The best example of such a plan is the Larkin Company plan. Around the year 1880 Mr. Elbert Hubbard conceived the idea of giving away as a premium, some silver spoons of Rogers' with every $10.00 box of soap purchased through this company. A group of women organized and pooled their purchases, to get the spoons. From this small beginning has grown, based on this plan, an organization whose sales run between $30,000,000.00 and $40,000,000.00 a year. At the present time, this company is said to have some 80,000 "secretaries," each with a group of five or more purchase-consumers. The "secretary" gets a reward in coupons to the "merchandise amount" of $12.50 per $50.00 purchases. Note that some of the prices in the catalogues conform very closely to those of the chain stores, yet others are found slightly higher. This has no serious effect on the sales because of the coupon system. In other words, a housewife can save up coupons and thus buy certain things which she may need in the home, where she might not otherwise have the money to purchase such goods. The success of this plan is assured. It has a wide following, especially in industrial towns where "saving and thrift" are watchwords.

Straight Premiums

Such incentives may be in cash or merchandise, such as, for example, are given with purchases in grocery stores and department stores. H & H Green Stamps, coupons (United Cigar Stores), a set of dishes with a stove, $25.00 for your old radio, are good examples of this method.

Profit-Sharing Plan for Consumers

Such a plan was launched a few years ago by the Commonwealth Press, Chicago, and provided that all excess profits, above 6%, were to be distributed among consumers buying more than $250.00 worth of printing for three months, according to amount of purchases. This plan, however, was discontinued this year on account of competition, and the "lukewarm" acceptance by consumers.

Reduced Prices

Such incentives are, generally, lowered prices, such as used during "Fire Sales"; special close-outs; cut-rate sales; or due to "self-service" such as created by store plans employed by Piggly-Wiggly, and other chain stores. Many of these have proven quite successful.

Quantity Purchases, Discounts

Such incentives may be created by advertising quantity sales or special sales, such as the Rexall One-Cent Sales; "Three Collars for $1.00" Sale; combination packages; Dollar Day Sales, etc.

Club Sales with Premiums

The well-known "Club Aluminum" plan has proven that such incentives may be successful.

Special Deals

Such incentive plans are in extensive use, especially in the cosmetic trade, where a bottle of after-shaving lotion is given free with a tube of shaving cream, or a bottle of perfume with a box of face powder, etc.

Commission for Leads Secured from other Consumers

Such plans are in extensive use by some automobile distributors who offer $5.00 to $20.00 each for leads that are closed, supplied by regular customers. A similar plan has been used with washing machines and vacuum cleaners with success.

Installment Plan to Facilitate Payments

You are all familiar with the increased sales made by installments in all lines of manufacture, hence I shall not spend much time on this point. It has been proven to us; but may I show you just one or two examples of what incentives of this type may accomplish?

I was talking recently with a distributor of a well-known refrigerator who told me, and showed me, that during the first four days of June of this year, he had sold as many refrigerators as during the entire month of June the previous year, due to the introduction of a liberal installment plan.

Only a few days ago I was discussing this important point with the sales manager of a Public Utilities Company in the northeast. His department had sold 200 refrigerators in 1928; by June 1st this year, he had sold 336; this remarkable increase was due solely to the fact that last year he sold refrigerators on the basis of 25% down, and a year to pay, whereas, this year they were being sold on the basis of $10.00 down and thirty months to pay.

Here you have proof enough of the efficiency of a popular incentive plan for consumers.

Prize Contests for Consumers

Such contests are frequently advertised in the national magazines and undoubtedly you are all familiar with them. The largest one today I believe, and the one which is best known at the present time, is the Eastman Kodak $25,000.00 Contest which is running now, and which is being watched with a great deal of interest. Other contests along this line are very effective.

Non-Financial Incentives for Consumers

While such incentives are more intangible and difficult to trace, yet we have constant evidence that they pay. The great majority of non-financial incentives are promoted by advertising, crystallizing the potential demand by kindling our dormant desires, and by stirring consumers to action and making them buy and pay the price.

Purchase Appeals, and Buying Motives

By far the most powerful incentives are the imaginary or real features created either by the product itself, or by its use, and exploited by the distributor, by the salesmen and by advertising which will make consumers voluntarily buy more of your products, without any apparent effort on your part.

I believe here is a point which we often overlook, but it is true that the most economical incentive, just as the least expensive publicity, is the direct word-of-mouth enthusiasm spread around by satisfied consumers. Not only that, but the play on our emotions (done directly or indirectly) is a very powerful incentive, in that we are made to feel that by purchasing certain products, or services, we are "keeping up with the Joneses." In other words, we are made, or automatically become "salesmen" for certain products through our pride and vanity, and that helps to increase sales at minimum expenses.

It looks to me as if, in the near future, we are going to pay more and more attention to our research departments, and to develop those special features of the product or service which make for automatic demand, and, therefore, for increased net profits. Such demand may be established through incentives commonly known as "purchase appeals" such as creation of style, beauty, color, utility (sometimes with an implied guarantee as often understood, or assumed, by the average consumer, that whatever is advertised nationally is carrying a guarantee of quality to the consumer), value, sometimes price, and certainly always appearance.

Consumer Helps

Remember that we referred briefly to this in the previous section. But let us remember that consumer helps, whether applied directly to consumers, in their homes or at the business places of distributors, form a very powerful incentive. For example, demonstrations, such as used with vacuum cleaners and washing machines—often sent on approval—are very effective. Also demonstrations, usually tried out through "schools" such as cooking schools, sewing schools, dressmaking schools; or the offer of free educational literature, such as recipe booklets, household hints, and what-not, all attract customers and certainly help to build sales at a very low expense.

Space does not permit the enumeration of dozens of effective non-financial incentives for consumers. Almost every company uses some, in one form or another.

Summary

Considering now the cost and results of incentives applied, let us illustrate this with at least one case. In one company manufacturing and distributing plumbing and heating apparatus, years ago there was practically no thought about incentives in distribution. When this company started some years ago, it was small. Then it gradually established branches and increased sales. Branch managers were first paid on a salary basis, but this incentive proved insufficient. They were then paid on a commission scale, which, due to a "boom," drove the income of branch managers way out of reason. A new plan was then instituted, of salary and bonus, which was successful from the start, in that it practically doubled sales. Then some years later, this company changed the distribution method from selling to dealers, to selling to jobbers as well as to dealers, and again increased sales. Considerable service work was rendered free of charge to jobbers and dealers, as well as sales promotion work, with several incentive plans for both dealers and jobbers. This naturally had its constructive effect. Finally this company put into motion an installment plan for consumers, and about the same time launched a national advertising campaign to educate the public to the use of its products. As a result, the total sales have grown in a few years from a small beginning of five or six million dollars, to almost $100,000,000.00 per year.

What was the price? This company paid about three to four million dollars for all of incentives above mentioned; but note that their profits have gone up from between three to four million dollars per year ten years ago, to about $12,000,000.00 last year, accredited partly to standardization and manufacturing economics, but mostly to distribution incentives.

So we see, incentives applied in the right way, in the right place and at the right time, pay heavy dividends.

If we are organizing to increase our profits, it behooves us to study incentives, through the entire chain from factory to consumer, regardless of where they are to be applied, regardless of where we are going to use the money—for executives, for distributors, or to create automatic demand from the consumers, or a combination method—do not be afraid of spending the money. The market is there and the possibilities are there, and it is our job, as distribution executives, to move merchandise at a profit. This we can do better with the help of you accountants than without it.

National Association of Accountants
Committee on Research
1987-88

RATE THIS BOOK

WHAT DID YOU THINK OF *RELEVANCE REDISCOVERED?*

NAA would appreciate hearing from you. Please take a few minutes to complete this reader survey. Merely drop this postage paid business reply card into the mail.

1. How did you learn of this study? ______________________

____

____

2. Regarding this research report:

	High 5	4	3	2	Low 1
a. Was the <u>content</u> of interest and relevance to you?	❑	❑	❑	❑	❑
b. Did it communicate its message easily and clearly?	❑	❑	❑	❑	❑
c. Were you able to apply the material in your job?	❑	❑	❑	❑	❑
d. Was this of general business interest?	❑	❑	❑	❑	❑

FOLD HERE

3. I would like to see NAA research the following topics or subjects:

____

____

Thank you.

Name: ______________________________________
Please Print

Title: ____________________ Date: ____________________

Company: ____________________________________

Address: ____________________________________

____

NAA Member: Yes ❑ Member No.: ____________________

No ❑ Please send me membership information.

DETACH, FOLD & SEAL

NO POSTAGE
NECESSARY
IF MAILED
IN THE
UNITED STATES

BUSINESS REPLY CARD

FIRST CLASS PERMIT NO. 50 MONTVALE, N.J.

POSTAGE WILL BE PAID BY ADDRESSEE

NATIONAL ASSOCIATION OF ACCOUNTANTS
ATTN: DIRECTOR OF RESEARCH
10 PARAGON DRIVE
MONTVALE, NJ 07645-9989

FOLD HERE

DETACH, FOLD & SEAL